AFRICAN HISTORICAL DICTIONARIES
Edited by Jon Woronoff

Historical Dictionary of Tunisia

Second Edition

Kenneth J. Perkins

African Historical Dictionaries, No. 45

The Scarecrow Press, Inc.
Lanham, Md., & London
1997

SCARECROW PRESS, INC.

Published in the United States of America
by Scarecrow Press, Inc.
4720 Boston Way
Lanham, Maryland 20706

4 Pleydell Gardens, Folkestone
Kent CT20 2DN, England

British Library Cataloguing in Publication Information Available

Library of Congress Cataloging-in-Publication Data

Perkins, Kenneth J.
    Historical dictionary of Tunisia / Kenneth J. Perkins. —2nd ed.
        p.   cm.—(African historical dictionaries ; no. 45)
    ISBN 0-8108-3286-0 (alk. paper)
    1. Tunisia—History—Dictionaries. I. Title. II Series.
DT244.P47   1997
961.1′003—dc21   96-51075
                                            CIP

ISBN 0-8108-3286-0 (cloth: alk. paper)

∞™ The paper used in this publication meets the minimum requirements of
American National Standard for Information Sciences—Permanence of
Paper for Printed Library Materials, ANSI Z39.48–1984.
Manufactured in the United States of America.

Contents

Editor's Foreword

Although not particularly large, populous, or rich, Tunisia has long played a disproportionately significant role in international affairs. This is due in large part to its location and its unique function as a bridge between the Arab world, Africa, and Europe. As it steered its own fairly steady course through the many currents and countercurrents of political, economic, and social change in the years after its independence in 1956, Tunisia often served as a model of development for newly emergent African and Asian nations.

Tunisia's traditional function as a link between divergent cultures was enhanced by the impressive efforts of Habib Bourguiba, the country's president for three decades (1957–1987) and the guiding spirit of the struggle for independence before that. As an outspoken champion of development in the Arab and African worlds, Bourguiba attained a commanding presence abroad. Indeed, for many, Tunisia and Bourguiba seemed to be one. Ultimately, however, he also evolved into a domineering and inflexible leader at home. When a growing national sentiment for change unseated him, his successor, Zine el-Abidine Ben Ali, introduced significant changes that attempted to preserve Tunisia's progressive secular traditions while maintaining stability in the face of an internal opposition increasingly centered on Islamic political movements rather than, as in the past, on the left. Thus far, Ben Ali's balancing act has generally succeeded.

Consequently, Tunisia has avoided sinking into the chaos that has befallen some of its regional neighbors, most notably Algeria. On the contrary, the country has evolved into a privileged partner of Europe and the moderate Arab and African countries. As a result, despite its limitations of size and natural resources, Tunisia continues to play a significant international role. This revised edition of the *Historical Dictionary of Tunisia* will enrich outsiders' understanding of this crucial country by elucidating the historical context in which its leaders and people are rooted. The chronology has been updated, entries have been added or expanded, and the enlarged bibliography provides access to many new and relevant works. As before, the information is cogent and the style eminently readable.

This second edition was written by the author of the first, Kenneth J. Perkins. Professor Perkins is a specialist on modern North Africa, with an abiding interest in Tunisia. He has visited the region regularly since the late 1960s. Among other works, he is the author of *Tunisia: Crossroads of the Islamic and European Worlds* and a coeditor of *The Maghrib in Question: Essays in History and Historiography*. Like Perkins's other works, this book opens the door to a fascinating country with which anyone interested in international affairs should be familiar.

Jon Woronoff
Series Editor

Spelling and Alphabetization Note

Where conventional Anglicized forms exist for Arabic place-names, they have been used in preference to the more precise, but less familiar, formal transliterations. Thus, "Sfax" appears in place of "Safaqis," "Kairouan" rather than "Qairawan," and "Sousse," not "Susa." By the same token, spellings of the names of contemporary figures that have acquired general acceptance in English language books, articles, and news reports have been adopted. Thus, "Habib Bourguiba" rather than "Habib Abu Ruqaiba" and "Zine el-Abidine Ben Ali" rather than "Zain al-Abidin ibn Ali." The transliteration of the names of figures from earlier periods, however, adheres to more formal scholarly practice except for the omission of the diacritical marks and symbols conventionally used in such systems. The same applies to Arabic common nouns. Inasmuch as nonspecialists sometimes find these orthographic markings confusing and specialists readily recognize the names or words without them, the symbol ᶜ to represent the Arabic letter ᶜ*ain* and the symbol ' to represent *hamza,* a glottal stop, have been utilized only in the titles of Arabic books and newspapers mentioned in the entries.

Arabic has only three vowels (a, i, and u), and these are not written if they are short. In addition, some letters have similar sounds (to a non-Arabic speaker). These two phenomena can lead to variant transliterations of the same word. As a general rule in this work, vowels not used in Arabic have been avoided, and similar-sounding consonants have been rendered in precise transliteration. As a result, "Maghrib," not "Maghreb," is the spelling of the generic term for the western Arab lands; "funduq," not "fonduq" or "fondouk," the spelling for a combination warehouse and hotel; and "Muhammad," not one of its many variants, the form for the most frequently occurring male name in Arabic, except in those cases where contemporary figures have themselves adopted the widely used "Mohamed."

For the purposes of alphabetization within the *Dictionary,* the Arabic article "al-" and titles, such as "bey," "dey," and "pasha" are not taken into account.

Chronology

1203	Yahya ibn Ghaniyya captures Tunis
1205	Restoration of Tunis to al-Muwahhids by Abd al-Wahid ibn Abi Hafs
1228–1249	Consolidation of Hafsid control over Tunisia by Abu Zakariyya
1270	Crusade of King (later Saint) Louis IX
1347–1349	Banu Marin, a Moroccan tribe, control Tunisia
1357–1358	Second Marinid occupation of Tunisia
1534	Khair al-Din, Turkish ruler of Algiers, seizes Tunis
1535	Charles V, Hapsburg emperor, ousts Turks and returns Tunis and La Goulette to Hafsids
1569	Ilj Ali, Ottoman pasha of Algiers, captures Tunis
1573	Hapsburg troops restore Hafsids
1574	Ottoman navy evicts Hapsburgs from La Goulette, Hafsid dynasty collapses; Tunisia becomes a province of Ottoman Empire
1591	Deys seize power in military coup in Tunis
1631	Ottoman sultan recognizes authority of Murad Corso Bey; beginning of Muradid dynasty
1673	Murad II suppresses deylical insurrection
1686	Algerian troops occupy Tunis
1694–1695	Algerian troops again occupy Tunis
1702	Assassination of Murad III by Ibrahim Sharif
1705	Husain ibn Ali claims title of bey; beginning of Husainid dynasty
1708	Ottoman sultan grants Husain title of pasha, acknowledging his power in Tunisia
1729–1740	Rebellion of Ali Pasha ends in his assumption of power
1746–1756	Civil war returns Husain's heirs to throne
1782–1814	Reign of Hammuda Bey marked by general economic prosperity
1807	Algerian invasion repulsed
1837–1855	Reign of Ahmad Bey; first attempts at political and social reforms
1857	Muhammad Bey issues Ahd al-aman
1861	Muhammad al-Sadiq Bey promulgates constitution
1863	Government contracts first international loan
1864	Increased taxation triggers rural revolts
1869	Tunisia's creditors form International Finance Commission
1873–1877	Reform ministry of Khair al-Din al-Tunsi
1878	Congress of Berlin condones eventual French control of Tunisia
1881	French occupation of Tunisia; Treaty of the Bardo

1882	La Marsa Convention establishes French protectorate
1891	Consultative Conference, advisory body to resident general, formed
1896	Founding of the Khalduniyya Society
1907	Limited Tunisian participation in Consultative Conference authorized
1911	Jallaz Cemetery incident
1912	Young Tunisian boycott of Tunis tram system
1920	Publication of *La Tunisie Martyre;* organizing of Dustur Party
1924	Founding of the Confédération Général des Travailleurs Tunisiens (CGTT)
1934	Dustur Party dissidents, led by Habib Bourguiba, form Neo-Dustur Party
1938	Neo-Dustur leaders arrested following violent anti-French demonstrations
1942	German troops occupy Tunisia; U.S. and British forces invade Tunisia from Algeria
1943	Allied liberation of Tunis; Bourguiba returns
1944	Nationalist groups issue Manifeste du Front Tunisien
1945	Bourguiba flees to solicit international support for Neo-Dustur; formation of the Union Générale des Travailleurs Tunisiens (UGTT)
1952	Neo-Dustur attempts to place Franco-Tunisian question on agenda of United Nations; French militants assassinate Farhat Hached
1954	Neo-Dustur begins negotiations with France to modify Tunisia's political status
1955	France accords internal autonomy to Tunisia
1956	
March 20	Independence granted
August 14	Independent government passes innovative Personal Status Code
1957	
March 9	Accord with France gives Tunisia full control over judicial system
May 5	Municipal elections; Tunisian women vote for first time
July 25	Amin Bey deposed; Habib Bourguiba becomes president of the Republic of Tunisia
August 5	Funds and property of beylical family confiscated
September 9	After months of clashes between French and Tunisian forces, state of emergency declared in areas along Algerian frontier

1958	
June 17	Withdrawal of French troops from all of Tunisia except for Bizerte naval base and the Sahara
November	Introduction of the dinar as the national currency
1959	
June 1	Constitution promulgated
November 8	Habib Bourguiba reelected president
1960	
February 18	President Bourguiba publicly discourages Ramadan fast
June 5	Concessions to explore for oil and to construct a refinery at La Skirra granted to ENI, Italian state petroleum corporation
November 13	Government seizes 250,000 acres of French-owned farmland; offers 1 million dinars in compensation
1961	
January 12	Ahmad Ben Salah appointed minister of planning; ambitious state intervention in economy begins
July 11–20	Bizerte crisis; French forces and Tunisian soldiers and civilians clash in Bizerte and at nearby naval base
July 22	United Nations orders cease-fire at Bizerte
August 12	Opposition leader Salah Ben Yusuf assassinated in Germany
August 21	United Nations General Assembly emergency session on Bizerte crisis
August 26	United Nations General Assembly resolution urges French evacuation of Bizerte
September 22	France and Tunisia sign evacuation accord
October 3	French evacuation of Bizerte completed; status of naval installation remains uncertain
1962	
February 16	Decision taken to nationalize major public service industries
April 12	Habib Bourguiba marries Wassila Ben Ammar
December 12	Planning Minister Ahmad Ben Salah calls for substantial foreign aid in support of ten-year plan
1963	
October 15	Last French troops leave Bizerte naval base
1964	
May 12	All remaining foreign-owned farmland nationalized
May 28	All communally owned tribal land brought under state control
June 25	Commercially exploitable quantities of oil discovered in the Sahara
July 9	Agreement with the Vatican closes most Catholic

	churches, nationalizes church property, and requires government approval for appointment of archbishop of Tunis
October 22	Neo-Dustur renamed Parti Socialiste Dusturien (PSD); Habib Bourguiba reelected party president
November 9	Habib Bourguiba reelected president of Tunisia
1965	
January 8	Major oil strike at al-Borma
1966	
June 10	Pipeline from al-Borma to La Skirra opened
July 14	First oil exports
1967	
March 15	President Bourguiba suffers heart attack
June 7–12	Anti-Israeli demonstrations during Arab-Israeli war; token Tunisian forces sent to Egypt
1969	
March 28	Tunisia signs partial association agreement with European Economic Community (EEC)
June 24	National Assembly passes investment law designed to promote foreign participation in economy
September 9	Disgrace and dismissal of Ben Salah
September 20	National Assembly reforms cooperative farms structure
November 2	Habib Bourguiba reelected president of Tunisia
December 19	Government rejects imposition of state planning against will of citizens but vows to continue to lay down broad planning outlines
December 29	Constitution amended to allow prime minister to succeed president in case of death or disability
1970	
March 24	Former planning minister Ahmad Ben Salah arrested on charges of treason
May 24	Ben Salah sentenced to ten years at hard labor
1972	
January–February	Antigovernment student protests at University of Tunis
April 14	Tax exemptions and other financial concessions granted to export-oriented industries to encourage increased foreign investment
1973	
February 5	Ben Salah escapes from prison
1974	
January 12	Foreign Minister Muhammad Masmoudi announces plans for merger between Libya and Tunisia
February 11	Masmoudi suspended from Parti Socialiste Dusturien

September 14	National Assembly names Habib Bourguiba president for life
1976	
March 12	Commercial quantities of oil discovered in the Gulf of Gabès
March 19	Ahmad Mestiri calls for approval of organized opposition outside Parti Socialiste Dusturien
1977	
June 10	Tunisia and Libya agree to submit dispute over claims to Gulf of Gabès oil fields to International Court of Justice
October 24	President Bourguiba and opposition leader Ahmad Mestiri agree to a national pact that will liberalize the political process
1978	
January 26	General strike sparks violent demonstrations in Tunis, Sousse, and Kairouan; state of emergency declared in most serious outbreak of political and economic disorder since independence
January 29	Labor leader Habib Achour arrested in connection with rioting
July 19	Trials of labor leaders accused of fomenting January disorders begin
October 10	Twenty-four labor leaders, including Habib Achour, sentenced to prison terms for their part in precipitating January rioting
1979	
June 28	Arab League meets for first time in Tunis; Chedli Klibi elected secretary-general
1980	
January 28	Commando attack on Gafsa by Tunisian dissidents allegedly trained in Libya
April 17	Thirteen prisoners executed for taking part in January Gafsa raid
1981	
September 5	Prison sentences imposed on scores of Mouvement de la Tendance Islamique (MTI) members
November 1	Parti Communiste Tunisien (PCT) takes part in the first multiparty legislative elections since independence; all National Assembly seats won by Parti Socialiste Dusturien candidates or independents
1982	
March 30	Islamic militants implicated in student riots at University of Tunis

August	Palestine Liberation Organization (PLO) transfers its headquarters to Tunis
1983	
January	Goverment crackdown on Islamic organizations provokes antigovernment sentiments that trigger sporadic violence throughout year
March 19	Algeria and Tunisia sign Maghrib Fraternity and Cooperation Treaty; other North African states invited to adhere to pact
October 20	Government decides to remove subsidies on bread and other basic commodities
November 1	Fathia Mzali becomes first female member of cabinet
November 19	Mouvement des Démocrates Sociales (MDS) and Mouvement d'Unité Populaire-2 (MUP-2) legalized
December 16	First congress of the Mouvement des Démocrates Sociales
December 29	Rioting erupts in south over increases in prices of basic commodities necessitated by removal of government subsidies
1984	
January	Severe disorders continue throughout the country
March 17	President Bourguiba cancels price increases
October 29	Zine el-Abidine Ben Ali named secretary of state for national security in government effort to crack down on dissidents
1985	
January–March	Student riots at University of Tunis
March 9	President Bourguiba designates Prime Minister Mzali as his successor
August	Libya expels 90,000 Tunisian workers
October 1	Israeli air raid on PLO compound at Hammam-Chatt
October 23	Zine el-Abidine Ben Ali named minister of national security
November–December	Labor unrest as government attempts to bring unions under its control
1986	
January 19	President Bourguiba accuses wife, Wassila, and son, Habib Jr., of conspiring against him; ousts them from entourage
February 22	Five opposition parties express solidarity with labor in conflict with government
April 28	Zine el-Abidine Ben Ali named minister of interior

June 22	President Bourguiba personally names members of Parti Socialiste Dusturien central committee
July 8	President Bourguiba dismisses Prime Minister Muhammad Mzali
August 1	President Bourguiba divorces Wassila Bourguiba
November 3	All opposition parties boycott National Assembly elections
1987	
March 13	Rashid Ghannushi, leader of the Mouvement de la Tendance Islamique, arrested
August 2	Bombs explode at tourist hotels in Sousse and Monastir; government attributes responsiblity to Mouvement de la Tendance Islamique
September 27	Sixty-nine Mouvement de la Tendance Islamique members, including Rashid Ghannushi, sentenced to prison terms or death
October 2	Zine el-Abidine Ben Ali named prime minister
November 7	Prime Minister Zine el-Abidine Ben Ali declares President Bourguiba medically incapable of fulfilling presidential duties and assumes office of president
1988	
February 27	Parti Socialiste Dusturien renamed Rassemblement Constitutionnel Démocratique (RCD)
April 16	PLO official Khalil al-Wazir (Abu Jihad) murdered by Israeli commandos at his suburban Tunis home
April 28	National Assembly passes legislation authorizing the creation of opposition political parties
April–May	Presidential pardons accorded to prominent political and religious critics of the Bourguiba administration, including Ahmad Ben Salah and Rashid Ghannushi
June 10	Summit meeting in Algiers ends with commitment of all Maghrib heads of state to work toward Maghrib unity through policy coordination
July 22	Presidential pardons accorded to over 700 political prisoners
July 25	Constitutional amendments limit president to two five-year terms and call for succession of speaker of National Assembly in event of presidential death or disability
July 31	Ben Ali becomes president of the Rassemblement Constitutionnel Démocratique
1989	
February 17	Union du Maghreb Arabe (UMA) linking Mauritania, Morocco, Algeria, Tunisia, and Libya formed in Marrakesh, Morocco

April 2	In national elections, Ben Ali captures the presidency with over 99 percent of the votes and candidates of the Rassemblement Constitutionnel Démocratique secure all parliamentary seats despite a strong showing by Islamist candidates forced to run as independents
June 8	al-Nahda, the former Mouvement de la Tendance Islamique, is denied permission to organize a political party
1990	
January–February	Nationwide student strikes follow protests at faculty of theology, University of Tunis
April 18	Ahmad Ben Salah, in exile since escaping from prison in 1972, returns to Tunisia
August 14	Demonstrations in support of Iraq following its invasion of Kuwait
September 10	Arab League members vote to return headquarters to Cairo
October–December	Recurrent antigovernment demonstrations by Islamist militants
1991	
January 24–29	Demonstrations throughout country against Gulf War
February 17	Islamist extremists attack office of Rassemblement Constitutionnel Démocratique
May 8–12	Antigovernment demonstrations at universities in Tunis, Sousse, and Kairouan leave five students dead
May 22	More than 300 persons arrested in alleged Islamist conspiracy to overthrow the government
September 28	Government accuses al-Nahda of plotting to assassinate Ben Ali
October 9	Execution of three al-Nahda members found guilty of murder in the February attack on Rassemblement Constitutionnel Démocratique offices
December 10	Three hundred intellectuals and members of the liberal professions issue public statement denouncing government's constraints on free expression
1992	
March 4	Amnesty International charges government with human rights abuses and torture in its treatment of Islamist dissidents
June 14	Ligue Tunisienne des Droits de l'Homme (LTDH) dissolves itself in protest over legislation banning its members from participating in political party activity
July 9–	Trials of hundreds of al-Nahda members

August 30	accused of plotting against the government result in 11 life sentences and numerous lesser penalties
December 12	Ministry of the Interior announces the "complete dismantling" of radical militant networks within the Islamist movement

1993

March 27	Ligue Tunisienne des Droits de l'Homme resumes activity upon suspension of legislation that had banned members' participation in political parties
December 23	Parliament passes new electoral law guaranteeing parliamentary representation to opposition parties

1994

March 20	Ben Ali returned to the presidency in national elections; all legislative seats except those set aside for opposition candidates won by the Rassemblement Constitutionnel Démocratique
June 13–15	Ben Ali assumes presidency of Organization of African Unity at annual summit held in Tunis
June 15	Closure of most PLO offices in Tunis; transferral of organization's headquarters to Jericho in the West Bank begins
July 11	Yasser Arafat leaves Tunis for Gaza

1995

May 21	In local elections, Rassemblement Constitutionnel Démocratique candidates gain control of the country's 257 municipal councils, although opposition candidates win council seats for the first time since 1956
July 17	Tunisia and the European Union reach an agreement promoting free trade

1996

January 22	Agreement to establish official facilities (interest sections) in each other's countries formalizes Tunisian recognition of Israel

Rulers of Tunisia, 800–1996

* Indicates entry in dictionary

The Aghlabid Dynasty

* Ibrahim ibn Aghlab	800–812
Abd Allah I	812–817
* Ziyadat Allah I	817–838
Abu Iqal	838–840
Muhammad I	841–856
Ahmad	856–863
Ziyadat Allah II	863–864
Muhammad II	864–875
* Ibrahim II	875–902
Abdallah II	902–903
* Ziyadat Allah III	903–909

The Fatimid Dynasty

* Ubaidallah	909–934
al-Qaim	934–946
al-Mansur	946–953
* al-Muizz	953–972

The Zirid Dynasty

* Buluggin ibn Ziri	973–984
* al-Mansur	984–996
Badis	996–1016
* al-Muizz	1016–1062
Tamim	1062–1108
Yahya	1108–1116
Ali	1116–1121
al-Hasan	1121–1148

The Hafsid Dynasty

* Abd al-Wahid ibn Abi Hafs	1207–1221
* Abu Zakariyya Yahya	1228–1249

* al-Mustansir	1249–1277
al-Wathiq	1277–1279
Abu Ishaq	1279–1283
Ibn Abi Umara [usurper]	1283–1284
* Abu Hafs Umar	1284–1295
Abu Asida	1295–1309
Abu Yahya Abu Bakr al-Shahid	1309
Abu'l-Baqa	1309–1311
Ibn al-Lihyani	1311–1317
Abu Darba	1317–1318
Abu Yahya Abu Bakr	1318–1346
Abu'l-Abbas Ahmad	1346–1347
Abu Hafs	1347

[Marinid Control of Tunisia, 1347–1349]

al-Fadl	1349–1350
Abu Ishaq	1350–1369

[Marinid Control of Tunisia, 1357–1358]

Abu'l-Baqa Khalid	1369–1370
* Abu'l-Abbas	1370–1394
Abu Faris	1394–1434
al-Muntasir	1434–1435
Uthman	1435–1488
Abu Zakariyya Yahya	1488–1489
Abd al-Mumin ibn Ibrahim	1489–1490
Abu Yahya Zakariyya ibn Yahya	1490–1495
Abu Abd Allah Muhammad	1495–1526
al-Hasan	1526–1543
Ahmad	1543–1569

The Muradid Dynasty

* Murad Corso	1613–1631
* Hamuda Pasha	1631–1659
* Murad II	1659–1675
Ali [pretender]	1675–1686
* Muhammad Bey	1686–1696
Ramdan	1696–1699
* Murad III	1699–1702

The Husainid Dynasty

* Husain ibn Ali (Husain I)	1705–1735
* Ali Pasha (Ali I)	1735–1756
* Muhammad ibn Husain (Muhammad Bey)	1756–1759
Ali II	1759–1782
* Hamuda	1782–1813
Uthman	1813–1814
* Mahmud	1814–1824
* Husain II	1824–1835
Mustafa	1835–1837
* Ahmad	1837–1855
* Muhammad	1855–1859
* Muhammad al-Sadiq	1859–1882
Ali III	1882–1902
Muhammad al-Hadi	1902–1906
* Nasir (Muhammad al-Nasir)	1906–1922
Muhammad al-Habib	1922–1929
Ahmad II	1929–1942
* Munsif (Muhammad al-Munsif)	1942–1943
* al-Amin	1943–1957

Residents General of the Tunisian Protectorate

* Paul Cambon	1882–1886
Justin Massicault	1886–1892
Urbain Rouvier	1892–1894
* René Millet	1894–1900
Georges Benoit	1900–1901
Stephen Pichon	1901–1906
Gabriel Alapetite	1906–1918
Etienne Flandin	1918–1920
* Lucien Saint	1920–1929
Joseph Manceron	1929–1933
* Marcel Peyrouton	1933–1936
Armand Guillon	1936–1938
Erik Labonne	1938–1940
Jean Esteva	1940–1943
Charles Mast	1943–1947
Jean Mons	1947–1950
Louis Périllier	1950–1952
* Jean Marie François de Hautecloque	1952–1953
* Pierre Voizard	1953–1954

Pierre Boyer de la Tour	1954–1955
Roger Seydoux (High Commissioner)	1955–1956

Heads of State of the Republic of Tunisia

* Habib Bourguiba	1957–1987
* Zine el-Abidine Ben Ali	1987–

Abbreviations

B.C.E.   Before the common era
C.E.   Common era
CGTT   Confédération Générale des Travailleurs Tunisiens
LTDH   Ligue Tunisienne des Droits de l'Homme
MDS   Mouvement des Démocrates Sociales
MR   Mouvement de la Rénovation
MTI   Mouvement de la Tendance Islamique
MUP   Mouvement d'Unité Populaire
MUP-2   Mouvement d'Unité Populaire-2
OAPEC   Organization of Arab Petroleum Exporting Countries
OPEC   Organization of Petroleum Exporting Countries
PCT   Parti Communiste Tunisien
PLO   Palestine Liberation Organization
PSD   Parti Socialiste Dusturien
PSL   Parti Social Libéral
PSP   Parti Social du Progrès
PUP   Parti de l'Unité Populaire
RCD   Rassemblement Constitutionnel Démocratique
RSP   Rassemblement Socialiste Progressiste
SHTT   Société des Hôtels Tunisiens Touristiques
UDU   Union Démocratique Unioniste
UGET   Union Générale des Etudiants Tunisiens
UGTE   Union Générale Tunisienne des Etudiants
UGTT   Union Générale des Travailleurs Tunisiens
UMA   Union du Maghreb Arabe
UNFT   Union Nationale des Femmes Tunisiennes
UNTT   Union Nationale Tunisienne du Travail

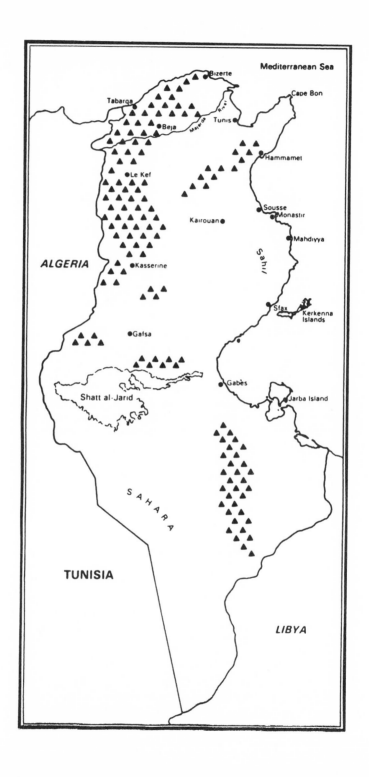

Introduction

Geography

Tunisia lies on northern Africa's Mediterranean coast, midway between the Atlantic Ocean and the Nile valley. Its location at the convergence of three distinct cultures (Arab, sub-Saharan, and European) has exposed Tunisia to a wide variety of contrasting influences and has made it a bridge between these disparate societies.

An abrupt southern turn of the African shoreline gives Tunisia two faces on the Mediterranean. From its northern coast, the country stretches some 850 kilometers (500 miles) south into the Sahara, while it extends an average of 250 kilometers (150 miles) inland from its eastern coast. Encompassing roughly 162,000 square kilometers (63,000 square miles), Tunisia shares land frontiers with Libya and Algeria. No natural boundaries separate it from these neighbors. Throughout much of its history, what is now Tunisia either was divided among competing powers, some indigenous and some alien, or constituted part of a larger entity that included territory now controlled by one or another of its neighbors.

Despite its relatively small size, Tunisia has great geographical and climatic diversity. The Dorsal, an extension of the Atlas Mountains of Morocco and Algeria, traverses Tunisia in a northeasterly direction from the Algerian border in the west to the Cape Bon peninsula. The country's highest peak, Jabal Shambi (1,544 meters; 5,066 feet), is in the Dorsal near Kasserine, but the range's elevations diminish as it approaches the sea. North of the Dorsal is the Tell, a region characterized by low, rolling hills and plains, although in the extreme northwestern corner of Tunisia, the land reaches elevations in excess of 1,050 meters (3,500 feet).

The climate of the Tell is typically Mediterranean, with mild, dry summers and cool, wet winters. The rich soil of the Tell is nourished by an annual rainfall averaging at least 400 millimeters (16 inches), although accumulations can range as high as 900 millimeters (36 inches) in the northwest. This level of precipitation, combined with the presence of the Majarda River, Tunisia's only significant perennial watercourse, has made the Tell the most productive farming area in the country. Since Roman times, cereal cultivation has been the mainstay of its agriculture, but other crops, including vegetables, grapes, citrus fruits, and olives also thrive there.

A second important agricultural region is the Sahil, the plain along Tunisia's eastern Mediterranean coast. Annual rainfall amounts diminish from north to south, varying from 500 millimeters (20 inches) north of

1

Sousse to fewer than 200 millimeters (eight inches) in the southeast, where the desert extends almost to the shores of the Mediterranean. Although there are no rivers in the Sahil, abundant underground water and moisture from the sea support agriculture, even in areas where precipitation is light. Very high summer temperatures, however, limit the range of suitable crops. An olive monoculture prevails in the Sahil, which is the country's main olive-producing region. The island of Jerba, off the southern end of the coastal plain, and the Kerkenna Islands, near Sfax, share the ecology of the Sahil mainland.

Inland from the Sahil, between the Dorsal and a range of hills south of Gafsa, are the Steppes. As is true along the coast, precipitation declines from the north, where as much as 350 millimeters (14 inches) may fall annually, to the south, where the yearly total may be as little as 175 millimeters (seven inches). In some portions of the Low Steppes that abut the coastal plain the limited cultivation of cereal and other crops is feasible, but the poor quality of the soil, the high summer temperatures, and the inconsistent rainfall increase the risks of farming. Herding is a more common livelihood, as it is in the High Steppes farther west. The rocky soil and rugged terrain of the lands along the Algerian border virtually preclude agricultural pursuits.

The northernmost limits of the Sahara occupy the southern half of Tunisia, where rainfall seldom exceeds 175 millimeters (seven inches). Even within the desert, however, there are diverse ecological and environmental zones. Around the extensive dry salt lakes south of the Steppes, in an area called the Jarid, are a number of oases in which sedentary farmers cultivate date palms and a few other crops. Farther east, the inhabitants of the small villages of the Zahr Mountains (also called the Mountains of the Ksour) south of Gabès supplement a primarily herding economy with limited farming dependent on irrigation systems that capitalize on the area's occasional torrential downpours. The extreme southwestern corner of Tunisia offers a stark contrast to areas of the desert that are capable of sustaining at least limited sedentary societies. There the edges of the Great Eastern Erg, a region of undulating sand dunes, spill across the border from Algeria. Until oil was discovered there in the 1960s, this barren, inhospitable territory, inhabited only by a few nomadic tribes, was of little interest to the outside world.

Population

In contrast to its geographical diversity, Tunisia has a population that is, by and large, homogeneous—ethnically, linguistically, and religiously. More than 98 percent of the country's 8.7 million citizens are Arabs. The rest are Berbers, descendants of the earliest identifiable ethno-linguistic group to inhabit what is now Tunisia. The Berbers rejected assimilation by a succession of outside rulers who dominated northern Africa after the ninth century B.C.E. Only Islam, introduced by the Arab conquerors of the region in the seventh century C.E., proved a sufficiently attractive and powerful vehicle for integrating the Berbers into an alien culture.

Despite their acceptance of Islam, the Berbers retained their own identity. Not until several centuries after the initial conquest, when large numbers of Arab tribes began to settle in northern Africa, did the Berbers start to assimilate the Arabs' manners, customs, and language. In the course of the extensive social interaction that followed, distinctive Berber characteristics were diluted, producing a predominantly Arab society. Prolonged subsequent contacts have rendered the terms *Arab* and *Berber* more meaningful as linguistic descriptions, indicating an individual's first language, than as racial ones.

Although considerably less numerous than the Arabs and Berbers, other groups have also contributed to modern Tunisia's ethnic heritage. Thousands of Spanish Muslims fleeing from the Reconquista found refuge in Tunisia's cities or established farming communities in the Majarda valley. The years of Ottoman influence in North Africa brought Turks, as well as many other subjects of the sultan, to Tunisia in a variety of official and private capacities. Blacks, introduced as slaves from sub-Saharan Africa, added another element to the population. So did the early nineteenth-century influx of Italian, Sicilian, and Maltese peasants and artisans, although by far the most extensive wave of European immigration occurred during the French protectorate between 1881 and 1956.

Parts of Roman Africa, including what is now Tunisia, were important centers of Christianity early in the religion's history. After the introduction of Islam, however, the native Christian community gradually died out. Today, with the exception of a few adherents of the Kharaji sect of Islam living on the island of Jerba, virtually all Tunisians are Sunni Muslims. Jerba is also the home of a small Jewish community, although most of Tunisia's estimated 4,000 Jews reside in the capital.

More than half the country's 8.7 million people reside in cities and towns. Almost all the rest are sedentary farmers. Since independence, the annual rate of urban population growth has fluctuated between 3 and 4 percent—a figure representing as much as twice the rate for Tunisia as a whole, which fell below 2 percent in the 1990s. As in many developing countries, a steady flow of migrants from rural areas to the cities in search of better economic opportunities accounts for the disproportionate rates. It also explains an annual rural growth rate that has dipped below 1 percent during times of economic crisis and has never exceeded 2 percent.

This rural to urban demographic shift has created serious problems. Housing facilities, social services, and transportation and communication systems are inadequate for the rapidly expanding population in almost every city. The magnet effect of Tunis, the capital and largest urban conglomeration, has been especially dramatic. Between 1956 and 1994, the city's population increased by more than 50 percent, from just over 400,000 to approximately 650,000. Of even greater significance is the 1994 enumeration of roughly 1.8 million persons, or about one-fifth of the country's total population, in the district of Tunis (which includes the governorates of Tunis, Ariana, and Ben Arous). Sfax, the next largest city, has fewer than half as many people as Tunis (250,000). Like Tunis and Sfax, most other important cities are in either the Tell or the Sahil, by far the most heavily urbanized and densely populated regions. These include Sousse, Gabès, and Bizerte, each with about 100,000 inhabitants, and smaller regional centers such as Le Kef and Béja, whose populations are less than 50,000. Kairouan, with a little more than 100,000 residents, lies in a transitional zone between the Sahil and the Low Steppes, while Kasserine, in the High Steppes, and Gafsa, a mining and industrial center at the southern edge of the Steppes, have populations of some 50,000 and 65,000 respectively. The largest urban centers in the Saharan portion of the country are Tozeur and Tataouine. The former, in the Jarid, supports fewer than 25,000 inhabitants; the latter has a slightly larger population of some 35,000.

Economy

The industrial and service sectors employ almost two-thirds of Tunisia's labor force. During the first three decades of independence, the state's extensive participation in industrial development ranged from directly owning some industries and public utilities to providing technical and financial assistance to selected private entrepreneurs. Beginning in 1985, however, the government embarked on an economic restructuring program that included a long-term campaign to privatize nonstrategic and monopolistic public sector industries and businesses, many of which had long operated at unsatisfactory levels. Commerce, banking, and other components of the service sector, including the tourism industry (which has long been a major supplier of foreign exchange) have also experienced a similar transition from public to private management.

The extraction and processing of mineral resources, most notably phosphates and petroleum, were, for many years, the country's most important industries. Generally employing fewer than 3 percent of the workforce, they derived their significance less from the jobs they provided than from the value of crude oil, phosphate rock, and phosphate by-products on the international market. By the end of the 1980s, however, textiles had supplanted minerals as the most important source of national export revenue. Other industries are more oriented to domestic consumption. Steel mills and cement factories satisfy some of the demand for building materials, but many essential products must still be imported. The food processing industry has reduced the importation of foodstuffs and, although intended primarily to meet internal needs, has also promoted the marketing of olive oil, tuna fish, and other commodities whose supply exceeds domestic demand.

A third of the labor force is engaged in farming, herding, or fishing. Mechanization and the introduction of modern agricultural techniques have increased the quantity and quality of yields in many areas, but as much as half of the country's arable land continues to be cultivated by traditional labor-intensive methods. This is especially true of marginal farmland, much of it in the Steppes and the Saharan oases. Another reason for maintaining traditional agriculture is that olives, the most important crop except for cereals, require a measure of conservation and upkeep that only human labor can provide. Livestock raising, once limited almost exclusively to nomadic tribes, is now more widely practiced by sedentary peoples, often in conjunction with agricultural pursuits. Despite Tunisia's 1,350 kilometers (800 miles) of Mediterranean coastline, relatively few persons derive their livelihood from fishing, and many of those who do fish utilize traditional methods and equipment. The richest fishing grounds are in the waters off the Sahil and around the island of Jerba.

History

Beginning early in the first millennium B.C.E., Phoenician merchants established trading centers throughout the central and western Mediterranean basin. Among these was Carthage, whose founding, not far from the modern city of Tunis, is traditionally dated at 814 B.C.E. In the following centuries, the Carthaginians built a commercial empire based on overseas trade that brought them into conflict with Rome. Between 263 and 146 B.C.E., Carthage and Rome engaged in three bitter rounds of warfare that ended with not only the military defeat of Carthage but also its physical destruction.

Under Roman rule, Africa, as the formerly Carthaginian territory was called, shifted its economic focus from commerce to agriculture. Its flourishing farms earned it the sobriquet "granary of Rome." Prosperity fostered the creation of many new urban centers. Even Carthage was rebuilt and by the second century C.E. had become the third most important city in the empire, behind only Alexandria and Rome itself.

The Roman presence continued until the fifth century, although not without opposition from the Berbers, who resented losing much of their best land. The Vandals, a Germanic tribe that had crossed the Mediterranean from the Iberian peninsula, captured Carthage in 439. Despite their military skills, these new rulers lacked the political acumen to create a viable state, and they controlled Africa for barely a century. In 533, the Byzantine emperor Justinian, anxious to assert his authority over as much of Rome's former empire as possible, dispatched a force that easily crushed the Vandals.

Byzantine efforts to replace the Vandals as masters of Africa encountered sharp Berber resistance. Always wary of Berber attacks, the Byzantine garrisons remained ensconced in defensive positions along the coast and in a few enclaves in the interior.

In a series of dramatic military campaigns following the death of the prophet Muhammad in 632, bedouin warriors occupied the Fertile Crescent and the Nile valley, bringing with them the tenets of their new Islamic faith. A raiding party from Egypt inflicted a defeat on the Byzantines as early as 647, but a permanent Arab-Muslim presence in Africa awaited the founding of Kairouan in 670. Like their predecessors, the Arabs encountered occasionally fierce Berber resistance, but the prospect of joining the Muslim armies and sharing the profits of their future victories induced many Berbers to convert to Islam.

Tensions soon developed between the Berber majority of Ifriqiya (the Arabized form of the Latin "Africa") and the Arab conquerors. Governors sent to the province from the Middle East favored the recently arrived Arab tribes over the indigenous Berber Muslims. The relegation of the Berbers to second class status drew them to the doctrines of Kharajism, a sectarian movement that asserted the equality of all Muslims. It also spawned a series of Berber revolts in the eighth century.

In the hope of restoring order to the troubled province, the caliph appointed Ibrahim ibn Aghlab, a military figure, as its governor. On the condition that his autonomy, as well as that of his descendants, be recognized in military and civil matters, Ibrahim accepted. The Aghlabids sought to affirm their legitimacy through the expansion of Islam and economic growth. In pursuit of those goals they conquered Sicily. At the same time, they cultivated the Mediterranean commerce that provided an outlet for goods brought to Ifriqiya in the trans-Saharan trade, which they also encouraged.

The Aghlabids, too, experienced difficulties in dealing with the Berbers. The latter's distaste for all manifestations of central authority enhanced their receptivity to criticisms of the Sunni Aghlabids voiced by Shii propagandists who began preaching among them late in the ninth century. One such agent provocateur, Abu Abdallah, raised a Berber force that overthrew the Aghlabids in 909. The victors acknowledged Ubaidallah, a descendant of the Shii imam Ismail, as their ruler. Although the Fatimids, as the new dynasty was known, consolidated their hold over Ifriqiya with relative ease, they evinced little interest in the province except as a springboard for expansion into the eastern Islamic heartlands. When, in 969, they shifted their seat of government to the Nile valley, they left Buluggin ibn Ziri, a Berber ally, in control of Ifriqiya.

After almost a century of vassalage to the Fatimids, Buluggin's descendants declared their independence. The need to regain a share of the trans-Saharan trade, significant portions of which had been diverted from Ifriqiya to Egypt, figured as prominently in this decision as did the desire to be rid of Fatimid supervision. The Fatimids punished the Zirids' disloyalty by sending the Banu Hilal, Arab bedouins then in the Nile Valley, into Ifriqiya. The influx of large numbers of nomads disrupted the agrarian economy of the region and, perhaps of greater importance in the long run, insured its eventual Arabization.

Beset not only by the Banu Hilal but also by European Christian attacks along the coast, the Zirids crumbled in the middle of the twelfth century. The al-Muwahhid rulers of western and central North Africa stepped into the resultant power vacuum, annexing Ifriqiya to forestall a Christian takeover. Early in the following century, the al-Muwahhid empire began to fragment. The descendants of Abd al-Wahid ibn Abi Hafs, a prominent al-Muwahhid general and governor of the province from 1207 to 1221, took control of Ifriqiya.

The Hafsids remained in power for more than three centuries. Despite their Berber origins, they collaborated with the Arab tribes, which they increasingly drew into governmental and military affairs. The gradual consolidation of the dynasty's position at home enabled it to challenge Christian naval domination in the central Mediterranean by promoting the activities of Muslim corsairs. Even amid this undeclared naval war, however, trade between North Africa and Europe continued. One indication of the Hafsids' interest in commerce was the decision to locate their capital at Tunis rather than in the interior, which had generally been the political center of gravity since the seventh century. Under Hafsid patronage, Tunis developed into a major commercial entrepôt. The city's significance, both politically and economically, was such that the term *Tunisia* gradually replaced *Ifriqiya* as the common designation of the region.

The projection of Ottoman power into the central and western Mediterranean in the sixteenth century worried the Hafsids, who regarded the newcomers as a threat to their position. A defeat at the hands of Turkish troops based in Algiers thrust the Hafsids into an alliance with the Ottoman Empire's most virulent enemy, the Spanish Hapsburgs, in 1534. The Hapsburgs did restore the Hafsids' throne, but in doing so established a protectorate over Tunisia that greatly circumscribed the family's power. The Ottomans seized Tunis for a second time in 1569 but were again repelled by the Hapsburgs. Their alliance with the Christians had deprived the Hafsids of virtually all popular support, however, and a final Ottoman assault in 1574 swept the dynasty aside.

As elsewhere in North Africa, direct Ottoman rule was short-lived. Less than two decades later, a revolt of the deys of Tunis, junior Ottoman officers, severely weakened Istanbul's hold over the province. The urban-based soldiers who engineered this uprising were soon compelled to yield their preeminence to the beys, officers whose responsibility for policing the countryside enabled them to mobilize the support of the rural tribes. Early in the seventeenth century, Murad Corso, by far the most adept of these men, succeeded in passing to his son the unprecedented powers he had amassed, thus initiating a dynasty that presided over Tunisia for the rest of the century. Although the Muradid beys profited from corsair raiding, the growth of European naval power made it imperative for them to stress peaceful commerce more emphatically than earlier rulers had.

Following a period of political unrest, Husain ibn Ali, a cavalry officer of the Muradids, proclaimed himself bey in 1705. As international trade continued under the Husainids, contacts with Europe intensified during the eighteenth century and stimulated Tunisian agriculture and industry. In the first third of the nineteenth century, however, the debilitating effects of a series of disastrous harvests, followed by outbreaks of famine and disease, took their toll on the economy. To make matters worse, the depression of the post-Napoleonic European economy reduced the demand for, as well as the value of, Tunisian exports at the very time that European imports, on which Tunisians had begun to rely, were becoming more costly. Many Tunisian entrepreneurs, including members of the royal family, fell heavily into the debt of European businessmen whose aggressive tactics enabled them to gain control over important facets of the country's economy.

The French occupation of neighboring Algeria in 1830 added to the gravity of the situation. Members of the Husainid elite were persuaded that the spread of European influence in their society could be curbed only by the selective adaptation of the concepts and technology from which the West apparently derived its strength. Accordingly, they initiated a series of political, economic, and social reforms. Not all Tunisians approved of this strategy. Some questioned the wisdom of turning to the West for a model; others feared that the changes, if effective, would create a more powerful central government more capable than ever before of imposing its will. Still others objected to the cost of the reforms. Even with drastic tax increases, the government's internal resources proved inadequate to finance the reforms. Forced to borrow money abroad, Tunisia slipped further into the sphere of European economic influence.

Moreover, several major reforms, including a guarantee of civil and religious rights, along with a constitution, were not of Tunisian inspiration, but were imposed on the bey by European consuls concerned more with the welfare of foreign nationals than with native Tunisians. A serious attempt to restructure the society along lines more compatible with its Arabo-Islamic traditions came too late to reverse the trend of Tunisian subordination to Europe. The reformers postponed, but could not avert, European control.

France declared a protectorate over Tunisia in 1881. Under its terms the bey remained on the throne but with his authority greatly circumscribed. At first, colonization proceeded slowly, but by the turn of the century French and other European settlers had gained control of much of the richest land in the country. The economic and political practices of the protectorate favored the settlers, whose influence belied their small numbers. At no time in the 75 years of the French presence did they constitute more than 7 percent of the total population.

Some Tunisians welcomed the French occupation, regarding it as an opportunity to introduce beneficial aspects of modern European society into their own. Giving satisfaction to their plea that the protectorate government treat Tunisians and Frenchmen equally, however, threatened to jeopardize the privileged status of the settlers, who vigorously resisted such policies. The rejection of even this modest demand set the stage for the emergence, at the end of World War I, of the Dustur Party. This nationalist organization more openly challenged the French role in Tunisia and called for a greater measure of Tunisian involvement in governmental affairs.

The Dustur leaders, most of whom came from traditional upper middle-class backgrounds, refrained from organizing a mass movement, preferring to engage in legalistic debates rather than more activist forms of political protest. These attitudes frustrated younger, more militant party members. In 1934, led by Habib Bourguiba, they organized the Neo-Dustur Party, which quickly supplanted the Dustur as the embodiment of nationalist aspirations. For the next two decades, Franco-Tunisian relations fluctuated between acute repression of all manifestations of nationalism and more or less genuine attempts to find compromises acceptable to both sides. Rising levels of violence inside the country in the early 1950s underscored the need for a solution to the Tunisian problem. Beginning in 1954, the pace of the negotiating process accelerated, culminating in the termination of the protectorate in 1956.

With the deposition of the last Husainid bey in the next year, Bourguiba became president of the Republic of Tunisia. At the same time, he continued at the helm of the Neo-Dustur which, until the 1980s, was Tunisia's only legal political party. Following several uncontested re-elections to the presidency, the National Assembly named Bourguiba president for life in 1974. Independence having been achieved, Bourguiba and his colleagues in the Neo-Dustur turned their attention to improving the quality of national life by promoting significant social and economic change. This entailed programs to provide more numerous, more accessible, and better quality educational and medical facilities. It also included campaigns to raise the traditional status of women and to involve them more actively in the country's development. The ultimate success of many of these undertakings depended on state control over matters traditionally within the purview of Muslim religious authorities. The government's incorporation of religious schools in the public education system and its abolition of Islamic courts were steps that engendered great animosity among those who did not approve of independent Tunisia's secular orientation. Lacking the wherewithal to confront the state, they acquiesced in these arrangements, but their smoldering resentment contributed to the emergence, in the 1980s, of an organized movement demanding a return to Islamic values and practices.

The Neo-Dustur, officially renamed the Parti Socialiste Dusturien (Socialist Dustur Party) in 1964, endorsed a program of careful planning and significant state intervention as the surest path toward economic development. Widespread discontent with such policies became apparent, particularly among small farmers and businessmen, toward the end of the 1960s. Such resentment triggered a shift toward more liberal economic practices, although the government's role in the economy remained substantial. In the more open atmosphere of the following decade, consumer prices rose far more rapidly than wages, while the gap between the value of Tunisia's exports and imports widened dangerously. A general strike in January 1978 degenerated into the worst rioting since the era before independence.

Discontent over the economy increasingly fused with anger over the Parti Socialiste Dusturien's monopoly on the political process. Renewed outbreaks of violence in 1980 and 1984 lent urgency to the search for an economic middle ground between the extremes of earlier policies, as well as to the effort to liberalize the political process. The government took some halting steps toward both objectives in the middle of the decade. In the economic realm, it accepted, in 1987, the terms of a Structural Adjustment Program demanded by the World Bank and the International Monetary Fund (IMF) as the price for their continued assistance. A key objective of the plan was the eventual privatization of most of the almost 500 public enterprises that controlled more than two-thirds of the national economy—a goal attainable only at considerable cost to both workers and consumers.

At about the same time, Islamist groups, many of which seized upon the deteriorating economy to mobilize popular discontent with the government, began to make their presence felt. These organizations obsessed Bourguiba, who demonized them as mortal threats to Tunisia's essentially secular society. Fearful of their growing strength, he rejected all measures of political liberalization that might facilitate the further enhancement of their influence. The president's uncompromising demand for the draconian punishment of the Islamists persuaded many of his advisers and ministers that senility and ill health prevented him from carrying out the duties of his office responsibly. In accordance with a constitutional provision regulating the succession in the event of the incapacity of the chief executive, Prime Minister Zine el-Abidine Ben Ali declared Bourguiba unfit to govern and replaced him as president on November 7, 1987.

Proclaiming his commitment to a system of political pluralism and economic liberalism, Ben Ali quickly legitimized a number of previously proscribed parties, eased restrictive press laws, granted amnesty to thousands of political prisoners, and opened negotiations with the Islamists, although he declined to recognize al-Nahda, their political party. Running unopposed for the presidency in 1989, Ben Ali won 99 percent of the vote, while the Rassemblement Constitutionnel Démocratique (the Democratic Constitutional Rally, the former Dustur Socialist Party, whose leadership he had also assumed in 1987) swept every seat in parliament. Nevertheless, Ben Ali's decision to continue the Structural Adjustment Program, associated in the public mind with high unemployment and the aggravation of other social ills, encountered significant criticism not only from his opponents, some of whom were arrested, but also from his supporters.

The 1989 elections convinced the Islamists that Ben Ali opposed their engagement in the political process no less than Bourguiba had, leading extremists within their camp to resort to violence as a means of pressuring the government. With the support of the many Tunisians who dreaded the prospect of their nation descending into the kind of internecine sectarian violence then plaguing Algeria, Ben Ali responded to the campaign of coercion and terrorism with vigorous repressive measures that by 1992 effectively crippled the movement.

National elections in 1994 overwhelmingly returned Ben Ali to office, but also modified the composition of the parliament in a manner that presented at least the appearance of pluralism. The ban on al-Nahda continued, but a new law set aside a small number of legislative seats for opposition parties that garnered a specified percentage of the total vote, thereby guaranteeing them representation even if their candidates failed to win seats in head-to-head electoral competition. Although the Rassemblement Constitutionnel Démocratique did in fact capture all the places not specifically reserved for the smaller factions, the emergence of a multiparty parliament constituted a new departure in Tunisian politics. By 1995, some opposition leaders had begun to criticize Ben Ali's contrived experiment in pluralism, demanding a more open political environment that included a meaningful role for their parties. The arrests of several prominent politicians in 1995 awakened fears within the opposition of a reversion to the authoritarian practices of the late Bourguiba era.

On the economic front in 1995, Tunisia became the first Maghrib state to enter an association agreement with the European Union. Its terms will take effect over an extended period ending in 2007. Although the accord's requirement to open previously protected Tunisian markets to free trade will almost certainly create some short-term problems, the overall impact of the arrangement is likely to prove highly beneficial.

The Dictionary

-A-

Abbasids; Abbasid Dynasty. Descendants of Abbas, an uncle of the prophet Muhammad, who held the office of caliph (q.v.) from 750 until 1258. The Abbasids quickly recognized the impossibility of directly governing their vast domains, which stretched from Spain to China, from their capital in Baghdad. Consequently, they made little effort to deter regional governors and military officers from asserting their autonomy, so long as they acknowledged the caliph's spiritual leadership and paid an annual tribute to Baghdad. Among the earliest beneficiaries of this approach were the Aghlabid (q.v.) governors of Ifriqiya. The increasing fragmentation of the Abbasid empire weakened the caliphs, ultimately depriving them of political authority and leaving them with only attenuated spiritual powers by the time of the dynasty's demise at the hands of pagan Mongol invaders. After the Abbasid collapse, some Muslims acknowledged the sultans of the Hafsid dynasty (q.v.) as the rightful heirs to the caliphate, but Tunisia's distance from the center of gravity of the Muslim world made it impossible for the Hafsids to take advantage of such support.

al-Abbasiyya. Fortress on the outskirts of Kairouan erected by Ibrahim ibn Aghlab (q.v.) around 810. Factionalism, frequently stemming from traditional tribal rivalries in Arabia, permeated Ibrahim's army. After repressing two military uprisings in which the townspeople of Kairouan had also participated, Ibrahim took up residence at al-Abbasiyya, where he surrounded himself with Arab troops of proven loyalty and a contingent of slave soldiers.

Abd al-Wahid ibn Abi Hafs (r. 1207–1221). al-Muwahhid commander who governed Ifriqiya for sixteen years after defeating the al-Murabit loyalist Yahya ibn Ghaniyya (q.v.) in 1205. Although his initial hopes of establishing an independent dynasty were thwarted, one of his sons, Abu Zakariyya (q.v.), did come to the throne in 1227. His descendants ruled Ifriqiya until 1574.

Abdallah ibn Saad (?–ca. 657). Leader of the first Arab raiding party to enter Ifriqiya. In 647, he defeated the Byzantine exarch Gregory (q.v.) at Sbaitla. The unwilling to risk his forces in assaults on the well defended coastal cities, ibn Saad secured a war indemnity and returned to Egypt in 648. Arab warriors did not again appear in force in Ifriqiya until 665.

Abu Abdallah (?–911). Shii propagandist whose success in rallying Berber support to the cause of the Ismaili Ubaidallah (q.v.) led to the overthrow of the Aghlabid dynasty (q.v.) in 909. When many of Abu Abdallah's Berber followers became disillusioned with the policies of the new regime and revolted, Ubaidallah ordered his assassination in 911.

Abu Hafs Umar [al-Mustansir II] (r. 1284–1295). Hafsid who came to the throne amid a family power struggle with the backing of the Banu Sulaim (q.v.) Arab nomads. Breaking with past practices, he rewarded his supporters with land grants, thereby increasing the bedouins' political and economic power.

Abu Yazid (ca. 883–947). Leader of an unsuccessful Kharaji (q.v.) insurrection against the Fatimids (q.v.) in the Jarid in 934. He was arrested, but escaped and launched a second uprising in 947, capturing Tunis and Kairouan. He was defeated by the Fatimids outside Mahdiyya and then executed, bringing the Kharaji threat to Ifriqiya to an end.

Abu Zakariyya (r. 1227–1249). Son of Abd al-Wahid ibn Abi Hafs (q.v.) and founder of the Hafsid dynasty (q.v.). His strong army, drawn mostly from Moroccan tribesmen with links to his family, assured stability in Tunisia and enabled him to take advantage of the al-Muwahhids' decline to extend his control over territory as far west as Tlemcen. His willingness to receive Andalusian Muslims seeking refuge from the Spanish Reconquista introduced into Tunisia a vibrant group that contributed greatly to the region's prosperity. Abu Zakariyya's policies did much to help forge a Tunisian identity that was distinct from the rest of North Africa.

Abu'l Abbas (r. 1370–1394). Ruler who oversaw the reunification of the Hafsid domains and the revival of the family's fortunes following almost a century of internal strife during which the Marinid dynasty of Morocco occupied Tunisia for several brief periods.

Achour, Habib (1913–). Secretary-general of the Union Générale des Travailleurs Tunisiens (UGTT; q.v.), 1963–1965, 1971–1978, and 1984–1985. His work as a labor organizer began in the French Confédération Générale du Travail in Sfax in the 1940s. Displeased with the strong communist influence in the CGT, Achour joined Farhat Hached (q.v.) in creating the UGTT in 1945. He quickly acquired a large following among the phosphate workers and longshoremen of the south.

The UGTT and the Neo-Dustur cooperated closely in the decade prior to independence. Achour's skill in rallying his supporters behind Habib Bourguiba at the 1955 Neo-Dustur congress in Sfax enabled the party leader to fend off a challenge from his rival, Salah Ben Yusuf (q.v.). In the following year, at the urging of the party's leaders, Achour broke with the UGTT's secretary-general, Ahmad Ben Salah (q.v.), and established a rival group, the Union des Travailleurs Tunisiens, which he headed until the two bodies were reunited in 1959. Within five years, Achour had been elected secretary-general of the UGTT (1963) and become a member of the political bureau of the Parti Socialiste Dusturien (PSD, 1964; q.v.). Tensions developed, however, when Achour resisted the efforts of two of the most powerful political figures in the country, PSD director Muhammad Sayah (q.v.) and Ben Salah, now the minister of planning, to subordinate the union to the party. The independent-minded Achour was stripped of his posts in the union and the party in 1965 but regained them a few years after Ben Salah's disgrace at the end of the decade.

In the troubled economy of the 1970s, Achour campaigned assiduously on his constituents' behalf. In the process, he built the UGTT into the most powerful organization in the country aside from the PSD itself, and the only one capable of seriously challenging the establishment. Achour's charge that Prime Minister Hadi Nouira (q.v.) had failed to abide by a "social contract" negotiated between the government and the unions in 1977 spawned a series of work stoppages culminating in the "Black Thursday" (q.v.) riots of January 26, 1978, which left scores dead. In the wake of these disorders, the government took control of the UGTT and arrested Achour.

When Muhammad Mzali (q.v.) replaced Nouira as prime minister in 1980, Achour and other union figures were released. Although Achour won election as UGTT president in 1981, the more important position of secretary-general evaded his grasp until 1984. In the interim, the authorities took advantage of differences within the union leadership to foster the creation of a new labor organization, the Union Nationale Tunisienne du Travail (UNTT; q.v.), which they hoped would neutralize the UGTT. Achour's continued criticisms of the government led to his arrest at the end of 1985. He remained under detention until the removal of Habib Bourguiba (q.v.) from the presidency in November 1987. Thereafter, he was pardoned by Zine el-Abidine Ben Ali (q.v.), the new chief executive, on condition that he endorse the merger of the UNTT and the UGTT before withdrawing from participation in union activity.

L'Action Tunisienne. Newspaper begun by Habib Bourguiba (q.v.) in 1932, following his disillusionment with the Dustur Party leadership. It was the first vehicle for conveying the sentiments of the younger generation of nationalist leaders who subsequently formed the Neo-Dustur Party. Despite the western education of Bourguiba and most of his collaborators on *L'Action Tunisienne,* the paper defended traditional Tunisian practices against French criticisms and promoted a strong sense of Tunisian identity. The protectorate authorities suspended its publication in 1933.

When Bourguiba and his colleagues formed the Neo-Dustur in the following year, an Arabic language version of *L'Action Tunisienne, al-Amal* (q.v.) served as the organ of the new party until restrictive press laws and the arrest of the Neo-Dustur leadership crippled it in 1936. *L'Action Tunisienne* reappeared during the year or so of relatively free political expression permitted in the protectorate by France's Popular Front (q.v.) government. In this atmosphere, the paper called for independence in association with France, a constitution, and an end to government support for colonization. In 1938, political violence erupted in Tunis. Government officials, attributing this situation at least in part to Bourguiba's militant editorials, again banned *L'Action Tunisienne,* which then appeared only sporadically until independence.

The paper, renamed simply *L'Action,* resumed publication only in 1955, and then as a weekly. Bourguiba, deeply involved in the negotiations to terminate the protectorate, delegated its management to a team of Neo-Dustur colleagues who invited Moroccan and Algerian nationalists, as well as French sympathizers, to join them in publishing the paper. Although technically a component of the party, *L'Action* no longer confined itself to Tunisia, but was distributed throughout North Africa and in France. Amid the turbulent political rivalries that followed independence, the opinions expressed in *L'Action* did not always coincide with those of the party establishment. Following a public disagreement between the paper's editorial staff and the Neo-Dustur leadership over Tunisia's response to the French bombing of Saqiyat Sidi Yusuf (q.v.) in 1958, the political bureau reasserted its control over *L'Action* and halted its publication.

Despite these problems, party leaders were aware of the need for a French-language paper to disseminate their views, particularly among western-educated Tunisians. In 1962, a French section was added to the party's now daily Arabic publication, *al-Amal,* but by the end of the year this cumbersome arrangement was abandoned in favor of the daily publication of *L'Action* as a separate entity. After 1965, the Société Tunisienne d'Edition et de Presse, a corporation established by the party, published *L'Action*. As part of a party reorganization in early 1988, following the accession of President Ben Ali, the paper's name was changed to *Le Renouveau*.

Africa Proconsularis. Roman province created in 27 B.C.E. by merging the province of Africa (the territory earlier controlled by Carthage) and portions of the Roman protectorate of Numidia (in what is now eastern Algeria). An important agricultural region, Africa Proconsularis was often referred to as the "granary of Rome."

Afrique-Action. Weekly newspaper established in 1960 by Muhammad Masmudi (q.v.) and his associates, many of whom had worked at *L'Action* (q.v.) prior to its suspension in 1958. *Afrique-Action* addressed issues of interest to the entire developing world in an attempt to appeal to an international, rather than a purely Tunisian, audience. Despite its organizers' links with the party, the journal did not hesitate to criticize high officials, including President Bourguiba (q.v.). This led to a 1961 order that the word *Action,* long associated with official publications of the Neo-Dustur, be dropped from its title. The weekly continued to appear in Tunis under the title *Jeune Afrique* for several months. In 1962 its offices were moved to Paris, where they have remained ever since.

Aghlabids; Aghlabid Dynasty (800–909). Ibrahim ibn Aghlab (q.v.) detached the Abbasid province of Ifriqiya from the direct control of Baghdad. His descendants ruled as autonomous princes, or amirs, for the next century. Military campaigns in Sicily and Italy increased their territory, augmented their prestige, and produced revenues for the development of Ifriqiya. However, Aghlabid excesses in levying taxes, frequently to finance lavish royal projects, and their haughty attitude alienated their subjects, leading to the overthrow of the dynasty by Berber tribes.

Agriculture. Since antiquity, when the Roman province of Africa Proconsularis earned a reputation as the "granary of Rome," dry farming has been the principal method of cultivation in Tunisia. The construction of more than a dozen major dams, primarily in the 1970s and 1980s, however, has brought over 200,000 hectares (500,000 acres) of land under irrigation. Wheat, barley, and other cereals are the most widely grown crops, but olives, citrus fruits, grapes, dates, and a wide variety of vegetables also figure prominently in agricultural production. The agricultural sector employs approximately a third of Tunisia's workforce, but accounts for only about 15 percent of gross domestic product.

The persistent decline in the percentage of agricultural workers in the years since independence reflects the increasing mechanization of Tunisian agriculture. Relatively few highly mechanized large-scale agro-industrial enterprises cultivate the vast majority of the country's arable land. A much larger number of individual farmers, on the other hand, work small labor-intensive plots, many of them covering five hectares (12.5 acres) or less and of only marginal productivity.

Attempts in the 1960s by Ahmad Ben Salah (q.v.), then minister of planning, to collectivize agriculture encountered strong resistance and ended in failure at the close of the decade. Although state corporations continued to work some land, more than two-thirds of the cultivated area had reverted to private hands by the middle of the 1970s, and 80 percent was privately owned by 1985. To expedite private investment in agriculture, two organizations, the Agence de Promotion des Investissements Agricoles (APIA) and the Banque Nationale du Développement Agricole (BNDA), were created in 1982 and 1983 respectively. In 1990, the BNDA merged with the Banque Nationale de Tunisie to form an agriculturally based commercial bank, the Banque Nationale Agricole (BNA).

Opposition to Ben Salah's methods stemmed not only from farmers' dissatisfaction with the concept of collectivization but also from official displeasure with the agricultural sector's 1.5 percent rate of annual growth in the 1960s. So sluggish a performance made it clear that collectivization would achieve neither the greater agricultural self-sufficiency nor the heightened agricultural efficiency promised by Ben Salah. In the four-year plan of 1973–1976, the annual rate of growth in the agricultural sector doubled, but recurrent adverse weather conditions prevented significant growth surges during either of the next two five-year plans, although 13 percent of the plan's total investment was allocated to agriculture in 1977–1981, and 16 percent in 1982–1986. In the plan for 1987–1991, one-fifth of all expenditures were earmarked for agricultural projects. Despite a highly successful harvest in the closing year of that plan, the value of agricultural exports continually lagged behind the cost of imported foodstuffs and other agricultural products. Still intent on achieving national self-sufficiency, the drafters of the plan's agricultural component for 1992–1996 hoped to increase productivity by attracting more private investors to agro-industries and food-processing enterprises.

Wheat is Tunisia's largest cereal crop but, given its heavy dependence on rainfall, harvests fluctuate greatly. The frequent discrepancy between wheat supplies and demand contributes significantly to the chronic need for agricultural imports. For example, a record harvest of some 1.78 million metric tons occurred in 1991, but inadequate rains in 1994 reduced the yield to less than 500,000 metric tons. Tunisian farmers produced a barley crop of 145,000 metric tons in 1994, in contrast with one that usually ranges between 400,000 and 600,000 metric tons. It had dropped to a meager 131,000 metric tons in the particularly poor harvest of 1986. Other cereal crops, such as maize, oats, and sorghum, whose recent combined production has normally totaled about 45,000 metric tons a year, are similarly affected by the weather.

The harvest of olives (q.v.) also fluctuates, not only because of the weather but also owing to the lengthy period before new plantings bear fruit and the tree's subsequent two-year production cycle. In the first half of the 1990s, the annual yield ranged between 375,000 and 1,325,000 metric tons, most of which was used to manufacture between 75,000 and 260,000 metric tons of olive oil, an important export commodity.

The production of oranges, tangerines, lemons, limes, grapefruits, and a few other citrus fruits generally hovers around 250,000 metric tons. Oranges are the most widely cultivated citrus fruit, with Tunisian farmers usually harvesting from 100,000 to 150,000 metric tons annually. The southern oases produce between 75,000 and 90,000 metric tons of dates yearly, while the country's almond trees yield from 40,000 to 50,000 tons of nuts. In the colonial period, and for some time after independence, much of the grape harvest, which has sometimes exceeded 100,000 metric tons annually, was used to make wine. More recently, however, Islamist groups' objections to the production of wine have resulted in a decline in the grape crop, with a harvest of only 60,000 metric tons in 1994.

Other important crops (and their 1994 harvests) include tomatoes (470,000 metric tons), melons (particularly watermelons; 350,000 metric tons), sugar beets (350,000 metric tons), potatoes (220,000 metric tons), peppers (170,000 metric tons), peaches (40,000 metric tons), beans (17,000 metric tons), onions (90,000 metric tons), chickpeas (15,000 metric tons), apples (75,000 metric tons), apricots (24,000 metric tons), and tobacco (7,000 metric tons).

Government efforts to promote commercial fishing, begun in the mid-1970s, steadily increased the size of the annual catch, which peaked at just over 100,000 metric tons of fish, crustaceans, mollusks, and sponges in 1988. Thereafter, however, the trend reversed itself, declining to some 78,000 metric tons in 1994. Cork forests, located in the mountainous region of the northwest, produce about 11,000 metric tons of cork each year.

Herding, once a mainstay of the nomadic population, now provides the exclusive livelihood for very few Tunisians. The most abundant forms of livestock are sheep, numbering more than 7.1 million; goats (1.4 million); cattle, many of them on dairy farms (660,000); and poultry (39 million), which produced more than 55,000 tons of eggs in

1992. There are now fewer than 250,000 camels, almost all of them in the south.

Ahd al-Aman (Security Covenant). Decree issued by Muhammad Bey (q.v.) in 1857, largely in response to European pressure for political and judicial reforms in the aftermath of the Sfez Affair (q.v.). It guaranteed civil and religious equality for all Tunisians, abolished government monopolies, and pledged the government to modify the legal system to provide increased protection for foreign residents.

Ahmad Bey (1806–1855; r. 1837–1855). Tenth Husainid ruler. He initiated important reforms designed to protect Tunisia from foreign encroachment. Ahmad superimposed many ideas and institutions borrowed from the West on a political and social system still bound to traditional values and practices. In the military field, he purchased up-to-date equipment, hired European officers as advisers, created a military training school at the Bardo Palace (q.v.), and inaugurated the practice of conscripting Tunisian peasants for military service. In support of his army, and to enhance Tunisia's self-sufficiency, he also established foundries, textile mills, and other small factories. Ahmad hoped his abolition of the slave trade (1841) and subsequent emancipation of slaves in his realm (1846) would persuade the European powers of his progressivism and discourage any thoughts of intervention. Although these reforms proved ruinously expensive, with few projects surviving Ahmad's death, the years of his reign gave many of Tunisia's future leaders their first real exposure to Western practices and ideology.

Aix-la-Chapelle, Congress of. Meeting of the European powers held in 1818. Its primary purpose was to preserve the peace concluded at the 1815 Congress of Vienna following the Napoleonic Wars. It also addressed the issue of the North African corsairs (q.v.), whose activity had escalated during the European fighting. The congress empowered Great Britain and France to make joint representations to the North African rulers insisting on the cessation of corsair raids and threatening military action if they persisted. Although the bey acceded to these demands, the outbreak of the Greek Revolution in 1820 drew the attention of the powers from North Africa to the eastern Mediterranean and precipitated another round of Tunisian corsair activity.

Algeria. Tunisia's western neighbor has figured prominently in its history since Carthaginian times. Beginning with the Romans, the populations of the two regions were frequently subjected to common outside rulers, culminating in the establishment of French control over both Algeria and Tunisia in the nineteenth century.

Ironically, Algeria provided the newly independent Tunisian government with its first foreign policy quandary in 1956. Neo-Dustur leaders sympathized with the objectives of the Front de Libération Nationale, which had launched the Algerian rebellion in 1954. But they also recognized the need for good relations with France in order to retain desperately needed financial and technical assistance. The political activities of FLN leaders in Tunis created problems with France, but the Tunisian government's refusal to evict Algerian civilian refugees and FLN soldiers from camps in western Tunisia near the Algerian frontier proved a more direct irritant to Franco-Tunisian relations. The French army attempted to seal the border by building an electrified fence, the Morice Line (q.v.), in 1957. In the following year, a French attack on the Tunisian village of Saqiyat Sidi Yusuf (q.v.), resulted in its destruction and the loss of at least 80 lives. Despite its high cost, Tunisian support for the FLN did not waver. Later in 1958, when Algerian leaders formed a provisional government in exile, they chose Tunis as its headquarters.

In the waning days of the war, however, as the likelihood of Algerian independence increased, Tunisia did attempt to profit at its neighbor's expense by claiming portions of the Algerian Sahara known to have substantial oil reserves. Although the claims were rebuffed, FLN officials resented the Tunisian maneuver. This, along with Habib Bourguiba's discomfort with the radicalism of Algerian presidents Ben Bella and Boumedienne, resulted in a deterioration in relations after Algerian independence in 1962. Tunisia's shift toward a more capitalist economy during the 1970s further alienated the Algerians, who remained strongly committed to the concept of a state controlled economy.

Not until well after Boumedienne's death in 1979 did the situation change. Such cooperative projects as a pipeline from Algeria's oil fields to the Tunisian port of La Skirra (q.v.) underscored the warming trend encouraged by Algerian president Chedli Ben Jadid, as did the Maghrib Fraternity and Cooperation Treaty signed by Ben Jadid and Bourguiba in 1983. In this accord, the two leaders pledged to promote closer ties among the states of North Africa with an eye toward eventually achieving political unity. Tunisian friendship with Algeria not only provided a counterweight to another powerful neighbor, Libya, but also made possible linkages between the country's uncertain economy and the far more prosperous one of Algeria. The rapid improvement in Libyan-Tunisian relations following the replacement of Bourguiba by Zine el-Abidine Ben Ali in 1987 proved a prelude to broader regional interaction. Less than two years later, in February 1989, Tunisia joined Algeria, Libya, Morocco, and Mauritania in establishing the Union du Maghreb Arabe (UMA) (q.v.) to foster development and economic cooperation.

Far more than the guidelines of the UMA, however, it was the presence of Islamist opposition groups in both Tunisia and Algeria that shaped the relationship between the two countries after 1989. Following the Tunisian elections in April of that year—just as Ben Jadid was easing the restrictions on political activity that had characterized FLN rule since 1962—a number of Islamist critics of the Ben Ali government went into exile in Algeria, opening contacts with the predominant Islamist movement there, the Front Islamique du Salut (FIS). In these circumstances, Tunisia welcomed the military coup in January 1992 that ousted Ben Jadid and canceled the legislative elections that the FIS was poised to win. With both Algeria and Tunisia facing political challenges of a similar nature, although of quite different orders of magnitude, relations between the two improved. As the situation in Algeria degenerated into full-scale civil war, however, Tunisians worried about the security of their borders and the possibility that their own most radical Muslim groups might emulate their Algerian counterparts. Consequently, Ben Ali supported the Algerian government's hard line toward the Islamists, discouraging compromises that he feared might embolden his Tunisian adversaries.

Ali ibn Ghaniyya (?–1188). al-Murabit follower whose effort to unite the tribes of the central and eastern Maghrib against al-Muwahhid rule ended with his defeat in the Jarid in 1188.

Ali ibn Ghdahem (?–1867). Leader of an 1864 tribal revolt. Ostensibly sparked by the government's imposition of increased taxes, the revolt also reflected fears that reforms strengthening the central government would curb tribal autonomy. As the revolt collapsed in the face of vigorous government repression, Ali and many of his followers fled the country. He returned to Tunisia in 1865, was arrested, and died in prison in 1867.

Ali ibn Khalifa (1801–1884). Qa'id of the Naffat, a tribe from the region between Sfax and Gabès. With beylical rule collapsing in the summer of 1881, he organized resistance against the invading French forces. Ali's hopes of Ottoman support did not materialize, nor was he able to persuade the settled communities of his region to join the struggle. By the end of the year, French troops had defeated Ali's warriors and driven them into Tripolitania. There he and his followers proved an embarrassment to the Ottoman provincial authorities. Wishing to avoid a conflict with France, they urged Ali and his supporters to accept the pardon offered by the protectorate government and return to Tunisia. Ali died before agreeing to the offer of amnesty, but by 1885 virtually all of his supporters had done so.

Ali Pasha (1689–1756; r. 1740–1756). Nephew of, and for a time heir apparent to, Husain ibn Ali (q.v.). He rebelled against his uncle in 1729, after the latter altered the succession in favor of his son, Muhammad (q.v.). Aided by the Turkish rulers of Algiers, who promoted civil strife in Tunisia as a means of increasing their influence in the country, Ali defeated Husain in 1740. He was himself overthrown in 1756 when his former allies backed Husain's descendants in a counterrevolution. Ali's success in winning over some tribes during the civil war created animosities that lingered long after the immediate issues of the revolt had been resolved.

Alim (plural, ulama). Religious official versed in traditional Islamic disciplines. In addition to their scholarly role as students and interpreters of the faith, the ulama provided instruction in Muslim schools and staffed the sharia (q.v.) courts. Beginning with the Husainid dynasty (q.v.), many ulama also began to occupy important clerical and administrative positions in the government.

Almohades. *See* **al-Muwahhids**

al-Amal. Arabic newspaper created in 1934 by members of the recently established Neo-Dustur party, including Habib Bourguiba (q.v.), its director, and Tahar Sfar (q.v.), its editor in chief. The use of Arabic circumvented an official ban on *L'Action Tunisienne* (q.v.), the Neo-Dustur's French paper, but the language choice also represented an effort to make the party's ideas more widely available to the Tunisian populace. Suspended by the authorities after only a few months of publication, *al-Amal* enjoyed a brief revival when the Popular Front (q.v.) eased press restrictions in 1937 but, like other nationalist publications, was again suppressed in 1938. *al-Amal* resumed publication in 1955, for the first time on a daily basis, and has since remained the official Arabic newspaper of the ruling party. In 1988, following the accession of President Ben Ali, its name was changed to *al-Hurriya,* meaning freedom.

al-Amin [Lamine] Bey (1879–1962; r. 1943–1957). Nineteenth and last Husainid (q.v.) ruler of Tunisia. Amin enjoyed good relations with the nationalists in the early 1950s, appointing several members of the Neo-Dustur to the 1954 ministry formed to negotiate an autonomy accord with France. In 1957, however, independent Tunisia's Constituent Assembly deposed the elderly bey in favor of a republican form of government.

Amir. Prince. Title taken by Aghlabid (q.v.) and Zirid (q.v.) rulers to underscore their independence from outside control and their full secular authority within their domains.

al-Andalus. Arabic term, "land of the Vandals," given to the region of southern Iberia conquered by the Muslims beginning in 711. During the Spanish Reconquista (q.v.), a Muslim exodus from al-Andalus to all parts of North Africa occurred. The Hafsid (q.v.) rulers welcomed these refugees, incorporating many of them into their bureaucracy and army while encouraging others to establish new agrarian communities, especially in the Majarda valley (q.v.).

Andrea Doria (1466–1560). Genoese statesman and commander of the city-state's fleet in a series of engagements with North African corsairs and the Ottoman navy early in the sixteenth century. An important ally of Charles V (q.v.), he participated in the Hapsburg (q.v.) capture of Tunis in 1535.

Anglo-Tunisian Bank. Joint venture established in 1857 to promote British investment. While helping to incorporate Tunisia into the international monetary system, it epitomized the Anglo-French rivalry in the country. The bank counted many Tunisian government employees among its investors and officers and quickly acquired a monopoly on the issuance of notes of legal tender, leading France to object to its privileged status. After a lengthy dispute, the Tunisian government succumbed to French pressure and disavowed its links with the bank.

Anglo-Tunisian Convention of 1863. Accord granting British subjects residing in Tunisia the same status as Tunisians in commercial, judicial, and legal matters. Although both parties to the convention regarded it as a means of diminishing French influence, its provisions angered Tunisians concerned with the growth of foreign leverage in general.

Antalas (fl. 530–548). Berber chieftain whose defeat of the Vandal king Hilderic (q.v.) in 530 precipitated the takeover of Africa by Hilderic's former ally, the Byzantine Empire. In a revolt against the new rulers in 544, Antalas put the Byzantine army on the defensive for several years before he was subjugated in 548.

Arab League. International organization of Arab states that Tunisia joined in 1958. To indicate its disapproval of the Egyptian-Israeli Peace Treaty in 1979, the League moved its headquarters from Cairo to Tunis. The general secretariat remained there until 1990 when, following Egypt's reintegration into the league, it returned to Cairo. Several specialized agencies of the league, including the Arab Fund for Technical Assistance to African Countries, the Arab Atomic Energy

Agency, the Arab States Broadcasting Union, and the Arab League Educational, Cultural, and Scientific Organization (ALECSO) are headquartered in Tunis.

Art. Statuary, mosaics, jewelry, and other everyday objects were the most common art forms in Carthaginian and Roman times. The National Museum, located in the Bardo Palace (q.v.) near Tunis, houses a superb collection of ancient art that includes some of the world's finest Roman-era mosaics from Carthage (q.v.), Bulla Regia, Thuburbo Majus (q.v.), Dougga (q.v.), and other sites in Tunisia.

The rigorously monotheistic Muslims' initial contacts with Byzantine Christianity in the eastern Mediterranean convinced them that the inclusion of icons and sculptures in churches differed little from the polytheistic worship of idols in pre-Islamic Arabia. To preclude the possibility of a similar situation developing within Islam, such art forms were banned in any religious context. The conviction of some pious Muslims that sculpting and painting were presumptuous human mirrorings of the divine act of creation provided the rationale for applying this prohibition, at least in theory, in the secular realm as well. In Tunisia, as elsewhere in the Muslim world, sculpture virtually vanished, but figural representation, although limited, was never entirely repressed.

Instead, arabesques and complex geometric patterns constituted the most common decorative motifs, often appearing in the pottery, metalwork, leather goods, jewelry, and carpets produced by generations of Tunisian artisans. Artisanal production thrived until the nineteenth century, when cheaper and often more durable European manufactured products became readily available on the Tunisian market. Since independence, however, a significant artisanal revival, attributable in large part to foreign tourists' demand for Tunisian handicrafts, has occurred.

The reawakening of interest in western art forms was another consequence of Tunisia's increased exposure to European culture in the nineteenth and twentieth centuries. Not surprisingly, the pioneers of modern Tunisian art closely imitated European conventions. In 1912, Abdulwahab Jilani (1890–1961) became the first Tunisian artist to exhibit his work at the Salon Tunisien, a prestigious annual show that had featured paintings by European artists since 1894. During the interwar years, only a few other Tunisian artists, by far the most influential of whom was Yahya Turki (1901–1968), gained admission to the salon. His experiments with expressionism broke with the more conventional methods and styles that had continued to dominate the work of Tunisian artists even as new trends were sweeping the European art world. Given painting's novelty as a form of Tunisian artistic expression, Turki's enthusiasts were either highly westernized

Tunisians or liberals from the European colonial community who were willing to reach out to talented young Tunisians.

Under the guidance of Turki, Ammar Farhat (b. 1911), who had first displayed his work in the Salon in the late 1930s, and a few supportive French artists, the "Ecole de Tunis" coalesced after World War II. Its most successful members included Jellal ben Abdallah (b. 1921), Ali Bellagha (b. 1925), Abdelaziz Gorgi (b. 1928), and Zoubeir Turki (b. 1924), all of whom were reaching their artistic maturity early in the postwar years. These artists did not embrace a single style or method, but were united by a desire to create an authentically Tunisian artistic personality that valued the country's traditions and symbols but expressed them in modern forms. The école attained the height of its influence and popularity in the 1950s and 1960s. Because the quest to define and articulate a national identity went hand in glove with Tunisian nationalists' goals in the decade leading up to independence in 1956 and in the years immediately thereafter, the artists of the école assumed a significant role in the forging of a national artistic heritage.

Independence facilitated Tunisian artists' contacts with the rest of the world, leading many of them to move beyond their own cultural parameters to embrace a variety of contemporary trends. The two most prominent figures in this cosmopolitan movement were Hatim el-Mekki (b. 1918) and Hédi Turki (b. 1922). The eclectic tastes of the former had already resulted in the production of works in a wide array of styles, while the latter, a long-time affiliate of the Ecole de Tunis, had become enamored of abstractionism after spending several years as a student in Europe and the United States. Some young Tunisian artists followed Turki into abstractionism; others turned to figurative styles such as expressionism, pop art, and surrealism. Amid the interest in abstract art in the 1960s and 1970s, Nja Mahdaoui (b. 1937) and Najib Belkhodja (b. 1933) enjoyed great success by employing Arabic calligraphy as a link between the genre and Tunisian traditions.

A coterie of naive artists has also thrived since independence. The best of them—Baghdadi Chniter (b. 1938), Ali Chtita, Mehrezia Ghaddhab (b. 1934, the first woman to carve a niche for herself in the Tunisian art world), and Ali Guermassi (b. 1923)—have made important contributions to the preservation of traditional manners and customs by depicting aspects of Tunisian society that have been rapidly disappearing in the face of modern development.

The Ecole des Beaux-Arts was founded in Tunis in 1923. Opportunities for artistic study were expanded in 1973 with the creation of the Institute of Technology for Arts and Architecture, which trains both teachers and practitioners of the fine arts. Since shortly after independence, the Union Nationale des Arts Plastiques (UNAP) has striven to promote the interests of Tunisian painters and sculptors and to enhance public appreciation of their work, some of which is displayed in the Musée d'Art Moderne, the home of the official state art collection.

Association des Anciens Elèves du Collège Sadiqi/Association of Sadiqi College Graduates. Association of Sadiqi College (q.v.) alumni organized in 1905 under the leadership of Ali Bash Hamba (q.v.) and Bashir Sfar (q.v.). Proponents of a modern educational system, these young graduates offered evening classes, at first in French and later in Arabic, on a variety of subjects that were not part of the traditional Tunisian curriculum.

Association pour la Sauvegarde du Coran/Association for the Preservation of the Quran. Organization established by faculty and students at the Zaituna Mosque-University (q.v.) in 1970 to express their concerns about Tunisia's declining moral standards, which they attributed to the government's emphasis on modernization and the accompanying disintegration of traditional values. It advocated renewed attention to Islam as the most effective means of correcting this problem. The growing gap between social classes, magnified by the government's 1969 shift away from socialist policies, also disturbed the association's members. By not interfering with the group's activities, national leaders hoped to undermine criticisms that they had deliberately and consistently pushed Islam into the background since independence. Many of them viewed the association as a useful counterweight to the more numerous and potentially troublesome leftist movements developing at the same time and often expressing similar grievances. After the political and economic upheavals of 1978, the association joined with like-minded societies to form the Mouvement de la Tendance Islamique (MTI; q.v.). Many of the men who emerged as leaders of this new organization had been members of the Association pour la Sauvegarde du Coran while students at Zaituna.

-B-

Baccouche, Hachemi (1917–). Novelist and essayist whose writings convey the trauma experienced by many westernized Tunisians with the termination of the protectorate. Baccouche's French education and his family's economic and political connections with French businessmen and administrators left him ambivalent about independence, and he emigrated to France in 1957. In the following year, he published *Ma foi demeure,* a novel exploring the complexities of a mixed

Franco-Tunisian marriage that stands as a metaphor for the extensive linkages between Tunisian Muslims and Frenchmen that had evolved in the colonial era. The book was well received in France but widely criticized in Tunisia, where its sympathetic treatment of the French and its pleas for reconciliation were viewed as excessive and incongruent with the prevailing spirit of decolonization. Baccouche's second novel, *La Dame de Carthage*, was published in 1961. A work of historical fiction set amid the Spanish-Ottoman-Tunisian conflicts of the sixteenth century, it likewise took as its central theme the problems of intercultural relations. The same topic also formed the heart of Baccouche's best-known piece of nonfiction, *Décolonisation— Grandeurs et Servitudes de l'Anti-Colonialisme,* an essay that also appeared in 1961.

Baccouche, Hedi (1930–). Neo-Dustur activist whose service as prime minister from 1987 to 1989 capped a long political career. Baccouche joined the party after World War II as a secondary-school student. In the 1950s, while attending the Sorbonne and the Institut d'Etudes Politiques, he presided over the Federation of Tunisian Dusturian Students in France. He served as governor of Bizerte, Sfax, and Gabès during the 1960s and headed several national agencies, including the Social Security Fund and the National Fisheries Office, in the 1970s. Following a succession of diplomatic appointments in Europe and Algeria from 1979 to 1984, he became director of the Parti Socialiste Dusturien (PSD; q.v.). In April 1987, he became minister of social affairs.

On his accession to the presidency in November, Zine el-Abidine Ben Ali (q.v.) appointed Baccouche (who had worked closely with him to engineer Bourguiba's removal) prime minister. Baccouche also rose to the number-two position in the Rassemblement Constitutionnel Démocratique (RCD; q.v.), becoming its vice president in 1988. He remained prime minister through a series of cabinet shuffles in which most of the other ministers who had served in the last Bourguiba government were cast aside. Baccouche resisted the rapid pace of reform recommended by Ben Ali and criticized the rigorous austerity measures imposed on Tunisia by the World Bank with the support of the president. As a result, he was dismissed in September 1989 and subsequently lost his RCD positions.

Bairam al-Khamis, Muhammad (1840–1889). Vigorous advocate of Islamic reform. A member of a most distinguished family of ulama in Tunis, he both studied and taught at the Zaituna Mosque-University (q.v.). During the ministry of Khair al-Din (q.v.), whose ideas he shared, Bairam served as the first director of the Habus Administration (q.v.), as editor of the official gazette, *al-Ra'id al-Tunisi* (q.v.), and as supervisor of the government printing press. Although he retained some of these positions after Khair al-Din's fall in 1877, he emigrated to Egypt two years later, living there for the last decade of his life. Bairam's extensive writings dealt primarily with modernist interpretations of Islam, but he also authored one of the most detailed studies of nineteenth-century Tunisia, *Kitab Safwat al-Iᶜtibar bi Mustawdaᶜ al-Amsar wa' l-Aqtar,* published in Cairo in 1884.

Baldiyya. Term used after the Ottoman conquest to denote native Tunisian urban residents, especially those of the capital, as distinct from both the foreign ruling class and the rural population. Close adherence to a code of conduct firmly rooted in Islamic traditions characterized the baldiyya and endowed it with considerable social prestige. Primarily involved in business pursuits, the members of this group rarely participated in the government, although their social status and marital links with the ulama, many of whom did hold government posts, ensured that their views carried some weight with the rulers, particularly in the Husainid era.

Banu Ghaniyya. al-Murabit supporters from the Balearic Islands who sought to undermine al-Muwahhid authority in the eastern and central Maghrib in the late twelfth and early thirteenth centuries. Their first campaign, under Ali ibn Ghaniyya (q.v.), failed in 1188, but Yahya ibn Ghaniyya (q.v.) succeeded in capturing Tunis in 1203. Forced to abandon the city two years later, Yahya's forces continued to harass the al-Muwahhids until his death in 1238.

Banu Hilal. Arab bedouins forced by the Fatimids (q.v.) to migrate, in the mid-eleventh century, from Upper Egypt to Ifriqiya. The Fatimids hoped these nomadic tribes would create difficulties for their disloyal Zirid (q.v.) vassals. Zirid efforts to stem the Arab tide failed and in 1057 Kairouan was sacked. This "Hilalian invasion" resulted in an increase in nomadism, disrupting agricultural activity and overland trade. More importantly, it greatly swelled Ifriqiya's hitherto small Arab population, paving the way for the region's eventual Arabization.

Banu Sulaim. Arab nomads encouraged by the Hafsids (q.v.) to migrate from the Tripoli area to the region around Kairouan early in the thirteenth century in the hope that they would displace the Banu Hilal (q.v.) nomads whom the dynasty had found extremely difficult to control. Rewarded with grants of land and official positions by later Hafsid rulers, the Banu Sulaim prospered, hastening the Arabization of the Tunisian countryside.

Barbary Pirates. *See* **Corsairs**

Bardo Military School. Institution founded at the Bardo Palace (q.v.) in 1840 by Ahmad Bey (q.v.) to train a cadre of officers for the updated army he was organizing. Between 40 and 60 cadets, many of them royal mamluks (q.v.) or scions of well-established families, attended the school at any given time. During their six to nine years in residence they studied, in addition to military subjects, the applied sciences, mathematics, and engineering, all under the supervision of European officers. Another segment of the curriculum focused on traditional Quranic studies. Their social backgrounds and their modern educations thrust many of the Bardo School's socially prominent graduates into important positions in the civilian bureaucracy as well as the army, giving them considerable influence in the mid-nineteenth century. The school ceased operations in the reign of Muhammad al-Sadiq Bey (q.v.).

Bardo Palace. Royal residence in the western suburbs of Tunis begun in the Hafsid era and expanded under later rulers. It was the primary residence of the Husainid beys prior to the inauguration of the protectorate. In 1888 the main building was converted into a museum housing a collection of antiquities that includes a number of exceptionally fine Roman mosaics. Since independence, the National Assembly has met in a building on the palace grounds.

Bardo, Treaty of the. Accord imposed on Tunisia after the 1881 French invasion. It left the monarchy intact but greatly diminished the bey's prerogatives. The treaty placed France's resident-minister in charge of Tunisia's foreign affairs and turned the direction of the Tunisian army over to a French general. The agreement is also known as the Treaty of Ksar Said.

Bash Hamba, Ali (1876–1918). French-trained lawyer and Young Tunisian (q.v.) activist. A graduate of Sadiqi College (q.v.), in 1905 he established the Association des Anciens Elèves du Collège Sadiqi (q.v.) as both a fraternal organization for the school's alumni and a vehicle for acquainting other Tunisians with Europe through its sponsorship of lectures and courses open to the public. One of the founders and the political director of *Le Tunisien* (q.v.), Bash Hamba wrote extensively for the paper and oversaw the initiation of its Arabic version in 1909. An adherent of pan-Islamic ideas, he actively solicited Tunisian support for Tripolitanian Muslims in the wake of Italy's 1911 invasion of that territory. The protectorate authorities, who suspected Bash Hamba of having a part in instigating the Jallaz Cemetery incident (q.v.), exiled him in 1912 for his role in organizing a boycott of the Tunis tram system that aimed at securing equal treatment for its Tunisian and European employees. Following a brief stay in France, he resided in Istanbul, where he participated in Ottoman efforts to promote pan-Islamic ideas during World War I.

Ben Ali, Zine el-Abidine (1936–). Second president of the Republic of Tunisia, acceding to the office in 1987. Ben Ali served in the armed forces from 1958 until 1980, attaining the rank of general and holding the office of director general of national security from 1977 until 1980. After several years as Tunisian ambassador to Poland, he returned to his national security post in 1984. A series of ministerial appointments followed, including minister of national security in 1985 and minister of the interior in 1986. Ben Ali's designation by President Habib Bourguiba (q.v.) as prime minister in October 1987 placed him constitutionally first in line for the presidential succession. In the following month, a medical team found Bourguiba no longer capable of carrying out his official responsibilities and Ben Ali assumed the office on November 7.

As president, he moved quickly to liberalize the political environment. Renaming the Parti Socialiste Dusturien (PSD; q.v.), whose leadership Ben Ali had also assumed from Bourguiba, the Rassemblement Constitutionnel Démocratique (RCD; q.v.) symbolized the intention of building a more inclusive party than had existed in the past, while the legal recognition accorded to other parties foreshadowed the emergence of a system of political pluralism. Press laws were relaxed and more than 10,000 prisoners, many of them political detainees, were amnestied in the first three years of the Ben Ali presidency. His national security work in the closing days of the Bourguiba era had convinced him of the importance of not making martyrs of the adherents of the growing Islamist movement. Consequently, his government complied with a number of minor, essentially cosmetic, demands enunciated by the newly formed al-Nahda party (q.v.), although its denial of formal recognition to al-Nahda prevented the party from contesting the 1989 parliamentary elections. To balance these concessions, Ben Ali vigorously defended the provisions of the Personal Status Code of 1956 (q.v.), vowing not to allow religious groups to erode the rights it guaranteed the nation's women. Running unopposed for the presidency in 1989, Ben Ali won 99 percent of the vote. Moreover, his party swept every seat in parliament, much to the distress of al-Nahda, whose candidates secured 15 percent of the national vote running as independents. It remained effectively excluded from the political process.

On the basis of his overwhelming electoral mandate, the president resumed the implementation of a structural adjustment program, first adopted in 1986, designed to promote privatization, to bolster competition among Tunisian manufacturers, to reduce public spending, and to enhance exports. Disagreements over the wisdom of pursuing this course of action, in which economic success was purchased at the price of high unemployment and the aggravation of other social ills, led Ben Ali to fire prime minister Hedi Baccouche (q.v.); opposition figures critical of the president were imprisoned. Such actions encouraged Ben Ali's opponents, particularly among the leaders of al-Nahda, whose bitterness over the party's treatment in the elections continued unabated, to portray the president in an increasingly unflattering, autocratic light. In late 1990, Ben Ali ordered a government crackdown on Islamist activists that culminated two years later in trials at which hundreds of al-Nahda members and sympathizers were found guilty of plotting the assassination of the president and a coup d'état.

At its second congress, held in 1993 to prepare for national elections scheduled for the following year, the RCD renominated Ben Ali as its presidential candidate. Shortly thereafter, in fulfillment of a pledge that opposition parties would play a role in the new legislature, the chief executive unveiled a modified electoral law guaranteeing a small percentage of seats to parties winning a minimal number of votes. Because the new code forbade political organizations based on religion, however, al-Nahda continued to be excluded from the arena of legitimate political activity. The legally recognized opposition parties agreed not to run presidential candidates against Ben Ali in 1994 and only Moncef Marzouki the head of the Ligue Tunisienne des Droits de l'Homme (LTDH; q.v.), attempted, unsuccessfully, to challenge him for the presidency. Ben Ali polled over 99 percent of the presidential vote and led the RCD, whose candidates captured all the legislative seats not specifically set aside for the opposition, to another overwhelming victory. Engaging the major parties in the elections served to lessen criticisms, but Marzouki and a handful of other adversaries of the regime who publicly denounced the process were briefly incarcerated. With the RCD's secular and religious critics effectively silenced, Ben Ali again made economic concerns his primary focus.

His containment of the Islamist opposition and ostensible commitment to political pluralism helped Ben Ali to preserve the western support for Tunisia that had generally characterized the Bourguiba era. At the same time, however, he viewed the Maghrib as the most important arena of Tunisian foreign policy. Soon after assuming the presidency, relations with Libya, which had frequently been strained under Bourguiba, improved markedly. More committed to genuine regional cooperation than his predecessor, Ben Ali led Tunisia into the Union du Maghreb Arabe (UMA; q.v.) in 1989 and ensured that his country played an important role in the organization thereafter.

Circumstances within the Maghrib allowed the harmonious relationship with the west to survive Ben Ali's condemnation of the dispatch of multinational forces to the Arabian peninsula following the Iraqi invasion of Kuwait in 1990. Convinced of the dangerous ramifications of this step, he traveled to Iraq in an unsuccessful effort to persuade Saddam Hussein to negotiate. This approach reflected widespread Tunisian sympathy for Iraq, but it also strained the country's important links with the Gulf states, creating rifts which, in some instances, endured until the middle of the decade. The descent, beginning in 1992, of neighboring Algeria (q.v.) into a civil war pitting militant Islamists against an intransigent secular government made the preservation of stability elsewhere in the Maghrib particularly important to the west and guaranteed its support for, or at least the absence of its criticism of, the president's tactics regarding al-Nahda and its offshoots.

Ben Ammar, Tahar (1889–1985). Political figure and head of the beylical government whose negotiations with France secured internal autonomy for Tunisia in 1955 and full independence in 1956. Born at Sabila Ben Ammar, some fifteen kilometers (ten miles) northwest of Tunis, he attended the Lycée Carnot and the Collège Alaoui in the capital, where he participated in the activities of the Young Tunisians (q.v.) before that group's disintegration in 1911. Following World War I, Ben Ammar was among the founders of the Dustur Party (q.v.) and was elevated to its executive committee after leading a delegation to France to publicize the party's views in 1921. In the next year, however, he broke with the Dustur's leaders over their total rejection of reforms proposed by the French. After a brief association with the Parti Réformiste (q.v.) of Hassan Guellaty (q.v.) in 1927, Ben Ammar avoided political party affiliation, preferring to work independently for a restructuring of the protectorate that would safeguard Tunisians' political, economic, and social rights.

He was a member of the Tunisian chamber of the Grand Council (q.v.) from 1928 until its suspension in 1934, becoming its president when it was reconstituted after World War II. In the interwar years he also presided over the Northern Tunisia Chamber of Agriculture. In the particularly difficult economic circumstances of the late 1920s and 1930s, Ben Ammar worked hard to shield vulnerable lands from additional European encroachment and to defend the interests of Tunisians, both peasants and owners, whose livelihood depended on the land. In this regard, his efforts were instrumental in ending the judicial sale of land and in facilitating debt restructuring. He also helped create a government office of cereal production and won acceptance into the protectorate's agricultural school for Tunisians.

In a 1944 meeting between members of the Grand Council and Free French leader Charles de Gaulle, Ben Ammar expressed his hope that France would promulgate a Tunisian constitution. This echo of the original, but now largely abandoned, Dustur platform conflicted with the demand for internal autonomy that had by then become the goal of the mainstream Tunisian nationalists of the Neo-Dustur Party (q.v.) under the leadership of the recently repatriated Habib Bourguiba (q.v.). Nonetheless, Ben Ammar supported the government formed by Mhamed Chenik in 1950 with the express purpose of negotiating an autonomy agreement. When those talks broke down, Ben Ammar led a boycott of the Grand Council in an unsuccessful attempt to extract concessions from the French.

As one of the few political figures still at liberty with the arrest of Bourguiba and his associates in the wake of Neo-Dustur protests over the collapse of the autonomy negotiations, Ben Ammar acted as a spokesman for the nationalists. He was also a member of the Conseil des Quarante (Council of Forty), a group of notables and officials representing all shades of Tunisian opinion that the bey convened in 1952 for the dual purpose of advising him on the political situation and providing him with a forum at which to enunciate his sympathy for nationalist objectives. Buoyed by the 1954 decision of Premier Pierre Mendès-France (q.v.) that only a renewed dialogue could contain the deteriorating crisis in Franco-Tunisian relations, Ben Ammar formed a government that negotiated an internal autonomy accord in 1955 and then arranged the formal termination of the protectorate in March 1956. He resigned as prime minister in the following month, after the election of a constituent assembly.

In 1958, Ben Ammar answered to a variety of criminal charges, apparently lodged through the machinations of political enemies resentful of his history of seeking accommodation with the French. He was accused of treason (for opposing the deposition of the bey and the formation of a republic) and of other crimes ranging from financial fraud to receiving stolen goods, the latter allegation stemming from his safekeeping of some of the crown jewels. President Bourguiba granted amnesty to Ben Ammar, who then retired to his estate, eschewing politics for the remainder of his life.

Ben Ammar, Wassila (1912–). Member of a prominent family of financiers and the second wife of Habib Bourguiba (q.v.), whom she married in 1962. As the president's confidante and close adviser for almost a quarter of a century, she acquired considerable influence in both governmental and party circles, but also made many enemies. After his 1984 heart attack, Bourguiba came increasingly under the influence of a group of conservative political advisers who argued that the thinking of Prime Minister Muhammad Mzali (q.v.) and of a few others in the president's entourage threatened his longtime monopoly of political power. Among their targets was Wassila, who had advocated a constitutional amendment clarifying the succession process in order to avoid a crisis when Bourguiba died. Taking the advice of his counselors, the chief executive dismissed Mzali in 1986 and denounced both his son, Habib Bourguiba Jr. (q.v.), and his wife, whom he also divorced. Wassila left the country, but returned in 1988 after Zine el-Abidine Ben Ali had replaced her former husband as president.

Ben Ayad, Mahmud (ca. 1805–1880). Close associate and financial adviser of Ahmad Bey (q.v.). His flight to France with a sizeable portion of the Tunisian treasury in 1852 drove the country to the brink of bankruptcy and was often cited by later reformers as evidence of the need to curb the unrestrained powers of the bey and his entourage.

Ben Salah, Ahmad (1926–). Neo-Dustur activist and secretary-general of the powerful Union Générale des Travailleurs Tunisiens (UGTT) (q.v.) whose mobilization of organized labor in support of Habib Bourguiba (q.v.) enabled the latter to overcome a challenge for the leadership of the party mounted by Salah Ben Yusuf (q.v.) just prior to independence in 1956. Appointed to the post of minister of planning in 1961, Ben Salah was, for a time, widely considered to be President Bourguiba's choice as his successor.

He introduced a 10-year plan built around socialist development projects and intended to promote self-sufficiency and to raise living standards. Ben Salah enjoyed considerable success in the industrial sector. But he provoked widespread antagonism in rural areas because of his insistence on organizing state-run agricultural cooperatives and his goal of bringing all cultivable land under state management. Accusations of corruption and mismanagement followed, and in 1969, fearful that popular opposition to Ben Salah was weakening the government, President Bourguiba renounced him. The former minister was arrested and imprisoned, but escaped from custody in 1973. In exile, Ben Salah organized the Mouvement de l'Unité Populaire (MUP; q.v.), an opposition group embodying the socialist principles he had attempted to apply while in office. President Ben Ali pardoned Ben Salah in 1988. Although he returned to Tunisia, he refrained from publicly engaging in political activity and left the coordination of the MUP to Brahim Haydar.

Ben Yusuf, Salah (1910–1961). Neo-Dustur activist and head of a radical wing of the party that challenged Habib Bourguiba's (q.v.) leadership in 1955. The more revolutionary Ben Yusuf rejected Bourguiba's moderation, epitomized by his acceptance of a French offer of internal autonomy in 1954. Ben Yusuf also strongly supported pan-Arabism, whereas Bourguiba preferred to focus on specifically Tunisian issues. Following his unsuccessful bid to take control of the Neo-Dustur, Ben Yusuf left the country. But he continued to criticize Bourguiba until he was assassinated in Cairo in 1961. Despite the failure of the Yusufist movement, its vigor alarmed Bourguiba and played a major role in shaping his generally negative attitude toward all forms of opposition.

A rehabilitation of Ben Yusuf occurred in the more pluralistic political environment that developed after Bourguiba's removal from office. First, President Zine el-Abidine Ben Ali (q.v.) invited Ben Yusuf's widow, who had accompanied him into exile in 1956, to return to Tunisia, which she did in 1988. Then he released Ben Yusuf's supporters, who had been incarcerated since the 1960s, as part of an amnesty of political prisoners later in the same year. The process culminated in 1991 when Ben Yusuf's remains were returned to his homeland for burial.

Berbers. The earliest identifiable ethno-linguistic group inhabiting the area of modern Tunisia. The first Berbers represented an amalgamation of the neolithic peoples associated with Capsian culture and migrants of west Asian origin who entered North Africa from the south and east. Their name derives from *barbaroi* (barbarians), the derogatory term by which the ancient Greeks referred to them.

The Berbers vigorously resisted Carthaginian, Roman, Vandal, and Byzantine efforts to subjugate them, although they sometimes forged alliances with the alien rulers and assimilated some facets of the more sophisticated Mediterranean cultures. Widespread Berber conversions to Islam occurred in the wake of the Arab conquest of North Africa in the seventh century, creating an atmosphere conducive to the gradual spread of the traditions, customs, and language of the Arabs as well as their religion. In Ifriqiya, the Berbers retained their numerical majority for several centuries, but the influx of the Banu Hilal (q.v.), the Banu Sulaim (q.v.), and other nomadic Arab tribes beginning in the eleventh century assured the triumph of the Arabization process that had already begun. Subsequent centuries of Arab-Berber contact led to the virtual disappearance of a pure Berber stock, although Berber dialects and traditions persisted.

In the modern era, the word *Berber* has taken on a primarily linguistic (rather than racial) meaning, signifying an individual whose first language is a Berber dialect. Estimates of Tunisia's present population place the number of such persons at fewer than 250,000. Most live on the island of Jerba or in the Saharan regions of southern Tunisia.

Bey. Military title of Turkish origin. First used in Tunisia early in the Ottoman era, it indicated the officer charged by the dey (q.v.) with overseeing the rural regions beyond direct Turkish control. Toward this end, the beys mounted a semiannual expedition (mahalla) (q.v.) and organized tribal warriors into auxiliary cavalry units. In the process, they established closer links with the Tunisian population than did other members of the Ottoman ruling class. Beginning in the 1630s, the bey Murad Corso (q.v.) and his descendants amassed increasing powers in their own hands, ultimately displacing the deys as the real rulers. The Husainids (q.v.), the Muradids' successors, also used the title from their accession in 1705 until the abolition of the monarchy in 1957.

Bizerte. Tunisia's major seaport, located on the northern coast. Extensive French improvements at Bizerte in the 1890s, many of them in connection with the establishment of a French naval base, made its harbor and port facilities among the finest in the Mediterranean. France retained control of its base after independence and refused Tunisian demands for its evacuation in 1961. The French army's attempt to break a blockade of the base led to bloody confrontations with hastily mobilized Tunisian civilians and paramilitary units. Responding to a Tunisian appeal, the United Nations called for negotiations in regard to the future of the base. After lengthy delays, France abandoned the installation in late 1963.

Black Death. Like the rest of the Mediterranean basin and Europe, Tunisia experienced devastating outbreaks of bubonic plague during the fourteenth-century epidemic. The first eruption of the disease in 1346 wreaked economic and social havoc in and around Tunis. Over the next 500 years, periodic recurrences of the plague ravaged the countryside, seriously disrupting the agrarian economy. Not until the 1820s did the threat of pestilence finally vanish from the region.

Black Thursday. January 26, 1978, the date on which the Union Générale des Travailleurs Tunisiens (UGTT; q.v.) organized the first nationwide general strike since independence to protest the government's mismanagement of the economy and its growing intolerance toward opposition sentiments. In an explosion of pent-up frustrations that had been building for several years, strikers clashed with security forces, producing the most acute violence in the country in more than two decades. Estimates of fatalities on Black Thursday range as high as 200 persons, while hundreds more, including UGTT leader Habib Achour (q.v.), were jailed. Although these demonstrations elicited few immediate changes, they starkly revealed the fragility of the country's political and economic situation.

Boniface (?–431). Roman military governor of Africa Proconsularis who revolted in 429. The Vandals (q.v.) took advantage of the ensuing instability to invade and establish their control over the province.

al-Borma. Oil field near the Algerian frontier, approximately 250 kilometers (150 miles) southwest of Gabès. It was discovered in 1964 by the Italian national oil company, Ente Nazionale Idrocarburi (ENI), which developed al-Borma in a partnership with the government. This marked the beginning of Tunisia's oil industry. Until natural gas (q.v.) production began at the Miskar field in the Gulf of Gabès in 1995, al-Borma was also Tunisia's major source of that commodity. An oil pipeline links al-Borma with the petroleum export terminal at La Skirra (q.v.).

Bourguiba, Habib (1903–). Nationalist leader, founder of the Neo-Dustur Party, first prime minister of independent Tunisia, and president of the republic from 1958 until his removal for medical reasons in 1987. He left his native Monastir to obtain his secondary schooling in Tunis. He attended both Sadiqi College (q.v.) and the Lycée Carnot, an institution primarily for the children of the colons (q.v.). Despite joining the Dustur Party in 1922, Bourguiba received a scholarship to the University of Paris in 1924. While studying law in France, he met and married Mathilde Louvain, who returned to Tunis with him in 1927.

Political activity quickly became more important for Bourguiba than his law practice. Beginning in 1931, he manifested his impatience with the Dustur leadership's conservative views in a number of articles written for the Dustur-sponsored paper *La Voix du Tunisien* (q.v.). In the next year, along with Mahmoud Matari (q.v.), Tahar Sfar (q.v.), and his brother M'hammad, he founded *L'Action Tunisienne* (q.v.), a newspaper that expressed the more radical views of the younger, French-educated segment of the party that he epitomized. In the pages of *L'Action Tunisienne,* Bourguiba forcefully addressed controversial issues that the more timid Dustur directors preferred to avoid. His vigorous defense of Islamic values earned him considerable acclaim, especially his outspoken opposition to the protectorate government's plan to allow Tunisians who had accepted French citizenship to be buried in Muslim cemeteries. He also censured French economic policy in the protectorate and demanded full independence. Because of the blunt attacks of Bourguiba and his colleagues, publication of *L'Action Tunisienne* was suspended and the Dustur was suppressed in the spring of 1933. Several months later, Bourguiba's spirited opposition to the resident general's proposal to allow the reconstitution of the Dustur in return for a modulation of its policies resulted in his expulsion from the party.

At a March 1934 meeting in Ksar Hellal, Bourguiba and his fellow dissidents created the Neo-Dustur Party, underscoring the transition to a new generation of nationalist leaders. The militant declarations of Bourguiba and the rest of the party hierarchy led, before the end of the year, to their arrest and consignment to internal exile at Bordj Le Boeuf in the Sahara. In the months prior to his detention, however, Bourguiba had overseen the organization of an effective cellular structure that enabled the Neo-Dustur to continue functioning during the incarceration of its leaders.

The arrival of a new resident general in 1936, followed by the electoral victory of the Popular Front (q.v.) in France, paved the way for Bourguiba's release and the resumption of Neo-Dustur political activity. He revived his demands for independence, but also acknowledged the desirability of maintaining a cooperative relationship between the two states. Some French liberals supported Bourguiba, but colon intransigence, combined with senior French generals' emphasis on the strategic importance of North Africa in the event of a European war, blocked any move toward a redefinition of the protectorate arrangement before the fall of the Popular Front in mid-1937. The inability to achieve a breakthrough, even with a reasonably sympathetic French government, frustrated Bourguiba. But the deteriorating economy and the return from exile of Abd al-Aziz Thaalbi (q.v.), the founder of the Dustur Party, left no time to lament past failures. Thaalbi hoped to take charge of the nationalist movement, and although Bourguiba had no intention of yielding to him, the older man's reputation and prestige made him formidable. After a brief period of wary cooperation, Bourguiba felt strong enough to break with Thaalbi openly. Neo-Dustur militants disrupted the speeches of the Dustur leader, whose resort to French police protection gave credence to Bourguiba's assertion that he, not Thaalbi, represented Tunisia's future.

The French authorities carefully monitored the situation in Tunisia throughout 1937, but elsewhere in the Maghrib they took more decisive measures, arresting key Moroccan and Algerian nationalist leaders. In November, Bourguiba called a strike to demonstrate Tunisian solidarity with the other North Africans, while in his *L'Action Tunisienne* columns he rallied popular support for a confrontation with France. Mahmoud Matari, president of the Neo-Dustur since its founding, disapproved of these increasingly radical steps. His resignation in early 1938 left Bourguiba in complete control of the party. Escalating tensions produced a series of violent demonstrations in April. Bourguiba was again arrested, and the Neo-Dustur was dissolved. To avoid arousing nationalist passions, the French authorities arranged for his trial to take place in France. After several months of delay, Bourguiba and a number of other political prisoners were transferred to France just before it fell to Germany in the spring of 1940. The trial never occurred.

Bourguiba feared that the fall of France would tempt Neo-Dustur leaders still at liberty in Tunisia to consider cooperating with the Axis powers as the surest means of ending the protectorate. He considered this view both naive and dangerous, and even from prison, he warned Tunisians against such collaboration. Nevertheless, when the Germans entered previously unoccupied southern France following Operation Torch (q.v.) in November 1942, they freed Bourguiba and other Tunisian nationalist prisoners in the hope of winning over the Neo-Dustur leader. Bourguiba spent the early months of 1943 in Rome making propaganda broadcasts that condemned French colonialism but still consistently spurned German and Italian overtures, ostensibly because they did not guarantee Tunisian independence after the war, but also because of his acute distaste for fascism. In April 1943, he was permitted to return to German-occupied Tunisia. Later in the spring, as Allied troops closed in on Tunis, Bourguiba's rejection of an Axis offer to evacuate him made clear his preference for dealing with the French.

Almost immediately, he began lobbying protectorate officials to secure for Tunisians the political rewards that he believed their loyalty to France during the war had earned them. With an eye toward more effectively mobilizing Tunisian opinion, he encouraged the creation of interest groups, including the important Union Générale des Travailleurs Tunisiens (UGTT; q.v.), with which the party maintained close links. The minimal concessions offered over the next two years, however, convinced Bourguiba that only concerted international pressure would alter the French government's views on Tunisia.

In April 1945, he secretly left the country to begin a four-year international campaign publicizing Tunisian grievances and soliciting support for the Neo-Dustur. He traveled first to Egypt and the Middle East, where the increasingly contentious Palestine question was the primary concern of the newly formed Arab League (q.v.). To draw attention to North African problems, Bourguiba, along with prominent Moroccan and Algerian nationalist exiles in Cairo, established the Comité de la Libération du Maghreb Arabe (q.v.) in March 1947. During these years he also visited the United States, attending the December 1946 session of the United Nations. While in the United States, he sought support for the Neo-Dustur among American trade unionists, many of whose leaders had become familiar with the UGTT through international labor organizations. They sympathized with its goals and recognized the ties between them and the Neo-Dustur. In the end, however, Bourguiba's efforts produced few concrete results in either the Arab world or the West.

While he was abroad, followers of the more radical Neo-Dustur secretary-general, Salah Ben Yusuf (q.v.), lost patience with Bourguiba's slow-moving tactics. Spurning the gradualism and negotiations that characterized the latter's philosophy, they advocated taking whatever steps were necessary to achieve immediate and unrestricted Tunisian independence. In September 1949, Bourguiba returned to the country at the invitation of the protectorate authorities, who hoped his presence would deepen the rift in the nationalist movement. The warm welcome he received during a tour throughout Tunisia in the winter of 1949–1950 confirmed his leadership of the party, although Ben Yusuf continued as its secretary-general. Conscious of the importance of organizing and mobilizing ordinary Tunisians, and aware of the benefits the Neo-Dustur derived from its close association with the UGTT, Bourguiba guided the party in forming auxiliary societies grouping together farmers, craftsmen, merchants, women, students, and other special-interest groups.

Armed with this impressive backing, Bourguiba initiated a dialogue with France. The talks opened on a promising note, with the French negotiators accepting the principle of internal autonomy for Tunisia. In return, the Neo-Dustur permitted Ben Yusuf to participate in a ministry formed to work out the details of this arrangement. Bourguiba, who had no official status, did not take part in these discussions. By the fall of 1950, however, the talks had bogged down and France appeared ready either to impose the limited reforms it believed were in order, regardless of Tunisian views, or to break off the negotiations entirely. A wave of protest strikes erupted throughout the protectorate. In February 1951, Bourguiba again departed on an international mission to clarify the Neo-Dustur's position in Asia, Europe, and the United States. Late in the same year, he traveled to Paris in an attempt to break the lingering deadlock. He arrived just as the French government presented a final, and unacceptable, offer that rang down the curtain on the negotiations.

Returning to Tunisia, Bourguiba orchestrated Neo-Dustur protests, which were augmented by strikes called by the UGTT and most of the party's auxiliary organizations. Arrested along with other party activists in January 1952, he was at first imprisoned in the Sahara and then on the island of Galite, near Tabarka. After incarcerating the Neo-Dustur leadership, the French sought, but failed to find, Tunisians unaffiliated with the party with whom they could conduct meaningful negotiations. In the meantime, however, Tunisian frustrations manifested themselves in the form of the fallaqa (q.v.), members of an armed resistance movement. In the spring of 1954, the government of Pierre Mendès-France (q.v.), recognizing the urgency of resolving the Tunisian crisis, pronounced itself ready to negotiate an accord granting internal autonomy. Bourguiba was brought to France to conduct the negotiations. The process lasted for almost a year, and Bourguiba came to realize that for a variety of political reasons the Mendès-France government could not go beyond the concept of internal autonomy to that of full independence, which he would have preferred. Therefore, Bourguiba decided to accept what the prime minister could offer as a steppingstone to eventual independence, and an agreement was reached in April 1955.

In June, he returned to Tunisia to a hero's welcome, although Ben Yusuf and his militant followers rejected internal autonomy as inadequate and accused Bourguiba of caving in to the French. At the Neo-Dustur Congress in October, Ben Yusuf mounted an unsuccessful challenge to Bourguiba's leadership. He was expelled from the party, leaving Bourguiba in absolute control. When France terminated the Moroccan protectorate several months later, Bourguiba demanded the same consideration for Tunisia, which was granted on March 20. Neo-Dustur candidates easily triumphed in the elections for a Constituent Assembly, and Bourguiba became the prime minister of the first independent government. He continued to serve in that capacity until 1970, although he preferred the designation "chef du cabinet" (head of the cabinet) after 1959.

Shortly after independence, the Constituent Assembly deposed the aging Amin Bey (q.v.) and declared the formation of a republic, bestowing on Bourguiba the additional title of president in 1957. In an arrangement calculated to permit the enormously popular Neo-Dustur leader to determine the thrust of the new nation, the constitution vested considerable powers in the president while depriving the legislature of any real authority. For more than a decade and a half, Bourguiba faced no challengers, being reelected in 1964 and 1969. In 1974 the National Assembly confirmed him as president for life.

Bourguiba utilized his extensive presidential powers and his popularity to initiate far-reaching programs of social change. His goal was to replace the traditional values and attitudes prevalent among many Tunisians with more modern and progressive ones that would enhance the country's ability to cope with the contemporary world. Because Islam played a central role in the lives of most Tunisians, many of Bourguiba's early reforms focused on traditional Islamic institutions and practices. He tried to alter or terminate religious practices that he regarded as no longer viable. Bourguiba personally spearheaded campaigns to abolish both public and private habus (q.v.) lands; to eliminate the sharia (q.v.) courts; to introduce civil, commercial, and criminal codes that all but negated the influence of Islamic law; to enact the Personal Status Code (q.v.), which outlawed many customary practices involving women and the family; and to bring all education under the control of the state. The latter process reflected his conviction that education would play the most crucial role in the transformation of Tunisian attitudes. With that in mind, he worked assidu-ously to expand and improve the country's school system. Bour-guiba's most brazen action regarding Islam was to publicly break the Ramadan fast in 1960. He asserted that a developing country such as Tunisia could not afford the decline in productivity occasioned by this observance. When the ulama of Kairouan launched protest demon-strations, Bourguiba moved vigorously and quickly to repress them, accusing the religious authorities of seeking to protect their traditional power at the expense of the national good. Within five years of inde-pendence, Bourguiba had succeeded in bringing virtually the entire re-ligious establishment under state control. An uneasy truce developed between the president and the religious leadership, but memories of the wholesale dismantling of Islamic institutions in the early days of the republic, combined with the belief that Bourguiba's secular poli-cies had created many problems of their own, gave rise in the 1970s and 1980s to a potent, religiously based opposition.

No less than on social issues, Bourguiba's thinking shaped indepen-dent Tunisia's economic policies. Although the president had initially adopted a laissez-faire philosophy, by 1961 he concluded that only a dramatic reversal of this approach could revive the stagnant economy. Consequently, he named Ahmad Ben Salah (q.v.), a longtime propo-nent of expanding state involvement in the economy, minister of plan-ning. Against the advice of some of his associates who mistrusted the ambitious Ben Salah, Bourguiba gave him a free hand to orchestrate the country's economic development, making it clear that he supported the younger man's proposals. Many Tunisians believed this appoint-ment constituted Bourguiba's endorsement of Ben Salah as his politi-cal heir apparent. Nonetheless, when the minister's socialist strategies, especially his plans to bring all cultivable land under state control, aroused widespread opposition in the late 1960s, the politically adept Bourguiba did not hesitate to break with his protégé. Accusing Ben Salah of deliberately deceiving him about the health of the economy and of condoning corruption within the ministry, Bourguiba had him arrested and tried for treason. He was convicted in 1969.

Ben Salah's disgrace prompted even some party stalwarts to ques-tion Bourguiba's almost total domination of the political environment. In addition to his state office, Bourguiba presided over the Neo-Dus-tur or, as it was known after 1964, the Parti Socialiste Dusturien (PSD; q.v.). Critics of his poor judgment in bestowing such extensive au-thority on Ben Salah demanded checks on the powers of the presi-dency. At the same time, there were calls for the liberalization of party procedures so as to break the monopoly on decision making enjoyed by the old guard that had crystallized around the chief executive. Bourguiba's recurrent bouts of ill health and his extended trips abroad for medical treatment in the early 1970s gave his opponents additional reasons for trying to loosen his control over both the party and the government. Although the prestige he enjoyed as the "supreme combatant," a sobriquet he had earned in the 1930s, enabled Bourguiba to weather this storm of protest, he fully grasped its significance. In 1974, with his health restored, he strengthened his hold on the party by expelling his most outspoken opponents and engineering his appointment as party president for life.

Even as these political issues were being thrashed out, efforts were under way to repair the damage done to the economy during the Ben Salah years. Beginning in 1970, Prime Minister Hadi Nouira (q.v.) had, with Bourguiba's approval, launched a free-market economy specifically designed to attract the foreign capital deemed essential for the rebuilding process. Although hundreds of international investors, lured by tax concessions and other incentives, did build factories in Tunisia, most of them were concentrated in the already industrialized capital region. They produced almost exclusively for export rather than for the local market and, because they were highly mechanized, provided only limited employment opportunities for Tunisians. At the same time, the agricultural sector, on which many Tunisians still depended, deteriorated. In the final analysis, only a handful of Tunisian capitalists benefited from these policies. For the bulk of the population, prices climbed more rapidly than salaries. Unemployment and underemployment persisted in a situation that aggravated existing class disparities.

Although Nouira had been the architect of these economic policies, Bourguiba's vigorous reaffirmation of authority in the mid-1970s made it impossible for him to dissociate himself from decisions that had proven unwise or to shield himself from the growing public resentment over the economy. Perhaps recalling the difficulties his critics had created in the wake of the Ben Salah affair, the president condoned government efforts to stifle protests. The inability of UGTT leaders, many of whom were veteran party activists, to impress upon him the seriousness of the workers' grievances served only to heighten tensions. Their explosion in the violence-ridden general strike on January 26, 1978, represented the most serious challenge to Bourguiba since independence.

The Black Thursday (q.v.) disorders split the upper echelons of the Parti Socialiste Dusturien between those who advocated extensive reforms to correct social and economic ills and those who argued that a crackdown on the regime's opponents was the best means of stabilizing the situation. Bourguiba resisted adhering fully to either course of action. Instead, he preferred to discipline the demonstrators while offering minimal concessions that only marginally altered the status quo. The uprising in Gafsa on the second anniversary of Black Thursday, however, underscored the need for more substantial action.

A few months later, Bourguiba took advantage of Nouira's ill health to install Muhammad Mzali (q.v.) as prime minister, with instructions to liberalize the political environment and to find an economic middle ground between the socialism of Ben Salah and the free-market approach of Nouira. Mzali enjoyed some success in both these areas, at least to the extent that his reforms did not threaten Bourguiba's position at the apex of the political system. In legalizing opposition political parties, for example, the prime minister specifically enjoined them from challenging the president personally.

Despite his advanced age and occasional infirmity, Bourguiba continued to monitor the Tunisian political and economic scene attentively, not hesitating to intervene directly whenever he so desired. In January 1984, the most violent rioting since independence broke out when Tunisia's international creditors pressured the Mzali government to remove subsidies from several basic commodities. Seeking to distance himself from this extremely unpopular action, Bourguiba immediately ordered the subsidies reinstated. By thus undermining the authority of his prime minister, the president made it virtually impossible for him to pursue new initiatives that might have similarly disruptive effects. Nevertheless, Bourguiba ignored the demands of party conservatives that he dismiss Mzali, preferring to keep him in office with no capacity for independent action. A heart attack suffered by Bourguiba later in the year enabled the prime minister to reassert himself for a time, but as the president recovered, close associates opposed to the pluralism Mzali had tentatively introduced persuaded Bourguiba in the summer of 1986 not only to dismiss Mzali but also to divorce his wife Wassila and to break with his son Habib Jr. (q.v.), both of whom had supported Mzali. For the next year, Bourguiba backed the often heavy handed efforts of the new prime minister, Rashid Sfar, to control the opposition, which was concentrated in the labor unions, the political parties legalized by Mzali, and the increasingly active Mouvement de la Tendance Islamique (MTI; q.v.). Bourguiba's anxiety over the potential danger possed by the latter organization contributed substantially to his downfall. Scores of MTI members were tried in September 1987. Several received death sentences, and many received lengthy prison terms. Bourguiba was happy to thus rid himself of some of his most outspoken and persistent critics, but interior minister Zine el-Abidine Ben Ali (q.v.) persuaded him to commute the death sentence of MTI leader Rashid Ghannushi (q.v.) so as to avoid providing the group with a martyr.

The president accepted Ben Ali's advice and promoted him to the office of prime minister in October. In the following month, however,

Bourguiba appeared to be on the verge of reversing his decision regarding the MTI executions. On November 7, 1987, Ben Ali, attributing this and other erratic behavior to Bourguiba's poor health and increasing senility, arranged for a team of physicians to examine Bourguiba. They declared him medically incapable of executing his presidential duties, enabling Ben Ali to succeed him as president of the republic in accordance with the provisions of article 57 of the constitution. The former chief executive lived for a time at a presidential estate in Mornag, near Tunis, before retiring to his hometown of Monastir in late 1988.

Although he had clearly precipitated Bourguiba's removal, Ben Ali took pains to assure the public that his government would accord Bourguiba the respect to which his long career had entitled him. The blame for the worst abuses of Bourguiba's last years in office was invariably laid at the feet of members of his entourage, several of whom were tried and sentenced to prison for their misdeeds. Nonetheless, Ben Ali quickly set about dismantling the cult of personality that had developed around Bourguiba during the half-century in which he had dominated Tunisian political life. The title of president for life was abolished in 1988. Shortly thereafter, the statues of Bourguiba that were fixtures in virtually every town in the country were quietly taken down. Similarly, the many thoroughfares and institutions named in the ex-president's honor received new designations. The culmination of this process was the relocation of a large equestrian statue of Bourguiba that had become a landmark of downtown Tunis to a far less conspicuous site in the suburb of La Goulette. Prior to the 1989 elections, the former leader made a public appearance to endorse Ben Ali's candidacy for the presidency. Thereafter, however, he remained in seclusion. Rumors concerning the deterioration of his physical and mental health circulated widely.

Bourguiba, Habib Jr. (1927–). Son of and adviser to Habib Bourguiba (q.v.). Like his father, he received his secondary education at Sadiqi College (q.v.) and earned a law degree in France (in 1954). In the early years of independence, he held many key diplomatic posts, including ambassador to Italy (1957–1958), France (1958–1961), and the United States (1961–1963). Elected to the political bureau of the Parti Socialiste Dusturien (PSD; q.v.) in 1964, he filled various party offices, acted as a counselor to his father, and served on the boards of a number of public and private companies during the next two decades. Political differences between Bourguiba and his father surfaced as the president's health deteriorated following his 1984 heart attack. In 1986, President Bourguiba denounced several members of his entourage, including his wife and his son, whom he believed were conspiring against him.

Bourguibism. Political philosophy of moderation espoused by Habib Bourguiba (q.v.), particularly during the nationalist struggle and the first two decades of independence. It was characterized by compromise, by a step-by-step approach intended to provide tactical flexibility in the pursuit of ultimately inflexible principles, and by efforts to avoid permanently alienating political opponents. The upsurge in political and economic unrest beginning in the late 1970s prompted the abandonment of this philosophy in favor of less conciliatory strategies.

Buluggin ibn Ziri (?–984). Founder of the Zirid dynasty (q.v.). Buluggin was a Berber ally of the Fatimids (q.v.) whom they appointed to govern Ifriqiya when their court moved to Egypt in 973. While never renouncing his allegiance to the Fatimids, he continually tested the limits of his independence and paved the way for his descendants' eventual break with Cairo.

Byzacenia. Roman province created early in the fifth century in the coastal and predesert region south of Africa Proconsularis (q.v.).

Byzantine Empire. For slightly more than a hundred years in the sixth and seventh centuries, portions of modern Tunisia's coastal plain and its immediate hinterland were ruled by the Byzantine Empire. Soon after Vandal nobles overthrew King Hilderic (q.v.), an ally of Emperor Justinian, in 530, a Byzantine force was dispatched to Africa. In addition to avenging Hilderic, the expedition also served Justinian's goal of attempting to restore the grandeur and territory of the Roman Empire at its height. Subsequent efforts to stimulate the economy of the province and to extend control over new lands triggered Berber raids against towns and villages that persisted throughout the Byzantine era. The effectiveness of imperial rule was further diminished by Justinian's attempt to impose a Monophysite theology on his African Christian subjects and by Emperor Heraclius's later advocacy of Monothelite concepts. These religious tensions influenced the governor, Gregory (q.v.), to declare his independence from Constantinople in 646. The almost simultaneous incursions of the Arab Muslims, however, thwarted Gregory's plans and Byzantine authority crumbled throughout North Africa.

-C-

Caecilian (fl. ca. 300–315). Cleric who responded weakly to the Roman emperor Diocletian's persecution of Christians in 303. As a result, he was condemned by many church leaders when he became bishop of Carthage a decade later. His most outspoken critic, Donatus (q.v.), organized a popular resistance movement against Caecilian and his supporters that lasted for more than a century.

Caliph; Caliphate. Westernized form of the Arabic *khalifah,* a successor, the word designated the successors of the prophet Muhammad as spiritual and political head of the Muslim community. In Tunisia, the first Fatimid ruler, Ubaidallah (q.v.), took this title to underscore his claim of universal Muslim leadership and also to challenge the legitimacy of the Abbasid family (q.v.), which had claimed the office since 750. The al-Muwahhid rulers also styled themselves caliphs, as did their Hafsid (q.v.) retainers who assumed control of Tunisia in the thirteenth century. When the Abbasid dynasty collapsed under Mongol pressure in 1258, some Muslims in the Middle Eastern Islamic heartlands acknowledged the head of the Hafsid family as caliph. But he asserted no authority in that capacity, and the title fell into disuse until the Ottomans revived it in the nineteenth century.

Cambon, Paul (1843–1924). First French resident general in Tunisia (1882–1886). His initial task was to oversee the implementation of reforms agreed to in the La Marsa Convention (q.v.). In so doing, Cambon enshrined the practice of maintaining the appearance of beylical sovereignty while reserving real power for himself and his cadre of French administrators.

Cap Nègre. Promontory on Tunisia's northern coast where a French trading station was established in 1666. The site, called Tamkart in Arabic, was ceded to France in accordance with the terms of a 1685 commercial treaty. The export of wheat across the Mediterranean from Cap Nègre revealed an increasing Tunisian interest in international commerce and saw a decline in corsair activities, at least temporarily. Concerned over the European domination of this growing and potentially profitable trade, Ali Pasha (q.v.) ordered the closure of the Cap Nègre entrepôt in 1741.

Capsa; Capsian Culture. Ancient site near the modern city of Gafsa at which the remains of a Neolithic culture dating from the tenth millennium B.C.E. have been unearthed.

Carthage. City on the Gulf of Tunis founded by Phoenician merchants in the ninth century B.C.E. The Carthaginians dominated Mediterranean commerce from the sixth to the third centuries B.C.E. through a network of trading posts. In the Punic Wars (q.v.) of the third and second centuries B.C.E., Carthage sustained a series of defeats at the hands of Rome, the most powerful rival it had yet confronted. These wars ended when Rome destroyed the city in 146 B.C.E. Julius Caesar ordered its reconstruction in 27 B.C.E., and Carthage quickly emerged as the principal city of Roman Africa and one of the major urban centers in the empire. Later it became an early center of Christianity. Carthage preserved its importance until the end of the seventh century C.E., when the Arabs abandoned it in favor of Tunis, whose location further inland made it less vulnerable to attacks from the sea. It is now a fashionable beach suburb of the capital.

Charles V (1500–1558). Hapsburg emperor who also ruled Spain as Charles I. In 1535, he responded to a request from the Hafsids (q.v.), whom the Ottoman admiral Khair al-Din Barbarossa (q.v.) had ousted from their capital in the previous year, for help against their common Turkish enemy. After Spanish troops had regained Tunis and La Goulette for the Hafsids, the emperor instituted a protectorate that lasted until the weakened Hafsids finally succumbed to the Ottomans in 1574.

Charles of Anjou (1226–1285). Brother of King Louis IX (q.v.) and ruler of Sicily from 1266 until 1282. Unlike earlier Christian rulers of the island, he showed little interest in North Africa, making no effort, for example, to continue the Norman (q.v.) practice of extracting tribute from the Hafsids (q.v.). When he failed to dissuade his brother from undertaking a crusade against the Hafsids in 1270, he reluctantly brought his army to Tunisia. Upon his arrival, he found Louis dead and his troops decimated by the plague. Charles took command and hastily signed a peace treaty with al-Mustansir I (q.v.) that guaranteed religious freedom for Christians in Tunisia. Then he withdrew the crippled army, ending the ill-fated expedition.

Chatti, Habib (1916–1991). Journalist, diplomat, and international civil servant. A Neo-Dustur activist from his youth, Chatti pursued a career in journalism, which led to his appointment as independent Tunisia's first director of information services in 1956. Following ambassadorial appointments in several Middle Eastern and North African countries and in Great Britain between 1958 and 1972, he served as minister of foreign affairs from 1974 until 1977. From 1980 until 1985 he served as secretary general of the Organization of the Islamic Conference, playing an active role in a wide variety of matters of importance to the world Muslim community.

Cinema. Albert Samama was a Jewish-Tunisian entrepreneur who developed an interest in the cinema around the turn of the century. He shot several silent films in the country in the 1920s. Later in the interwar years, some French directors availed themselves of the protectorate's favorable climate for filmmaking, but Tunisians had neither the inclination nor the opportunity to follow in Samama's footsteps. At the time of independence, no Tunisian film industry existed and few Tunisians possessed cinematic training or experience.

In 1957, the Tunisian government created a state-owned company, the Société Anonyme Tunisienne de Production et d'Expansion Cinématographique (SATPEC), to manage the importation and distribution of foreign films, as well as to promote the development of indigenous production. But it was only a decade later that such an enterprise began to take shape, with SATPEC building a film production complex in the Tunis suburbs in 1966. Later in that year the first Tunisian feature film, *L'aube,* directed by Omar Khlifi (a man with no formal cinematic training), was released. Khlifi and a cadre of Tunisians that included Sadoq Ben Aicha, Abdellatif Ben Ammar, Brahim Babaï, Rachid Ferchiou, and Naceur Ktari, all of whom had studied filmmaking in Europe, established themselves in the late 1960s as influential pioneers in the country's fledgling film industry. The biennial Journées Cinématographiques de Carthage film festival, which acquired international renown following its 1966 inauguration, was an important by-product of this era.

By the late 1970s, the government had ended SATPEC's monopoly on the industry as part of a general trend toward privatization, although the company continued to function until 1988. The creation of new film studios in the 1970s and 1980s, many of them engaged in international cooperative ventures, not only expanded the opportunities available for already active filmmakers but also facilitated the emergence of a younger generation. Ridha Behi's 1977 cinematic condemnation of tourism, *Soleil des hyènes,* won great critical acclaim, as did the debut feature films of Mahmoud Ben Mahmoud (*Traversées,* 1982); Taieb Louhichi (*L'ombre de la terre,* 1982); Nouri Bouzid (*L'homme de cendres,* 1986); and Ferid Boughedir, whose 1990 *Halfaouine* proved to be the greatest box-office success in the history of the Tunisian cinema. The entry into the directors' ranks of Selma Baccar (1978) and Neija Ben Mabrouk (1982) paved the way for such later female filmmakers as Moufida Tlatli, whose 1994 feature *Les silences du palais* was widely regarded as one of the best Tunisian productions ever released.

Climate. Except for the desert regions in the southern half of the country, Tunisia's climate is typically Mediterranean, with warm, dry summers and cool, moist winters. The average July temperature in Tunis is 26 degrees Centigrade (79 degrees Fahrenheit), while the January average stands at 10 degrees Centigrade (50 degrees Fahrenheit).

Similar norms prevail elsewhere along the coast, although one of the highest temperatures ever recorded on earth—55 degrees Centigrade (131 degrees Fahrenheit)—was registered at Ben Gardane on the southeastern coast. In the interior, temperatures are generally lower in winter, with subfreezing readings not uncommon at the higher elevations, and higher in summer.

Annual precipitation varies considerably from one part of the country to another. The greatest amounts fall in the area northwest of the Cape Bon peninsula. Between 400 and 600 millimeters (16 and 24 inches) a year, coming mostly between October and March, is the norm. The mean annual precipitation at Ain Draham, by far the wettest place in the country, exceeds 1,500 millimeters (60 inches) a year, some of which occasionally falls as snow, while Tabarka, on the coast near the Algerian border, has an annual mean of approximately 1,000 millimeters (40 inches). In the Sahil, normal precipitation ranges from 425 millimeters (17 inches) around Tunis to only 200 millimeters (eight inches) in the south, where the desert encroaches on the coastal plain. On the steppes, rainfall increases from 150 millimeters (six inches) in the west to 300 millimeters (12 inches) in the east. The Saharan oases rarely receive more than 125 millimeters (five inches) of rain a year.

Colon. Settler or colonist. The term originally had an agricultural denotation but eventually came to designate all Europeans residing in France's overseas territories.

Comité de la Libération du Maghreb Arabe/Committee for the Liberation of the Arab Maghrib. Organization created in Cairo in 1948 by Habib Bourguiba (q.v.) and other North African nationalists to coordinate their campaigns against the French and to win the support of other Arab nations for their causes.

Communist Party. *See* **Parti Communiste Tunisien.**

Confédération Générale des Travailleurs Tunisiens (CGTT)/ General Confederation of Tunisian Workers. Labor organization founded in 1924 by Muhammad Ali (q.v.) to articulate Tunisian workers' grievances. Among its goals were the protection of workers' rights, the enhancement of their skills and productivity, and the formation of consumer cooperatives. The Dustur (q.v.) cautiously supported the union at first, but severed its connections after a wave of strikes and the arrest of Muhammad Ali in 1925. The French crushed the CGTT easily and no effective labor organization arose in Tunisia for the next two decades.

Congress of Berlin. Meeting in 1878 at which the European powers acknowledged French claims to a privileged position in Tunisia. The congress rejected similar Italian demands concerning Tunisia, but did recognize Italy's special interests in Tripolitania.

Constitution of 1861. Promulgated by Muhammad al-Sadiq Bey (q.v.), this organic law was the first such document enacted in the Muslim world, where the Quran had traditionally been considered the only guide necessary for governing. The impetus for the constitution came from the pressure of the European powers, especially France, on Muhammad Bey (q.v.) to institutionalize the commitments made in the 1857 Ahd al-aman (security covenant). Tunisian views on the constitution were divided. The religious leadership and urban merchants generally opposed it as another manifestation of growing European influence in the country, but many government officials, especially those familiar with earlier attempts at reform, saw it as a means of creating a stronger and more efficient state.

Distress over the increased strength of the central government and the injurious nature of the European economic penetration of the country, both circumstances facilitated by the constitution and the Ahd al-aman, fueled a widespread rebellion in 1864. Fearful that the bey's inability to curb the revolt would trigger the intervention of its rivals and diminish its own influence in the country, France took the ironic step of compelling Muhammad al-Sadiq to rescind the very document it had pressed him to issue only a few years earlier, thereby terminating the brief constitutional experiment.

Consultative Conference. Advisory body to the resident general established in 1891. The protectorate authorities entirely excluded Tunisians from its deliberations until 1907 and thereafter permitted only a limited number to participate. As a result, the conference served only the interests of the colon population.

Contrôleurs Civils. Corps of civilian administrators organized by Resident General Cambon (q.v.) in 1884 as an intermediate level between French officials in the capital and regional Tunisian administrators. Their primary tasks were to supervise tribal qa'ids and shaikhs, especially in their collection of taxes, and to facilitate colonization.

Corsairs. As Tunisia's Hafsid (q.v.) rulers attempted to recover from the political, economic, and social crises that had shaken their domains in the fourteenth century, they found themselves hemmed in by European military and commercial domination of the central Mediterranean basin. To counter widespread attacks on Muslim shipping, the

Hafsids encouraged North African seamen not only to engage enemy warships but also to conduct raids of their own against European merchant vessels. The Europeans' inability to check the undeclared war that ensued during the 1400s added to the Hafsids' prestige among their fellow Muslims. It also added to their income, for although the corsairs operated independently of the state, the treasury took a share of the profits from the sale of captured ships and cargoes and from the ransoms paid to secure the release of prisoners.

Early in the sixteenth century Spain, flushed with its victories over the last Muslim states in Iberia, attempted to carry the Reconquista (q.v.) into Africa and eliminate the Barbary corsairs in the process. These campaigns met with only partial success. The Spaniards did make some gains in the Maghrib, imposing a virtual protectorate over the emaciated Hafsids from 1535 until 1574. But they drove several corsairs, including Khair al-Din Barbarossa (q.v.) and Darghut (q.v.), to seek help from the Ottoman Empire.

After the Ottoman conquest of Tunisia, its new rulers identified themselves even more closely with the corsairs than had the Hafsids. The pashas, and the deys and beys who followed them, could hardly have done otherwise. They could not depend on a steady flow of taxes from the interior and were ill-equipped, as a result of the centuries of European commercial domination, to foster peaceful maritime trade. Sailors from Ottoman lands in the eastern Mediterranean, immigrants from Andalusia, and Christian renegades figured prominently among the leaders of the corsair enterprise during its golden age in Tunisia in the late sixteenth and early seventeenth centuries. For Europeans of this era, the Barbary "pirates" epitomized greed, cruelty, and terror. From the North African point of view, however, the corsair raids were not piracy but, as they had been from their inception, legitimate belligerent acts that provided the only mechanism for Muslims to acquire a share of the lucrative Mediterranean commerce from which the more powerful European navies and merchants had excluded them.

Political, economic, and social upheavals throughout the continent prevented the European states from forcefully addressing the corsair threat until the latter half of the seventeenth century. In 1662, England and Holland mounted a joint naval expedition that imposed on the bey a treaty protecting their merchant vessels, while France negotiated commercial treaties with Tunisia in 1665, 1672, and 1685. The concurrent deterioration of the Muradid dynasty (q.v.) diminished its capacity to resist such European overtures.

The agreements did not end corsair activity, but they did pave the way for its gradual subordination to more customary forms of commerce. The volume of trans-Mediterranean trade increased in the 1700s but in the continuing absence of a Tunisian merchant fleet most goods still moved in European ships. Raids persisted, albeit on a considerably reduced scale. Vessels from the smaller European states and, after its independence, the United States provided the easiest and most frequently attacked targets.

A general resurgence of corsair attacks occurred while Europe was preoccupied with the Napoleonic Wars. At the end of those hostilities, the powers took steps to eliminate the corsairs once and for all. A British fleet bombarded Tunis in 1816 and after a second show of force three years later the bey acceded to the demands of the Congress of Aix-la-Chapelle (q.v.) and renounced maritime raiding. Nonetheless, Tunisian corsairs engaged in a brief spurt of activity during the Greek Revolution. It was not until the establishment of a European presence in the Maghrib, with the French occupation of Algeria in 1830, that the Barbary corsairs totally vanished from the Mediterranean scene.

Cosovereignty. Concept advanced by the French government to counter the growth of opposition to the protectorate after World War II. At its heart lay an attempt to satisfy some nationalist demands without granting full independence by allowing Tunisia a degree of internal autonomy. While making limited concessions in 1951, France dragged its heels on Neo-Dustur calls for a completely Tunisian government and an assembly mirroring the country's demography. Few colons accepted the assurances of Habib Bourguiba (q.v.) that their interests would be respected in such an altered political atmosphere. Thus, the notion of cosovereignty foundered on the twin rocks of colon and nationalist intransigence, pushing both sides toward more extreme positions. Only after armed violence erupted in 1954 did the protectorate government and the nationalist leadership agree on a plan for internal autonomy. Even then, however, the two parties to the arrangement interpreted it quite differently, with the French viewing internal autonomy as an end in itself and Bourguiba regarding it as a political way station on the road to unqualified independence.

Crusade (Eighth). The attack on Tunisia by King Louis IX (q.v.) in 1270 was the eighth and last major campaign in a series of wars, begun late in the eleventh century, to regain formerly Christian lands throughout the Mediterranean basin from their Muslim rulers.

-D-

Darghut [Draghut; Turghut] (?–1565). Corsair captain who attacked Christian shipping from bases on the island of Jerba. He became governor of Tripoli after the Ottomans captured the city in 1551. A series of aggressive campaigns enabled Darghut to extend his control over formerly Hafsid (q.v.) territories as far afield as Kairouan. Spanish forces seized Jerba in 1560, but Darghut's counterattack destroyed their fleet and ensured Muslim hegemony in the central Mediterranean.

Democratic Constitutional Rally. *See* **Rassemblement Constitutionnel Démocratique (RCD).**

Dépêche Tunisienne, La. Daily newspaper established in 1889 with the financial backing of Resident General Justin Massicault. The editors of *La Dépêche Tunisienne* hoped to offset criticisms of the protectorate expressed in the colon-dominated French-language press by voicing strong support for government policies. The paper flourished throughout the colonial era, not only because it provided an outlet for the expression of official views but also because it surpassed its French language competitors in its ability to convey timely and accurate news reports from Europe. Despite its denunciations of nationalist activities since the late 1930s, *La Dépêche Tunisienne* continued publication for several years after independence. Its last issue appeared in 1961, when a law was enacted, following the Franco-Tunisian confrontation over Bizerte, that severely restricted the participation of foreign nationals in business enterprises.

Dey. Junior officer rank in the Ottoman army. A group of deys took control of Tunis in 1591 after mounting a coup that deposed the governor appointed by Istanbul. Thereafter, they effectively dominated the urban areas but chose to entrust the supervision of the countryside to other soldiers, the beys (q.v.), who eventually challenged their authority. Relegated to secondary status by the bey Murad Corso (q.v.) and his descendants, the deys revolted. Their defeat in 1673 guaranteed the preeminence of the beys.

Donatism. Christian schism of Roman Africa. Its adherents argued that church leaders who had not resisted the persecutions of Emperor Diocletian in 303 were unworthy of their positions and could no longer administer the sacraments. The greatest support for the movement came from rural Berbers and the urban lower classes. Both groups saw Donatism not only in religious terms but also as a means of protesting the economic crisis that had afflicted the province for nearly a century, for which they blamed the Roman and Romanized ruling class emblemized by the church hierarchy.

Donatus (?–ca. 355). Christian bishop. He and his followers split with the church over their insistence on the condemnation of clerics who had failed to oppose the persecutions of Emperor Diocletian.

Don John of Austria (1547–1578). Commander of the Christian forces that captured Tunis from the corsair Ilj Ali (q.v.) in 1573. In keeping with the concept of a Hapsburg (q.v.) protectorate over Tunisia, Don John restored the Hafsid (q.v.) sultan to the throne.

Doolittle, Hooker (1889–1966). American consul in Tunis from 1941 to 1944. First posted to North Africa in 1933, he spent eight years in Tangier and was familiar with both nationalist aspirations and the interests of French colonialists. After Tunis was liberated in the spring of 1943, Doolittle openly criticized the Free French for their treatment of the Arabs and made no effort to hide his sympathy for the Tunisian nationalists. His contacts with leaders of the Neo-Dustur led France to demand his dismissal. Accordingly, the Department of State reassigned Doolittle to Alexandria. French accusations that he was abetting the Neo-Dustur persisted throughout the four years that he served in Egypt.

Dorsal. Mountain range extending southwest to northeast from the Algerian border near Kasserine to Cap Bon. An extension of the Atlas Mountains of Morocco and Algeria, it separates Tunisia's tell and steppe regions. The country's highest mountain, Jabal Shambi (1,544 meters; 5,066 feet), lies in the Dorsal some seven miles northwest of Kasserine.

Dougga. Ancient city that dates to Phoenician times located some 125 kilometers (75 miles) southwest of Tunis. Because it was the residence of Numidian rulers allied with Rome during the Third Punic War (q.v.), Dougga suffered no ill effects when Carthage fell. Rome annexed the city in 46 B.C.E., and its population gradually assimilated Roman ways. It experienced great affluence in the early centuries of Christianity. The city was abandoned after the Vandals (q.v.) arrived. Although the Byzantines revived Dougga briefly, it had no real importance at the time of the Arab invasion. Systematic archeological excavation of the site began in 1899.

Dustur Party. Political party founded by Abd al-Aziz Thaalbi (q.v.) in 1920. Its name means "constitution" and was derived from the party's demand for the restoration of the Constitution of 1861 (q.v.). Party leaders rather unrealistically presented the constitution's revival as a panacea for Tunisia's problems. The party also called for the formation of a government responsible to an elected assembly and for guarantees of Tunisians' basic rights. Most of the Dustur's support came from the Tunis bourgeoisie, which had suffered economically and politically under the protectorate.

The party might have used the links it forged with the labor movement in the mid-1920s as a way of broadening its base. But most Dustur leaders disdained both the working class and the radical forms of protest they associated with trade unionism. In any event, they were more interested in restoring their own lost power and privileges than in pursuing social issues that they did not see as affecting them directly.

Unwilling to challenge the French authorities openly, the Dustur lapsed into inactivity. In the early 1930s, a group of outspoken young men with more populist views rose to prominence in the party. Their demands for Tunisian independence precipitated a threat from the authorities to dissolve the party, opening a serious rift in its ranks. Many of the younger radicals resigned or were expelled from the Dustur. Under the leadership of Habib Bourguiba (q.v.), they established the Neo-Dustur party in 1934. Although the Dustur continued to exist after World War II, it never again played an important role on the Tunisian political scene.

Dustur Socialist Party. *See* **Parti Socialiste Dusturien**

-E-

Education. Prior to the nineteenth century, education in Tunisia was controlled by the ulama (q.v.) and, beyond its most elementary levels, was available only to males. Until the age of about nine, boys attended the kuttab, or Quranic school, whose curriculum consisted primarily of memorizing the scriptures. Then some went on to the madrasa, a secondary school with a broader core of studies that also emphasized religious subjects. At the apex of this system stood the Zaituna Mosque-University (q.v.), at which young men from Tunisia and elsewhere in the Muslim world received the training that qualified them for membership in the ulama class.

The rising power and influence of the West convinced the Husainid beys of the need for modern, secular schools. But for many years only a handful of elites within their entourage studied in them. During the protectorate, Franco-Arab schools (q.v.) offered an essentially French curriculum with instruction in the French language to a limited number of students. To acquaint traditionally educated Zaituna students with European languages and scientific thinking, the Young Tunisians (q.v.) organized the Khalduniyya (q.v.) in 1896. Not until the establishment of the Institut des Hautes Etudes in 1947, however, did nonreligious higher education become available in Tunisia.

Habib Bourguiba (q.v.), who had studied at the best schools in Tunisia and France, regarded mass education as a valuable tool for forging a sense of national unity and creating a supply of skilled workers capable of systematically furthering Tunisia's development. The early independent governments devoted considerable resources, sometimes amounting to as much as one-third of the national budget, to education. This high rate of expenditure, much of it allocated to building the educational infrastructure that the protectorate authorities had deemed unnecessary, declined in later years. Nevertheless, in the first half of the 1990s, between 15 and 20 percent of Tunisia's annual budget still went to the support of education.

The absence of sufficient numbers of adequately trained Tunisians resulted in a bilingual arrangement, since the educational system relied heavily on French teachers for several years after independence. The use of the French language was also consistent with the importance assigned by the ruling elite to literacy in a western language. Until the late 1970s, instruction at the primary level was generally in a mixture of Arabic and French, with French predominating thereafter. At that time, in keeping with the government's stated objective of Arabizing the curriculum, Arabic was made the sole language of instruction for the first three years of primary school. A few years later, however, the study of French, beginning in the second year of primary school, was mandated. Thus, Arabization proceeded slowly and erratically. Even as the use of Arabic spread at the lower levels, higher education, particularly in the sciences, remained in French. For many students, particularly those committed to the Islamist movement and its emphasis on Tunisia's Arabo-Islamic cultural heritage, this situation stimulated a sense of deracination that provoked demands for broader Arabization.

Although schooling has never been compulsory, both the government and the Neo-Dustur party and its successors have actively encouraged school attendance. At independence, the number of pupils in state-run primary schools, following a six-year cycle ending at about age eleven, was 209,438. It rose to 1,472,844 in 1995, 46 percent of whom were girls. Another 9,000 children attended private primary schools. In the same year, 58,279 teachers—roughly a tenfold increase over 1956—staffed the country's 4,000 schools. The spread of primary education helps to account for Tunisia's 65 percent literacy rate, one of the highest in the Arab world.

An examination that students write at the conclusion of primary school determines which students will proceed to the seven-year secondary curriculum. In 1995, there were 662,222 students, 47 percent of them young women, in 712 state secondary schools, with another 75,000 students in private schools at that level. In order to continue their educations beyond the secondary level, students must again pass a rigorous examination, the baccalauréat. In 1992, about 23,000 students (some 35 percent of those who took the baccalauréat) passed it.

Unsuccessful students may repeat the process three times, or until they reach the age of 23.

The University of Tunis, established in 1961, grants both undergraduate and graduate degrees. In 1993, 81,385 students, about 40 percent of them women, were pursuing higher education under the guidance of more than 5,000 faculty members. In 1988, using a model borrowed from France, the government divided the university into several distinct units with specific academic emphases. Since then, the University of Tunis I has specialized in the arts, letters, and human sciences; the University of Tunis II in science, technology, and medicine; and the University of Tunis III in law and economics. The former Zaituna Mosque-University, which had functioned as a faculty of theology within the University of Tunis since the 1960s, was recognized as a separate institution. All of these institutions are located in Tunis and its suburbs. Students outside the capital are served by two smaller institutions founded in 1986, the University of the Center at Monastir, with branches in Sousse and Kairouan, and the University of the South at Sfax, with branches at Gafsa, Gabès, and Jerba. In addition, there are teacher training schools in Bizerte, Sousse, and Tunis.

Egypt. The contrasting philosophies of Habib Bourguiba (q.v.) and Egyptian president Gamal Abdel Nasser, especially in regard to Palestine (q.v.) and Arab unity, resulted in tense relations between their two countries for more than a decade after Tunisia became independent. Bourguiba's distaste for the Egyptian leader was sharpened by the enthusiasm that Salah Ben Yusuf (q.v.), his main rival in the mid-1950s, had for Nasser and his policies. Until 1958, Bourguiba opposed Tunisian membership in the Arab League (q.v.) in protest of Egypt's domination of the organization. Bourguiba's 1965 suggestion that the PLO, then dominated by Egypt, temper its tactics toward Israel precipitated a campaign against him in the Egyptian media that was so vicious that Tunisia severed diplomatic relations with Egypt.

The June 1967 war between Israel and its Arab neighbors, however, fostered a reversal in Tunisian-Egyptian relations. The eruption of spontaneous demonstrations in Tunisia during the war revealed a level of grassroots commitment to the Arab states and the Palestinian cause far in excess of the government's position. Bourguiba responded by restoring relations with Egypt and acknowledging the Palestinians' need to engage in an armed struggle with Israel. Nasser's death in 1970 paved the way for Tunisia to participate more fully in Middle Eastern affairs.

Like most Arab states, Tunisia condemned the visit of Egyptian president Anwar Sadat to Jerusalem in 1977 and broke relations with Egypt following its 1979 peace treaty with Israel. The Arab League's decision to locate its headquarters in Tunis following Egypt's expulsion from the league in 1979 indicated how dramatically Tunisian official views on the issues most critical to the eastern Arab world had changed since the 1950s.

The Iran-Iraq War of the 1980s underscored the need for Arab solidarity. Egyptian willingness to aid the Iraqi war effort facilitated informal contacts between Egypt and other Arab states, including Tunisia. But diplomatic relations with Egypt were not restored until early 1988, after Zine el-Abidine Ben Ali (q.v.) had succeeded Bourguiba as president. Following the 1990 Iraqi invasion of Kuwait, Ben Ali opposed the deployment of foreign forces in the Gulf region and condemned the Arab states, including Egypt, that supplied troops to the coalition arrayed against Iraq. Demonstrators in Tunis and other cities denounced the policies of Egypt (and the United States and Saudi Arabia) throughout the crisis that culminated in the Gulf War (q.v.), placing additional strains on bilateral relations. Once Kuwait had been liberated, however, Tunisia succeeded in moving swiftly beyond these ruptures, largely because of mutually shared concerns about postwar regional stability. With the Egyptian and Tunisian governments both having to contend with well-organized, highly critical Islamist movements, each recognized the advantages of a cooperative relationship that could reinforce the barriers against religious extremism throughout the region.

Eucharistic Congress (1930). Assembly of French Catholics that convened in Carthage. Many Tunisians were offended by the decision to hold such a meeting in an overwhelmingly Muslim country, viewing it as a conscious French insult. Habib Bourguiba (q.v.) later singled out the Eucharistic Congress as a conclusive demonstration of France's insensitivity to Tunisian concerns. It persuaded him of the need to adopt an approach to the protectorate government that was more militant than the one advocated by the Dustur's leaders.

European Economic Community (EEC); European Union (EU). The European Economic Community accorded Tunisia associate membership in 1969, paving the way for an agreement that promoted the export of Tunisian agricultural products to Europe, especially olive oil, which was exempted from duties. Although the community collectively became Tunisia's major trading partner, accounting for more than 80 percent of its exports and 70 percent of its imports by 1994, rivalry in the marketing of certain products created occasional strains. The growth of the Tunisian textile industry in the 1970s, for example, prompted the EEC to impose quotas on the importation of Tunisian textiles and clothing toward the end of that decade. Conversely, the entry of Greece into the EEC in 1981 and of Spain and Portugal in 1986 aroused Tunisian fears that these agricultural competitors (especially in olives and olive oil) would drive its products from important European markets. An EEC guarantee to maintain agricultural imports from Tunisia at the level of the early 1980s, however, helped to assuage such anxieties.

Plans for the creation of a single European market, which materialized with the establishment of the European Union in 1993, persuaded Tunisia and its North African neighbors of the desirability of formulating common policies to ensure both the maximum exploitation of the benefits an economically united Europe would offer and the successful management of the challenges posed by the new situation. Such thinking played a major role in the organization of the Union du Maghreb Arabe (UMA; q.v.) in 1989. Even before the crystallization of the EU four years later, concern over the potentially deleterious impact of the steadily rising tide of Maghribi immigrants to Europe prompted the EEC to initiate in 1991 the most generous developmental assistance package in its 13-year history of providing aid to the Maghrib. The community awarded Tunisia 284 million ECU (more than $350 million) with the aim of stimulating an expansion of the economy that would create new jobs (thus stemming the flow of worker migration to Europe) and would raise living standards (thus undercutting government critics, especially within the Islamist camp, whose popularity was fueled by poverty and despair). EEC leaders believed that socioeconomic and political malaise in the Maghrib, if left to fester, would inevitably translate into instability in their own countries.

In 1995, Tunisia became the first state in North Africa or the Middle East to negotiate an association agreement with the EU. The accord stipulated the creation of a free-trade zone over a 12-year period, guaranteed European economic assistance during this transitional phase, provided for increased educational and scientific exchanges, and envisaged extensive cooperation in such areas as communication, transportation, and tourism.

Exmouth, First Viscount [Edward Pellew] (1757–1833). British naval officer whose fleet bombarded Tunis in 1816 to punish the bey for a resurgence in the activity of the corsairs (q.v.), which had coincided with the Napoleonic Wars, and to compel him to release Europeans held as prisoners in Tunis.

-F-

Fallaqa. Literally, bandits. The term refers to militant nationalists who launched an armed resistance movement against the French in 1954 with raids on government installations and colon property in rural areas. The unprecedented violence of the fallaqa came in reaction to French attempts to ignore the Neo-Dustur in the search for a resolution to the Tunisian crisis.

Fatimids; Fatimid Dynasty (910–973). The heirs of Ubaidallah (q.v.), who ruled Ifriqiya from 910 until their departure for Egypt in 973. A militant branch of the Shia regarded Ubaidallah's ancestor Ismail (q.v.) as the proper seventh imam (q.v.). Urged on by Abu Abdallah (q.v.), many Berber tribesmen who were dissatisfied with their lot under the Aghlabids (q.v.) acknowledged Ubaidallah as the mahdi (q.v.), a figure destined to inaugurate an era of justice under Shii leadership. The Aghlabids' defeat at the hands of these Berber warriors paved the way for Ubaidallah's rise to power. The decision to identify itself as "Fatimid" reflected the dynasty's wish to emphasize its legitimacy by asserting that it was descended from Fatima, the prophet Muhammad's daughter.

Its rulers' choice of the title "caliph" (q.v.) symbolized their ultimate objective of displacing the Abbasid (q.v.) caliphs as the universal leaders of Islam, since in theory there could be but a single caliph. Thus to the Fatimids, control of Ifriqiya was not an end in itself. It provided them with a base from which to launch assaults against Abbasid controlled territories to the east. Military and naval expeditions against Egypt began as early as 913, but internal rebellions and challenges from external rivals, especially the Spanish Umayyads (q.v.) and their Zanata Berber (q.v.) allies, preoccupied the Fatimids for several decades. After successful campaigns in Egypt in the 960s, the Fatimids founded the city of al-Qahira (Cairo) in 969. Four years later, the Fatimid court took up residence in its new capital on the Nile, relegating Ifriqiya to the status of a minor dependency.

Finances. Tunisia's gross domestic product stood at 395 million dinars at the time of its independence in 1956. It had risen to approximately 18 billion by 1995. The 1956 state budget of 37.3 million dinars swelled to 7.2 billion in 1996. The most important sources of government receipts have been direct and indirect taxes, including a value added tax (VAT) first imposed in 1988 but already generating almost a third of all tax receipts by the early 1990s; income from the petroleum and natural gas industries; profits earned by state monopolies; and, as privatization spread, proceeds from the sale of state-owned corporations.

Spending on education (q.v.) has consistently constituted one of the largest single components of the national budget. In the early 1990s, government spending in this area varied between 637 million and 770 million dinars annually; in the same period, the provision of health, social, and community services cost the state between 760 million and 920 million dinars each year. The 1996 budget allocated well over half its total outlay (60 percent) to what were described as "ministries of a social nature."

Defense spending, which had declined steadily through the first half of the 1980s, began to rise after Zine el-Abidine Ben Ali (q.v.), a soldier by profession, replaced Habib Bourguiba (q.v.) as president in 1987. By 1992, it had reached 237 million dinars. The new administration pointed to the emergence of antigovernment movements in the 1980s, some of them wedded to militant tactics, to justify strengthening all aspects of the state's security apparatus. Disbursements in support of public order and safety, for example, a category that appeared as a separate budgetary item for the first time in 1985, jumped from an initial 100 million dinars to almost three times that level in 1992.

Persistent budget deficits necessitated a reduction in government investments in the economy toward the end of the Bourguiba era. The shortfalls diminished somewhat under Ben Ali, dropping from about 405 million dinars in 1986 to a projected 385 million in 1996. The first budget drawn up under Ben Ali's supervision (in 1988) committed approximately 670 million dinars to investments. The funds dedicated to this portion of the budget continued to rise steadily, if modestly, in the years that followed.

Severe fluctuations in the price of and the demand for Tunisia's major exports have contributed to a recurrent deficit in the balance of trade. Although the gravity of this problem has been concealed occasionally by remittances from workers living abroad and tourism (q.v.), the trade deficit skyrocketed from about 90 million dinars in the early 1970s to just under 2 billion dinars in 1994. Foreign aid (q.v.) in the form of loans and investment credits have also added to Tunisia's financial hardships. In the mid-1970s, the total external debt stood at 1.5 billion dinars. By 1993, however, it had more than quintupled (amounting to roughly half the gross domestic product), and the debt-service ratio hovered around 19 percent.

The Banque Centrale de Tunisie solely issues the dinar, controls the nation's money supply, and regulates banking operations in the country. In 1995, the bank held $4.8 million in gold reserves, $1.6 billion in foreign exchange, and International Monetary Fund drawing rights worth $7 million.

In addition to 12 commercial banks with branches throughout the country and eight "offshore" banks located in Tunis, there are eight development banks that formulate, implement, and finance investment projects both within and outside Tunisia. One such institution is narrowly linked to a specific sector of the economy (the Banque Nationale de Développement Touristique), but the others, which include joint ventures with Saudi Arabia, the United Arab Emirates, Kuwait, Qatar, and Libya, pursue more diversified interests.

Fishing. *See* **Agriculture**

Foreign Aid. Since 1956, Tunisia has been the recipient of substantial foreign aid. For several years after independence, the contributions of France (q.v.) far exceeded those of other aid donors, as the former colonial power not only helped to fund development projects but also supplied the Tunisian government with badly needed teachers and technicians. Tunisian displeasure with French conduct of the war in Algeria (q.v.), the French refusal to evacuate the naval base at Bizerte (q.v.), and the Tunisian government's expropriation of colon property all created strains in the Franco-Tunisian relationship that led to a serious, if temporary, decline in French aid in the mid-1960s.

At about the same time, other important donors, including the United States and the World Bank, limited assistance because of their doubts about the wisdom of the development schemes advocated by planning minister Ahmad Ben Salah (q.v.), particularly in the agricultural sector. Driven close to bankruptcy by the failed economic policies of the 1960s, Tunisia required generous infusions of foreign aid to restore its economic health. The liberal economy forged by Prime Minister Nouira (q.v.) after Ben Salah's downfall in 1969 created a climate conducive to such a scenario, and foreign assistance accounted for 40 percent of all development expenditures in the transitional four-year plan for 1969 to 1972.

The World Bank, the African Development Bank, and the European Investment Bank soon became Tunisia's most important multilateral donors, while France resumed its status as the country's major bilateral contributor in the 1970s. Other members of the European Economic Community (q.v.)—most notably West Germany and Italy—and the United States (q.v.) also allocated substantial sums (in the case of the United States some $730 million between 1970 and 1990) for a wide variety of Tunisian projects. By contrast, aid from the communist bloc over the same twenty-year period totalled only $410 million.

During the 1980s, Arab petroleum-producing countries and multilateral Arab aid agencies began to figure more prominently in Tunisian economic development than they had previously. Bilateral aid from these sources amounted to considerably more than $500 million in the course of the decade. Tunisia's opposition to the allied coalition arrayed against Iraq in 1990 and 1991, however, resulted in a drastic curtailment in aid both from the Gulf states (dropping from $100 million in 1990 to less than $3 million in 1991) and the United

States (declining from $31 million in 1990 to $8 million in 1991). Although relations were quickly mended after the war, neither the United States nor the Gulf countries immediately restored assistance to its previous levels. Of the $405 million in aid Tunisia received from all sources in 1992, fellow Arab states contributed $6.6 million and the United States a mere $1 million. Multilateral donors supplied just over $100 million, roughly half of it contributed by Arab agencies. In 1993, however, an American grant of $32 million in economic assistance actually surpassed prewar amounts.

Foreign loans and investment credits were essential to the success of development projects, but by the time Habib Bourguiba was removed from the presidency in 1987 they had driven Tunisia's external debt up to a staggering 3.2 billion dinars. Although the new administration assured traditional donors that it would devise budgets calculated to retire this debt in a systematic fashion, it continued to mount, reaching some 9.2 billion dinars by 1994.

Forestry. *See* **Agriculture**

France. Beginning in the European Middle Ages, France took an active interest in developments in Tunisia. The emergence of the Hafsid dynasty (q.v.) as a powerful central Mediterranean force challenged French interests. Political as well as religious concerns inspired the thirteenth-century Crusade of King Saint Louis IX (q.v.). Later, transactions with Tunisia figured prominently in securing for Marseilles merchants a strong position in trans-Mediterranean trade. To nurture and protect that trade, the French government, on several occasions during the latter half of the seventeenth century, forced the Muradid dynasty (q.v.) to adhere to commercial treaties modeled on Franco-Ottoman accords. Thereafter, French merchants all but controlled Tunisia's international exchanges.

The beginning of French rule in neighboring Algeria in 1830 aroused fears of French ambitions in Tunisia, not only within the Husainid dynasty (q.v.) but also in Great Britain, which had no desire to see France acquire too strong a position in North Africa. The next half-century was marked by an intense Anglo-French competition over Tunisia. This rivalry ended only when the European powers agreed, at the 1878 Congress of Berlin (q.v.), to acknowledge many of each other's interests within the Ottoman Empire, including those of France in Tunisia. Three years later, France declared a protectorate over the beylical government.

During the protectorate era, French officials oversaw, and in some cases took over directly, the management of the Tunisian government. As colons (q.v.) acquired the country's richest lands and enjoyed preferential treatment from the authorities, Tunisian resentment grew.

Around the turn of the century, the Young Tunisians (q.v.) put forward relatively modest demands that France grant Tunisians equality with the country's foreign residents. At the end of World War I, the newly formed Dustur Party (q.v.) formulated a more detailed platform based on the restoration of the Constitution of 1861 (q.v.), assurances of basic rights for all Tunisians, and the formation of a government responsible to an elected assembly. The Dustur leadership shunned a full-scale confrontation with France, but by the 1930s protectorate officials faced a new generation of more vociferous Tunisians. Prepared to act forcefully to secure their political rights, these men formed the Neo-Dustur Party (q.v.). After more than 20 years of activism, their efforts culminated in the termination of the protectorate in 1956.

The end of the protectorate did not, however, mean severing all Tunisian ties with France, which continued to support the newly independent state in a wide variety of ways. For as long as shortages of adequately trained Tunisians persisted, linguistic and historical affinities encouraged the recruitment of French educators. Similarly, the French government supplied political and economic advisers and technical personnel to Tunisian ministries to ease the transition to independence. In still another area, the newly organized Tunisian armed forces initiated a heavy reliance on French equipment and training that subsequently remained the norm. In return, colons were permitted to retain their land, and some French troops remained in the country.

France's war with the Algerian Front de Libération Nationale constantly irritated Franco-Tunisian relations. Tunisian protests following the French bombing of Saqiyat Sidi Yusuf (q.v.) in 1958 prompted France to withdraw most of its forces from the country, leaving only those stationed at its large naval base in Bizerte (q.v.) and at a few posts in the Sahara. Efforts to expand operations at the Bizerte base provoked a crisis in 1961. After demanding the complete evacuation of the installation, Tunisian president Habib Bourguiba (q.v.) ordered Neo-Dustur militants to blockade the base. Determined not to give up Bizerte while the revolution in Algeria continued, France dispatched troops to break the siege. In the fighting that ensued, the irregular Tunisian forces sustained thousands of casualties. Tunisia placed the Bizerte issue on the agenda of the United Nations, which instructed France to return to the confines of the base as a prelude to negotiations on its future, but France delayed talks until after the conclusion of the Algerian War. Not until 1963 did the last of its forces depart. A year later, the Tunisian government, responding to sentiments aroused by the Bizerte affair, expropriated the land still remaining in European hands.

Despite these contretemps, relations between the two countries never broke down entirely. Habib Bourguiba's admiration for the principles of French liberalism, even in the depths of political crises that pitted Tunisia and France against each other, certainly facilitated the forging and maintenance of this postcolonial relationship, but Tunisia's French connection went well beyond personalities. The emergence of radical regimes in Algeria and Libya in the 1960s impressed upon Tunisians the value of France as a potential ally against their much larger and more powerful neighbors, at the same time that it created a situation naturally drawing France closer to its progressive and western-oriented former protectorate. In the years that followed, France provided substantial funds for development assistance, furnished the bulk of Tunisia's imports, and provided the most important market for its exports. After taking the lead in securing associate membership in the European Economic Community (q.v.) for Tunisia in 1969, France customarily supported Tunisia's campaign to enhance its position in the European market.

After Bourguiba's forced retirement in 1987, France was the first non-Arab state visited by Zine el-Abidine Ben Ali (q.v.), the new chief executive, while French president François Mitterrand was the first foreign head of state to travel to Tunisia. The continuity in constructive Franco-Tunisian relations symbolized by this exchange was briefly interrupted by Tunisia's condemnation of the multinational coalition (which included France) arrayed against Iraq following its invasion of Kuwait in 1990.

Shortly after the end of the Gulf War, however, the necessity of managing potentially explosive bilateral issues restored the relationship to a more even keel. The persistent flow of Tunisians (and other North Africans) driven to France by the absence of political freedom and economic opportunity in the Maghrib aroused French fears that the militant activities of Algerian and Tunisian opposition Islamist groups might spill over into Europe. To counter this scenario, France urged its European associates to join it in helping to strengthen the Tunisian economy as an essential first stage in eliminating the root causes of discontent. This approach culminated in the European Union's signing a sweeping commercial partnership agreement with Tunisia in 1995. France encouraged the Ben Ali government to move toward genuine political pluralism as another important mechanism for alleviating the fundamental grievances of many Tunisians.

Franco-Arab Schools. Schools with curriculums based on the French primary system and open to both French and Tunisian students. The language of instruction was French, but French-speaking students also studied Arabic. The concept was conceived by Louis Macheul (q.v.), the first director of public education in the protectorate. Because the Franco-Arab schools attracted only a small percentage of eligible students and because the colons opposed substantial expenditures on educating Tunisians, the hope that they would facilitate interracial understanding never materialized. By the mid-1890s, colon fear of competition from educated Tunisians compelled the protectorate authorities to emphasize vocational, rather than academic, training for Tunisians.

Funduq. Combination warehouse and residence for Europeans trading in Tunisia. The al-Muwahhids were the first rulers to authorize the construction of such buildings. They subsequently became the sites of flourishing commercial activity, often pursued even in periods of Muslim-Christian political and military friction.

-G-

Gafsa. City in the southern steppe region and center of the phosphate (q.v.) mining industry. In the conceptualization of economic development plans after independence, the government invariably paid less attention to the south than to other regions. As a result, the general economic downturn of the 1970s, characterized by inadequate wages and high unemployment, hit the already depressed south especially hard. Frustration over the deteriorating economy and the government's increasingly authoritarian stance sparked a nationwide general strike on January 26, 1978. Economic and political troubles persisted, however, and on the second anniversary of the strike serious violence erupted in Gafsa.

On January 26, 1980, guerrillas seized key police and military installations in the city, hoping to provoke a general uprising. The attackers effectively controlled Gafsa for several hours before army and police reinforcements arrived, restored order, and captured many of them. According to official estimates, 37 soldiers and civilians died in the raid, with another 108 sustaining injuries, but other observers placed casualty figures much higher. The government claimed that the guerrillas, most of whom were Tunisians, had entered the country from Libya, where they had been trained as part of a Libyan campaign to undermine the Bourguiba regime.

Despite their various grievances against the government, opposition political leaders unanimously condemned the Gafsa attack. At the same time, however, they urged the authorities to learn from it and to address the fundamental economic and political disorders that had created the environment that gave rise to the attack. Tunisia's most important allies, France and the United States, acted quickly to demonstrate their support for the government by dispatching naval vessels to Tunisian waters and by taking steps to increase economic and military assistance.

At the March trials of those accused of participating in the raid, sentences ranging from 20 years in prison to death were meted out to some 30 persons. Despite the president's insistence on the Libyan inspiration of the Gafsa incident and the continuing loyalty of the vast majority of the country's citizens, the attack exposed the regime's fragility after years of political and economic turmoil. By revealing the potentially catastrophic consequences of the government's internal and external adversaries joining forces to mobilize popular opposition, the events of January 1980 also demonstrated the urgent need for serious economic and political reforms.

Genseric [Gaiseric] (?–477). Vandal king whose successful assault on Carthage in 439 forced Rome to recognize Vandal dominion over Africa Proconsularis and Byzacenia.

Ghannushi, Rashid (1941–). A founder, in the late 1970s, of the Mouvement de la Tendance Islamique (MTI; q.v.), a society dedicated to promoting an Islamic way of life in Tunisia. Born in al-Hama, near Gabès, his primary and secondary schooling took place exclusively in a traditional milieu. Without a working knowledge of French, he had to leave Tunisia to pursue a higher education, going initially to Egypt and subsequently to Syria, where he completed a degree in philosophy and social science at Damascus University. His stay in the eastern Arab world left him disillusioned with Arab nationalism and favorably disposed to the thinking of Islamic activists. Ghannushi returned to Tunis in 1968 as a secondary school teacher.

Distressed by his students' casual attitudes toward Islam and alarmed that foreign influences were spreading at the expense of traditional values, Ghannushi organized study groups in secondary schools and mosques to encourage the restoration of Islamic values in Tunisian society. He also established links with organizations, such as the Association pour la sauvegarde du Coran (q.v.), that promoted goals similar to his own and wrote articles focusing on doctrinal and moral issues in *al-Maᶜrifa* (q.v.), an Islamist newspaper. Through the decade of the 1970s, he gained a substantial following, particularly among secondary and university students. By 1979, the Mouvement de la Tendance Islamique had emerged as a distinct and identifiable force under the leadership of Ghannushi and his colleague Shaikh Abd al-Fattah Mourou.

His public pronouncements became more openly critical of the government in the early 1980s, and he was imprisoned from 1981 to 1984. Three years after his release, Ghannushi was again arrested, along with scores of others known to be affiliated with Islamic groups. All were alleged to have committed acts of terror and to have collaborated with foreign states (specifically Iran) to overthrow the government. Ghannushi denied the charges, but was found guilty and condemned to life imprisonment in a trial that attracted international attention with accusations of torture and other violations of the defendants' rights.

A few weeks later, Zine el-Abidine Ben Ali (q.v.) replaced Habib Bourguiba (q.v.) as president of Tunisia. The new chief executive did not share his predecessor's conviction that harsh measures were the only effective deterrent to Islamist activism. He released Ghannushi and other members of the MTI in 1988 and attempted to cool the overheated political environment by agreeing to some of the more superficial demands in Ghannushi's quest for the Islamization of Tunisia, such as broadcasting the call to prayer and setting aside prayer areas in factories and offices. Ben Ali's government did not, however, grant official status to the Hizb al-Nahda, or Renaissance Party, as the MTI recast itself early in 1989.

In elections for the National Assembly held later that year, Ghannushi (and other members of al-Nahda) evaded the ban on the party's participation by standing as independent candidates, Ghannushi in the Tunis suburb of Ben Arous, where he polled almost a third of the votes. But like every candidate not affiliated with the ruling Rassemblement Constitutionnel Démocratique (RCD; q.v.), he was defeated. Accusing the authorities of rigging the elections, Ghannushi chose to go into exile, first in France and then in Algeria. Abd al-Fattah Mourou, in his capacity as secretary-general of the still illegal party, took over its day-to-day management, but Ghannushi remained its spiritual and political guide.

Following the Iraqi invasion of Kuwait in August 1990, Ghannushi joined two other prominent Islamist leaders, Abbasi Madani of the Algerian Front Islamique du Salut (FIS) and Hassan Turabi of the Sudanese National Islamic Front (NIF), as a mediator between Iraq and Saudi Arabia. Pointing to the sanctity of the Islamic holy places, Ghannushi and his colleagues shuttled back and forth between Baghdad and Riyadh in an ultimately unsuccessful attempt to avert the dispatch of non-Muslim troops to the Arabian peninsula.

At the height of the subsequent allied military operations against Iraq, in February 1991, a deadly assault by al-Nahda militants on an RCD office in Tunis sparked a renewed government crackdown on the Islamist movement, prompting Ghannushi to call for the formation of a provisional government to supervise new elections. Over the course of the next year, Tunisian officials made repeated accusations, which Ghannushi vehemently denied, that under his leadership al-Nahda was plotting a coup aimed at the establishment of an Islamic state. In the summer of 1992, Ghannushi (in absentia) and several hundred other al-Nahda members and sympathizers were brought to trial on charges of conspiring to overthrow the government. In a reprise of his 1987 case, he received a sentence of life imprisonment in a proceeding marred by allegations of legal irregularities and torture.

Concerned about his future in a France growing increasingly wary of the spillover effect of Maghribi Islamist organizations on its own soil, Ghannushi sought and was granted political asylum in Great Britain in 1993. He persisted in his criticisms of Ben Ali's government, reserving his strongest contempt for its pretensions of political pluralism while continuing to refuse to recognize al-Nahda and barring it from elections.

La Goulette [Arabic: Halq al-Wadi]. Seaport of Tunis. The capital is located on a shallow lake joined to the Mediterranean by a narrow channel only. This location provided security but made access difficult for large vessels. Some 15 kilometers (10 miles) from Tunis, La Goulette lies on a narrow strip of land near the channel linking the lake with the sea. La Goulette's position near the sea lanes connecting the eastern and western portions of the Mediterranean gave it great strategic value in the sixteenth-century Ottoman-Hapsburg struggle for ascendancy in the Mediterranean. A Hapsburg (q.v.) garrison occupied the fortress at La Goulette, ostensibly to protect the Hafsids (q.v.) from 1535 until 1574, when the Ottomans seized it. In 1880, an Italian-built railroad crossed the lake and facilitated connections between the capital and the port.

Grana. The colloquial Tunisian-Arabic name for Livorno, this term designated Jews of European origin. Between the fifteenth and seventeenth centuries, thousands of Spanish Jews joined Iberian Muslims seeking refuge from persecution in Tunisia. Other Spanish Jews who had originally settled in Livorno immigrated to Tunisia in the eighteenth and early nineteenth centuries, giving rise to the use of the word *Grana*, rather than the previously common *Andalusian*, to distinguish European Jews from the indigenous Jewish community. Familiar with Europe and versed in its languages, many Livornese Jews grew rich as middlemen and agents for Tunisian corsairs (q.v.), but from the early nineteenth century on, the development of more usual commercial transactions and the increasing number of European businessmen in Tunisia deprived them of such opportunities.

The Grana in Tunis, estimated to number about a thousand in the mid-nineteenth century, were primarily small businessmen, although a few had acquired positions of considerable influence within the ruling elite. In the capital, more than half the Grana took advantage of their European roots to claim the protection of one or another power, effectively removing themselves from the jurisdiction of the Tunisian government. Their business and familial networks in Tunisia and Europe, combined with their status as European protégés, enabled the Grana to resume their profitable roles as middlemen for the loans and other financial transactions in which the beys became embroiled in the decades preceding the inauguration of the protectorate.

Grand Council. Legislative body instituted in accordance with provisions of the Constitution of 1861 (q.v.). The bey's ministers were responsible to the Grand Council, whose 60 members, a third of them government officials, the monarch himself appointed. With the abrogation of the constitution in 1864, the council ceased to exist.

Following World War I, France made several minor concessions in the hope of mollifying nationalist sentiment without seriously weakening its position in the protectorate. One such concession was the creation of a second Grand Council, this one with separate European and Tunisian chambers. The former had 56 members, more than half of whom were elected by the colons themselves; the latter had only 40 members, none of whom were directly elected. Although the makeup of the council, with its disproportionate representation of the colons, angered many Tunisians, restrictions on its legislative capacity rendered it impotent in any case. Nevertheless, the Tunisian section was suspended in 1934, ending any pretense of shared rule until after World War II.

Gregory (?–647). Byzantine exarch (governor) of Africa whose declaration of independence from Constantinople in 646 came just before the first Arab raids into the Maghrib. Gregory marshaled his forces against the invaders, but was defeated near Sbaitla in 647, giving the Arabs control of the steppe and desert areas of the province.

Guellaty, Hassan (1880–1966). French-educated lawyer and Young Tunisian (q.v.) activist. He wrote for *Le Tunisien* (q.v.), served as president of the Khalduniyya Society (q.v.), and was a member of the committee formed in 1912 to organize a boycott of city trams and to lobby protectorate officials for comparable treatment of European and Tunisian workers. Arrested and expelled from the country, he returned after World War I. Guellaty rejected the view of Abd al-Aziz Thaalbi (q.v.), another former Young Tunisian, that colonial rule had obliterated a Tunisian golden age, but expressed a greater willingness than the Dustur leaders to cooperate with the French in engineering a program of reforms. Toward this end, he founded the Parti Réformiste (q.v.) in 1921. Although some French moderates endorsed Guellaty's efforts, his inability to generate a substantial popular following doomed him and his political organization to obscurity.

Gulf War (August 1990–February 1991). The Iraqi invasion of Kuwait in August 1990 and the subsequent dispatch of an international military force to the Arabian peninsula elicited an outpouring of Arab nationalist sentiment in Tunisia. Asserting that intra-Arab crises should be resolved without outside intervention, President Zine al-Abidine Ben Ali (q.v.) boycotted the Arab summit meeting, held in Cairo in the week following the invasion, that endorsed Saudi Arabia's appeal for military assistance from the international community and sanctioned the organization of a multinational force. Ben Ali's position had the support not only of his own Rassemblement Constitutionnel Démocratique (RCD; q.v.) but also of the opposition parties and the majority of the Tunisian population. What misgivings about the Iraqi invasion did exist were blunted by the formation of the American-led coalition, which evoked nearly universal condemnation, gave rise to a significant measure of national unity, and occasioned the first authorized public demonstrations since the overthrow of Habib Bourguiba (q.v.) in 1987. As the crisis deepened, however, Ben Ali's government stressed that it did not condone the invasion but sought to find an Arab solution to the catastrophic situation it had set in motion.

Several organizations supportive of Iraq soon coalesced, the most active of which was the Comité National pour Repousser l'Aggression contre le Monde Arabe et Soutenir l'Irak (National Committee to Resist Aggression against the Arab World and to Support Iraq). Joining the Union Générale des Travailleurs Tunisiens (UGTT; q.v.), which was the moving force behind the committee, was the Mouvement des Démocrates Sociales (MDS; q.v.), whose leader, Muhammad Mouada, accompanied a ministerial-level delegation on an unsuccessful negotiating mission to Iraq in September, and other opposition parties, including the Parti de l'Unité Populaire (PUP; q.v.), the Rassemblement Socialiste Progressiste (RSP; q.v.), and the Parti Communiste Tunisien (PCT; q.v.). National organizations, such as the Union Générale des Etudiants Tunisiens (UGET; q.v.), the Union des Ecrivains, the Association des Femmes Démocrates, and the Ligue Tunisienne des Droits de l'Homme (LTDH; q.v.) also associated themselves with the work of the committee.

Among Tunisia's Islamist activists, on the other hand, the crisis had a divisive effect. After initially denouncing the Iraqi invasion, al-Nahda (q.v.) altered its official position with the arrival of American and other international military forces in Arabia, asserting that their presence profaned the holy places of Islam. Rashid Ghannushi (q.v.), the movement's exiled leader, positioned himself squarely in the Iraqi camp, vigorously attacking the intervention and the political leaders of the peninsula who had requested it. On the other hand, Abd al-Fattah Mourou (q.v.), al-Nahda's leader inside the country, justified Saudi Arabia's plea for foreign military assistance on the grounds that such a step had become necessary to protect Islam. Mourou's views on the situation in the Gulf contributed to his marginalization within al-Nahda.

Military operations launched against Iraq in January 1991 sparked vociferous public demonstrations against the allied coalition throughout Tunisia. The government carefully supervised these protests, however, in order to prevent al-Nahda extremists from seizing control of them and turning them into forums demanding the formulation of a more aggressively pro-Iraqi foreign policy than the RCD intended to pursue. Because party and government leaders recognized the acute damage that more active Tunisian support of Iraq might cause to their fragile economy, they balked at severing beyond hope of restoration the ties that had linked Tunisia, often quite profitably, with many of the multinational coalition partners prior to the invasion of Kuwait. Even so, the annual revenue derived from tourism (q.v.) declined by more than a third in 1991, reflecting western vacationers' hesitancy to travel to the Arab world in general, but particularly to a state that had failed to censure Iraq. Following its liberation, Kuwait banned the importation of Tunisian products. It was not until 1994 that the emirate restored full diplomatic relations with Tunisia and resumed investing in the country.

Gunderic (fl. 409–429). Leader of the Vandal army that invaded Roman Africa in 429. His victories paved the way for his successor, Genseric (q.v.), to eliminate the last vestiges of Roman control in the region.

-H-

Habus. In Islamic law, a form of unalienable property set aside as a pious trust. Revenue produced by such property was earmarked by the individual establishing the endowment either for the support of religious and charitable institutions (public habus) or for the sustenance of his heirs (private habus).

When the protectorate began, approximately a quarter of all land in the country, much of it prime agricultural acreage, fell into this category. Colon demands for access to habus property led the French authorities to pressure the Habus Administration (q.v.) to make some of its land available for settlement.

In 1956, as part of the newly independent state's efforts to consolidate its power by minimizing the role of traditional Islamic institutions, remaining public habus lands were confiscated. In the following year, a second law ordered the distribution of private habus assets among the heirs of the founder as their own private property.

Habus Administration. Government agency created by Khair al-Din al-Tunsi (q.v.) in 1874 and charged with oversight of habus (q.v.) property. Beginning in 1896, protectorate officials forced it to turn over several thousand acres of habus land annually to the Directorate of Agriculture for sale to settlers. The independent government abolished the Habus Administration in 1956.

Hached, Farhat (1913–1952). Labor organizer and founder, in 1945, of the Union Générale des Travailleurs Tunisiens (UGTT; q.v.). An outspoken opponent of French rule, he worked closely with the Neo-Dustur, often mobilizing workers' strikes to give added clout to party demands. Hached's 1952 assassination by the Red Hand (q.v.), a colon terrorist group, set off a spiral of violence throughout the country and created the nationalist movement's first true martyr.

Haddad, Tahar (1899–1935). Zaituna Mosque-University (q.v.) alim (q.v.) and advocate of enhanced rights for Muslim women. In his most famous book, *Imra'tuna fi'l-shari ᶜa wa'l-mujtamaᶜ* (Our Women in the Law and Society), he presented an innovative, liberal interpretation of Quranic passages dealing with women. Haddad's bold views angered many of his Zaituna colleagues, ultimately costing him his position there. His ideas about women's role in society, as well as his philosophy on other social issues, greatly influenced the organizers of the Neo-Dustur early in their political careers. Most of the improvements in women's status enacted by the party soon after independence bear the stamp of Haddad's thinking.

al-Hadira. The weekly organ of the Young Tunisian (q.v.) movement. It circulated from 1888 until 1910 and was the first private Arabic-language newspaper published by Tunisians. *al-Hadira* called for social change in an Islamic context, but also stressed the need for Tunisians to adopt the positive features of western culture. Because protectorate officials believed *al-Hadira* served a useful purpose by promoting Franco-Tunisian harmony, they subsidized its publication throughout its existence.

Hafsids; Hafsid Dynasty (1227–1574). Descendants of Abd al-Wahid ibn Abi Hafs (q.v.), a Moroccan Berber general of the al-Muwahhid army who served as governor of the province of Ifriqiya early in the thirteenth century. Shortly thereafter, the collapse of the al-Muwahhid empire enabled the Hafsids to seize much of its former territory, gaining recognition throughout the Maghrib and Andalusia as the predominant Muslim power in the West. In 1253, the Hafsid ruler Abu Abdallah took the title of caliph (q.v.). After the eradication of the Abbasid caliphate (q.v.) by the Mongols in 1258, this claim to universal Muslim leadership acquired some supporters in the Islamic heartlands. But

Tunisia's physical separation from those areas made its implementation impractical, and subsequent Hafsid rulers confined their ambitions to the Maghrib.

In the consolidation and expansion of their authority, the Hafsids found it expedient to ally themselves with Tunisia's nomadic Arab tribes. Within a century, Arabs formed the core of the Hafsid army and held crucial positions in the bureaucracy as well. This situation led to a blurring of Arab-Berber distinctions in Tunisia as well as an acceleration of the process of Arabization. In conjunction with the Hafsids' creation of a viable state administered from Tunis, it also helped to forge a distinctively Tunisian identity.

Internal rivalries plagued the Hafsids, often tempting external powers to challenge their regime. Twice in the fourteenth century, family feuds allowed the Marinid rulers of Fez to capture and briefly hold Tunis. Shocked by these invasions, the next several Hafsid rulers sought to strengthen their authority and stabilize their domains. They initiated reforms ushering in an era of prosperity that marks the fifteenth century as the Hafsid golden age.

The most serious threat to the Hafsids came from Europe. As early as 1270, their forces had repelled a Christian attack that was inspired more by political and economic motives than by religious motives, despite its designation as a crusade. At about the same time, the rulers of Aragon, hoping to take advantage of splits within the dynasty, continually meddled in Hafsid affairs. European domination of the central and western Mediterranean sea lanes at the time of the Hafsid revival in the late fourteenth century, often achieved through the exploits of maritime raiders licensed by the Christian powers, provoked the Hafsids to encourage similar activities by Muslim seamen. As a result, corsair (q.v.) operations became a matter of course in the 1400s. These operations did not, however, significantly disrupt the seaborne commerce that had contributed significant revenues to the state's coffers from the beginning of the Hafsid era.

Spain's growing domination of the western Mediterranean through the fifteenth century and the Ottoman Empire's forays into the area early in the sixteenth century squeezed the Hafsids between the two powers at a time when quarrels within the ruling family were again rife. The Ottoman presence in Algiers after 1510, despite its ostensible objective of helping North Africa's Muslims fend off Spanish aggression, distressed the Hafsids, who viewed it as a threat to themselves. Following an unsuccessful Tunisian attack on Algiers in 1534, the Turks mounted an offensive of their own, seized Tunis, and deposed the Hafsid ruler.

In desperation, the dynasty turned to Spain for help. Grasping the strategic importance of Tunisia and the need to deny it to their Ottoman enemies, the Hapsburgs (q.v.) helped the Hafsids recover their throne, but at the price of creating a Spanish protectorate over Tunisia. The Ottomans recaptured Tunis in 1569, but the Hapsburgs ousted them for a second time and restored the Hafsids in 1573. During these years, however, the dynasty's obvious weakness and its willingness to consort with the Spaniards had deprived it of any semblance of popular support. An Ottoman assault in 1574 once again unseated the Hafsids, this time ringing down the curtain on the dynasty and incorporating Tunisia into the Ottoman sphere.

Haidaran. Site northwest of Kairouan of a decisive battle between the Banu Hilal (q.v.) and the Zirid (q.v.) army in 1052. The Zirids' hopes of containing Arab nomadic incursions into Ifriqiya's settled lands were dashed by their defeat at Haidaran, after which the Banu Hilal spread unchecked throughout the province.

Hammad ibn Buluggin (r. 1015–1029). Son of Buluggin ibn Ziri (q.v.). After Buluggin's death the task of administering the territory entrusted to the family by the Fatimids on their departure for Egypt was divided. His son Mansur retained control of Ifriqiya (q.v.), and another son, Hammad, took responsibility for the lands west of it. Attempts by Hammad's relatives to prevent his sons from succeeding him provoked a civil war in 1016 that led to the creation of separate Hammadid and Zirid states, the former in the central Maghrib, the latter in Ifriqiya proper.

Hamuda Bey (1759–1814; r. 1782–1813). Fifth Husainid ruler. Economic setbacks marked the first half of Hamuda's reign, but at the time of his death Tunisia was experiencing an era of prosperity induced primarily by events in Europe. The Napoleonic Wars heightened the demand for Tunisian commodities, especially grain, while the Europeans' inability to police the Mediterranean occasioned a resurgence in corsair activity. The resulting affluence, along with Hamuda's decision to decrease the number of janissaries and to rely more heavily on local tribal forces in his army, made him one of the most popular Husainid rulers.

Hamuda Pasha (r. 1631–1666). Son and successor of Murad Corso (q.v.) as bey of Tunis. He used his influence, derived from beylical control of the tribes in state service, to guarantee the appointment of weak deys, thus strengthening his own position. To offset the antagonism of the deys, he forged strong links with the Tunisian bourgeoisie, especially the ulama. He reminded them that he, unlike the foreign deys, had been born in the country and considered himself a Tunisian.

This overture was a first step toward connecting Tunisia's governors with the governed and reconstituting the sense of national identity that had existed in embryonic form in Hafsid times but had been missing since that dynasty's deterioration a century and a half earlier. Aware of his limitations as well as his power, Hamuda carefully balanced initiatives toward native Tunisians with professions of allegiance to the Ottoman sultan, from whom he received the title "pasha" in 1658.

Hanafi Madhhab. One of four major Sunni schools of thought (madhhab) on the interpretation of the sharia. It takes its name from Abu Hanifa, an Iraqi alim of the eighth century. The school's relative flexibility appealed to rulers seeking some latitude in legal matters, making it the favored madhhab of the Abbasids (q.v.), the smaller dynasties (such as the Aghlabids [q.v.]) which broke with them, and the Ottomans. Tunisia's ruling elite frequently adhered to the Hanafi madhhab, but that preference had almost no impact on the bulk of the population, which followed the more conservative Maliki (q.v.) school.

Hannibal (247–182 B.C.E.). A leading citizen of Carthage and commander of its army in the Second Punic War (218–202 B.C.E.) (q.v.). Convinced of the need to carry the war into Roman territory, he marshalled his forces at Carthaginian bases in Iberia, crossed the Alps, and launched a surprise attack on Italy from the north. Hannibal's forces bogged down, however, when they failed to win a decisive victory. After isolating the Carthaginians by cutting their supply lines, the Roman general Scipio (q.v.) seized the initiative, invaded Africa, and demanded the surrender of the defenseless Carthage in 203. Hannibal could not extricate his army in time to save the city, but he returned to Africa the next year in the hope of expelling the Romans. His defeat at the Battle of Zama (q.v.) brought the war to an end. For the next several years, Hannibal governed Carthage, but in 195 he fled to the eastern Mediterranean, where he allied himself with enemies of Rome and where he died in 1832.

Hanshir (plural, hanashir). Large rural estate of the precolonial era. Although sometimes privately owned, a hanshir often combined state property, acreage held by local notables, and habus (q.v.) lands. The beys and their relatives owned many of the most extensive hanashir. Like other large landowners, they employed khammas (q.v.) to work them. After 1881, the protectorate government's jurisdiction over state lands and the difficulty of establishing precise hanshir ownership facilitated European speculators' acquisition of control over much of this property.

Hapsburgs; Hapsburg Dynasty. Rulers of the Holy Roman Empire from 1452 until its collapse in 1806. In 1519, the crowns of the empire and of Spain were merged in the person of Charles V (q.v.). The Spanish Hapsburgs and the Ottomans engaged in naval warfare throughout the sixteenth century in a contest for control of the Mediterranean basin. In conjunction with this conflict, Hapsburg forces helped the Hafsids (q.v.) to eject the Ottomans from Tunisia, but established a Spanish protectorate over the country for most of the period between 1535 and 1574.

Hassan ibn al-Numan (?–699/700). Commander of the Umayyad army sent to Ifriqiya in 691. His mission was to subdue the Berber tribes that continued to resist Arab control and to conquer the remaining Byzantine strongholds in the area. Hassan quickly recaptured Kairouan from the rebellious Berbers, but stiff opposition persisted until he defeated their female leader, Kahina (q.v.), in 698. In the meantime, he drove the imperial forces from Carthage in 695 and devised a naval strategy that led to the defeat of a large Byzantine fleet. The Arabs failed to repel a Byzantine counterattack, however, and did not finally secure the city until 698. When they did, Hassan judged the site too vulnerable to attack from the sea, abandoned it, and founded a new city, Tunis, several miles inland.

Hautecloque, Jean Marie François de (1893–1957). France's resident general, 1952–1953. Reforms enacted in 1951 diminished his powers, and de Hautecloque spent much of his tenure in an unsuccessful search for a formula to implement the policy of cosovereignty (q.v.). Neo-Dustur attempts to bring international attention to Tunisian grievances by sending a delegation to the United Nations in 1952 provoked his wrath. When Amin Bey (q.v.) defied de Hautecloque's order to dismiss the prime minister who had authorized the delegation and to recall its members, the resident general ordered a crackdown on the Neo-Dustur. Violent public demonstrations erupted, and a state of emergency was imposed. Amin succumbed to de Hautecloque's directives, but the incarceration of the Neo-Dustur leadership only intensified the mounting crisis.

Herding. *See* **Agriculture**

Hilalian Invasion. *See* **Banu Hilal**

Hilderic (?–533). Vandal king and ally of the Byzantine Empire. During his reign, Berber incursions into productive agricultural lands imperiled the economy of Africa. Hilderic's weak military response to the Berber threat in 530 ended in his defeat and deposition by the Vandal aristocracy in favor of Gelimer. This palace coup provided the Byzantines with an excuse to intervene in Africa on Hilderic's behalf. In 533, their invading army crushed Vandal resistance. But rather than restoring Hilderic, the Byzantines absorbed Africa into their empire.

Husain Bey (1784–1835; r. 1824–1835). Eighth Husainid ruler. Economic problems characterized his reign as the cost of imports escalated and exports failed to keep pace, owing to the decrease in demand for them on depressed European markets. Beylical efforts to bolster the economy had centered, since 1820, on monopolizing the trade in olive oil, Tunisia's most lucrative agricultural product. The rulers' risky practice of securing ready cash by arranging oil sales to foreign buyers before the harvest precipitated a disaster when the crop failed in 1828. To meet his commitments, Husain had to purchase oil on the international market, incurring a massive debt, much of it to French businessmen. The French occupation of Algeria, midway through Husain's reign, further heightened that country's interest in and influence over Tunisia.

Husain ibn Ali (1669–1740; r. 1705–1740). Founder of the Husainid dynasty. He was the son of a Tunisian mother and a Greek father who served in the Muradid (q.v.) armed forces. Husain became a cavalry officer in the closing years of the Muradid era. In the turmoil following the assassination of Murad III (q.v.) in 1702, an Algerian army invaded Tunisia. After effectively mobilizing the resistance to this intrusion, Husain assumed the title of bey. Fearful of renewed Algerian aggression, the urban elite enthusiastically supported him, eventually going so far as to encourage him to establish a family dynasty. Husain's simultaneous cultivation of the tribes gave him solid connections in both urban and rural societies. His elevation by the Ottoman sultan to the rank of pasha (q.v.) in 1708 further cemented his power, but he systematically turned aside all Ottoman bids to gain ascendancy in Tunisia.

In 1724 Husain nominated his son Muhammad (q.v.) to be his successor. This alienated his nephew Ali (q.v.), whom he had long treated as the heir apparent. Ali rebelled in 1729 and began a bitter civil war, which even Husain's death on the battlefield in 1740 did not bring to a permanent conclusion.

Husainids; Husainid Dynasty (1705–1957). The descendants of Husain ibn Ali (q.v.) who presided over Tunisia during a period of increasing external pressures, which culminated in the establishment of the French protectorate in 1881. The family retained the title of bey throughout the years of French control that followed, but the office lacked any real power. In a major political reform soon after independence, Amin (q.v.), the last Husainid ruler, was deposed and the monarchy abolished in favor of a republican government.

The early years of the dynasty were plagued by the related threats of civil war and Algerian intervention. While generally successful in coping with these problems, the Husainids, who were not themselves natives of Tunisia, realized the necessity of developing as broad a base of support in the country as possible. With that in mind, the beys began to integrate tribal warriors into their army and to elevate members of the urban bourgeoisie, especially the ulama, to positions of responsibility in the government.

The dramatic upturn in the economy during the Napoleonic Wars helped to solidify the relationship between the beys and their subjects, but the absence of effective Husainid leadership following the death of Hamuda Bey (q.v.) in 1814 left the country weak and vulnerable. A series of disastrous harvests and a widespread commercial slump, aggravated by a depression gripping the Mediterranean world, provided European merchants with an opportunity to insinuate themselves into the center of the Tunisian economy by lending money to Tunisians on the verge of financial ruin. The French occupation of Algeria in 1830 heightened the already serious risk posed by this European economic penetration by placing a major creditor on Tunisia's borders, where its influence could easily be brought to bear on the bey's government. An Ottoman reassertion of direct control over Tripolitania in 1835 similarly jeopardized the bey's autonomy.

Determined to avert both French and Ottoman intervention in Tunisia, Ahmad Bey (r. 1837–1855; q.v.) launched a campaign to strengthen the central government and to make the country more self-sufficient. But the expense of such an undertaking necessitated tax increases that further undermined the economy. More importantly, Ahmad's unchecked spending left his successors with no choice but to borrow money abroad. The highly unfavorable terms of the loans they arranged set off a spiral of indebtedness that placed Tunisia firmly in the grasp of its European creditors.

In the quarter century between Ahmad's death and the imposition of the French protectorate, the Husainids struggled to maintain their autonomy. Those years were marked by intense competition between France and Great Britain for economic and political domination in the country. The eagerness of many of the beys' officials to enrich themselves by collaborating with foreign governments and by participating in the ventures of European businessmen in Tunisia produced a debilitating atmosphere of graft and corruption in the capital. In the hopes of appeasing the powers, the Husainids consented to demands for such "reforms" as the Ahd al-aman (q.v.) and the Constitution of 1861 (q.v.), but this agenda primarily served the Europeans' own purposes and failed to bring either political or economic stability to the country. When statesmen at the Congress of Berlin (q.v.) reached an agreement on the disposition of Tunisia, a French occupation became inevitable.

The Treaty of the Bardo (q.v.), signed in the wake of the French invasion in 1881, left Muhammad al-Sadiq (q.v.) on the throne, but without any real authority. For the next 75 years, the Husainids reigned but did not rule, their powers circumscribed by French officials. This long period of political impotence, the beys' lack of interest in (or sympathy for) the nationalist movement (with the possible exception of Munsif [q.v.]), and the enormous popularity of Habib Bourguiba (q.v.) all contributed to the ease with which the monarchy was abolished and to the lack of controversy that its demise aroused after independence.

-I-

Ibn Abi Diyaf, Ahmad (1802/03–1874). Author of *Ithaf ahl al-zaman bi akhbar muluk tunis wa ʿahd al-aman,* an important chronicle of Tunisian history. The study opens with the Arab conquest and continues into the reign of Muhammad al-Sadiq Bey (q.v.), but concentrates on the latter part of the eighteenth century and the first half of the nineteenth. This was an era about which Bin Diyaf (as his name appears in colloquial Tunisian Arabic) had an abundance of accurate personal information. For more than 30 years, beginning in 1827, he acted as private secretary to each successive bey. Bin Diyaf's inclusion in the chronicle of an extensive biographical dictionary of major personages makes the work a key reference source for the period.

Ibn Khaldun, Abd al-Rahman (1332–1406). Alim and political figure who served several North African and Middle Eastern dynasties in secretarial, advisory, academic, and judicial positions. He was born in Tunis, where his ancestors, residents of Andalusia since the Muslim conquest, had resettled in the previous century as refugees from the early stages of the Christian Reconquista (q.v.). After briefly holding a minor position in the Hafsid (q.v.) bureaucracy, Ibn Khaldun traveled to Fez in 1354 to further his education. He found employment there at the court of the Marinid sultan, but his involvement in palace intrigues earned him both enemies and occasional prison sentences. Within a decade he had migrated to Granada and thereafter lived and worked for various periods of time in Bajaia, Tlemcen, Tunis, and Cairo.

Ibn Khaldun's most famous work, and his most enduring legacy, is the *Muqaddima* (*Introduction*) to his universal history, written in the late 1370s. In it he drew heavily on his own experiences to posit a philosophy of history and of the evolution of human societies based on a cyclical theory of rising and declining group solidarity (*asabiyya*). The *Muqaddima* secured for Ibn Khaldun recognition as one of the most respected scholars of the Muslim Middle Ages. Contemporary scholars know him as the "father of sociology."

Ibrahim ibn Aghlab (r. 800–812). Founder of the Aghlabid dynasty (q.v.). Originally from Khurasan, a province of eastern Persia, Ibrahim came to the Maghrib as an officer in the Abbasid (q.v.) army. In 795 he was named governor of the Zab, a cluster of Saharan oases. Discerning Ibrahim's military skills, the caliph (q.v.) Harun al-Rashid ordered him to Ifriqiya in 800 to suppress the Kharaji (q.v.) inspired uprisings then plaguing that region.

Ibrahim accepted this mission on the condition that the caliph recognize him as an autonomous amir and allow his heirs to succeed him as governors of Ifriqiya. In return, he agreed to pay an annual tribute to Baghdad and to acknowledge the caliph's spiritual leadership of the Muslim community. The Abbasids judged it pointless to expend valuable resources in an attempt to curb the ambitions of so distant a provincial commander and were content with Ibrahim's fiscal commitment and acceptance of the caliph's spiritual authority. Thus they accepted the arrangement.

Ibrahim II (r. 875–902). Ninth amir (q.v.) of the Aghlabid dynasty (q.v.). Initially a popular ruler, he alienated his subjects when he imposed harsh taxes to finance the construction of the royal city of Raqqada (q.v.), near Kairouan. His paralysis in the face of an organized Shii (q.v.) propaganda campaign among the discontented Berbers dismayed his nominal sovereign, the Abbasid caliph (q.v.), who encouraged Ibrahim II's relatives to force his abdication.

Ibrahim Sharif (r. 1702–1705). Turkish cavalry officer whose coup d'état in 1702 resulted in the death of Murad III (q.v.) and ended the Muradid dynasty (q.v.). Ibrahim assumed the offices of both dey and bey, but any prospect of acquiring popular backing collapsed when he proved unable to thwart an Algerian invasion and was himself captured by the attackers. The resistance then fell to Husain ibn Ali (q.v.), paving the way for his rise to power.

Ifriqiya. Arabic form of the Latin "Africa." The Arabs used this term for the areas called Africa Proconsularis (q.v.) and Byzacenia (q.v.) at the time of their first incursions into North Africa. The designation was used until the era of the Hafsid dynasty (q.v.), when it was replaced by the name "Tunisia."

Ilj Ali [Turkish: Uluç Ali] (ca. 1508–1587). Ottoman pasha (q.v.) of Algiers whose attack on Tunis in 1569 obliged the Hafsids (q.v.) to seek refuge with the Spanish garrison at La Goulette. Aided by the Spaniards, the Hafsids retook Tunis in 1573. In the following year, Ilj Ali, whom the sultan had appointed head of the Ottoman navy after he successfully led the North African galleys at the Battle of Lepanto in 1571, dispatched a fleet that again seized Tunis, this time deposing the Hafsids and bringing their domains into the Ottoman orbit.

Imam. Literally, leader. The term is commonly used to designate the leader of Muslim communal prayers. The title was also accorded to the descendants of Muhammad, through his daughter Fatima and his son-in-law Ali, whom Shii Muslims (q.v.) recognized as the only rightful leaders of the Muslim community.

Industry. The earliest industries to develop following independence were outgrowths of traditional crafts (textiles, ceramics, and leather) or involved processing Tunisian raw materials. For example, the food processing industry originated as an import substitution measure, and the chemical industry, which was closely linked to phosphate production, manufactured primarily for the export market.

Food processing and textile manufacturing continued to account for approximately half of Tunisia's industrial production in the first half of the 1990s. Food processing plants annually produced, depending on harvest conditions, between 120,000 and 280,000 metric tons of olive oil, 465,000 to 565,000 metric tons of semolina, 540,000 to 657,000 metric tons of flour, 50,000 to 70,000 metric tons of refined sugar, and thousands of metric tons of canned goods ranging from tomato paste to tuna. In 1992, textile plants manufactured 142 million pieces of ready-to-wear garments, 17 million pairs of hosiery, and 39,000 metric tons of cloth. Other locally produced consumer goods include some 7 million pairs of shoes, small appliances, and a wide variety of furniture, glass products, and plastic goods.

Among heavier industries, the nation's steel mills during the early 1990s had a combined annual capacity of some 340,000 metric tons, produced primarily at the al-Fouladh mills in Menzel Bourguiba. Cement factories turned out more than 4 million metric tons a year. Under contract with General Motors, the American automotive corporation, a plant in Kairouan produced a small number of cars (about 1,000 a year) for sale in the Maghrib. A farm machinery complex manufactured several hundred tractors annually, along with combines and other smaller agricultural equipment for the domestic market. The chemical industry's production of some 30,000 metric tons of superphosphate, 700,000 to 820,000 metric tons of triple superphosphate, and 800,000 to 970,000 metric tons of phosphoric acid in each of the first four years of the 1990s contributed significantly to the country's export earnings.

Tunisia's industrial development has been heavily concentrated around Tunis, partly because of the region's proximity to both foreign and domestic markets and partly owing to the larger pool of skilled and semiskilled labor available there. This situation created economic imbalances that triggered unrest in less favored areas of the country, particularly the south. To promote labor-intensive industries that would create new jobs, especially outside the capital area, the government's four-year plan of 1973–1976 allocated 32 percent of total investment to the industrial sector. The plan fell short of its goal, however, with the sector expanding by 7 percent rather than the anticipated 10.

Uneven industrial growth marked the 1977–1981 plan, but many of the potentially damaging aspects of this situation were offset by increased petroleum production during those years. The next plan, in effect from 1982 to 1986, reduced investments in industry to 20 percent of the total but encouraged foreigners to undertake large-scale projects, a strategy that resulted in a 9 percent growth rate in manufacturing industries over the life of the plan. A drastic decline in oil revenues in the mid-1980s compelled planners to emphasize smaller and less grandiose industrial sector ventures, funded in increasingly larger proportions by private capital, both foreign and Tunisian, during the 1987–1991 plan. By then, private investors provided almost two-thirds of the investments endorsed by the Agence de Promotion des Investissements (API), a government agency set up in the midst of the economic liberalism of the 1970s to promote private investment in industries geared to domestic production. Private investors also accounted for roughly 90 percent of the jobs created through API-approved enterprises. The stress on private investment also characterized the 1992–1996 plan, which envisioned manufacturing as the principal engine driving a projected 6 percent increase in gross domestic production.

In the early 1990s, as much as a third of all foreign investment in Tunisia was concentrated in manufacturing industries. Government support for privatization greatly facilitated efforts to attract foreign entrepreneurs to this sector of the economy. Since independence, state-owned corporations had been an important component of the industrial sector, particularly in heavy industries manufacturing primary products. This arrangement began to change in the last years of the presidency of Habib Bourguiba (q.v.), however, and modifications accelerated after he left office. In 1988, the government of Zine el-Abidine Ben Ali (q.v.)

embarked on a four-year program sponsored by the World Bank and the International Monetary Fund (IMF) that was designed to curb Tunisia's spiraling deficit. One of its key provisions called for restructuring inefficient state-run industries and privatizing others. The continuation of this process during the 1990s posed both challenges and opportunities to the Tunisian economy. By the middle of that decade, industrial enterprises were contributing some 36 percent of the gross domestic product while employing just over a third of the workforce.

International Finance Commission. Agency established in 1869 by the bey's leading creditors (France, Great Britain, and Italy) to oversee fiscal reforms. Its right to allocate a portion of Tunisia's revenue for the retirement of foreign debts partially removed the management of state funds from Tunisian hands. The reform-minded Khair al-Din al-Tunsi (q.v.) chaired the commission until his elevation to the post of prime minister in 1873. Under his guidance, it sought to curb the foreign concessions that had produced the debt, but many powerful Tunisians who had profited from business dealings with the Europeans did all they could to impede the commission's work. The organization continued to function until 1884, when the protectorate government guaranteed Tunisia's remaining international liabilities.

Inzal. A form of contract providing for the permanent leasing of habus (q.v.) land. In their efforts to open as much land as possible to European agricultural development, the protectorate authorities encouraged this legal fiction, which condoned the transfer of otherwise inalienable real estate. A royal decree of 1886 sanctioned European acquisition of habus lands as inzal with rents fixed in perpetuity. The property itself was also referred to as inzal.

Islamic Tendency Movement. *See* **Mouvement de la Tendance Islamique (MTI)**

Ismail (?–ca. 765). Acknowledged as the seventh imam (q.v.) by some Shii Muslims (q.v.). His followers, called Ismailis, actively conspired to overthrow Sunni regimes that they viewed as illegitimate. Abu Abdallah (q.v.) spread Ismaili propaganda among Ifriqiya's Berbers in the early tenth century. Ubaidallah (q.v.), the founder of the Fatimid dynasty (q.v.), claimed descent from Ismail.

Italy, Italians. Contacts between Tunisia and the Italian peninsula, begun in Carthaginian times, naturally intensified during the centuries that Rome controlled North Africa. The earliest Muslim commanders in Ifriqiya focused their attention on the region's interior rather than its Mediterranean coastline, but the Aghlabid dynasty (q.v.) conquered Sicily in the 800s and used the island as a base for forays against the Italian mainland. In a reversal of this situation, the Norman (q.v.) rulers of Sicily subjugated much of Ifriqiya's coast in the eleventh and twelfth centuries. Even amid these rivalries (and ultimately of greater importance) strong commercial ties developed. Italy was a natural market for the goods of the trans-Saharan trade and merchants from Venice, Genoa, Pisa, and Livorno all did business in Tunisia, especially from Hafsid (q.v.) times onward. At the end of the eighteenth century, a community of Jews of Livornese origin, called Grana (q.v.), settled in Tunisia and played a particularly important role as middlemen between Tunisian and European entrepreneurs.

Shortly afterward, the small, and until then primarily mercantile, Italian population of Tunisia began to increase. Small farmers fleeing the demographic pressures of Sicily and mainland Italy settled in the country, while the elaborate projects of Ahmad Bey (q.v.) created a demand for skilled and semiskilled laborers to which many Italian workers responded. Moreover, unstable political conditions in Italy contributed a substantial number of refugees and exiles. Despite the growth of Anglo-French commercial rivalry in early nineteenth-century Tunisia, Italy maintained its status as one of the country's major trading partners, as revealed by its participation in the International Finance Commission (q.v.), established in 1869.

At the 1878 Congress of Berlin (q.v.), Italy attempted, on the basis of its investments and the sizeable Italian population in the country, to secure international recognition of its claim to Tunisia, but failed. Even after the French protectorate was installed, Italian migration to Tunisia continued and the Italian community remained the single largest foreign group in the country until the 1930s. Because many of these Italians were small farmers or laborers, they were more likely than Frenchmen to compete with Tunisians for the same economic opportunities, leading to some friction between the two groups. Dissatisfied with French treatment of Italians in Tunisia, Fascist Italy briefly entertained the hope of gaining control of the protectorate, but the Axis defeat in North Africa in 1943 ended all such expectations. On the contrary, the Allies made Tunisia, once again, the launching pad for an invasion of Sicily and the Italian mainland.

Italy has been an important supplier of imports to independent Tunisia, second only to France. Italy was also the second-largest recipient of Tunisian exports until Germany surpassed it in 1993. An Italian company, Ente Nazionale Idrocarburi (ENI), discovered Tunisia's first oil field at al-Borma (q.v.) in 1964 and assisted in its subsequent development. Thereafter, ENI and its subsidiaries remained active participants in the Tunisian petroleum industry. In the early 1990s, Italy stood third as a source of foreign investment in Tunisia, while its substantial economic assistance program totaled some $500 million between 1988 and 1993. All of these linkages, combined with the historical association of the two countries and their physical proximity, helped to make Italy a common destination for Tunisian immigrants in search of better economic opportunities or a more liberal political environment.

-J-

Jallaz Cemetery Incident. In 1911, the Tunis Municipal Council ordered a land survey in a neighborhood encompassing the Jallaz Muslim cemetery. Fears that the burial grounds would be defiled, along with the suspicion that the survey was the first step toward the land's expropriation and sale to Europeans, incited angry demonstrations that resulted in the loss of lives and the arrest of scores of Tunisians. Protectorate officials accused the leaders of the Young Tunisian movement (q.v.) of orchestrating the demonstrations. They expressed their dismay that the Young Tunisians, many of whom they themselves had cultivated, remained so willing to address crucial issues primarily from an Islamic perspective. Despite these contentions, however, French prosecutors could not link any prominent Young Tunisian with the incident in the ensuing trials.

Jalluli Family. Entrepreneurs from Sfax with a tradition of public service dating to Hafsid (q.v.) times. Their close ties with the Husainid dynasty (q.v.) made them one of the most powerful clans of the nineteenth century. Family members often held key positions in Sfax, including governor, but the most influential of them served in Tunis. The Jallulis were among a handful of individuals rich enough to bid successfully at auctions of the government's most lucrative offices. Since receipts collected in such posts then accrued to the officeholder as profits, Mahmud Jalluli greatly augmented the family fortune during his years as chief customs collector in the early nineteenth century. Along with other wealthy businessmen, the Jallulis made substantial loans to the government in 1829 to avert bankruptcy in the wake of the reckless financial dealings of Husain Bey (q.v.). In return, they received additional tax farming concessions in the Sahil that further augmented their affluence. The family's awareness of shifting political currents enabled it to retain considerable influence even after the inauguration of the protectorate. Jallulis continued to serve in important central government positions well into the twentieth century.

Janissary. Turkish term for infantryman. Despite frequent references to the janissaries as Turks, many were not, since the pasha of Tunis, like other Ottoman regional commanders in the Maghrib, recruited janissaries from all over the Mediterranean world. In 1591, a group of janissary junior officers, the deys (q.v.), seized power in Tunis. Because they lacked the capacity to bring rural land outside the capital effectively under their control, corsair activities provided the economic underpinning of their regime, resulting in the establishment of close connections between the corsair captains and many of the janissaries.

The prestige of the deys was later eclipsed by the beys (q.v.), officers whom they had entrusted with expanding their authority into the countryside. The beys built a power base of their own among the tribes, initiating an urban-rural rivalry. The failure of a 1673 janissary revolt to dislodge the reigning bey and restore deylical authority assured the superiority of the beys. As their ability to influence political events declined, the janissaries engaged in vicious infighting over the exercise of what little of their power remained.

The last serious janissary bid to restore the old order coincided with the Algerian invasion following Ibrahim Sharif's (q.v.) coup in 1705. Their attempt to place one of their officers in control of the capital was foiled by the popular support enjoyed by Husain ibn Ali (q.v.), who organized the resistance against the Algerians.

Although the Husainid dynasty continued to recruit janissary troops, it relied increasingly on local resources for its military needs. A janissary revolt in 1811 prompted Hamuda Bey (q.v.) to pare down the corps significantly, while another uprising in 1816 further discredited the foreign soldiers. Ahmad Bey's (q.v.) military reforms, and especially the introduction of conscription, virtually eliminated the janissaries as a credible force in the country.

Jarid. An oasis region in the southwest, near the Algerian frontier, and the country's major date-producing area. Its seclusion attracted Kharaji Muslims (q.v.), who established communities in Tozeur and other towns in the region as early as the eighth century. Owing to Kharaji involvement in the trans-Saharan trade, the Jarid developed into an important commercial center. Fatimid (q.v.) hostility toward the Kharajis ignited the 934 revolt of Abu Yazid (q.v.), which originated in the Jarid. But even the Fatimids' departure for Egypt did not lessen the tension between the oases and the heartland of Ifriqiya, for the realignment of the major trans-Saharan routes after 969 antagonized the Kharaji merchants and turned them against the Zirids (q.v.). In the waning years of the twelfth century, the Banu Ghaniyya (q.v.) took advantage of the Jarid's isolation and its tradition of political opposition to make it a center of their attempt to overthrow the al-Muwahhid dynasty.

The Jarid, which continued to be oriented more toward the Sahara than toward Tunisia proper, frequently escaped the effective control of the central government until the protectorate period, when the technology available to the French authorities, both in the military and civilian spheres, permitted its firm incorporation into the Tunisian state.

Jawhar (?–991). Fatimid (q.v.) soldier who led the conquest of Egypt in 969. Probably of European Christian origin, he was a freedman in the service of the Fatimid caliphs and first achieved prominence as the commander of the expedition sent to the central and western Maghrib by the caliph al-Muizz (q.v.) in 958. His skill in this operation persuaded al-Muizz that Jawhar could accomplish the Fatimid goal of expansion into the Nile valley. After achieving this objective, Jawhar built the new city of al-Qahira (Cairo), from which he ruled Egypt until the Fatimid capital was transferred there in 973.

Jerba. Island off the southeastern Tunisian coast. Some literary sources have identified it with the land of the lotus eaters in Homer's *Odyssey,* and there is archeological evidence of settlement on the island in the Carthaginian and Roman eras. Jerba's relative isolation made it an ideal refuge for minorities, including a Jewish community that still exists in the main town, Houmt-Suq.

Because the island became a Kharaji (q.v.) center early in the Islamic period, its people had limited contact with the rest of Ifriqiya. In 1284, the Aragonese captured Jerba, then nominally under Hafsid (q.v.) rule, and made it a base for raids on Muslim shipping in the central Mediterranean. The Spaniards' harsh treatment of the islanders, however, spurred an uprising that ended in a Hafsid restoration by the middle of the fourteenth century. But Jerba's strategic position made it too valuable a prize in the contest for maritime supremacy in the Mediterranean to abandon lightly. Aragonese attempts to retake it continued until the failure of a major expedition in 1432 temporarily checked Spanish ambitions.

In response to the Hafsid decline after 1535 and the increase of Hapsburg (q.v.) influence in Tunisia that accompanied it, Darghut (q.v.) and other Muslim corsairs seized Jerba and made it their headquarters for attacks on Christian vessels. The Hapsburgs severely damaged Darghut's fleet off Jerba in 1551 and briefly captured the island in 1560, only to lose it, this time definitively, in a counterattack in which Ottoman forces from Tripoli aided Darghut.

After independence, Jerba became a center of the Tunisian tourist industry. In the 1960s, several large hotels intended primarily for European vacationers were built, and an international airport opened. Further development in the next decade virtually blanketed the island's beaches with hotels and accorded primacy to tourism in Jerba's economy, which previously had been oriented toward agriculture and maritime activities.

Jeune Afrique. *See Afrique-Action*

Jews. *See* **Grana**

Journal Officiel de Tunisie. Official gazette created in 1883 to publicize government policies among non-Arabic speakers in the protectorate. After independence, the title of the *Journal Officiel de Tunisie* was changed to *Journal Officiel de la République Tunisienne.*

Jugurtha (160–104 B.C.E.). Berber chieftain who led a rebellion against Rome in 113 B.C.E. Jugurtha aspired to bring all the Numidian territory once controlled by his grandfather Masinissa (q.v.) under his rule. As the revolt faltered, Jugurtha was captured and later died in prison. Nineteenth- and twentieth-century nationalists occasionally cited him as an example of local resistance to foreign domination.

-K-

Kahina (?–698). Female warrior who led the last concerted Berber effort to halt the Arab advance into the Maghrib. Defeated near Tabarka by the soldiers of Hassan ibn al-Numan (q.v.) in 698, Kahina fled to the Aurès Mountains in modern Algeria where she was killed later in the same year.

Kairouan. Founded by Uqba ibn Nafi (q.v.) in 670, Kairouan served as the capital of the province of Ifriqiya. It was the first Arab administrative center in the Maghrib, the site of the region's first major mosque (named after its builder, Sidi Uqba), and the point from which Islam spread throughout North Africa. These links with Tunisia's earliest Muslims made the city a place of pilgrimage and clothed succeeding generations of its ulama with great prestige. Kairouan's location on the steppe at the edge of the Sahara distinguished it from earlier urban centers in the area and underscored the Arabs' propensity for the hinterland rather than the coast.

The Arabs were evicted from Kairouan by the Berbers in 683 and did not regain the city until 691. For the next century, Berber rebels, often inspired by Kharaji (q.v.) doctrines, harassed the capital and occupied it on several occasions. The Aghlabids (q.v.) ruled from Kairouan, turning the city into a major commercial center through which goods from sub-Saharan Africa passed en route to markets in the Middle East. They also appended to the original city a royal suburb,

Raqqada (q.v.). The Fatimids (q.v.) and the Zirids (q.v.) maintained Kairouan as their capital, with the latter adding another new suburb, al-Mansuriyya (q.v.).

The Fatimid departure for Egypt and the growth of the al-Murabit confederation in the western Maghrib altered trans-Saharan trade routes, producing a shift in Ifriqiya's commercial activity away from the desert-oriented Kairouan and back toward the settlements along the Mediterranean. This setback was aggravated by the appearance of the Banu Hilal (q.v.) tribes, which sacked Kairouan in 1057. The Zirid rulers retreated to Mahdiyya (q.v.), on the coast, and Kairouan never again functioned as a political center of gravity.

Nevertheless, its rich Islamic heritage assured its lasting importance as a religious center. In 1961, Kairouan was the scene of vigorous demonstrations against President Habib Bourguiba's (q.v.) first attempts to circumscribe the powers of the ulama and to draw a clear distinction between the religious and the secular spheres. More than two decades later, in the waning days of the Bourguiba era, the Islamist groups that had begun to assert themselves on the Tunisian political scene enjoyed considerable support among the people of Kairouan.

By the mid-1990s, the population of Kairouan had edged over the 100,000 mark.

Kasserine Pass, Battle of. American units that had participated in Operation Torch (q.v.), but had seen little subsequent combat, were assigned to hold the area around the Kasserine pass in western Tunisia as the Allies moved into the country in early 1943. In February, Axis forces retreating from Egypt and Libya defeated the Americans, broke through the pass, and threatened to overwhelm the Allied armies until a hastily organized counterattack checked their advance.

Le Kef. Regional economic and administrative center of western Tunisia. Early in the Christian era, the Romans, who knew the site as Sicca Veneria, maintained a prosperous agricultural colony there. Especially in the late seventeenth century, Le Kef's proximity to the Algerian frontier on a main route linking Tunisia and Algeria gave it strategic importance. Several attempts by the deys of Algiers to extend their influence eastward precipitated battles in and around Le Kef, prompting the Muradid bey Muhammad to erect a substantial fortress there in 1679.

Khair al-Din Barbarossa (1466?–1546). Corsair captain of eastern Mediterranean origin. He became ruler of Algiers after defending the city against a Spanish attack in 1510. When he later acknowledged Ottoman sovereignty, the Hafsids (q.v.) (who regarded the Turks as a threat to their dominions) became so alarmed that they attacked Algiers in 1534. Aided by the Ottomans, Khair al-Din repulsed the assault and launched a counteroffensive that resulted in his occupation of Tunis and portions of its hinterland. He held these territories only until 1535, when the Hapsburgs (q.v.) restored the Hafsids to their throne. In recognition of Khair al-Din's efforts to secure the central Mediterranean for the Ottomans, the sultan appointed him admiral of the imperial fleet in 1534.

Khair al-Din al-Tunsi (ca. 1822–1890). A favorite mamluk (q.v.) of Ahmad Bey (q.v.), he became the most prominent Tunisian statesman of the nineteenth century. After Ahmad's death, he served as minister of maritime affairs under Muhammad Bey (q.v.) and then as president of the Grand Council (q.v.) established by Muhammad al-Sadiq Bey (q.v.) in 1860. He resigned from that office in 1862 following a dispute with his political nemesis, Mustafa Khaznadar (q.v.), then the prime minister, over the advisability of the government's borrowing money abroad. Khair al-Din opposed this policy, arguing that it would augment the already substantial influence of the European powers in Tunisia, whereas Khaznadar, who had reaped enormous profits from his dealings with European businessmen, favored the idea.

Khair al-Din resided in Europe from 1862 until 1869. In 1867 he published *Aqwam al-masalik li ma^{c}rifat ahwal al-mamalik* (*The Surest Path to Knowledge concerning the Conditions of Countries*), a book describing the material situation of the West and, more importantly, outlining an approach to government that he believed would bring stability and prosperity to Tunisia. Khair al-Din viewed governance as a matter of stewardship, with the ruling elite responsible for the welfare of its subjects, who did not themselves participate directly in the political process. Thus, he stressed the need for a strong, but just, state ready to protect its citizens from arbitrary abuses of power. As a good Muslim, Khair al-Din believed that government functioned best with the cooperation and participation of the ulama, and much of *The Surest Path* was an appeal to those men. While impressed by the technological assets of Europe, Khair al-Din rejected the wholesale adoption of western ideas and devices, preferring instead the selective adaptation of the material and intellectual products of western culture.

He returned to Tunisia in 1869 to chair the International Finance Commission (q.v.). Khaznadar's warm and lucrative relationship with British government officials and investors in Tunis alienated the other European members of the commission, who called for his dismissal as prime minister. In 1873, the bey complied, naming Khair al-Din to the post. For the next four years, he pursued a policy, based on the principles expounded in *The Surest Path,* intended to restore confidence in the government, to bring justice and prosperity to Tunisians, and to prevent any further European encroachment.

Toward these ends, Khair al-Din completely overhauled the inequitable tax system and offered small farmers economic incentives to expand their land under cultivation. He introduced reforms modernizing the curriculum of the Zaituna Mosque-University (q.v.), a traditional source of government clerks, and created a new secondary school, Sadiqi College (q.v.), modeled on the French lycée, to be a training ground for young men destined for government service. He also advocated a close relationship with the Ottoman Empire as an example of Muslim solidarity in the face of western pressure.

The latter policy drew Khair al-Din close to Great Britain, the longtime European patron of the Ottomans. But British support for the empire was on the wane and British enthusiasm for a protracted role in Tunisia was diminishing. Consequently, other European powers rushed to stake their claims. The continuation of Khair al-Din's reform program, however, threatened to jeopardize all European interests in the country. In 1877, a coalition of the prime minister's foreign and domestic enemies convinced the bey to remove him from office. Khair al-Din retired to Istanbul, where he lived until his death, serving as grand vizier of the empire under Sultan Abd al-Aziz in 1878–1879.

Khalduniyya. Educational society founded by the Young Tunisians (q.v.) in 1896 and named in honor of the fourteenth-century Tunisian intellectual, Ibn Khaldun (q.v.). Intended to acquaint Tunisians who were illiterate in western languages with the contemporary European world, it offered instruction (in Arabic) in a wide variety of subjects. The organizers of the Khalduniyya especially targeted Zaituna Mosque-University (q.v.) students in order to broaden their horizons, which were circumscribed by the school's still largely traditional curriculum.

Khammas. Sharecropper. The word is derived from the Arabic for one-fifth, the portion of the crop such individuals customarily received as payment for their labor.

Kharajism; Kharajis. Muslim sect popular among Berber tribes during the first several centuries of Arab rule in North Africa. It emphasized the equality of all believers and asserted that the leadership of the Islamic community should devolve upon its most pious member, regardless of familial or racial background.

Social and political discrimination against the Berbers by representatives of the Umayyad dynasty (661–750) triggered revolts couched in Khariji ideology as early as the 730s and 740s. The Umayyads' successors, the Abbasid dynasty (q.v.), pledged to accord impartial treatment to all Muslims, but many Berbers remained attracted to Kharajism. They made it their principal vehicle for political dissent, using its egalitarian doctrines to rally opposition to alien rule. This was manifested when Berber tribesmen seized Kairouan on several occasions in the late eighth century and when Abu Yazid (q.v.) revolted against the Fatimids (q.v.) in 934. The last significant political movement of Kharaji inspiration was an eleventh-century rebellion against the Zirids (q.v.). Always strongest in the southern reaches of Ifriqiya, Kharaji influence was gradually restricted to such remote areas as the Jarid (q.v.) and the island of Jerba, on which a small Kharaji community has survived to the present.

Khaznadar. Husainid official responsible for the state treasury. Generally entrusted to a close associate of the bey, the office carried with it great power and prestige.

Khrumir. Northwestern tribe whose lands straddle the Algerian frontier. Nineteenth-century French officials in Algeria frequently complained that segments of the tribe living on Algerian territory customarily fled to Tunisia to evade taxes, while others residing in Tunisia conducted raids across the border. The French government cited a series of Khrumir raids as the rationale for the invasion of Tunisia in 1881 that ended in the declaration of the protectorate.

Klibi, Chedli (1925–). Secretary-general of the Arab League (q.v.) from 1979 to 1990. Klibi assumed the leadership of the regional organization when its headquarters were relocated from Cairo to Tunis after Egypt was expelled from the league for signing a peace treaty with Israel. His decision to resign was bound up in the controversy occasioned throughout the Arab world by the Iraqi invasion of Kuwait. It was also a protest against the abrupt return of the league's headquarters to the Egyptian capital shortly after the invasion. Supporters of Saddam Hussein criticized Klibi for the league's condemnation of Iraq at an emergency summit over which he presided. Conversely, the Iraqi leader's opponents attacked his lack of enthusiasm for military action to protect Saudi Arabia and to liberate Kuwait.

Klibi's opposition to the use of armed force in the Gulf reflected the policies of the Tunisian government, which he had long served in a number of capacities prior to his association with the league. A journalist and academician at the time of independence, Klibi served as director general of Tunisian Radio and Television from 1958 until 1961. During the 1960s, he held a series of positions in the ministry of culture and information, which he headed from 1971 to 1973. Following a division of the ministry's functions, Klibi served as minister of cultural affairs between 1976 and 1978 before taking up his post as secretary-general of the Arab League.

Kouloughlis. Offspring of mixed marriages between Tunisian women and Turkish soldiers. Initially, their career options were limited to service in the army. In their desire to build a strong base of local support, however, the Husainid beys (q.v.) opened civilian government posts to the kouloughlis, some of whom also engaged in commercial activities.

Ksar Hellal. Sahil town. Habib Bourguiba (q.v.) and other members of the Dustur who had been expelled from or had broken with the party met there in March 1934. At this Ksar Hellal Congress, the Neo-Dustur party was founded.

Kusaila (?–688). Leader of Berber resistance against the earliest Arab occupation of Ifriqiya. His followers harassed the Arabs with hit-and-run raids and ambushes, one of which took the life of Uqba ibn Nafi (q.v.). Kusaila occupied Kairouan in 683 and held the city until Hassan ibn al-Numan (q.v.), commanding the largest Arab force ever sent to the Maghrib, dislodged him eight years later.

Kutama. Berber tribe forming the core of the force assembled by Abu Abdallah (q.v.) to overthrow the Aghlabids (q.v.). Although the Kutama initially constituted the mainstay of the Fatimid (q.v.) army, they were disappointed by the regime's refusal to allow them to pillage Ifriqiya's settled lands or to acknowledge them as a privileged group. As a result, Abu Abdallah led the Kutama into revolt. His assassination, on orders from Ubaidallah (q.v.), antagonized the tribe further. A renewed insurrection was checked only when the ruler relented and allowed the Kutama to plunder freely, including in Kairouan, which they attacked in 911.

Suspicion and mistrust continued to permeate relations between the tribe and the central government, however. As the Fatimids gradually solidified their position, they diverted the attention of the Kutama from Ifriqiya by encouraging them to participate in campaigns designed to weaken potential Fatimid enemies in the central and western Maghrib. Even after the Fatimids moved to Egypt, they made use of the tribe by promoting Kutama discontent in order to prevent the Zirids (q.v.), to whom they had entrusted Ifriqiya, from becoming too powerful.

-L-

Ladgham, Badi (1913–). Neo-Dustur activist and observer at the United Nations from 1951 until 1955. He worked to safeguard Tunisian interests in the international organization and also to convey nationalist objectives to the American public. Ladgham was secretary general of the Neo-Dustur and then of the Parti Socialiste Dusturien (PSD) from 1955 to 1971 and prime minister in 1969 and 1970. The ouster of Ahmad Ben Salah (q.v.) in 1969, followed by President Bourguiba's (q.v.) extended stay outside the country for medical treatment, greatly enhanced Ladgham's influence. More tolerant of Islamic values than was Bourguiba, he was also more favorably disposed toward Egypt and the other Arab states of the Middle East, with which he restored good relations. In 1970, he successfully mediated between King Hussain and Yasser Arafat to stop the fighting in Jordan between the army and the PLO.

Lamine Bey. *See* **al-Amin Bey.**

Lasram Family. One of the most powerful political families of the eighteenth and nineteenth centuries. The Lasram family was descended from the original Arab settlers of Kairouan. Their loyalty to the Husainids (q.v.) during the civil strife of the eighteenth century catapulted family leaders into important political posts, most notably that of bash katib, or head clerk. The family virtually monopolized that office through the first half of the nineteenth century, while also filling other less crucial positions in the administration. Even under the protectorate government, members of the family continued to retain influential posts. One of them, Muhammad Lasram (1858–1925), also participated actively in the Young Tunisian movement (q.v.) and played a major role in organizing the Khalduniyya Society (q.v.).

Lavigerie, Charles-Martial (1825–1892). French Catholic clergyman and missionary appointed bishop of Algiers in 1866. In 1868 he created the Society of Missionaries of Algiers, better known as the White Fathers. His zeal for proselytizing brought him into conflict with the authorities. Despite official reservations about missionary work, Lavigerie regarded the extension of French political control in North Africa as essential to the spread of Christianity. This conviction led to his initial involvement with Tunisia.

In 1873, he undertook a campaign to restore the shrine of King Saint Louis IX (q.v.) to French control. Built in the 1840s at the presumed site of the crusader king's death on the plateau of Byrsa overlooking Carthage, the shrine had fallen into disrepair. Well aware of French interests in Tunisia, the politically astute Lavigerie persuaded the pope to staff the shrine with White Fathers, the first of whom arrived in 1875. Named apostolic administrator of Carthage and Tunis in 1881, the archbishop moved his residence from Algiers to Tunis to capitalize on the symbolism of the restoration of the See of Carthage in spreading Christianity in Africa. Elevated to the rank of cardinal in 1882, he was designated cardinal-archbishop of Carthage and Algiers in 1884, the same year in which he initiated the construction of the basilica of Saint Louis at Carthage.

Despite the deterioration of church-state relations in France in the 1880s, Lavigerie worked hard to promote cooperation between these two bastions of the French presence in the protectorate. At the same time, the White Fathers, under his close personal supervision, both ministered to the resident Catholic population and aggressively pursued their missionary calling. In addition to preaching, members of the order built schools and orphanages, frequently assisted by the White Sisters, an order of nuns Lavigerie had organized. The cardinal's vehement attacks on Islam, his repeated charges of Muslim fanaticism, and his taste for ostentatious displays of the Christian presence (at Carthage and elsewhere) alienated Tunisian Muslims, aggravating the misunderstandings between them and the French. Lavigerie suffered a fatal stroke during a visit to Algiers in 1892. He was buried in the basilica of Saint Louis, but after Tunisian independence his remains were transferred to the headquarters of the White Fathers in Rome.

Libya. For most of their histories, what are now the nations of Libya and Tunisia shared very similar experiences. Tribes in southern Tunisia ignored the borders drawn up by the Ottomans, with many who had resisted the French occupation in 1881 fleeing to Libya. The traditional links between the two regions made it inevitable that events in Libya occasionally caused repercussions in Tunisia. The Italian invasion of Libya in 1911, for example, aroused the anger of the Young Tunisians (q.v.), while Libya's acquisition of independence in 1951 provided encouragement to Tunisian nationalists.

After oil was discovered in Libya in the late 1950s, the country's booming economy provided jobs for thousands of unemployed Tunisian workers. Although the 1969 coup that brought Colonel Muammar Qadhdhafi to power did not immediately disturb the good relationship between the two countries, the new government's radical positions on regional issues and its insistence on moving swiftly toward Arab unity soon posed problems.

Qadhdhafi regarded Tunisian president Habib Bourguiba (q.v.) as a vestige of a bygone era who advocated philosophies and techniques that were no longer appropriate. In 1974, taking advantage of the president's poor health and momentary lack of control over the decision-making process, Qadhdhafi persuaded Foreign Minister Muhammad Masmudi (q.v.) to sign a unity agreement. Bourguiba's renunciation of the accord shortly afterward initiated a feud between the two leaders that precipitated a number of serious incidents. Over the next several years, Libya supported opposition groups inside Tunisia. Qadhdhafi also used the Tunisian workers in Libya as a political weapon, periodically expelling many of them to force the Tunisian government to cope with the anger of deported laborers, few of whom could find jobs in their own country. Such actions embarrassed Tunisia by underscoring its reliance on labor migration, but Tunisian officials had few effective means of retaliation beyond mounting propaganda campaigns and strengthening relations with France, the United States, and other critics of the Libyan regime. The animosity between the two countries culminated in January 1980, when Tunisian dissidents trained in Libya attacked the southern city of Gafsa (q.v.). Tunisia immediately severed diplomatic relations with its neighbor, which reciprocated by expelling 10,000 Tunisian workers.

In 1982, however, as Libya came under increasing fire from western nations as well as moderate Middle Eastern and African states, it sought to improve relations with Tunisia. Qadhdhafi visited Tunis several times; the two states agreed to a ruling by the International Court of Justice that delimited their territorial waters in the oil-rich Gulf of Gabès; discussions opened on a number of joint development projects utilizing Libyan funds and Tunisian workers; and Tunisian labor migration to Libya resumed. This thaw proved short-lived, however. By 1985, a downturn in the oil industry had taken its toll throughout the Libyan economy, which could no longer absorb large numbers of foreign workers. Qadhdhafi seized upon Tunisia's deportation of hundreds of Libyans accused of espionage as an excuse to expel more then 30,000 Tunisians. As a result, the two nations severed diplomatic ties, initiating a period of animosity that lasted until 1987.

During the final year of his presidency, however, Bourguiba moved toward a rapprochement, extracting a commitment from Qadhdhafi not to interfere in internal Tunisian affairs. Facing virtually global isolation as a result of his support for various guerilla organizations and for Libya's own military operations in Chad, Qadhdhafi viewed Tunisia's friendship as a mechanism for regaining a respectable place in the international community. Within a few weeks of Bourguiba's removal, Zine al-Abidine Ben Ali (q.v.) restored full diplomatic relations and resumed the talks that his predecessor had begun with other North African heads of state to explore the prospects for Libyan adhesion to the 1983 Maghrib Fraternity and Cooperation Treaty. These discussions culminated in the formation, in 1989, of the Union du Maghreb Arabe (UMA; q.v.), a regional organization linking Mauritania, Morocco, Algeria, Tunisia, and Libya. In the interim, Tunisia and Libya completed a series of bilateral accords designed to facilitate transportation and communication across their borders and to promote joint economic ventures, including the development of undersea oil fields in the Gulf of Gabès.

As Libyan-American relations degenerated into periodic bouts of armed conflict in the late 1980s, Ben Ali occasionally tried to utilize his access to both Washington and Tripoli to mediate the conflict. But his effectiveness was limited by the Tunisian public's tendency to sympathize with its Libyan neighbors and its opposition to outside intervention in the Maghrib. Tunisia abided by the sanctions on air traffic to and from Libya imposed by the United Nations in 1992 to force the surrender of Libyan citizens accused of committing acts of international terrorism. But roads across the frontier with Libya remained open, and ferry services between the two countries continued to operate. These routes quickly became crucial to ensuring Libyan connections with the rest of the world, engendering a boom in southeastern Tunisia's otherwise depressed economy. Ben Ali recognized that the deeply antagonistic relationship between Libya and the western powers leading the UN campaign (the United States, Great Britain, and France) posed a potential danger to other members of the UMA and threatened to damage their relations with the European Union. The Tunisian president tried, but failed, to mediate a compromise between Qadhdhafi and his critics in 1993. As a result, the sanctions, with their advantages and their drawbacks for Tunisia, remained in effect.

Ligue Tunisienne des Droits de l'Homme (LTDH)/Tunisian League of Human Rights. The first human rights organization in the Arab world. Saadeddin Zmerli founded the LTDH in 1977 to safeguard the individual liberties of Tunisian citizens as laid out in the United Nations' Universal Declaration of Human Rights and in the state's constitution. Since its creation, its members have represented a cross section of political views. In defense of the rights of trade unionists, students, and members of the Mouvement de la Tendance Islamique (MTI; q.v.), the league criticized the Bourguiba (q.v.) government for laws restricting the formation of organizations, for its press code, and for its practice of indefinitely detaining prisoners without charges. By the end of its first decade of existence, the league boasted more than 3,000 members and had opened lines of communication with other human-rights groups and widely respected newspapers (such as the Parisian *Le Monde*) that enabled it to disseminate information about Tunisia easily and quickly.

Following the LTDH's vigorous efforts to ensure proper treatment for MTI leaders jailed in 1987, its secretary-general, Khemais Chemari, was arrested. This arrest, along with the ruling Parti Socialiste Dusturien's (PSD; q.v.) creation of an auxiliary organization with ostensibly analogous goals, elevated the league's mistrust of the government to new levels. A few months after the accession of President Zine el-Abidine Ben Ali (q.v.), however, Chemari was acquitted of all charges brought against him. As further gestures of the new leader's willingness to coexist with the league, Zmerli was named minister of health in 1988 and another prominent LTDH figure, Muhammad Charfi, became the national director of educational and scientific research in 1989.

The conflict between the Ben Ali government and al-Nahda (q.v.; the Islamist political organization that had supplanted the MTI), which opened after the 1989 elections and continued into the 1990s, produced a spate of accusations alleging abuses of the human rights of adherents of that party and other members of the opposition. Anxious to offset attacks on its human rights record, some of which emanated from the highly regarded Amnesty International, the government in 1991 created an official commission, the Comité Supérieur des Droits de l'Homme et des Libertés Fondamentales (CSDHLF), to investigate these and similar charges. At about the same time, it imposed a variety of restrictions on the LTDH that made concurrent membership in it and participation in the work of political parties, in which many league members were activists, all but impossible. In mid-1992, the LTDH leadership voted to dissolve the organization rather than operate under such circumstances.

Despite the absence of any evidence of greater tolerance, the league was reconstituted early in 1994, a presidential election year in Tunisia. A week after the balloting, Moncef Marzouki, a former LTDH president, was arrested on charges of defaming the state (by calling for greater political freedom and the legalization of al-Nahda) in an interview published in a Spanish newspaper. Marzouki had earlier antagonized the authorities by his ultimately unsuccessful attempt to run against Ben Ali for the presidency. After spending several months in prison, he was released without being brought to trial. But the government's hostility towards the league, which it regarded as a pawn in the hands of its secular and Islamist political opponents, continued unabated.

Literature. The Zaituna Mosque-University (q.v.) made premodern Tunisia an important intellectual center of the Arab world. For many centuries, religious material dominated the literary output of the region. The writings of Imam Sahnun (q.v.), an eighth-century scholar, paved the way for the dissemination of legal interpretations based on the Maliki madhhab (q.v.) throughout the Maghrib. In a more secular vein, the talents of the poet and literary critic Ibn Rashiq, a resident of Kairouan in the eleventh century, were acknowledged throughout the Arab world.

The most famous premodern Tunisian writer, however, was Ibn Khaldun (q.v.). This fourteenth-century thinker began his career in the employ of the Hafsid dynasty (q.v.) and subsequently held a variety of offices elsewhere in North Africa, Spain, and the Middle East. In his best-known work, the *Muqaddima* (*Introduction*), he drew on his own experiences to formulate a theory of the evolution of human societies as well as a more general philosophy of history.

Such traditional genres as poetry, studies in the religious sciences, and chronicles characterized Tunisian literature well into the nineteenth century. Two of the most distinguished literary figures of the 1800s were Ahmad ibn Abi Diyaf, the author of the *Ithaf Ahl al-zaman bi akhbar muluk tunis wa ᶜahd al-aman,* a chronicle and biographical dictionary, and Muhammad Bairam al-Khamis (q.v.), much of whose work related to religious reform. He also wrote a detailed study of nineteenth-century Tunisia, the *Kitab safwat al-iᶜtibar bi Mustawdaᶜ al-Amsar wa al-Aqtar.*

Europe's growing encroachment on Tunisia's political, social, and economic affairs stimulated political treatises that proposed methods of confronting this challenge. Although it was aimed primarily at a Tunisian audience, the most important of these works, *Aqwam al-Masalik li Maᶜrifat Ahwal al-Mamalik,* by Khair al-Din al-Tunsi (q.v.), was also translated into French to provide inquisitive Europeans with a clearer comprehension of Tunisian aspirations. The translation gave European readers their first real insights into Tunisian society from a Tunisian perspective.

The spread of French education after the establishment of the protectorate expanded Tunisia's literary horizons by introducing genres such as the novel and drama that were not part of the classical Arabo-Islamic literary tradition. To the extent that this process also created a class of Tunisian intellectuals capable of expressing themselves fluently in French, it also gave rise to a linguistic controversy. As a counter to colonial efforts to equate French with the expression of sophisticated ideas and to relegate Arabic to secondary status in matters of the mind, early twentieth-century writers such as Abu'l-Qasim al-Shabbi (q.v.) and Tahar Haddad (q.v.) wrote in superb literary Arabic so as to emphasize the language's long and rich traditions and Tunisia's Arabo-Islamic heritage.

The Arabic literary environment in Tunisia in the 1920s and 1930s was, in fact, more fully developed than anywhere else in the Maghrib. At its center was the Jamaat Taht al-Sur, a circle of young writers whose contemplative and often existentialist themes Mahmoud al-Mesadi, a leading figure of the group, crystallized in his drama *al-Sudd.* The literary quality of this generation of Arabic authors' work generally outstripped that of its immediate successors. The latter's fiction and poetry, written in the closing days of the protectorate and the early period of independence, consisted primarily of didactic works intended to generate a spirit of patriotism and to promote nationalism. Thus, despite the fact that the most successful Tunisian political activists of the time were

French educated, the Arabic language and Arabic literature served as important vehicles for the expression of nationalist sentiment.

Although relatively few literary works in French were published in Tunisia before independence (in contrast with both Algeria and Morocco), there has been a steady stream of work in that language since 1956. Tunisia's most widely acclaimed francophone writer is Albert Memmi (q.v.), whose works explore themes of deracination and cross-cultural conflict, often based on his own experiences as a member of Tunisia's Jewish community. His writing has not been as extensively translated as Memmi's, but Hachemi Baccouche (q.v.), whose books include historical novels and an autobiography, is another francophone Tunisian author widely read in his own country and outside it. Some writers who have opted to express themselves in French have also chosen to live abroad. Memmi, who has resided in France since 1956, is the most prominent among them, but Tahar Bekri, Abdelwahhab Meddeb, and Hédi Bouraoui also fall into this category.

In keeping with the national objective of Arabizing Tunisian society, the generation of writers that has come of age since independence, and includes Ali al-Duaji, Rashid al-Hamzawi, Bashir Khrayyif, and Mustafa Tlili, has shown a marked preference for writing in Arabic. A few, such as Salah Garmadi, have published equally well received works in both languages. Others, of whom Meddeb is an example, continue to write primarily in French but incorporate cultural and linguistic aspects of Arabic into their work, thereby infusing it with an Arabo-Islamic spirit.

Louis IX (1214–1270). French king who invaded Tunisia in 1270. The immediate justification for this campaign was the Hafsids' (q.v.) refusal to pay Louis's brother, Charles of Anjou (q.v.), the tribute they had previously rendered to Christian rulers of Sicily. A stronger motivation was Louis's desire to participate in a crusade against the Muslims, although the true target of his zeal was Egypt, not Tunisia. His fear that the Hafsids would imperil his communication and supply lines to the east prompted the attack. While encamped at Carthage, Louis's army was decimated by dysentery, to which he himself fell victim. With his forces depleted, Charles negotiated a settlement with al-Mustansir I (q.v.) and withdrew the army. Louis was canonized by the Catholic Church in 1297.

-M-

al-Maᶜarifa. A monthly review founded in 1973 by adherents of the philosophy of the Egyptian Muslim Brotherhood. Successively edited by Rashid Ghannushi (q.v.), Hamida al-Naifar, and Salah al-Din Jourchi, *al-Ma^carifa*'s focus on religious issues offered an important journalistic outlet for the early proponents of incorporating Islamic values more fully into the Tunisian political and social culture. The publication's outspoken criticisms of government policies led to the confiscation of many of its issues and, ultimately, to its suspension by the authorities in 1979.

Macheul, Louis (1848–1922). French education official who served as the protectorate's director of public education from 1883 to 1908. His conviction that education held the key to good relations between Tunisians and Europeans led him to establish a Franco-Arab school system (q.v.). Despite the growth of colon opposition, Macheul promoted efforts to improve educational opportunities for Tunisian students throughout his career in the protectorate administration.

Madhhab. School of interpretation of Islamic law. Four such schools—Hanbali, Hanafi, Maliki, and Shafii—had acquired legitimacy throughout the Sunni Muslim world by the late ninth century. In Tunisia, the Maliki (q.v.) madhhab predominated from the outset, but the Hanafi (q.v.) madhhab, to which most Turks adhered, also established itself in the country during the Ottoman era.

Maghrib [commonly Maghreb in French]. An Arabic word meaning "the place where the sun sets," or the west. Early Arabs applied the word to the North African lands beyond the Nile valley. In modern times, the term generally refers to the states of Mauritania, Morocco, Algeria, Tunisia, and Libya.

Mahalla. Military expedition periodically dispatched by the central government to tribal areas. Its purpose was to collect taxes and demonstrate the government's ability to influence events in the hinterland. Although the practice had existed earlier, the deys (q.v.) institutionalized it at the end of the sixteenth century. By the 1800s, a mahalla traveled into the south each winter, and a second one, in the spring, visited the tribes in the western part of the country. The Husainid beys (q.v.) customarily entrusted the command of the mahalla to the crown prince in order to give him some military experience as well as an opportunity to familiarize himself with portions of the realm. Increasingly, however, the mahalla's function became more symbolic than real, often failing to collect sufficient taxes to pay for itself. Khair al-Din al-Tunsi (q.v.) ended the outmoded and no longer remunerative tradition in the 1870s.

Mahdi. Messianic figure whom Muslims believe will restore the purity of their community after a period of corruption and decay. The mahdi is an especially prevalent symbol in Shia Islam, although the concept also exists among Sunnis. In the early tenth century, Abu Abdallah (q.v.) rallied Berber support against the Aghlabids (q.v.) on behalf of Ubaidallah (q.v.), who claimed to be the mahdi.

Mahdiyya. Capital city built by the Fatimids (q.v.) in the decade after their rise to power. It was named for the first Fatimid ruler, Ubaidallah (q.v.), who claimed the title "mahdi" (q.v.). Their selection of a site on the Mediterranean Sea reflected the Fatimids' disgust with Berber uprisings around Kairouan, the former political center, as well as the dynasty's interest in expanding eastward in order to challenge the Abbasids (q.v.) more effectively. Although the Fatimids' Zirid (q.v.) successors at first ruled from the interior, they too moved the capital to Mahdiyya after the Banu Hilal (q.v.) sacked Kairouan and its suburbs in 1057.

Thereafter, the Zirids made Mahdiyya the headquarters of a Muslim effort to check Christian offensives in the central Mediterranean, raiding Christian ports and shipping from the city. In retaliation, a fleet of Genoese and Pisan vessels captured Mahdiyya in 1087 and compelled the Zirids to pay a substantial indemnity before returning it. Over the next century, as Zirid power waned, Mahdiyya changed hands several times. The Norman (q.v.) rulers of Sicily seized it, and much of the rest of the coast, in 1148, but the al-Muwahhids (q.v.) of Morocco, then the most powerful force in the Maghrib, countered this Christian assault on Ifriqiya with a campaign of their own. They retook Mahdiyya in 1159, but chose to make the less vulnerable Tunis their provincial capital. The corsair Darghut (q.v.) operated from Mahdiyya in the sixteenth century, provoking a Spanish attack that destroyed much of the city and ended its importance as a political or naval center.

Mahmud Bey (r. 1814–1824). Seventh Husainid ruler. Shortly after coming to the throne, Mahmud encountered heavy pressure from the European powers to curb his subjects' corsairing (q.v.) activities. Aware that maritime raiding had already lost its economic importance, he acquiesced to these demands following the dispatch of European and American fleets to Tunis in 1816, 1817, and 1819.

The remainder of his reign was troubled by a succession of poor harvests that caused economic disruption, diminishing state revenues and bringing widespread famine and misery to the countryside. Moreover, a simultaneous European depression closed many traditional continental markets to Tunisian goods. Nonetheless, the royal court lavishly consumed European luxury goods and accumulated substantial foreign debts. To shore up his finances, Mahmud monopolized the purchase of olive oil, the country's most valuable export. To raise enough cash to meet his obligations, however, he frequently authorized the sale of oil at below market prices. By the time Mahmud died, the treasury was in chaos, and the door had been opened for Europe's economic penetration of the country.

Majarda River. Tunisia's only perennial river. The Majarda rises in the mountains of northeastern Algeria, flows through the Tell (q.v.), and empties into the sea between Tunis and Bizerte. Its total length is just under 500 kilometers (300 miles), and it waters a basin of some 25,000 square kilometers (15,000 square miles). In the early Christian centuries, the substantial wheat harvests of Roman farms in the Majarda valley earned the province of Africa Proconsularis the title "granary of Rome." Later cultivators, including refugees from Andalusia and French colons, flocked to the agriculturally attractive Majarda basin, which remains the primary grain-producing region in the country.

Majba. Personal tax, levied as a capitation, which produced almost half the state's revenues in the mid-nineteenth century. The government pledged the majba receipts as a guarantee of the annual payments due on its 1863 loan. To honor this commitment, it had to double the rate of the tax and also impose it on some individuals, such as the villagers of the Sahil, who had not previously paid it. This fiscal policy played a major role in triggering the 1864 revolt, in response to which the government ultimately rescinded its plans for augmenting the majba.

Maliki Madhhab. System of Islamic legal interpretation based on the writings of the Medinese scholar Malik ibn Anas. One of four such schools recognized by Sunni Muslims, the Maliki madhhab gained widespread acceptance in Ifriqiya from its introduction there in the eighth century. Although the region's ruling elites, particularly those originating elsewhere in the Muslim world, often followed other schools, and occasionally even attempted to subjugate the Maliki ulama, the vast majority of the population never wavered in its loyalty to this madhhab.

Malta, Maltese. Overpopulation and a seriously depressed economy prompted tens of thousands of Maltese, most of them peasants or unskilled workers, to emigrate from their islands in the early nineteenth century. So many settled in Tunisia (less than 350 kilometers [210 miles] from Malta) that by midcentury they constituted the largest single foreign community, numbering some 7,000. British consul Richard Wood (q.v.) reached an understanding with the Tunisian government in 1856 that allowed the Maltese, who were British subjects, to acquire real estate in the country on the sole condition that any legal disputes arising from such transactions be settled in Tunisian courts. Many Maltese purchased parcels of rural land and settled outside Tunis, where virtually the entire Maltese population had previously been concentrated. The Maltese continued to immigrate to Tunisia during the protectorate, their numbers doubling to some 14,000 by the end of World War I. A 1923 law facilitated the acquisition of French citizenship by second-generation aliens born in Tunisia and automatically conferred citizenship on third-generation aliens born in the country. Classifying persons from a variety of European backgrounds as French makes demographic statistics on the Maltese (and other non-French communities) in Tunisia deceptive.

Although the independent Tunisian government's decision in 1964 to expropriate foreign-owned land deprived Maltese holders of the approximately 15,000 hectares (37,500 acres) still in their hands, relations between Tunisia and Malta, which secured its own independence in the same year, have generally been good. The two nations have manifested an especially cooperative spirit on such matters of mutual concern as controlling pollution in the Mediterranean Sea.

Mamluk. Non-Muslim youth purchased by agents of the Husainid beys (q.v.) in Ottoman slave markets. In Tunis, the mamluk received a superb education, usually along with his contemporaries among the princes of the royal family. His training included religious instruction culminating in conversion to Islam. At the conclusion of his formal education the mamluk embarked on a career of government service that frequently led to the highest positions in the army and the bureaucracy. The recruitment of mamluks assured the Husainids of a constantly replenished contingent of highly qualified government officials. Moreover, since their status derived solely from the largesse of the bey, they exhibited an intense loyalty to their patron. There were rarely more than a hundred mamluks at any given time, with only a dozen or so in the same age group. Owing to their limited numbers, their proximity to the center of power, and their close personal ties to the beys (whose daughters and sisters they often married), the mamluks constituted a powerful elite within the Husainid state.

Manifeste du Front Tunisien (Manifesto of the Tunisian Front). A 1944 declaration by a coalition of Tunisian leaders calling for self-government and an elected legislature. The manifesto was a reaction to French unwillingness to make concessions to Tunisian nationalism following the Allied victory, despite the nationalists' refusal to collaborate with the Axis during the war. It was signed by representatives of the Dustur, Neo-Dustur, and Communist Parties; partisans of the deposed Munsif Bey (q.v.); labor organizers; educators; and ulama. Differences of opinion among the signatories about the wisdom of demanding an end to the protectorate necessitated omitting any references to independence from the final document. The French authorities' decision to respond to the manifesto with only minimal compromises served to intensify demands for full Tunisian sovereignty.

Mansur ibn Buluggin (r. 984–996). Second Zirid (q.v.) ruler. Realizing the impossibility of effectively managing the entire region that the Fatimids (q.v.) had entrusted to his family, Mansur retained control of Ifriqiya but assigned responsibility for the land further west to his brother Hammad (q.v.). Although Mansur's occasional acts of defiance irritated the Fatimids, they refrained from undertaking a full-scale campaign to curb Zirid ambitions. Instead, they nurtured discontent among the volatile Kutama Berbers (q.v.). Consequently, Mansur faced several Fatimid-inspired revolts in Kutama territory during his reign. These uprisings were all repressed, but they precluded any serious move toward autonomy on Mansur's part.

Mansuriyya. Suburb of Kairouan built in the late 940s as a royal residence by the Fatimid (q.v.) caliph al-Mansur, for whom it is named. al-Mansur disliked Mahdiyya (q.v.), but hesitated to return to Kairouan itself because of that city's general antagonism toward his dynasty. The Zirids also used Mansuriyya as a capital, adding an important economic dimension to the locale by ordering Kairouan's merchants to relocate their businesses there.

Marabout [Arabic: Murabit]. French form of an Arabic word literally meaning "a man from a ribat" (q.v.). Because such a person dedicated himself to defending Islam against aggression, the word came to refer, throughout North Africa, to any pious individual locally regarded as a saint. The tomb of the marabout, who was often affiliated with one of the mystical orders of Islam, became a place of veneration and an object of regional pilgrimages. Some French sources also use the word *marabout* for such a tomb, characteristically a simple, whitewashed building with a dome, although a more accurate term is *qubba*.

Mareth Line. Defensive position established by Axis forces as they retreated from Libya in early 1943. Approximately 25 kilometers (15 miles) south of Gabès, the line extended from Mareth on the Mediterranean southwest into the desert. It fell to British general Sir Bernard Montgomery's Eighth Army on March 27, 1943. Its collapse cleared the way for an Allied drive toward Tunis, which fell on May 7.

Marinids; Marinid Dynasty. The Banu Marin, the Berber tribe that succeeded the al-Muwahhids (q.v.) in the western Maghrib. Anxious to expand their own domain and fearful that the bitter rivalries among the

Hafsids (q.v.) left them unprepared to defend Tunisia against Christian assaults, the Marinids occupied the country in 1347. Their attempts to control Arab tribes that had enjoyed considerable latitude under the Hafsid sultans sparked a series of rebellions, forcing them to withdraw to Morocco in 1349. A second Marinid invasion occurred in 1357, as the dynasty continued its campaign to bring the entire Maghrib under its control. Once more, Arab tribal resistance compelled the invaders to abandon their plans, this time after only a few months. The Marinid failure to master Tunisia on either of these occasions stemmed, in part, from the Hafsids' success in creating a sense of Tunisian identity separate from the rest of North Africa. After the second Marinid attack, the Hafsids built upon that identity to foster a political and economic renaissance that propelled the dynasty to the height of its influence and prestige in the century and a half that followed.

La Marsa Convention. Accord reached with Ali Bey (q.v.) on June 8, 1883, officially establishing a French protectorate over Tunisia. In signing the document, the bey agreed to the imposition of administrative, judicial, and financial reforms prescribed by the French resident general. Thus, Ali surrendered the pretense of sovereignty over internal matters that Muhammad al-Sadiq (q.v.) had managed to retain when he signed the Treaty of the Bardo (q.v.).

Masinissa (240–148 B.C.E.). Berber chieftain and ally of Rome in the Second Punic War (q.v.). As a reward for his services, he received large grants of land around Carthage. Although alienated by the Carthaginians' haughty attitude toward the Berbers, Masinissa found much to admire in their culture and tried to incorporate the best of it into Berber society. To the leaders of Carthage, however, he represented an obstacle to the city's revival. When an attempt to draw Masinissa into an alliance against his Roman patrons failed, the city prepared to go to war against him. Rome promptly intervened on the Berber leader's behalf, opening the Third, and final, Punic War.

Masmudi, Muhammad (1925–). Political figure and nationalist activist. Educated at Sadiqi College (q.v.) and the University of Paris, he acted as a European spokesman for the Neo-Dustur (q.v.) in the early 1950s. Masmudi secured a seat on the party's political bureau in 1955. In the following year, he became independent Tunisia's first ambassador to France, but returned home in 1958 to assume the position of minister of information. His control over the media provided him with a platform for denouncing Tunisia's single-party political structure and the powers vested in its president. By 1961, his criticisms had precipitated a break with Habib Bourguiba (q.v.), who dismissed Masmudi from the government and arranged to have him expelled from the party.

Reintegrated into the Parti Socialiste Dusturien (PSD) after the fall of his longtime rival Ahmad Ben Salah (q.v.), Masmudi was secretary-general of the party and minister of foreign affairs from 1970 until 1974. An ardent Arab nationalist, he concentrated on bettering Tunisia's fragile relations with the eastern Arab states during his tenure in office. His pursuit of this goal was facilitated by the poor health of President Bourguiba, who had long been wary of a rapprochement with Arab nationalism, and by the death of that movement's greatest spokesmen, Egypt's President Nasser, in 1970. Masmudi's political career ended in 1974, when he orchestrated a merger between his country and Libya. After initially giving his approval, the ailing Bourguiba rejected the plan, dismissed Masmudi from office, and expelled him from the party. The former minister went into exile for several years, but returned to Tunisia in 1977 to live under house arrest. In the early 1980s he was permitted to leave the country again. He returned only after President Bourguiba's removal from office in 1987, but did not publicly engage in political activity in the Ben Ali era.

Matari, Mahmud (1894–1972). Associate of Habib Bourguiba (q.v.) in the creation of the Neo-Dustur Party (q.v.) in 1934. A member of the French Communist Party as a student, Matari served as president of the Neo-Dustur until a falling out with Bourguiba occurred in 1937. In light of France's crackdown on Moroccan and Algerian nationalists after the collapse of the Popular Front (q.v.) government, Bourguiba discounted French promises of reforms for Tunisia. Instead, he advocated a militant, uncompromising approach to France. The more moderate Matari had little choice but to resign, having failed to dissuade Bourguiba from a course of action he regarded as counterproductive, and aware of the support Bourguiba enjoyed among the party's rank and file. He served briefly in a cabinet formed by Munsif Bey (q.v.) in 1943, but did not again play an active political role until the end of the protectorate. As an independent, Matari sat in the constituent assembly and also served in the first national assembly elected in 1959.

Memmi, Albert (1920–). Literary figure whose body of work received international acclaim and earned him recognition as one of the most distinguished French-language writers of the first postindependence generation in North Africa. Educated in French and Jewish schools in Tunis, Memmi received a degree from the University of Paris in 1949. He returned to Tunisia and lived there until he emigrated to France in 1956. His novels, short stories, and essays have explored themes drawn from his own experiences in Tunisia's Jewish community, including the psychological dimensions of colonial relationships and questions of identity. Among his works are *Le Statue de sel* (*The Pillar of Salt,* 1953) and *Agar* (*Strangers,* 1955), two essentially autobiographical novels that explore the debilitating impact of the colonial experience on the people who are colonized. Memmi develops very similar themes in the essay *Portrait du colonisé précédé du portrait du colonisateur* (*The Colonizer and the Colonized,* 1957), while three other essays, *Portrait d'un Juif* (1962), its sequel *La Libération du Juif* (1966), and *Juifs et Arabes* (*Jews and Arabs,* 1975) explore Jewish identity in the aftermath of the creation of a Jewish state and the social relations between Jews and Gentiles. Memmi returned to fiction in the late 1960s, publishing *Le Scorpion ou la confession imaginaire* (*The Scorpion*), which many critics regard as his most powerful work, in 1969. *Le Désert ou la vie et les aventures de Jubair Ouali El-Mammi* (1977) is a fictional account of a figure resembling the medieval Tunisian historian and sociologist Ibn Khaldun (q.v.). In *Le Pharaon* (1988), the narrator, a Tunisian Egyptologist, struggles to arrive at an understanding of the world in which he has lived and of the encounters he has had with major historical figures such as Habib Bourguiba (q.v.). In the decade of the 1980s, two studies in the psychology of oppression and racial conflict, *La Dépendance: Esquisse pour un portrait du dépendant* (*Dependence,* 1984) and *Le Racisme: Description, définition, traitement* (1982), established Memmi's reputation as a student of sociology as well as a writer.

Mendès-France, Pierre (1907–1982). Premier of France from 1954 to 1955. While deeply absorbed in the arduous process of extricating France from Indochina, his government also had to contend with a deteriorating situation in Tunisia, marked by the fallaqa (q.v.) uprising. Convinced that force, by itself, could not resolve the Tunisian question, and reluctant to begin a new round of colonial warfare in North Africa, Mendès-France opted for compromise and authorized negotiations with the nationalists in the summer of 1954. In April, 1955, his government agreed to grant Tunisia internal autonomy.

Mestiri, Ahmad (1928–). Parti Socialiste Dusturien (PSD) activist and government official whose criticisms of President Bourguiba's (q.v.) powers caused him to break with the party in the 1960s. Mestiri, along with other PSD leaders who regarded Ahmad Ben Salah's (q.v.) economic strategy as ruinous, believed the planning minister had remained in power, despite his ill-considered policies, only because he enjoyed the favor of the president, on whose prerogatives there were virtually no constraints.

Restored to good standing in the PSD after Ben Salah's disgrace in 1969, Mestiri undertook a campaign to open the transaction of important party business to broader participation and to establish institutional checks on the powers of the president. Elected to the PSD central committee in 1971, he advocated the direct election of the powerful Political Bureau by the party congress. The president's recurrent ill health enabled Mestiri to make some headway along these lines, but in 1974 a rejuvenated Bourguiba ejected Mestiri and his allies from the PSD, squelching the movement for change.

In 1978, portraying himself as the leader of a group seeking to reform, not overthrow, the government, Mestiri sought approval to organize a political party, the Mouvement des Démocrates Sociales (MDS; q.v.). Although his request was refused, he was widely acknowledged as the leader of a loyal opposition. In 1980, he was again rehabilitated by the party and even given a minor cabinet post. Mestiri accepted an invitation extended by the prime minister, Muhammad Mzali (q.v.), to political groups outside the PSD to participate in the 1981 elections, as well as Mzali's offer to officially sanction as political parties those polling at least 5 percent of the vote. The list compiled by the MDS failed to garner this requisite minimum, and official recognition was delayed until 1983.

After organizing a demonstration protesting the Tunisian government's failure to condemn the American bombing of Tripoli in April 1986, the MDS leader was arrested. His detention during the 1986 election campaign led his party to boycott the balloting. Mestiri was released in December 1987, a few weeks after Bourguiba was replaced by Zine el-Abidine Ben Ali (q.v.). Following protracted discussions with the new president on the issue of political pluralism, Mestiri rejected a suggestion that the opposition parties forge a coalition to contest the 1989 legislative elections. Instead, Mestiri orchestrated a campaign in which his party polled a scant 4 percent of the total vote and failed to secure a single seat in the National Assembly. Although the MDS attracted more of the electorate than any other party except for the ruling Rassemblement Constitutionnel Démocratique (RCD), this stunning defeat forced Mestiri to step down as secretary-general a few months later. Following a rift between his successor, Muhammad Mouada, and other prominent party officials in 1992, Mestiri resigned from the MDS and retired from politics altogether.

Milk. An Arabic word describing privately owned property that could be sold or otherwise transferred without legal constraint.

Millet, René (1849–1919). French resident general from 1894 to 1900. He sympathized with the Young Tunisians' (q.v.) hopes of serving as interlocutors between their countrymen and the West. With that in mind, he provided government subsidies for the publication of their newspaper, *al-Hadira* (q.v.), and endorsed the work of the Khalduniyya (q.v.), their society for disseminating instruction in modern subjects to Zaituna Mosque-University (q.v.) students. Millet's support of the Young Tunisians aroused the ire of the colons, whose protests in metropolitan France forced him to temper his policies and ultimately led to his removal.

Mollet, Guy (1905–1975). Socialist prime minister of France from 1956 to 1957. In order to focus French North African policy on the full-scale rebellion in Algeria, he agreed to Moroccan demands for independence early in 1956. Upon learning of this settlement, the Neo-Dustur insisted on similar treatment for Tunisia. Mollet's government formally acknowledged the termination of the protectorate on March 20, 1956.

Monastir. Sahil city dating from the Carthaginian period. Called Ruspina by the Romans, it was the headquarters for Caesar's African operations in 46 B.C.E. Early in the Islamic period, the Arabs protected the coast of Ifriqiya with a chain of fortresses, including one built at Monastir in 796. This ribat (q.v.) flourished for several centuries, gaining the gratitude and respect of Ifriqiya's Muslims. As a result, Monastir became an important religious center, especially after the sack of Kairouan in 1057. The region around the town produces substantial quantities of olives, but the development of Monastir's beaches has made it an important center of tourism, which has become the mainstay of the local economy.

Morice Line. Defense perimeter constructed by the French army along the Tunisian-Algerian frontier in 1957. After independence, Tunisia permitted the Algerian Front de Libération Nationale (FLN) to train soldiers in the country and to use Tunisian territory as a sanctuary. The purpose of the Morice Line, which included an electrified border fence, was to seal the frontier and prevent FLN forces from moving freely into and out of Tunisia.

Morocco. Morocco and Tunisia had few direct contacts prior to the end of French rule in both countries in 1956. Although President Bourguiba (q.v.) and Sultan Muhammad V held similar views on many issues, tensions flared briefly in 1960 when Tunisia supported the independence of Mauritania against Moroccan claims to sovereignty over the territory. Nor did Tunisia endorse Moroccan efforts to gain control over Western Sahara after it was evacuated by the Spanish in 1975. Tunisian policy derived from a belief in the Western Saharans' right to self-determination, and also a reluctance to antagonize its powerful neighbors, Libya and Algeria, who vigorously opposed Moroccan objectives. Tunisian officials consistently called for a negotiated settlement of the Western Saharan problem and worked to prevent Morocco's diplomatic isolation.

Consequently, the two countries remained on good terms even after the 1983 Maghrib Fraternity and Cooperation Treaty linked Tunisia with Algeria and Mauritania and Libya joined Morocco in a short-lived unity accord in 1984. Later in the decade, as key differences between Morocco and Algeria over Western Sahara began to move toward resolution, Tunisia stressed the need to include Morocco in future plans for Maghrib unity. These culminated in 1989 with the formation of the Union du Maghreb Arabe (UMA) (q.v.), a regional organization that all five North African states joined.

Alone among the Maghrib states, Tunisia contributed a contingent of peacekeeping troops to the United Nations Mission for the Referendum in Western Sahara (MINURSO), an agency organized in 1991 to oversee a self-determination vote in the disputed territory. Although scheduled for 1992, the elections were repeatedly postponed as Moroccan and Western Saharan negotiators squabbled over lists of qualified electors. Throughout the first half of the 1990s, this lingering inability to resolve the Western Saharan question cast a cloud over the UMA and hampered the goal of forging common policies among its member states.

Mourou, Abd al-Fattah (1948–). Religious activist and secretary-general of the Mouvement de la Tendance Islamique (MTI; q.v.) since its foundation in 1981. Born in Tunis, Mourou attended Sadiqi College (q.v.). He then earned a law degree from the faculty of theology and law (the former Zaituna Mosque-University [q.v.]) of the University of Tunis, where he was among the founders of the Association pour la Sauvegarde du Coran (q.v.). Before embarking on the practice of law in 1976, he served for six years as a judge in courts administering the Personal Status Code (q.v.). When the Association pour la Sauvegarde du Coran and other similar groups consolidated to form the MTI at the end of the 1970s, Mourou and Rashid Ghannushi (q.v.) emerged as the new movement's leading figures.

Although consistently critical of the secular orientation of the government of Habib Bourguiba (q.v.), Mourou advocated reforming the system by working within it, in contrast with Ghannushi and his more radical associates, who were inspired by the Muslim militants who successfully deposed the shah of Iran. MTI elections in 1981 reflected this contrast. Supported by the majority of the organization's members, Ghannushi became its amir, or leader, while Mourou was elected secretary-general, bearing responsibility for its day-to-day operations. Despite his relative moderation, Mourou was jailed, along with other

MTI leaders, from 1981 to 1984. Following a short period of renewed activism after his release, he left Tunisia in 1986 to work with the World Islamic League in Saudi Arabia. As part of a massive crackdown on the MTI, which Tunisian authorities alleged to have bombed a resort hotel, Mourou was tried in absentia and sentenced to a ten-year prison term in 1987.

He returned to Tunisia in 1988, the beneficiary of a pardon issued by Zine el-Abidine Ben Ali (q.v.), Bourguiba's successor. He resumed his duties as secretary-general of the Mouvement de la Tendance Islamique. Mourou strongly supported the MTI's participation in the first parliamentary elections of the post-Bourguiba era, even though doing so necessitated changing the movement's title to al-Nahda (q.v.) to comply with the electoral laws' prohibition on parties whose names or programs referred to religion. Nevertheless, the government denied al-Nahda recognition, and its candidates were forced to run as independents, without success. This failure to gain entry to the political process underscored the differences between Mourou and Ghannushi. The latter went into exile after the elections, but Mourou, despite his continued presence and activity in the country, clearly remained al-Nahda's second in command.

Subsequently, the differences between the two became increasingly apparent. They disagreed on an appropriate response to the outbreak of the Gulf War, with Ghannushi condemning the dispatch of the multinational coalition to the Arabian peninsula and Mourou, perhaps in deference to his former hosts, adopting a much less critical public posture. More importantly, the secretary general deplored al-Nahda militants' trend toward violence, a topic about which Ghannushi remained silent. Already marginalized, Mourou suspended his ties with al-Nahda when its members murdered a Rassemblement Constitutionnel Démocratique (RCD; q.v.) party worker in a 1991 assault on a party office in Tunis. A few months later, government allegations that al-Nahda was planning a coup led to the arrest of many known activists. Insisting on his commitment to democratic processes and peaceful change, Mourou announced his definitive break with the party he had helped to organize. Although he expressed an interest in forming a new party, he had not been successful in doing so by the 1994 legislative elections. The more charismatic Ghannushi, despite his continued absence from Tunisia, eclipsed Mourou, who gradually receded from public view.

Mouvement de la Rénovation (MR). *See* **Parti Communiste Tunisien**

Mouvement de la Tendance Islamique (MTI)/Harakat al-Ittijah al-Islami; Islamic Tendency Movement. One of a number of groups formed during the 1970s with the objective of fostering an Islamic society in Tunisia. Sermons delivered by the leaders of the Mouvement de la Tendance Islamique, Rashid Ghannushi (q.v.) and Abd al-Fattah Mourou (q.v.), and the editorials of the monthly Islamist review *al-Ma^carifa* (q.v.) initially stressed doctrinal and moral issues, but as the MTI grew into the largest Tunisian group of its kind by the late 1970s, it became increasingly politicized. Ghannushi criticized the government's reliance on alien ideologies and development models, which he found to be both inappropriate and unnecessary. Moreover, they brought in their wake materialism and the corruption that inevitably accompanied it.

As the quality of life declined for all but the small minority of Tunisians able to benefit from Prime Minister Nouira's (q.v.) economic overtures to the West, the MTI gained a substantial following among lower- and middle-class men and women whose expectations had been raised beyond the government's ability to satisfy them. The success of the Islamic revolution in Iran prodded the movement to adopt a more defiant stand. It developed a network of branches throughout the country and publicly called not only for a return to more moral and religious values but also for the fashioning of a more equitable economy and the introduction of political pluralism. As a result, *al-Ma^carifa* was banned in 1979 and Ghannushi was imprisoned in 1981.

The government's refusal, even after the legalization of other opposition groups, to allow the MTI to organize as a political party endowed it with an aura of persecution that attracted additional adherents. The arrest of many MTI sympathizers on the grounds that the organization had masterminded a spurt of rioting in January 1984 had a similarly counterproductive effect. Unable to produce evidence linking the MTI with the riots, the government released the detainees, including Ghannushi, later in the year. The MTI again came under attack in early 1987. Accusations of a conspiracy to overthrow the government led to the arrest of Ghannushi and hundreds of other MTI members. While they were awaiting trial, several bombs exploded at hotels in Monastir, a popular tourist resort and President Bourguiba's (q.v.) hometown. The MTI denied responsibility for the blasts, but pointed out the inevitability of such actions in the face of government tactics. In September, seven MTI members were sentenced to death and another 69, including Ghannushi, received lengthy prison sentences.

The usually hard-line interior minister, Zine el-Abidine Ben Ali (q.v.), opposed carrying out the death sentences to avoid creating martyrs and stimulating increased MTI activity. Bourguiba's subsequent orders to execute two of the condemned men may have helped to persuade Ben Ali, who had in the interim become prime minister (and thus first in line to succeed the president), of the chief executive's inability to grasp the situation and of the need to remove him. Within a few months, Ben Ali released hundreds of MTI prisoners (including Ghannushi), implemented some of the movement's demands for the public manifestation of Tunisia's Islamic identity, and began exploring mechanisms for bringing Ghannushi and his followers into the political process. Hoping to contest the 1989 legislative elections, the MTI reconstituted itself as a political party, al-Nahda (q.v.). Despite the new government's apparent receptivity to the Islamist agenda, it denied the party the official recognition needed to present candidates to the voters.

Mouvement des Démocrates Sociales (MDS)/Movement of Social Democrats. Political organization founded by Ahmad Mestiri (q.v.) in the mid-1970s, when he and other would-be reformers were ousted from the Parti Socialiste Dusturien (PSD). After denying the Mouvement recognition as a political party for several years, the government allowed its members to participate in the 1981 parliamentary elections, promising to recognize the MDS as a legal party if it polled a minimum of 5 percent of the vote. It failed to achieve this goal, however, and remained outside the officially sanctioned political spectrum until 1983. After its legalization, the MDS campaigned for a more liberal political environment. It boycotted the November 1986 elections to protest Mestiri's arrest earlier in the year for organizing a demonstration against the American bombing of Tripoli.

Like other opposition parties, the MDS hailed the 1987 removal of President Habib Bourguiba (q.v.) as a step toward the liberalization of Tunisian politics. President Ben Ali's (q.v.) prompt release of Mestiri and his willingness to implement a system of political pluralism greatly encouraged party members. In the 1989 elections for the National Assembly, the first in the post-Bourguiba era, however, the MDS sustained a staggering blow. It won a scant 13 percent of the vote, failed to secure a single seat in parliament, and was outstripped by Islamist candidates running as independents. Mestiri resigned as party secretary-general and was replaced by Muhammad Mouada. Subsequent accusations by Mustafa Ben Jaafar, a rival candidate for the leadership, that Mouada too readily acquiesced to the government opened a rift that ended only when Ben Jaafar and several of his key supporters were expelled in 1992.

Under a new electoral formula that set aside a small number of seats for officially recognized opposition parties, Mouada led the MDS into the 1994 legislative elections. The party fielded a slate of candidates in all 25 national election districts and substantially outpolled the other five opposition factions, accumulating almost 31,000 votes (of some 2.9 million cast) and winning 10 of the 19 opposition seats in the 163-member chamber. After the elections, the MDS parliamentary delegation and the party's weekly newspapers, *al-Mustaqbal* in Arabic and *L'Avenir* in French, demanded additional electoral reforms designed to broaden the artificially created pluralism of the National Assembly and to instill a genuinely functional multiparty system. In late 1995, Mouada published an open letter to the president criticizing the restrictive political environment. Shortly afterward, he was arrested. A second MDS leader, Khemais Chammari, was deprived of parliamentary immunity amid allegations that he and Mouada had conspired with foreign states against the government. In February 1996, Mouada received an 11-year prison term.

Mouvement de l'Unité Populaire (MUP)/Movement of Popular Unity. Political organization created by Ahmad Ben Salah (q.v.) after he fled from Tunisia in 1973. Conceived in exile and drawing a large measure of its support from Tunisians unable or unwilling to reside in the country, the MUP had a limited impact on national politics. In domestic affairs, its agenda championed sweeping social and economic reforms of the kind Ben Salah had attempted to implement as minister of planning in the 1960s; its foreign policy rested on the principle of Arab unity and cooperation. The MUP split in 1981 when dissidents opposed to Ben Salah's insistence on boycotting the electoral process broke with their leader and formed the Mouvement d'Unité Populaire-2 (q.v.) to contest elections.

Ben Salah returned to Tunisia in 1988, soon after Zine el-Abidine Ben Ali (q.v.) replaced Habib Bourguiba (q.v.) as president. The former minister refrained from publicly participating in politics, however, and named Brahim Haydar to lead the MUP. In keeping with its commitment to Arab unity, the party criticized the formation of the coalition arrayed against Iraq after that country's invasion of Kuwait in 1990. Although Ben Ali also opposed the dispatch of the multinational force to the Arabian peninsula, Haydar's attempts to organize pro-Iraqi demonstrations led to his detention for a time in 1991. Its lack of official recognition as a legally constituted party effectively prevented the MUP from exerting much influence on national politics.

Mouvement de l'Unité Populaire-2/Movement of Popular Unity-2. Splinter political party that broke away from Ahmad Ben Salah's (q.v.) Mouvement d'Unité Populaire (MUP; q.v.) in 1981. Its members advocated participating in the Tunisian political process rather than boycotting it, as Ben Salah insisted. Under the leadership of Muhammad Bel Hadj Amor, the MUP-2 retained the MUP's socialist and Arab-unity orientation, but showed greater tactical flexibility in moderating its demands and agreeing to the conditions laid down by Prime Minister Muhammad Mzali (q.v.) in exchange for being acknowledged as a political party.

The MUP-2 acquired formal recognition as the Parti d'Unité Populaire (PUP) in 1983. Like other elements of the opposition, it welcomed the removal of President Habib Bourguiba (q.v.) in 1987 and approved the willingness of his successor, Zine el-Abidine Ben Ali (q.v.), to discuss the prospects of pluralism with its leaders. The weaknesses of the PUP manifested themselves in 1989 in the first elections to the National Assembly of the post-Bourguiba era. The party managed to field candidates in only six of the 25 electoral districts and captured less than 1 percent of the vote. Even after several years of internal consolidation and institution building, the PUP performed only marginally better in the 1994 legislative elections. Its 118 candidates, running in 19 electoral districts, garnered fewer than 8,500 votes (of the roughly 2.9 million cast). A set-aside of 19 places in the National Assembly for opposition parties did, however, give the PUP two seats in the new parliament. The PUP publishes *al-Wahda,* a weekly newspaper whose title (*Unity*) reflects the party's pan-Arabist sentiments.

Muhammad Ali (ca. 1888–1928). Dustur Party activist and labor organizer. He organized the first Tunisian union, the Confédération Générale des Travailleurs Tunisiens (CGTT; q.v.). Of southern Tunisian origin, Muhammad Ali transported medical supplies gathered by the Young Tunisians (q.v.) to Tripoli during the Italian campaign of 1911. Subsequently, he lived in the Ottoman Empire and in Germany, where he may have studied economics, before returning to his country after World War I.

In 1924, when European longshoremen refused to support their Tunisian colleagues' demands for equal wages, the latter turned to the Dustur for support. One of the few members of the party genuinely attuned to the needs of the working class, Muhammad Ali was then working to form consumer cooperatives. He saw in the longshoremen's appeal an opportunity to tie the political grievances of the middle-class Dusturians with demands for social and economic justice for the masses, thus broadening the party's appeal and its constituency. Toward the end of the year, he organized, with Dustur approval, the CGTT. His hope that French leftists would support the campaign for equitable treatment of Tunisian workers was not realized, however, and only the communists backed his endeavors.

As CGTT leader, Muhammad Ali led several effective strikes in 1925, but the Dustur increasingly distanced itself from him, fearing that his association with the communists would give the protectorate authorities an excuse to crush the entire party. When he was arrested and deported during the 1925 strikes, Dustur leaders made no effort to help him. Deprived of his leadership, the CGTT collapsed almost immediately. Muhammad Ali died in Egypt in 1928.

Muhammad Bey (r. 1686–1696). Lost a Muradid (q.v.) family struggle for the office of bey (q.v.) in 1680. He joined forces with his former adversary a few years later when the dey (q.v.) of Tunis tried to usurp powers that the Muradid beys had exercised for decades. Muhammad enjoyed good relations with the rural tribes on whose support his family relied, but the tribal levies at the Muradids' disposal were no match for the Turkish soldiery available to the dey. To offset this disadvantage, the Muradids sought the assistance of the dey of Algiers. After their combined forces had overwhelmed the dey of Tunis, Muhammad executed his family rivals and assumed absolute power.

His policies soon antagonized the Turks in Algeria, who disliked his integration of Tunisian tribesmen into the officer corps and his use of Arabic as an administrative language. They also resented his attempts to assert control over tribes on the Algerian side of the frontier. Muhammad's behavior provoked an Algerian invasion in 1694 that ended in the capture of Tunis and his expulsion. He quickly rallied tribal support, however, and within a year evicted the Algerians.

Muhammad remained in power for only a brief time. Persistent tensions with Algeria contributed to the rise of the Husainid dynasty (q.v.), which suffered from Muhammad's legacy of strained relations with Algeria. Perhaps the most positive contribution of his troubled reign was a growing sense of Tunisian identity, which he instilled among the tribes.

Muhammad Bey (1811–1859; r. 1855–1859). Eleventh Husainid ruler. After the intensive westernization programs of his predecessor, Ahmad Bey (q.v.), Muhammad sought to inaugurate a period of retrenchment, which focused on lowering government expenditures as well as foreign influence. However, European interests proved too strong to permit him to pursue such a course. In 1857, Great Britain and France seized upon the execution of Batto Sfez (q.v.) to demand that Muhammad implement judicial reforms guaranteeing the basic rights of his own subjects and of foreigners resident in the country. At the same time, the powers also encouraged the bey to adopt a positive attitude toward Europeans wishing to do business in Tunisia. Aware that he had little choice, Muhammad issued the Ahd al-aman (q.v.) and agreed to begin drafting a constitution based on its principles.

Muhammad ibn Husain (1710–1759; r. 1756–1759). Son of Husain ibn Ali (q.v.), founder of the Husainid dynasty (q.v.). When the bey appointed Muhammad to command the mahalla (q.v.) in 1724, he signaled his designation as the new heir apparent, replacing Husain's nephew Ali (q.v.), who had previously been groomed for the succession. The decision precipitated a civil war from which Ali emerged victorious in 1740. Because both sides solicited tribal support, the war created deep rifts within the rural population. It also gave the Turkish rulers of neighboring Algiers an opportunity to influence events in Tunisia by intervening on behalf of one or the other faction. After his defeat, Muhammad bided his time until 1746. He then resumed the war and, with Algerian help, deposed Ali a decade later. He ruled until his death in 1759, but paid an annual tribute to Algiers in return for its part in his restoration.

Muhammad al-Sadiq Bey (1814–1882; r. 1859–1882). Twelfth Husainid ruler. Shortly after coming to the throne, he promulgated the Constitution of 1861 (q.v.), culminating the reform process started by the European powers during the reign of his predecessor, Muhammad Bey (q.v.). Persuaded that the reforms affirmed Tunisian autonomy vis à vis the Ottoman Empire, Muhammad al-Sadiq accepted them with more enthusiasm than had Muhammad.

His reign was characterized by European competition for influence in Tunisia and a variety of financial woes. Ill-conceived development projects, corruption in the bureaucracy, and royal extravagance all combined to create a spiraling debt that necessitated an extremely disadvantageous loan from France in 1863. Muhammad al-Sadiq's decision to increase the majba (q.v.) to pay off the loan helped spark the 1864 revolt. His brutal repression of the revolt earned him the enduring hatred of many of his subjects. The rebellion also added to his government's expense. Beginning in 1866, it could no longer meet its international monetary obligations, and three years later Muhammad al-Sadiq was compelled to agree to the creation of the International Finance Commission (q.v.).

Khair al-Din al-Tunsi (q.v.), prime minister from 1873 to 1877, introduced progressive political and budgetary reforms. Many of them aimed at curbing the bey's powers, which had become increasingly arbitrary since his suspension of the constitution (with French approval) during the rebellion. Throughout the decade, however, foreign intrigue in Tunisia continued to mount, ultimately forcing Khair al-Din from office and making a European takeover virtually inevitable. The French invasion of 1881 was the last crucial event in Muhammad al-Sadiq's long and troubled reign. As well as being too old to lead the resistance to the invaders, he was held in great contempt by many of his subjects for bowing to European pressure and for his savage repression of his own people. It was impossible for him to serve as an effective rallying point. The bey died less than a year after signing the Treaty of the Bardo (q.v.), which took away many of his powers.

Muhammadiyya. Village some 16 kilometers (10 miles) southwest of Tunis. Its name comes from Muhammad Bey (q.v.), who built a palace there in the 1750s. After Ahmad Bey's (q.v.) visit to Europe in 1846, he chose Muhammadiyya as the site for the construction of a new royal complex modeled on Versailles. The expenditures lavished on the Muhammadiyya project contributed significantly to the depletion of the treasury during Ahmad's reign.

al-Muizz (r. 953–975). Last Fatimid (q.v.) caliph to rule in Ifriqiya. Early in his reign, Muizz sent his Berber troops into the central and western Maghrib to counter rising Spanish Umayyad (q.v.) influence there. His eastern campaigns were of greater long-term significance, however. In 969, Fatimid soldiers advanced into Egypt, establishing a base from which the dynasty could more effectively challenge its Abbasid (q.v.) rivals in Baghdad. al-Muizz and his entourage followed, leaving Mahdiyya for Cairo in 973.

al-Muizz (r. 1016–1062). Fourth member of the Zirid (q.v.) family to act as Fatimid (q.v.) governor of Ifriqiya. Ultimately, however, he severed the connection between the Maghrib and Egypt. Aware of Sunni Muslims' resentment of the Shii (q.v.) Fatimids, Muizz endeared himself to the province's Sunni majority early in his administration by condoning the slaughter of Shiis throughout Ifriqiya and by cultivating close ties with the Maliki (q.v.) religious establishment in Kairouan. While clearly distancing himself from the Fatimids, Muizz continued to maintain correct relations with them for over three decades.

The definitive break came only in 1049. Fatimid commercial growth in Egypt had led to a shift in trans-Saharan caravan routes away from Ifriqiya, stifling the region's economy and sparking widespread rebellions by the 1040s. Strapped for revenue, Muizz instituted a series of monetary reforms that included a ban on Fatimid coinage and the inauguration of a mint of his own, both symbolic acts rejecting his former masters' authority. The Fatimids retaliated by unleashing on Ifriqiya the Banu Hilal (q.v.) nomads. These tribes defeated the Zirid army at the Battle of Haidaran (q.v.) in 1052 and sacked Kairouan in 1057. al-Muizz fled to Mahdiyya, which remained the Zirid capital until the dynasty's demise more than a century later.

Munsif [Moncef] Bey (1881–1948; r. 1942–1943). Eighteenth Husainid ruler. Most outspoken supporter of the nationalist movement among the beys who reigned during the protectorate. With the Neo-Dustur's best-known and most articulate leaders either in exile or in prison, less prominent party members saw no reason to dissuade Munsif from assuming the role of nationalist spokesperson, nor, given his position, could they have done so even if they wished. His demands that France (1) allow greater Tunisian participation in the government, (2) provide compulsory education in Arabic, and (3) guarantee Tunisians equal pay for equal work also earned him broad popular support. The French authorities particularly resented the bey's habit of taking initiatives without consulting them, as when he formed a ministry without the resident general's approval in late 1942.

When German military forces occupied Tunisia in response to the Operation Torch (q.v.) landings in Morocco and Algeria, Munsif maintained only formal and correct relations with them. Nevertheless, after the Allied liberation in the spring of 1943, the Free French accused the bey of having collaborated with the Nazis, expelled him to Algeria, and forced him to abdicate. No convincing evidence of treasonous behavior was ever produced, however, and Munsif's nationalist inclinations were almost certainly the true cause of his removal. He died in exile in 1947.

Murad II (r. 1666–1675). Grandson of Murad Corso (q.v.). In 1669, the dey (q.v.) of Tunis attempted to oust him and appoint an associate of his own as bey (q.v.). Recognizing in the plot a bid to restore the dey's power, Murad II marshaled his tribal forces and reaffirmed his domination after a brief period of fighting. His victory eliminated any prospect of a deylical resurgence. When Murad II died in 1675, another civil war broke out, this time with his own family contesting the succession.

Murad III (r. 1696–1702). Last Muradid (q.v.) bey. Hoping to end the persistent threat of Algerian intervention, he invaded his western neighbor in 1700, besieging Constantine. The city withstood the attack, however, and the bey retreated. The Algerian campaign had aroused widespread resentment because Murad III had financed it by extorting money from wealthy Tunisians. Moreover, his haphazard resort to torture both frightened and antagonized his subjects, while his insistence on controlling the city of Kairouan (which had maintained its autonomy from earlier Muradid rulers) assured him of considerable opposition from the ulama. He was assassinated in 1702 by a member of his entourage, Ibrahim Sharif (q.v.).

Murad Corso (fl. 1612–1631). Corsican renegade who became bey (q.v.) and founded the Muradid dynasty (q.v.). He assembled a personal tribal army whose campaigns against rebellious southern tribes brought him to the attention of the Ottoman ruler. Sultan Murad IV named him pasha (q.v.) of Tunis in 1631. At the same time, he gave Murad the right to hand down the office of bey to his heirs, thus greatly decreasing their dependence on the deys (q.v.).

Muradids; Muradid Dynasty (1631–1702). The descendants of Murad Corso (q.v.). As beys (q.v.), they theoretically ruled on behalf of the

Ottoman sultan, but in reality Istanbul exercised little influence over them. Political and economic upheavals marked the Muradid era, with the deys (q.v.) and beys engaging in a struggle for preeminence. The deys of Algiers frequently intervened in Tunisian affairs, members of the family squabbled over power, and the corsairing (q.v.) activities (long the major prop of the economy) gradually gave way to more peaceful commercial exchanges.

Contributing to the Muradid triumph over the deys was the dynasty's perception of itself as Tunisian, an identity the deys did not share. As a result, the Muradids made efforts to integrate both rural tribesmen and the urban bourgeoisie into the government. The enhanced sense of cohesion thus established served the Muradids well in rallying resistance to Algerian ambitions in the country.

The rise of mercantilism led the European maritime powers, and especially France, to use their vastly superior fleets to curb the Barbary corsairs. The Muradids were forced to sign commercial treaties with France in 1665, 1672, and 1685, each treaty enshrining substantial privileges for French merchants. The decline in corsairing enterprises led the beys to look for economic compensation in the interior. But poor harvests and their inability to assert adequate control over the hinterland inexorably drew them into the web of international Mediterranean commerce. The beys moved quickly to control the Tunisian end of this trade by creating government monopolies. Although they enjoyed some success in this endeavor, European merchants continued to dominate Tunisian commerce throughout the Muradid era.

Music. Classical music in Tunisia, as elsewhere in the Maghrib, derives from a corpus developed in Muslim Spain and carried across the Mediterranean in the fifteenth and sixteenth centuries by refugees from the Christian reconquest of the Iberian peninsula. The performance medium for this music of Andalusian origin, called maaluf, meaning customary or popular, is the nawba, a suite of instrumental and vocal pieces arranged according to rhythm in a traditionally established order. Since a nawba often lasts for several hours, the presentation of the suites in their entirety has become rare. In another modern modification, the traditional instruments of the orchestra have been supplemented with, and sometimes replaced by, roughly corresponding ones of western origin.

The tradition of transmitting the maaluf repertoire orally posed a danger to its full and accurate preservation. As early as the eighteenth century, however, systematic efforts to inventory and arrange this body of music had begun. Rashid Bey, a music aficionado who ruled Tunisia from 1756 to 1759, devoted much of his life to organizing and codifying the country's maaluf music. In the twentieth century, the French musicologist Baron Rudolphe d'Erlanger (1872–1932), working in close collaboration with Tunisian musicians, compiled an anthology of *Mélodies tunisiennes* that was published posthumously. His magnum opus was a six-volume study entitled *La Musique arabe,* which appeared between 1930 and 1959. It also stressed the musical heritage of the Maghrib, particularly Tunisia. A few years after d'Erlanger's death, several of his Tunisian associates established the Rashidiyya Institute (q.v.) to promote an appreciation of *maaluf* music. In 1963, another former assistant helped produce 18 programs devoted to Tunisian classical music for Radio-Télévision Tunisienne. Subsequently released on records, this series was part of a postindependence campaign to engender a sense of pride in the national heritage, as well as a sense of national identity. On the sixtieth anniversary of d'Erlanger's death in 1992, the Tunisian government opened a Center of Arab and Mediterranean Music dedicated to the preservation of the Arab musical patrimony and housed in the villa in the Tunis suburb of Sidi Bou Said where the French scholar lived and worked.

Tunisian popular music is almost invariably associated with dancing. The urban expression of Tunisian music generally derives from Andalusian music, and the rural expression of it from indigenous Arab or Berber traditions. But modern advances in transportation and communication, along with postindependence campaigns to instill an overriding sense of national rather than regional identity, have eroded many of the historic psychological and physical barriers between the cities and the countryside. The extensive rural-to-urban migration that has accompanied this transformation has promoted the interpenetration of local cultures, including music. Tourism (q.v.) has also had a considerable, if ambivalent, impact on Tunisian popular (and to a lesser extent, classical) music. Its presentation to visitors as an example of local culture has raised its profile, but it is frequently performed in versions that threaten the integrity of authentic forms and practices because they have been bastardized to appeal to foreign tastes.

The prototype of urban popular music is the *malhun,* whose many different varieties are distinguished by structure, rhythm, content, and in some cases the gender of the performer. Their subject matter is virtually limitless, and they are sung in local dialects (in contrast to the classical language used in the vocal music of the *nawba*). The *salhi* songs of the Sfax region are among the finest examples of Tunisian *malhun* music. Rural popular music is as diverse as the tribespeople who perform it and the regions in which it has evolved. It may celebrate events in the life cycle, extol the virtues of local people or places, describe romantic and amorous experiences, or provide an accompaniment to the performance of domestic, pastoral, or agrarian tasks.

The rituals of many Muslim religious fraternities (*tariqas*) in

Tunisia also feature an array of music, including instrumental pieces; songs that praise God, the prophet Muhammad, or the founder of the *tariqa;* the repetitious chanting of religious phrases; and dances that can induce ecstatic states among both participants and observers. Ceremonies involving music, singing, and dancing also take place around the tombs of revered figures (marabouts [q.v.] or walis), which are sites of local pilgrimages. Beyond these examples of essentially populist religious music, the à cappella chant calling Muslims to prayer five times each day and the stylized recitation of the Quran for liturgical or educational purposes are illustrative of more formal Muslim practices that share many of the tonal and rhythmic qualities of music even if they are not music, strictly speaking.

French and other European settlers living in Tunisia in the nineteenth and twentieth centuries naturally brought their musical tastes with them. Concerts, later supplemented by recordings and radio broadcasts, allowed them to continue to enjoy their musical heritage. Although some assimilated Tunisians chose to embrace, and even try their hand at, elements of western culture that were alien to their own heritage, the substantial tonal and rhythmic differences between Arab and western music precluded most Tunisians from developing a taste for the latter. Inevitably, however, professional musicians (most of whom came from traditional backgrounds and had not been educated in colonial schools) did acquire some familiarity with western music during the protectorate, although few made any obeisance to it. The growth of the nationalist movement during the interwar years and its culmination in the drive toward independence in the decade following World War II further diminished public receptivity to cultural forms linked with the colonizers.

The music of the eastern Arab world (the Mashriq), and especially of Egypt, exerted a much greater influence on Tunisia in the first half of the twentieth century. Introduced by touring Egyptian orchestras in the 1920s and then more widely disseminated by radio broadcasts, this music inspired the emergence of a new genre called *asria* (modern), which emulated the vocal and orchestral techniques of the Mashriq. The warm reception accorded to this musical style "imported" from the Arab heartlands signified the desire of many Tunisians to identify with an "Arab culture" so vibrant and diffuse that it was certain to survive even the powerful challenges posed by European colonialism. A renewed enthusiasm for classical Andalusian music paralleled this development and also represented an aspect of the quest to preserve indigenous traditions rather than assimilate those of European origin. The two trends intersected in the career of the Fathia Khairi (b. 1920), a popular entertainer who sang songs by both Egyptian and Tunisian composers and also frequently performed *maaluf* music with the orchestra of the Rashidiyya Institute (q.v.).

Although recordings by the Mashriq's most famous musical entertainers remained popular in Tunisia even after independence, links with the Arab east did weaken. With the end of the protectorate, Tunisian political leaders preferred to emphasize a national rather than pan-Arab culture that provided a focal point for identity and state building. A second important factor in the declining interest in the music of the Middle East was the impact of American and European popular music from the 1960s on. Young Tunisians' enthusiasm for this music may have run counter to the official policy of fostering local cultural forms, but the lure of a genre that was attracting devotees all over the world could hardly be resisted. What did emerge, however, were new musical forms blending aspects of contemporary western popular music, especially its instruments and performance techniques, with Tunisian traditions. The music of Hedi Habouba (b. 1949), for example, embodied a revival of Tunisian folk music by adapting it to the cosmopolitan tastes of young people of the 1970s and 1980s.

Mustafa Khaznadar (1817–1878). Powerful mamluk (q.v.) and chief minister of Ahmad (q.v.), Muhammad (q.v.), and Muhammad al-Sadiq (q.v.) Beys. He amassed a considerable personal fortune through his countenance of and participation in the graft and corruption that pervaded the nineteenth century Husainid bureaucracy. After the Ahd al-aman (q.v.) was issued in 1857, Khaznadar expanded his venal practices to European businessmen with hopes of investing in Tunisia, facilitating the implementation of their plans in return for payoffs or shares in their ventures. Among the more blatant of these arrangements was Khaznadar's appointment as an officer in the Anglo-Tunisian Bank (q.v.), a British-financed enterprise that had a monopoly on printing notes of legal tender in Tunisia. Khaznadar's vested interests made him an opponent of reforms designed to promote fair and responsible government, particularly as they were embodied in the Constitution of 1861 (q.v.).

In 1863, Khaznadar negotiated an international loan whose terms brought the country to the brink of financial ruin. In order to meet the exorbitantly high annual payments on the loan, the rate of the majba (q.v.), or personal tax, was doubled. The prime minister broke the back of the ensuing rebellion by cleverly combining a divide-and-conquer policy that exploited tribal differences with a heavy-handed military repression. Khaznadar contracted a new loan in 1865 to alleviate the economic distress occasioned by the revolt. In the following year, the government's inability to extract more tax revenue and its unwillingness to moderate its own expenditures forced the prime minister to suspend interest payments on the loan, signaling the country's bankruptcy and paving the way for the creation of the International Finance Commission (q.v.).

Even after the commission stepped in to supervise Tunisia's finances in 1869, however, Khaznadar continued his intrigues. Aware of Italy's limited ability to influence events in Tunisia and of France's preoccupation with Prussia, he arranged lucrative contracts for British investors, hoping thereby to ingratiate himself to Great Britain and gain a powerful ally. French and Italian members of the commission objected, demanding Khaznadar's removal. The bey, unwilling to antagonize his creditors further, complied and Khaznadar's longtime adversary, the reformer Khair al-Din al-Tunsi (q.v.), replaced him as chief minister in 1873. Khaznadar's subsequent efforts to undermine his rival bore fruit with Khair al-Din's dismissal in 1877. For several months he again held the post of chief minister, relinquishing it just before his death in the following year.

al-Mustansir I (r. 1249–1277). Throne name of the Hafsid ruler Abu Abdallah. His success in consolidating and managing the state forged by Abu Zakariyya (q.v.) made his reign the apogee of the Hafsid era. al-Mustansir's claim to the caliphate (q.v.) won brief acceptance in Egypt and Arabia after the collapse of the Abbasid dynasty (q.v.) in 1258, but his distance from the Muslim heartlands made it difficult for him to gain permanent recognition as caliph. Except for the abortive crusade against Tunisia by King Louis IX of France (q.v.), peaceful conditions characterized al-Mustansir's reign both at home and abroad. This tranquillity allowed al-Mustansir to focus his resources and attention on social and economic activities. His interest in education and his patronage of scholars significantly raised the level of intellectual pursuits in Tunisia, while his support for artists and craftsmen encouraged a building boom that left the capital with many new secular and religious structures of the highest quality. In economic matters, al-Mustansir promoted international trade and facilitated Christian mercantile enterprises in his domains. Under his aegis, Tunis developed into a Mediterranean city of the first rank.

The success of al-Mustansir aroused the jealousy of competitors in both North Africa and Europe, and it spawned tensions within the ruling family. Within a few years of his death the state was racked by revolts and weakened by foreign intrigues, ushering in a century of instability and decline that ended only with the accession of Abu'l Abbas in 1370.

al-Mustansir II. *See* **Abu Hafs Umar**

al-Muwahhids. Confederation of Berber tribes that gained control of Morocco in 1147. Led by the caliph Abd al-Mu'min and inspired by the puritanical theology of Ibn Tumart, the movement's founder, the al-

Muwahhids built an empire that encompassed much of North Africa and Spain. The Zirid ruler Hasan ibn Ali, harried by Norman (q.v.) raids and the unruly Arab nomads, at first welcomed the assistance of his powerful western neighbors. After ousting the Normans from Mahdiyya in 1159, Abd al-Mu'min proceeded to bring the rest of Ifriqiya into the al-Muwahhid sphere. His attempts to curb the nomads' independence by deporting many of them to Morocco, ostensibly for use in future campaigns in Spain, sparked a resistance that impeded the extension of al-Muwahhid authority. The caliph's death in 1163 further aggravated this situation. Ifriqiya became the scene of several major revolts, including one staged by the Banu Ghaniyya (q.v.), supporters of the al-Murabits, the rulers whom the al-Muwahhids had shouldered aside in their rise to power in Morocco. al-Muwahhid dominion over Ifriqiya was restored only in 1205 with the appointment of a strong governor, Abd al-Wahid ibn Abi Hafs (q.v.). Although Abd al-Wahid's rivals prevented his son from succeeding him as governor in 1221, the deterioration of the al-Muwahhid state left them unable to forestall such a transfer of authority indefinitely. In 1228, his son Abu Zakariyya (q.v.) assumed the governorship of Ifriqiya, marking a break with Morocco and the inauguration of the Hafsid dynasty (q.v.).

Mzali, Muhammad (1925–). Prime minister and secretary-general of the Parti Socialiste Dusturien (PSD) from 1980 to 1986. Educated at Sadiqi College (q.v.) and the University of Paris, he returned to Tunisia as a teacher in the early 1950s. Before being appointed prime minister, Mzali had served as minister of youth and sports (1969–1970) and had held a variety of other posts, which familiarized him with the aspirations and problems of young Tunisians. As a group, they were among the most seriously affected by the political and economic disorders of the late 1970s. Assuming office in the wake of those disorders, he initiated a series of reforms designed to mollify critics of the government by creating a more open political atmosphere. Toward that end, Mzali ordered the release of many opposition figures from detention. He also won approval from the 1981 PSD Congress to initiate a limited system of multiparty participation in the political process. Such policies earned Mzali the animosity of many PSD conservatives, but President Bourguiba's (q.v.) continuing support enabled him to stand his ground.

Mzali hoped to alleviate Tunisia's economic difficulties by striking a balance between the socialism of the 1960s and the liberalism of the 1970s, neither of which had proven entirely satisfactory. His five-year plan for 1982–1986 combined agricultural growth with badly needed industrial development. In a departure from the western orientation of his immediate predecessors, Mzali intended that as much as a third of the foreign investment needed for the plan's success should come from other Arab states. This accorded with the prime minister's general desire to improve Tunisian relations with the Arab world. His willingness to allow the PLO to establish a headquarters in Tunis after its expulsion from Beirut in 1982 and the increasing role played by Tunisia in such bodies as the Arab League (headquartered in Tunis between 1979 and 1990) and the Organization of the Islamic Conference bore witness to this aspiration.

Economic problems persisted during the first several years of Mzali's administration, with droughts and inadequate harvests impeding development plans. Moreover, an elaborate system of government subsidies on basic commodities strained the treasury. The subsidies partially offset the low industrial wages that the government argued were essential to ensure the competitiveness of Tunisian goods on international markets and to guarantee adequate profits to foreign investors. Toward the end of 1983, Mzali came under heavy pressure from the International Monetary Fund, a major aid donor, to remove most of the subsidies and to decrease the remainder. His reluctant compliance resulted in a drastic rise in the price of such staples as bread and semolina, sparking a two-week period of rioting throughout the country in January 1984. President Bourguiba quickly rescinded the price hikes, leaving the misimpression that the prime minister alone had been responsible for them. At the same time, however, the president dismissed Driss Guiga, the minister of the interior and one of Mzali's chief rivals in the government, accusing him of exploiting the disorders for his own political ends.

For the next two years, related problems of economic decline and political instability plagued Mzali's government. The ailing Bourguiba, increasingly influenced by a circle of conservative advisers opposed to Mzali, lost confidence in his prime minister. In a major governmental and party reshuffle in the summer of 1986, Mzali lost both the prime ministry and his position as secretary-general of the PSD. Fearful that additional reprisals would follow, he secretly fled the country. Before the end of the year, a Tunisian court imposed a three-year prison sentence on Mzali in absentia for defaming Tunisian leaders; another fifteen-year sentence for misappropriating government funds was handed down in 1987. Although Mzali had applauded Bourguiba's removal in November 1987, his request for a pardon in order to return to Tunisia was denied by the new government of Zine el-Abidine Ben Ali (q.v.), and he remained in exile in Europe.

-N-

al-Nahda. Political party organized in 1989. Owing to its religious roots, it was never accorded legal status by the government. The Mouvement de la Tendance Islamique (MTI; q.v.) changed its name to Harakat al-Nahda (Renaissance Movement) in order to comply with an electoral law banning political organizations based on religion and to become a signatory, along with the secular political parties, to the 1988 National Pact (q.v.). The name change included the word commonly used to denominate the campaign for Islamic reform that had swept much of the Arab world, including Tunisia, late in the nineteenth century. Even after this concession, however, the government of President Zine el-Abidine Ben Ali (q.v.) refused to authorize al-Nahda's participation in the first parliamentary elections of the post-Bourguiba era in April 1989. Consequently, al-Nahda candidates were forced to run as independents, contesting the elections in 22 of the 25 constituencies throughout the nation. They comprised the third largest electoral list, behind the government's Rassamblement Constitutionnel Démocratique (RCD; q.v.) and the main opposition party, the Mouvement des Démocrates Sociales (MDS; q.v.). In striking contrast to the dismal showing of the latter party, independent candidates affiliated with al-Nahda won approximately 15 percent of the total vote, garnering 30 percent or more in some electoral districts in and around Tunis.

Disheartened by the government's success in keeping al-Nahda out of the political arena, its leader, Rashid Ghannushi (q.v.), went into voluntary exile. The party's more moderate secretary-general, Abd al-Fattah Mourou (q.v.), continued to endorse democratic processes as the most constructive route to achieving al-Nahda's goal of forging a society in conformity with Islamic values. He took charge of the party's operations, although Ghannushi remained its head and political mentor. Mourou's uncharacteristically strong denunciation of government education reforms in late 1989, which he attacked as excessively secular and as being of foreign, non-Islamic derivation, underscored his continuing opposition to RCD policies and may have been intended to improve his image among more radical party members. Nevertheless, significant differences of opinion between Mourou and Ghannushi continued to surface. Among these were the appropriate al-Nahda responses to the 1990 Iraqi invasion of Kuwait, the subsequent dispatch to Saudi Arabia of a multinational military force, and the ensuing Gulf War (q.v.). Ghannushi vehemently opposed the western-led coalition. Mourou, who had lived for several years in Saudi Arabia and had maintained links with Islamist organizations based there, reacted with greater circumspection, although al-Nahda did organize a few relatively inconsequential anticoalition demonstrations and rallies. Mourou directly challenged Ghannushi's leadership for the first time during the crisis in the Gulf, asserting that his exiled colleague spoke as an individual, not as al-Nahda's leader. The majority of the rank and file, however, clearly regarded Ghannushi as its head.

Subsequent events provided further evidence of Mourou's diminishing influence. Convinced that there were no circumstances under which Ben Ali would legitimize al-Nahda, extremists within the organization, apparently without Mourou's knowledge or approval, began to plot the government's overthrow. In the last several weeks of 1990, Tunisian authorities arrested a number of alleged al-Nahda members, including policemen and soldiers, whom they accused of planning terrorist attacks. In February 1991, al-Nahda militants attacked an RCD office in Tunis, killing one person and injuring several others. The use of violence in the pursuit of political ends profoundly shocked many Tunisians. The unimplicated Mourou, along with two other prominent al-Nahda leaders, Fadhel Beldi and Benaissa Demni, suspended ties with the party.

A crackdown of unprecedented severity followed, culminating in hundreds of arrests amid charges that al-Nahda radicals had infiltrated many of the state's security organizations as a prelude to assassinating Ben Ali and staging a coup d'état. Trials held in 1992 included allegations of human rights abuses and widespread procedural irregularities. Hundreds of persons, including the absent Ghannushi, were sentenced to prison. Throughout this period, spokesmen for al-Nahda insisted, rather implausibly, that the accused were all members of a rival organization. Their assertion that Mourou and other party leaders in Tunisia had neither sanctioned nor participated in criminal activities, on the other hand, has greater credence.

The decline in public support for al-Nahda in the wake of these incidents bolstered the president's unwillingness to legalize it, and the party was again precluded from participating in national elections in 1994. Indeed, the government portrayed those elections as an opportunity to update the 1988 National Pact by securing the agreement of all the officially approved parties to work against the challenges posed by politicized Islam. With Mourou effectively marginalized and al-Nahda severely crippled inside the country, the strongest Islamist criticism of the elections came from the exiled Ghannushi, whom party loyalists still acknowledged as their leader.

Nasir Bey (1855–1922; r. 1906–1922). Fifteenth Husainid ruler. He initially disparaged the Dustur Party, which was formed during his reign, but he later threw his support behind the nationalist platform. In 1922, Nasir tried to pressure the French to negotiate with the Dustur by threatening to abdicate if the party's demands were not addressed. When Resident General Lucien Saint (q.v.) forced the bey's hand by ordering French troops to take up positions around the Bardo Palace (q.v.), Nasir relented. The Dustur's attempt to co-opt the bey damaged its image among moderate Frenchmen and cost it the support of those who viewed such overtures as omens of future unacceptable activities by the party.

National Pact (1988). Political charter intended by President Ben Ali (q.v.) to foster a formal national political consensus in the period leading up to the first elections of the post-Bourguiba era in 1989. In September 1988, Ben Ali convened the heads of labor, youth, women's, and other major national organizations; the leaders of the country's political parties, including several that had not yet been granted formal recognition; and a representative of the Mouvement de la Tendance Islamique (MTI; q.v.) to discuss the parameters of the pact. The document was officially signed on November 7, 1988, the first anniversary of Ben Ali's accession to office.

The pact crumbled, however, in February 1989. In an attempt to undermine the MTI, which had signed the National Pact and had applied for recognition as a political party under the name al-Nahda (q.v.), Ben Ali demanded that the signatories to the pact formulate a common list of parliamentary candidates for the April elections. The smaller parties found the offer appealing in that it offered them a better opportunity to secure parliamentary seats than might otherwise be the case, but its rejection by Ahmad Mestiri (q.v.), the leader of the Mouvement des Démocrates Socials (MDS; q.v.), the oldest and best-established opposition party, torpedoed the plan. As a result, Ben Ali's Rassemblement Constitutionnel Démocratique (RCD; q.v.) swept the elections, winning every parliamentary seat.

Natural Gas. Natural gas deposits were discovered in the Gulf of Gabès in 1974 in conjunction with exploratory drilling for petroleum (q.v.), but they remained unexploited for two decades. Only in 1992, with oil production flagging, did the Tunisian government reach an agreement with British Gas to develop the Miskar field, some 125 kilometers (75 miles) offshore. They also agreed to lay a pipeline connecting the field to the mainland and to construct a gas-processing plant near Sfax. Production from the field began in mid-1995 and was expected to reach 180 million cubic feet per day (the annual equivalent of a 1.5 million metric tons of oil) at its peak.

Natural gas drawn from the Miskar field gave Tunisia an overall hydrocarbon surplus and made it possible to increase oil exports, which had been limited since 1993 when the country had become a net petroleum importer. Moreover, the injection of Tunisian natural gas into the domestic market reduced the amount of Algerian gas drawn from the Transmed pipeline to Europe that crosses Tunisia, representing both a savings in purchase price and an increased income from transit fees collected by volume.

Neo-Dustur Party. Political party organized in 1934 by Dustur Party (q.v.) dissidents. These western-educated young men, many from middle-class Sahil families rather than the Tunis bourgeoisie that dominated the Dustur, were dissatisfied with the party leaders' failure to make any discernible progress in their dealings with the French. Their training in schools such as Sadiqi College (q.v.), and sometimes in French universities, led them to consider themselves more attuned to the contemporary political scene than the generally traditional Dustur hierarchy. At the same time, however, they resented French assimilationist policies that they feared would rob Tunisians of the Arab and Islamic identity which, despite their immersion in western culture, they continued to value. Far better than their staid elders, these men understood the benefits of garnering broad popular support. Toward that end they disseminated their ideas at the grassroots level. Habib Bourguiba (q.v.), for example, one of the most prominent dissenters within the Dustur, took on the editorship of *L'Action Tunisienne* (q.v.) in 1932. His outspoken criticisms of the protectorate challenged the conservative approach of the Dustur leaders and established him as a populist spokesman. The protectorate authorities, realizing the potentially dangerous impact of Bourguiba and his associates, ordered the dissolution of the Dustur when *L'Action Tunisienne* called for independence in 1933. Several months later, Bourguiba's vigorous opposition to the resident general's proposal to allow the reconstitution of the Dustur in return for a moderation of its policies resulted in his expulsion from the party. In March 1934, at Ksar Hellal, Bourguiba convened a meeting at which the Neo-Dustur Party was born. Its founding members also included Bourguiba's brother M'hammad, Mahmoud Matari (q.v.), who was its first president, Tahar Sfar (q.v.), and Bahri Guiga. The Neo-Dustur's principal demands included independence, an end to official colonization, the granting of a constitution, and a larger role for Tunisians in the political process.

One of the party's first goals was to create a countrywide organization. Copying the tactics, if not the ideology, of the communist organizers Bourguiba had observed in his student days, the Neo-Dustur established local cells linked to the party's central command in a pyramidal structure. The party benefited from its ability not only to organize Dustur malcontents but also to garner support in regions the older party had largely ignored. While the urban-based Dustur disdained the rural population, which had been especially hard hit by the deterioration of the economy in the 1930s, the Neo-Dustur worked assiduously and successfully to build party cells in the small towns and villages of Tunisia.

Bourguiba and most other Neo-Dustur leaders were jailed in September 1934, but the party structure they had carefully built proved its worth by continuing to function in their absence. In conjunction with members of the Confédération Générale des Travailleurs Tunisiens (CGTT; q.v.), Neo-Dustur members periodically staged demonstrations to protest the treatment of their leaders. The 1936 decision of the Popular Front (q.v.) government to release Bourguiba and his colleagues paved the way for a resumption of Neo-Dustur activity. The return of Abd al-Aziz Thaalbi (q.v.), the founder of the Dustur, to Tunisia in 1937 posed a challenge for the Neo-Dustur. Despite an initial show of cooperation, it quickly became apparent that the Neo-Dustur's secular, populist strategy precluded a permanent accommodation with Thaalbi. Instead, Neo-Dustur agitators systematically disrupted Thaalbi's public appearances, while party leaders continued to organize large public protests against the protectorate regime.

The Neo-Dustur was not, however, immune to disagreements among its chiefs over tactics. Bourguiba's insistence that the party not compromise on its demands alienated other prominent party members who advocated endorsing a reform program proposed by France in 1937. These included Mahmoud Matari, still the Neo-Dustur's president, who resigned from the party in protest. With the Popular Front now out of power, the French authorities responded vehemently to renewed Neo-Dustur demonstrations in April 1938, imprisoning party leaders and disbanding the organization. Once again, however, the Neo-Dustur's highly developed organization enabled it to continue to operate, albeit at a much reduced level. The outbreak of World War II again divided the party, some of whose members regarded collaboration with the Axis as the surest way of achieving their objectives. Bourguiba, steeped in the traditions of liberalism, decried such an alliance. From his prison cell, he urged his followers to stand by France in its confrontation with fascism.

The incarceration of the party's strongest leaders and Munsif Bey's (q.v.) brief bid for control of the nationalist movement left the Neo-Dustur quiescent in the early years of the war. Bourguiba's return to Tunisia just before its liberation by the Allies in May 1943, Munsif's deposition later in the year, and Thaalbi's death in 1944 paved the way for a resurgence of the Neo-Dustur. By helping labor leaders organize the new Union Générale des Travailleurs Tunisiens (UGTT; q.v.) in 1944 and 1945, the party not only reaffirmed its links with the workers' movement but also assured itself of influence in an important interest group that could be employed to mobilize public opinion. As soon as the war ended, Bourguiba left Tunisia to solicit support for the Neo-Dustur abroad, while at home Secretary General Salah Ben Yusuf (q.v.) continued to stress the party's demand, supported by virtually all politicized Tunisians, for complete and immediate independence.

Bourguiba returned in 1949 and immediately resumed control of the party. In contrast with the less patient Ben Yusuf, he counseled a policy of negotiation and gradualism that became the Neo-Dustur's official strategy for resolving conflicting French and Tunisian views on the protectorate's future. In 1951, France officially recognized the party, whose membership had been steadily increasing since the end of the war. Prominent Neo-Dustur members served in Tunisian governments that searched for an acceptable formula of cosovereignty (q.v.), but colon resistance to even minor concessions invariably undermined their efforts. When the frustrated Neo-Dustur again sought to bring the Tunisian issue to international attention, the equally frustrated French authorities ordered the arrest of the party's leaders in early 1952, triggering new riots. After an abortive effort to find creditable interlocutors among Tunisians not associated with the Neo-Dustur in 1954, the French government initiated talks that finally produced, in April 1955, an accord granting internal autonomy. Party radicals, led by Ben Yusuf, denounced Bourguiba's assertion that such a status would inevitably lead to full independence. The Neo-Dustur Congress in October 1955 was the scene of a bitter struggle between the two factions. Following his victory at the congress, Bourguiba expelled Ben Yusuf from the party, foreshadowing the intolerance that would thereafter characterize the Neo-Dustur.

Tunisia attained full independence in March 1956, and the party won a comfortable victory in the ensuing elections for a constituent assembly. The pyramidal structure that had held the party together through the colonial era remained in place after independence. Regional coordinating committees oversaw the activities of local Neo-Dustur cells whose constituents either were from the same community or worked in the same profession. At periodic party congresses, delegates chose a central committee to formulate policy. The central committee also selected the party's executive board, or political bureau, from among its own members. The party apparatus included a secretary general and a director to manage daily affairs, but real power in the party lay with Bourguiba who, in addition to his governmental functions, was its president. The distinctions between state and party became blurred through the combination of Bourguiba's personal popularity, his twin roles as head of government (as well as head of state after the deposition of Amin Bey [q.v.] in 1957) and head of the only legal political party, the practice of filling government jobs with veterans of the Neo-Dustur's anticolonial struggle, and the close conjunction between the Neo-Dustur's organizational structure and the subdivisions of the national government.

With independence attained, the party's goals shifted to the modernization of Tunisia through social change and economic development. The configuration of the Neo-Dustur and the presence of a cadre of committed, highly disciplined militants provided party leaders with an ideal mechanism for disseminating new ideas and mobilizing mass support for them at the grassroots level. The party also relied heavily on auxiliary organizations such as the Union Nationale des Femmes Tunisiennes (National Union of Tunisian Women) and the Union Générale des Etudiants Tunisiens (General Union of Tunisian Students) to promote its policies within special interest groups.

In the first several years of independence, the Neo-Dustur, over the objections of its powerful ally the Union Générale des Travailleurs Tunisiens, adopted a laissez-faire economic policy. By the early 1960s, however, economic stagnation necessitated a reconsideration of this decision. The 1961 appointment of one of the Neo-Dustur's most promising young leaders, Ahmad Ben Salah (q.v.), as minister of planning inaugurated a new era, not only in economic matters but throughout the society. Charged with designing a strategy that would foster self-sufficiency and raise living standards, Ben Salah and his associates crafted a ten-year plan predicated on intensive government participation in the economy. Other socialist development schemes followed throughout the decade. In 1964, to underscore the party's dedication to this new philosophy, it officially changed its name to the Parti Socialiste Dusturien (PSD; q.v.).

Normans. Norse adventurers who seized Sicily in the eleventh century, prompting the island's Islamic population to appeal for help to their fellow Muslims in Ifriqiya. After the Zirids (q.v.) took up residence in Mahdiyya (q.v.) in 1057, they launched naval raids in the central Mediterranean, including against Sicily, but were unable to dislodge the Normans. An uneasy truce evolved throughout the late eleventh and early twelfth centuries. In 1123, however, the Normans attacked Mahdiyya to prevent the declining Zirids from forging an alliance with the powerful al-Murabit confederation. Had such an arrangement materialized, the Normans would have faced a far more formidable challenge than before. The Zirid deterioration was so acute that less than a decade later the dynasty itself resorted to the rulers of Sicily for protection against domestic enemies. The Normans took advantage of this situation to whittle away the Zirid domains, capturing Jerba in 1135, Sfax in 1143, and Mahdiyya itself in 1148. They ruled almost the entire coast of Ifriqiya until 1159, when the combination of a popular uprising against Christian rule and an al-Muwahhid offensive dislodged them.

Nouira, Hadi (1911–1993). Longtime political ally of Habib Bourguiba (q.v.). Nouira organized the Neo-Dustur's youth movement in the 1930s. After independence, he served as director of the Tunisian Central Bank from 1958 until 1970 and as prime minister from 1970 until he suffered a stroke in 1980. His main task upon becoming prime minister was to foster an economic recovery from the disarray that the overzealous socialist planning of Ahmad Ben Salah (q.v.) caused. An economic liberal, Nouira vigorously promoted private investments but left intact most of the state enterprises created in the 1960s. He offered attractive concessions to foreign investors, especially those producing for the lucrative export market. Despite the growth of the industrial sector in the 1970s, new jobs did not keep pace with population growth, forcing many Tunisian workers to continue seeking employment abroad.

A small number of capitalists prospered during the decade of Nouira's government, but for most Tunisians economic conditions worsened. Small farmers were restored to their land when the agricultural cooperatives were dismantled, but not all of them adjusted successfully to the more competitive economy. Furthermore, European protectionism restricted markets for such important agrarian exports as citrus fruits and olive products. Many rural people were forced to sell their land, often to large entrepreneurs whose emphasis on mechanization rendered them redundant and fueled an exodus to the already overcrowded cities. In urban areas, disenchantment spread among industrial workers for whom the escalation of the cost of living far outpaced wage increases. Although Nouira's government attempted to alleviate this situation by instituting an elaborate program of subsidies on staple items, the gap between Tunisia's rich and poor widened dramatically in the decade of the 1970s.

Economic ills spawned political unrest as well, but Nouira maintained a hard line with respect to all opposition groups, including the fledgling Mouvement de Tendance Islamique (MTI; q.v.). He brooked no criticism and permitted no opportunity for the expression of dissenting views. His refusal to address the economic and political grievances of the Union Générale des Travailleurs Tunisiens (UGTT; q.v.), which had long been an important prop of the Parti Socialiste Dusturien (PSD; q.v.), created tensions that exploded on Black Thursday (q.v.), January 26, 1978. Workers and security forces clashed during a general strike organized by the UGTT, producing hundreds of casualties. Nouira reacted by ordering the arrest of scores of union leaders and other critics of the government. Mounting popular dissatisfaction with the government culminated in an uprising in Gafsa on the second anniversary of Black Thursday. Nouira's stroke a few months later gave other leaders in the PSD an opportunity to disavow the prime minister's political and economic approaches, which many had concluded were bankrupt and counterproductive, and to institute a more open government under the leadership of Muhammad Mzali (q.v.).

Numidia. Roman name for the territory west of Carthage (q.v.), encompassing what is now eastern Algeria and portions of western Tunisia. Because the Numidians had generally fought against Carthage in the

Punic Wars (q.v.), the Romans allowed the Berber (q.v.) chieftains to retain some power when they established a protectorate over the region after the wars. But recurrent insurrections by such ambitious leaders as Jugurtha (q.v.) resulted in the dissolution of the protectorate. In 27 B.C.E., Numidia was joined to the province of Africa to form the new province of Africa Proconsularis (q.v.).

-O-

Olives. Olives and olive oil have always played an important role in the Tunisian agricultural economy. The center of olive production is the Sahil, but the tree is also cultivated in the steppe region around Kairouan and in portions of the Tell. Since the Carthaginian era, Tunisian olive oil has been highly regarded for its superior quality and has figured prominently in the region's exports. Since olive trees produce no fruit for ten to twelve years after planting and do not normally bear uniform quantities in successive years, even under consistently favorable climatic conditions, a long-term commitment to cultivation is a prerequisite for success. In part because both cultivation and harvesting are labor-intensive processes that require considerable attention to pruning trees and thinning fruit to maximize yields, olive production in Tunisia has generally been the province of small-scale farmers enjoying full title to their land. Such growers in the Sahil protested government plans to collectivize olive cultivation in the late 1960s so vehemently that the authorities abandoned the scheme. This opposition was an important factor contributing to the downfall of Ahmad Ben Salah (q.v.), the planning minister who wanted to impose collectivization.

During the first half of the 1990s, olive production usually exceeded 600,000 metric tons, with a peak harvest of over 1.3 million metric tons in 1991. The amount of olive oil, the country's primary agricultural export, manufactured yearly fluctuated from approximately 140,000 metric tons to a record high of some 280,000 metric tons. Exports of olive oil ranged between 95,000 and 125,000 metric tons annually and earned over 300 million dinars in the strongest years and between 100 and 200 million dinars at other times.

Tunisia consistently ranks among the top five producers of olive oil in the world and is usually the third or fourth largest exporter of the commodity, along with Italy, Greece, and Spain. When Greece and Spain gained entry to the European Economic Community (EEC; q.v.) in the 1980s (Italy had belonged since its inception), the magnitude of Tunisia's olive oil exports loomed as an occasionally serious point of contention in its relationship with the EEC. The creation of a unified market with the formation of the European Union (EU) in 1993 threatened to further exacerbate the situation, but European awareness of the importance of shoring up Maghribi economies in the interest of regional security on both sides of the Mediterranean led to the negotiation of a partnership agreement between Tunisia and the EU in 1995 that laid the groundwork for the development, over a 12-year period, of a free-trade zone.

Operation Torch. Code name for the November 1942 British and American landings in Morocco and Algeria under the command of General Dwight Eisenhower. The ultimate objective of Operation Torch was the occupation of Tunisia, which was to serve as a base for the invasion of Italy. Germany reacted to the landings by pouring men and materiel into Tunisia to thwart the Allied advance. Fighting persisted through the winter of 1942–1943. In March, Eisenhower's army was joined by that of British Field Marshal Sir Bernard Montgomery, which was pushing into Tunisia from the east in pursuit of General Irwin Rommel's (q.v.) retreating Afrika Korps. The combined Allied forces liberated Tunis and Bizerte on May 7, and in the following week 275,000 Axis soldiers surrendered on Cape Bon, ending the campaign that the Torch landings had begun.

Organization of African Unity (OAU). Although most of its traditional connections with Africa were disrupted during the century preceding independence, Tunisia was a founding member of the Organization of African Unity in 1963. President Habib Bourguiba (q.v.) exhorted the emerging African states to follow his country's example by fostering economic and social development before embarking on plans for regional unity. Even after serious flaws appeared in the planned economy in the late 1960s, many African leaders continued to regard the early years of Tunisian independence as a model for development. In the following years, however, Tunisia's strong cultural links with the Arab world and profitable economic connections with Europe and the Middle East rendered slight its participation in the OAU, as well as its attention to sub-Saharan Africa in general.

President Zine el-Abidine Ben Ali (q.v.) took a greater interest in African affairs than had his predecessor and served as president of the OAU in 1994–1995. At the beginning of his term, with civil strife and international tensions rampant in many parts of the continent, Ben Ali enunciated a code of conduct for intra-African relations. At the same time, Tunisia became a member of the OAU's nine-country African Mechanism Apparatus for Preventing, Managing, and Resolving African Crises. Ben Ali used his OAU presidency to expand and solidify Tunisian links with the rest of the continent.

Ottoman Empire. The Ottoman conquest of Egypt in 1517 placed the empire in an ideal position to aid North African Muslims in their efforts to blunt Spanish Hapsburg (q.v.) thrusts across the Mediterranean. Despite the common bond of Islam, however, the declining Hafsids (q.v.) viewed the Ottomans as interlopers who threatened their control over Tunisia. Hafsid attacks against such Turkish allies as Khair al-Din Barbarossa (q.v.) provoked an Ottoman offensive that captured Tunis in 1534. In desperation, the Hafsids turned to Spain. A force commanded by Charles V (q.v.) evicted the Turks and restored nominal Hafsid authority in the following year. Corsair allies of the Ottomans seized Tunis in 1569, but the Hafsids again appealed to Spain for help, and the corsairs were displaced in 1573. Only in 1574 did the Ottomans conquer and hold Tunisia. Direct Turkish rule lasted, however, for less than a quarter of a century.

After a 1591 military coup overthrew the empire's chief representative in the country, the pasha (q.v.), real power rested with the deys (q.v.), junior Ottoman officers who superficially acknowledged the sovereignty of Istanbul but in fact acted independently. By the middle of the seventeenth century, the deys were themselves shouldered aside by the beys (q.v.), soldiers with stronger links to the Tunisian tribes. The subsequent creation of the Muradid (q.v.) and Husainid (q.v.) dynasties further eroded the ties between Tunis and Istanbul. Although Ottoman sovereignty continued in theory, the sultans exercised only limited power after 1600, generally doing no more than confirming the accession of each new bey with an official firman (edict) of investiture. The creation of the protectorate rendered the symbolism of even that act irrelevant. Nevertheless, Tunisia's official status as a part of the Ottoman Islamic state encouraged some critics of the government, both before and after the protectorate, to hope for an Ottoman intervention that would negate questionable practices (such as had sparked the 1864 revolt) or for the provision of at least moral support to movements linked to such broader issues as Islamic reform (as was the case with many of the Young Tunisians [q.v.]).

-P-

Palestine; Palestine Liberation Organization (PLO). For several years after the creation of the Palestine Liberation Organization (PLO) in 1964, President Habib Bourguiba (q.v.) openly criticized its policies and urged its leaders to pursue a more temperate course toward Israel. Convinced that Palestinian aspirations could not be attained by military confrontations with Israel, he advocated the revival of the 1947 U.N. partition plan for Palestine, believing that Israeli rejection of such a move would shift world public opinion in favor of the Palestinians. The PLO rebuked Bourguiba for his moderation, but failed in an attempt to have Tunisia ejected from the Arab League (q.v.). At the same time, Egyptian president Gamal Abdel Nasser, the PLO's principal supporter, severed diplomatic ties with Tunisia.

The Arabs' defeat at the hands of Israel in 1967 reaffirmed Bourguiba's views on the futility of war. Spontaneous rioting during the June War, however, revealed the intensity of Tunisian popular sympathy for the Palestinians and animosity toward Israel, prompting the government to reopen contacts with both the PLO and Egypt.

The mediation of Prime Minister Badi Ladgham (q.v.) helped end'the civil strife between Palestinians and Jordanians in 1970, but Tunisian relations with the PLO deteriorated as its activities threatened the stability of moderate Middle Eastern regimes. PLO participation in skyjackings and other extremist operations further contributed to Tunisia's reluctance to accord unwavering support to the organization. Periodically during the 1970s, Tunisian Arab nationalists such as Muhammad Masmudi (q.v.) assured the Palestinians of Tunisian concern over their plight, but it was not until Israel forced the PLO from Beirut in 1982 that Tunisia again became involved in Palestinian affairs.

With the Arab League already headquartered in Tunis, the PLO chose to relocate its central offices there as well. Somewhat reluctantly, Tunisia, urged on by the United States, agreed to host the Palestinians. Despite the country's distance from the eastern Mediterranean, this decision drew it directly into the Israeli-Palestinian conflict. In 1985, Israeli jets destroyed a PLO compound at Hammam-Lif near Tunis. Three years later, Israeli commandos assassinated Abu Jihad, a high-ranking PLO official, in his suburban Tunis home. The government vigorously protested these violations of its sovereignty, both of which resulted in the loss of Tunisian and Palestinian lives. Following the second raid, the United Nations Security Council issued a condemnation of Israel. Demonstrations displayed Tunisians' outrage over the attacks, and public opinion remained solidly supportive of the Palestinians. By the time the PLO and Israel signed their Declaration of Principles on Palestinian Self-Rule in 1993, the Palestinian community in and around Tunis numbered some 4,000.

Tunisia welcomed this breakthrough, as well as the May 1994 accord on its implementation. The two agreements not only held out the hope of a resolution of the Palestine question but also insulated Tunisia from the possibility of a repetition of the incidents of 1985 and 1988. After a Palestinian Authority was established in the Gaza Strip and in Jericho on the West Bank as a prelude to wider self-rule, PLO chief Yasser Arafat and many other Palestinian officials moved to Gaza in 1994. Only a few departments of the PLO remained behind in Tunis, primarily to continue soliciting international support and to oversee the repatriation of refugees. During the following year, the majority of these administrators were also transferred to Palestine, with only the PLO's foreign office maintaining its headquarters in the Tunisian capital by mid-1995.

At the start of 1996, Tunisia and Israel agreed to open official facilities (to be called interest sections) in each other's countries in order to expedite political consultations, travel, and trade. The accord formalized Tunisian recognition of the Jewish state.

Parti Communiste Tunisien (PCT)/Tunisian Communist Party. Although initially made up mostly of Europeans, the Tunisian Communist Party, founded in 1920 as a branch of the French party, frequently supported nationalist demands and defended the rights of Tunisian workers. Like the Dustur Party, the communists backed Muhammad Ali (q.v.) when he organized the Confédération Générale des Travailleurs Tunisiens (CGTT; q.v.) in 1924. But their support did not waver in the face of French opposition. When protectorate authorities moved against the CGTT following a series of strikes in 1925, many communists were also imprisoned. Although the ideologies of the Dustur and the communists were, in most respects, diametrically opposed, their common involvement with the CGTT permitted critics of each group to discredit it by its association with the other. Tunisian communists established their independence from the French party in 1934, but the simultaneous emergence and popularity of the Neo-Dustur made it difficult for the communists to recruit outside the European community and soon relegated them to the periphery of the political scene.

Nonetheless, the party survived. It was the only organized political opposition tolerated by the Neo-Dustur government in the first several years after independence, but despite its inability to mount a credible challenge to the Neo-Dustur it was banned in 1963. It operated clandestinely for the next 18 years, emerging only with the enunciation of the "open government" policy of Prime Minister Mzali (q.v.). The party, led by its secretary-general Muhammad Harmel, acquired full legal status in 1981, but legitimization did not substantially increase its membership, estimated at only 2,000. The communists joined other opposition parties in boycotting the first multiparty parliamentary elections in 1986 to protest the government's last-minute disqualification of a number of candidates.

When President Habib Bourguiba (q.v.) was replaced by Zine el-Abidine Ben Ali (q.v.) in 1987, party members felt heartened, as did other elements of the opposition. But the PCT quickly lost faith in the new administration's promises of political pluralism. Harmel accused the ruling Rassemblement Constitutionnel Démocratique (RCD; q.v.) of electoral fraud in by-elections for the National Assembly held only a few weeks after the change of regimes. Nevertheless, the communists participated, along with other opposition groups, in the deliberations on a national pact, presided over by Ben Ali in 1988. Still wary, however, the communists did not contest the 1989 legislative elections. A period of growth and consolidation ensued, during which the party abandoned, in 1993, its communist label (but not its communist ideology) in favor of the designation Mouvement de la Rénovation (MR; in Arabic, al-Taj-did). In the 1994 national elections, the party fielded a total of 71 candidates in 12 of the 25 constituencies and ran third behind the RCD and the Mouvement des Démocrates Sociales (MDS; q.v.), polling just over 11,000 votes and winning four of the 19 assembly seats reserved for the opposition. The MR has continued to publish the weekly newspaper begun by the PCT in 1981, *al-Tariq al-Jadid* (*The New Path*).

Parti Réformiste/Reform Party. Formed in 1921 by Hassan Guellaty (q.v.), this political party briefly challenged the Dustur for the leadership of the nationalist movement. Its members were more willing to accept French concessions and cooperate with the protectorate authorities than were Thaalbi (q.v.) and his followers, whom Guellaty denounced as radicals. The absence of popular support for its docile approach crippled the Parti Réformiste and it quickly faded into obscurity, giving the Dustur undisputed control of the nationalist crusade.

Parti Social du Progrès (PSP). *See* **Parti Social Libéral**

Parti Socialiste Dusturien (PSD)/Socialist Dustur Party. Official name of the Neo-Dustur Party from 1964 until 1988. Following the 1969 downfall of planning minister Ahmad Ben Salah (q.v.), a distinguished party member often assumed to be Habib Bourguiba's (q.v.) heir apparent before his disgrace, a number of prominent PSD leaders expressed their dismay over the extensive powers Bourguiba had accorded Ben Salah, despite their own frequently voiced reservations about his policies and their probable impact. Anxious to prevent the recurrence of such a situation, these men tried, in the early 1970s, to reform party mechanisms so as to restrict the prerogatives of the president. The adamant opposition of Bourguiba and his allies to such measures created disaffection, particularly among younger PSD members. After a period of relative political inactivity owing to ill health, during which his opponents appeared to accomplish some of their objectives, Bourguiba took the occasion of the 1974 PSD congress to reassert his control over the party. After his supporters secured his appointment as party president for life, he assumed personal responsibility for appointing the political bureau and proceeded to purge his critics. Several opposition political groups crystallized at this time, but until the reforms introduced by Prime Minister Mzali (q.v.) at the 1981 party congress, the PSD remained the only legally recognized party in the country.

Amid these political controversies, economic policies were also shifting. The party steered a more liberal economic course that encouraged private enterprise, but without abandoning its advocacy of state control over crucial sectors of the economy. In social matters, the party customarily espoused progressive ideals, but did not consistently implement them. The deterioration of conditions in the late 1970s convinced large numbers of working-class Tunisians that the party had lost interest in them. In addition to helping spawn the Black Thursday riots (q.v.) of 1978, this attitude also made party recruitment difficult, especially among the young. In an extremely youthful population, most of whom had no memories of the colonial era, the aura and prestige attached to the PSD as the party of those who had fought for and won independence mattered less and less.

The 1981 legalization of other parties theoretically ended the PSD's monopoly on political activity, but for as long as Habib Bourguiba dominated the political scene, the opposition showed little enthusiasm for contesting elections whose impartiality it doubted. By the mid-1980s, calls by the Mouvement de la Tendance Islamique (MTI; q.v.) to create an Islamic society in Tunisia constituted another, and potentially more serious, challenge to the Parti Socialiste Dusturien. Although denied formal recognition as a political party, the MTI championed solutions to the country's problems that offered alternatives to the apparently flawed approaches of the PSD and the other secular parties.

The close ties between the government and the Parti Socialiste Dusturien continued after Bourguiba was removed as head of state in November 1987. His successor as president of the republic, Zine el-Abidine Ben Ali (q.v.), had been secretary general of the PSD since 1987 and the new prime minister, Hedi Baccouche (q.v.), had served as the party's director since 1984. In February 1988, the name of the party was officially changed to the Rassemblement Constitutionnel Démocratique (RCD; q.v.), or Democratic Constitutional Rally.

Parti Social Libéral (PSL)/Liberal Social Party. Name adopted in 1994 by the Parti Social du Progrès (PSP), a small political party that had been founded by Mounir Béji in 1988. In a hastily organized campaign for the 1989 parliamentary elections, the PSP ran candidates in three of 25 national electoral districts, but won only 0.25 percent of the total votes cast. The renamed PSL performed little better in the 1994 elections. On a platform emphasizing human rights, an increase in social programs, and government decentralization, 35 of its candidates competed in seven electoral districts, but again failed to gain even 1 percent of the vote, winning fewer than 1,900 of the almost 2.9 million ballots cast. Despite 1994 amendments in the electoral law designed to give some parliamentary seats to opposition parties that achieved minimal success at the polls, the PSL's numbers fell short of the threshold and it was not represented in the new legislature. The party publishes a weekly newspaper, *al-Awfaq*.

Parti de l'Unité Populaire (PUP). *See* **Mouvement de l'Unité Populaire-2**

Pasha [Arabic: Basha]. Ottoman honorific title given to provincial governors and other notables. From 1574 until the military coup of 1591, Istanbul's representatives in Tunis bore this appellation. The beys (q.v.) of both the Muradid (q.v.) and Husainid (q.v.) dynasties continued to use the term to symbolize their status as deputies of the Ottoman sultan whose sovereignty, at least in theory, they acknowledged.

Personal Status Code of 1956. The centerpiece of President Habib Bourguiba's (q.v.) earliest efforts to initiate significant social change in independent Tunisia, this legislation banned or altered a number of customs relating to marriage and the family sanctioned by the sharia (Islamic law; q.v.). Widely regarded by contemporaries as one of the most sweeping revisions of traditional practices ever enacted anywhere in the Muslim world, the Personal Status Code clearly revealed the attitude of the new government toward many existing social structures. It also served as a model for other newly independent Muslim countries considering alterations in their own legal systems.

The code outlawed polygyny, set minimum ages for marriage, required women's consent to marriages arranged by their families, allowed either spouse to file for divorce in the secular courts, and legitimized marriages between individuals of different faiths. It also increased the proportion of the inheritance allotted to the wife on her husband's death.

So abrupt and dramatic were the changes introduced by the code that it came under attack from several quarters. The religious authorities objected to government interference in matters that previously lay within their domain, but the Neo-Dustur's popularity in the months just after independence, as well as Bourguiba's charge that the criticisms of the ulama were self-serving, rendered these protests ineffectual. Traditional males disliked the new law, and even many women, who were its intended primary beneficiaries, expressed discomfort with the pace and nature of the changes it imposed. Recognizing that acceptance and implementation of the code would take time and that, in any event, legislation alone could not guarantee that people would adopt new attitudes in such highly personal matters, the government worked to make modern schooling more accessible to both young men and young women in the hope that education would foster an atmosphere more conducive to the kinds of social change it envisioned. Eventually the code did gain broad approval among the Tunisian people.

But a minority never ceased to regard its provisions as illicit abrogations by the state of principles established by divine law. The emergence of an Islamist opposition to the government in the 1980s and Bourguiba's departure from the political scene in 1987 raised the possibility of eventually overturning the code. Although President Zine el-Abidine Ben Ali (q.v.) made a number of concessions to Islamist sentiments in his first several months in office, he also emphasized that his government would countenance neither the modification of the Personal Status Code nor any legal alteration in the status of women. This position was strengthened in November 1988 when opposition groups, including (albeit with little enthusiasm) the largest and most influential Islamist organization of the time, the Mouvement de la Tendance Islamique (MTI; q.v.), accepted the so-called National Pact (q.v.). In it the administration outlined the basic precepts by which Tunisia was to be governed.

Le Petit Matin. Newspaper established in 1922 to appeal to the liberal segments of the French community. Sympathetic to Tunisians' political and economic demands in the 1920s and 1930s, it frequently served as an outlet for nationalist writing when the government suspended Dustur and Neo-Dustur publications. *Le Petit Matin* was itself banned by the Vichy authorities, but it reappeared in 1944. Its criticisms of French protectorate policy resumed after the war. Despite a decline in circulation after independence, *Le Petit Matin* survived for more than a decade, publishing its last issue in 1967.

Petroleum. For two decades after the discovery of high-quality crude oil in exportable quantities in the mid-1960s, petroleum was Tunisia's most valuable commodity. At their height in the first half of the 1980s, exports of petroleum and petroleum by-products consistently exceeded 5 million metric tons a year. They accounted for almost half the country's foreign exchange, earning as much as 665 million dinars (more than $1.2 billion) in the peak year of 1980. The decline in production after 1987, combined with the worldwide collapse of oil prices in the mid-1980s, markedly lowered Tunisia's petroleum-generated income, enabling revenues earned by textile exports to outstrip it significantly. Owing to the international earning power of crude oil (even after these price setbacks), and in view of the limited capacity of Tunisia's single refinery at Bizerte, more crude was exported than was allocated for domestic needs. Consequently, even in the years of highest production, more than half of Tunisia's petroleum requirements were met with imports. Although output again reached 5 million metric tons early in the 1990s as new fields came on line, domestic consumption rose more rapidly than did production, forcing Tunisia to become a net petroleum importer beginning in 1993. Nevertheless, the country's proven reserves of some 1.7 billion barrels guaranteed almost another 50 years of production at the current rates of extraction.

Profitable oil discoveries in the Algerian Sahara encouraged European companies to explore the adjacent Tunisian desert regions, resulting in a strike at al-Borma (q.v.) near the Algerian frontier in 1964. Numerous other Saharan fields, developed as joint ventures between the government and various foreign investors, subsequently came into production. Some prospecting took place in the northern and central parts of the country, but it was offshore deposits in the Gulf of Hammamet and the Gulf of Gabès that proved most prolific and most profitable. Wells in the Ashtart field east of Sfax, for example, supplied about half of Tunisia's total petroleum yield in the boom years of the mid-1980s. Libya initially challenged some Tunisian claims in the Gulf of Gabès, but accepted a 1982 International Court of Justice adjudication of the controversy that enabled Tunisian exploration and development of the gulf to proceed systematically. As part of the rapprochement between the two countries following the removal of President Habib Bourguiba (q.v.) in 1987, a joint Tunisian-Libyan enterprise to pursue the exploitation of a promising field in the Gulf of Gabès was created in 1989.

Although never a member of the Organization of Petroleum Exporting Countries (OPEC), Tunisia was affiliated with the Organization of Arab Petroleum Exporting Countries (OAPEC) from 1982 until its declining output led it to withdraw in 1986. Almost all Tunisian oil exports (as well as crude oil destined for the Bizerte refinery) pass through the Gulf of Gabès port of La Skirra (q.v.), the terminus of a pipeline that links Algerian fields to the Mediterranean and into which Tunisia's desert fields also feed.

Peyrouton, Marcel (1887–1983). French resident general from 1933 to 1936. At the start of his administration, he offered the recently dissolved Dustur an opportunity to resume activity on the condition that it adopt a less contentious stand than Habib Bourguiba (q.v.) and other party militants were advocating. Peyrouton's proposition opened a split among the nationalists that led to the establishment of the Neo-Dustur in 1934. Alarmed by the nature and the platform of the new party, the resident general immediately ordered the arrest of its leaders. The Neo-Dustur survived this blow, however, and its members continued to agitate, often vehemently, against Peyrouton's repressive tactics until he was relieved of his position in 1936.

Phoenicians. Eastern Mediterranean people whose homeland encompassed the coastal regions of modern Syria, Lebanon, and northern Israel. Skillful navigators and enterprising merchants, they founded colonies throughout the Mediterranean basin. Among the most successful and important of these was Carthage (q.v.), established by settlers from Tyre in the late ninth century B.C.E. Although Carthage had become independent by the seventh century B.C.E., a steady influx of immigrants from the mother country kept Phoenician culture alive. Carthaginian governmental, social, and religious concepts, which profoundly influenced the surrounding Berber populations, had their origins in Phoenician practices.

Phosphates. The French geologist Philippe Thomas first discovered phosphate deposits near Metlaoui, some 40 kilometers (25 miles) west of Gafsa in 1886. Commercial exploitation of the mineral began a decade later with the formation of the Compagnie des Phosphates de Gafsa. Protectorate officials, hoping that Tunisia's abundant phosphate reserves (second only to those of the United States in the early twentieth century) would energize the sluggish economy, facilitated the mining and export of the mineral by building a railway between Matlaoui and Sfax in 1899. In the following decade, several new phosphate-producing regions discovered in the vicinity of Metlaoui were linked to the rail network.

Although exports exceeded 2 million metric tons annually by the early 1930s, the industry did not prove to be the panacea its supporters had anticipated. The price of phosphates on the world market dropped soon after extraction had begun in Tunisia and never again consistently attained the level needed for the benefits envisaged by protectorate economists. Substantial quantities of higher quality phosphates, primarily from Morocco, further damaged Tunisian prospects. After independence, the government assumed control of the company, provided a capital infusion that enabled it to upgrade the quality of phosphate exports, and promoted the construction of processing plants and factories that produced fertilizers and such other phosphate by-products as phosphoric acid and triple superphosphate (TSP), all of which enjoyed a greater demand than did the raw material itself. The persistence of low prices on the international market in the 1970s, however, translated into serious unemployment in the Gafsa region. This in turn contributed to the economic and political unrest that exploded in 1978 on Black Thursday (q.v.) and again in the guerrilla raid on Gafsa two years later. Efforts to revive the economy of the south in the 1980s hinged on expanding the exportation of phosphate rock and its derivative products. Production increased by more than 50 percent, from less than 4 million metric tons a year at the start of the decade to approximately 6 million at its close.

With output fluctuating around this figure during the early 1990s,

Tunisia retained its position as the world's fourth-largest phosphate producer. To offset persistently low world prices, annual exports of raw phosphates were more than doubled in the early 1990s. They exceeded 1 million metric tons in 1993, but produced only around 32 million dinars. The bulk of the phosphate ore mined in Tunisia, however, went to domestic chemical and fertilizer industries producing primarily for foreign markets. Exports of phosphoric acid surpassed 1 million metric tons in 1992. In the first half of the decade, the chemical-generated revenues reached as high as 155 million dinars in some years and never dropped to less than 120 million. Exports of triple superphosphates also edged toward the 1 million metric ton and 100 million dinar a year levels. Phosphatic fertilizer exports hovered around 1.5 million metric tons annually and earned between 175 million and 200 million dinars.

Popular Front. Left-wing coalition that governed France in 1936 and 1937. More sympathetic than its predecessors to nationalist grievances, the Popular Front released imprisoned Neo-Dustur leaders and permitted the resumption of political activity in the protectorate. Neo-Dustur hopes of achieving a breakthrough in these auspicious circumstances were thwarted, however, by concerted colon efforts to sabotage even minor concessions. The coalition's defeat in 1937 ended, for the time being, Neo-Dustur hopes of finding a viable interlocutor on the French political scene. As a result, Habib Bourguiba (q.v.), frustrated by the inability of even a liberal French government to deal effectively with Tunisian complaints, advocated more radical tactics than in the past, arguing that only such an approach would produce the desired outcome.

La Presse. See La Presse de Tunisie

La Presse de Tunisie. Liberal French daily newspaper established in 1935. It was suspended by the Vichy government but reappeared in 1943. At the end of the war it absorbed *La Tunisie Française* (q.v.), a more right-wing colon publication, and took the name *La Presse*. Although the paper voiced colon concerns and supported colon interests in the closing days of the protectorate, it continued to circulate after independence except for a short suspension in 1956 and 1957. When its publisher was accused of involvement in criminal activities in 1967, the government nationalized *La Presse*.

Punic Wars. Series of conflicts pitting Carthage against Rome in a struggle for domination of the central and western Mediterranean basin. Rome's victory in the First Punic War (263 B.C.E.–241 B.C.E.) derived from superior technology and the Carthaginians' inability to focus their full attention on the clash because of uprisings among the neighboring Berber tribes. As a result of the war, Carthage lost control of Sicily.

The Second Punic War (218 B.C.E.–202 B.C.E.) erupted as Rome attempted to extend its power over previously Carthaginian spheres of influence in the western Mediterranean. In Iberia, the Carthaginian leader Hannibal (q.v.) mounted an expeditionary force that crossed the Alps to attack Rome but was unable to win a decisive victory in Italy and was isolated there by Roman mastery of the sea. Taking advantage of this situation, a Roman army under Scipio (q.v.) invaded Carthage in 203 B.C.E. When Hannibal extricated his troops and returned to Africa in the following year, Scipio defeated him at the Battle of Zama (q.v.). Rome then imposed a treaty of alliance on Carthage. It also rewarded the Berber tribes that had fought on its side with grants of land in formerly Carthaginian territory.

The Third Punic War (146 B.C.E.) resulted directly from the humiliating settlement of the previous war. Carthage chafed under the terms of the peace treaty, but at the first sign of a rebellion Rome invaded. Determined to end the Carthaginian challenge once and for all, the Senate ordered the physical destruction of the city, thus guaranteeing Roman supremacy in the contested portions of the Mediterranean.

-R-

al-Ra'id al-Tunisi. Official newspaper that began publication in 1860. The first Arabic-language paper in the country, its weekly edition contained articles of general interest and reprints of items from papers appearing elsewhere in the Ottoman Empire along with copies of government decrees and other official communications. During the protectorate, *al-Ra'id al-Tunisi* served as an Arabic counterpart to the French *Journal Officiel* (q.v.). Since independence, the paper has been called *al-Ra'id al-rasmi li'l-jumhuriyya al-tunisi*.

Raqqada. Royal city built by the Aghlabid ruler Ibrahim II (q.v.). Located some eight kilometers (five miles) from Kairouan, it contained, in addition to a palace, an important market complex and a major mosque. To finance the expensive work at Raqqada, Ibrahim II imposed heavy taxes on the already overburdened peasantry. In conjunction with the reputation for luxury and decadence quickly acquired by Raqqada, particularly in contrast with the religious stature of Kairouan, this policy fueled the unrest that culminated in the Aghlabids' overthrow shortly after Ibrahim II's death.

Rashidiyya Institute. Organization established in 1934 to foster the preservation and promotion of classical Arabo-Andalusian music (*maaluf*) in Tunisia. Its name derives from an eighteenth-century bey of Tunis, Muhammad al-Rashid (1756–1759), an amateur composer who abdicated to devote himself to the study of the musical traditions brought to North Africa by Iberian refugees in the fifteen and sixteenth centuries. The guiding spirit behind the Rashidiyya Institute was the French musicologist Baron Rudolphe d'Erlanger, a resident of Tunisia and the leading European student of the country's musical traditions. Several prominent Tunisian musicians accompanied d'Erlanger to the First International Congress of Arab Music, which he organized in Cairo in 1932. Inspired by that symposium's recommendation to create organizations to safeguard local musical patrimonies, these musicians founded the Rashidiyya Institute shortly after their return from Egypt. The institute encouraged the performance of Arabo-Andalusian music not only to keep alive a vital component of the national heritage but also to offset the influence of Egyptian music, which had gained great popularity in Tunisia in the preceding decades. Following World War II, the Rashidiyya Institute added a school offering a variety of courses as a further means of promoting *maaluf* music. A heightened interest in all facets of the nation's culture accompanied the acquisition of independence. Senior members of the Rashidiyya Institute formed the nucleus of the National Conservatory of Music, while the Ministry of Cultural Affairs dispatched younger graduates of its school to local and regional cultural centers to help establish small-scale ensembles. The Rashidiyya Institute continues to promote Arabo-Andalusian music through educational activities, workshops for local and regional musical groups, and its own performances of maaluf both in Tunisia and abroad. *See* ***Music***

Rassemblement Constitutionnel Démocratique (RCD)/Democratic Constitutional Rally. The central committee of the Parti Socialiste Dusturien (PSD; q.v.) changed the party's name to the Rassemblement Constitutionnel Démocratique (RCD) in February 1988. It held its first congress a few months later. Zine el-Abidine Ben Ali (q.v.) was elected RCD president. He had assumed the chairmanship of the PSD political bureau after its incumbent, Habib Bourguiba (q.v.), was removed from the political arena in November 1987. The same congress reduced the party's political bureau from 22 to seven members, all of them supporters of Ben Ali. It also constituted a new 200-person central committee, well over half of whom were appointed directly by Ben Ali. As had been the case in Tunisia since independence, the ruling party and the national government were closely interwoven. Prime Minister Hedi Baccouche (q.v.) served as the RCD's vice president, and other prominent party leaders also held cabinet-level positions. Thus, despite the redesignation of the party and Ben Ali's insistence that he would bring a genuinely plural political system into being, little democratization occurred within the ranks of the RCD itself.

In the months that followed, however, the locus of power within the party was altered by (1) the return of dissidents who had previously deserted the PSD, (2) the inclusion of other civic leaders who had resisted joining a monopoly party, and (3) the advancement of younger party members whose involvement in PSD affairs had often been curtailed by the organization's old guard. That the diminishing influence of the latter also changed the nature of the party became especially clear when only 20 of the 125 party members who made up the outgoing parliament received RCD approval to stand for re-election in April 1989. As party president, Ben Ali was automatically the RCD's candidate in simultaneous elections for the nation's chief executive, which the RCD convinced the opposition parties not to contest.

Consequently, Ben Ali was elected with over 99 percent of the vote. Six parties participated in the parliamentary balloting, but the rejuvenated RCD won 80 percent of the vote and swept all 141 seats. Its only real competition came from candidates affiliated with al-Nahda (q.v.), an Islamist political party that the government had refused to recognize. Campaigning as independents, its adherents won some 15 percent of the vote nationwide and a much higher ratio in some regions. The legal opposition parties, whose combined vote represented only about 5 percent of the total, joined al-Nahda in denouncing the elections as fraudulent. Convinced that the RCD would not countenance a genuine challenge, the opposition parties boycotted municipal council elections in the following year, thereby allowing virtually unopposed RCD candidates to dominate those bodies as well. Mounting frustrations, particularly within the Islamist opposition, exploded when al-Nahda militants attacked an RCD office in Tunis in February 1991, causing the death of a party worker. The vigor of the ensuing government crackdown on the Islamists led the opposition parties to modulate their antiregime rhetoric, partly as a matter of self-preservation but also because most of them found the Islamists' agenda distasteful.

With new parliamentary elections scheduled for March 1994, the RCD held its second congress in July 1993. The party renominated Ben Ali for the presidency and began mobilizing its 1.6 million members for the campaign. Anxious to give the appearance of open, multiparty competition without jeopardizing the RCD's legislative control, Ben Ali oversaw a modification of the electoral law that took effect prior to the 1994 voting. At the local level 144 members of the new chamber were elected. As in the past, the party whose list came first in each electoral district won all of the seats assigned to that district on the basis of its population. An additional 19 seats, distributed in proportion to the number of votes they received nationwide, were assigned to parties that had participated in the election but whose lists had not come first in any district.

The RCD's campaign revolved around soliciting a vote of confidence in the policies it had pursued since 1989. Party candidates contended that the RCD had curbed political extremism and, by continuing the economic liberalization set in motion in the mid-1980s, had paved the way to an era of prosperity. In carrying over 95 percent of the votes in every circumscription but one (where it polled 94 percent), the RCD won all of the 144 seats contested locally. Four opposition parties secured enough votes to win between two and ten of the remaining 19 seats, thus achieving the goals of the system's designers. In the presidential poll, Moncef Marzouki (q.v.), a human rights activist, failed in an attempt to mount a challenge to the candidacy of Ben Ali, who again ran without opposition. Reflecting the influence of younger members of the party in the post-Bourguiba era, more than three-quarters of the new parliament's RCD deputies were less than 50 years old. Well over half were entering the legislature for the first time, and a mere five had been serving in parliament when Ben Ali assumed the presidency in 1987.

Although the magnitude of the RCD victory again raised the issue of electoral improprieties in some quarters, the monitoring of the elections by both foreign observers and representatives of the opposition parties kept serious fraud to a minimum. Rather, the vote revealed the considerable capacity of the RCD—in the tradition of its PSD and Neo-Dustur (q.v.) predecessors—to mobilize the electorate and the personal popularity of Ben Ali, which readily translated into votes for RCD candidates. Fears that the turmoil rampant in neighboring Algeria (q.v.) might spill across the Tunisian border served to enhance the stature of the president. Many voters believed that actions he took in 1990 and 1991 spared Tunisia from similar instability at the hands of radical Islamists and advantaged those seeking office on the same ticket. Ben Ali also benefited from the especially strong support of female voters who appreciated both his vow not to amend the Personal Status Code of 1956 (q.v.) and the expanded role within the RCD accorded to women during his tenure as party head.

In keeping with the trend set in the 1994 national elections, the RCD again convincingly demonstrated its political power in municipal elections held throughout Tunisia in May 1995. In that balloting, all but six seats, out of more than 4,000 contested, went to candidates of the ruling party.

Rassemblement Française de Tunisie/French Rally of Tunisia. Political party established by Tunisian colons in 1951. It opposed the

Neo-Dustur's call for a restructuring of the protectorate's political system and criticized France for introducing even minor changes in the status quo. The Rassemblement enjoyed an early triumph in derailing several moderate reforms, but ultimately proved unable to dictate to a French government experiencing increasing international pressures to decolonize. In the end, the party succeeded only in thoroughly poisoning relations between colons and Tunisian nationalists, creating a polarized atmosphere in which the Neo-Dustur experienced an upsurge in popularity and influence.

Rassemblement Socialiste Progressiste (RSP)/Progressive Socialist Rally. Political party established in 1983 by Nejib Chebbi. Although the government's decision to allow the RSP to publish a weekly newspaper, *al-Mawqif,* constituted a tacit recognition of its activities, formal legalization came only in 1988 after the replacement of President Habib Bourguiba (q.v.) by Zine el-Abidine Ben Ali (q.v.). With a program grounded in socialism and Marxism, the RSP occupied, along with the Parti Communiste Tunisien (PCT; q.v.), the extreme left wing of the political spectrum. Both before and after 1988, however, the party had to contend with recurrent internal disarray as its small but highly politicized membership debated the efficacy of various leftist trends.

In the 1989 parliamentary elections, the RSP offered lists in five of the 25 national electoral districts, but polled less than 0.5 percent of the total vote. Five years later, 50 RSP candidates stood in eight constituencies, but support for the party increased only marginally, with its nominees winning fewer than 1,800 votes out of some 2.9 million cast. Even under the terms of electoral laws that had been amended to ensure seats in the legislature for opposition parties, the RSP's showing failed to meet minimum requirements, and none of its members entered the parliament.

al-Ra'y. Newspaper established by Ahmad Mestiri (q.v.) in 1977 to voice opposition to Parti Socialiste Dusturien (PSD) (q.v.) policies. Like other dissenting publications, *al-Ra'y* was banned following the Black Thursday (q.v.) riots in January 1978. It reappeared with the liberalization of the political environment introduced by Prime Minister Mzali (q.v.) in 1980. Published weekly, *al-Ra'y* has a circulation of about 20,000.

Reconquista. A series of crusades, beginning in the eleventh century and lasting until 1492, that restored the whole of the Iberian peninsula to Christian control. In the course of the Reconquista, many Spanish Muslims fled to North Africa, including Tunisia, carrying with them a richly developed culture that blended European-Christian and Arabo-Islamic traditions and that came to assert a strong influence on Maghribi society. In the Hafsid (q.v.) era, upper- and middle-class refugees entered government service, in both the military and the civilian bureaucracy; numerous artisans from Andalusia enriched the commercial life of Tunisian towns; and peasant farmers built new villages reminiscent of their abandoned Iberian homesteads.

Red Hand. Terrorist organization created by extremist colons in 1952. Settlers committed to the retention of maximum French control over the Tunisian government resented the 1951 concessions to the nationalists. They also feared that Neo-Dustur appeals to the United Nations and international labor organizations might increase pressure on France to make additional compromises. When Resident General Jean de Hautecloque (q.v.) restricted nationalist activity in 1952, riots erupted throughout the country. The authorities imposed a state of emergency, but a minority of the most militant colons, believing a more drastic response was called for, formed the Red Hand. Their early attempts to cow Tunisians into submission culminated with the assassination, late in the year, of the internationally respected labor leader Farhat Hached (q.v.). In thus escalating the level of violence, the vigilante tactics of the Red Hand further soured Franco-Tunisian relations.

Le Renouveau. *See **L'Action Tunisienne***

Resident General. Title of the chief French official in Tunisia between 1882 and 1956. A representative of the Ministry of Foreign Affairs, the resident general (1) headed the protectorate administration, (2) closely supervised the bey's activities, including the promulgation of royal decrees, and (3) served as the ruler's foreign minister. The first resident general, Paul Cambon (1882–1886) (q.v.), unambiguously set the tone for the office. Through the enthusiastic exercise of his powers, he reduced the monarch to a figurehead without dismantling the appearance of beylical sovereignty.

Ribat. A fortified compound including a mosque and warriors' living quarters built on the coasts of Muslim territory to guard against attack. The men of the ribat customarily led ascetic lives. The town of Monastir grew up around such a ribat erected late in the eighth century as the centerpiece in a chain of similar structures intended to defend against a Byzantine naval assault. Other fortresses sprang up close to most important coastal settlements, including Sousse.

Roches, Léon (1809–1901). French consul general in Tunis from 1855 to 1863. His primary mission of strengthening French influence brought him into direct competition with Richard Wood (q.v.), his British counterpart. His knowledge of North Africa and of Islam, acquired during a decade in Algeria as secretary and interpreter to Abd al-Qadir and several years in the French consulate in Tripoli, enabled Roches to form a close personal relationship with Muhammad Bey (q.v.). Along with Wood, he persuaded the bey to issue the Ahd al-aman (q.v.)in 1857 and helped induce his successor, Muhammad al-Sadiq (q.v.), to proclaim the Constitution of 1861 (q.v.). Roches was on less favorable terms with the powerful prime minister, Mustafa Khaznadar (q.v.), whom Wood had carefully cultivated since his arrival in Tunis a few months before Roches. In 1858, Khaznadar rejected the French consul's offer to secure financial support for the government from the Rothschilds, but within five years the expenses of extravagant and ill-considered projects, some of them pressed on the bey by Roches himself, had made an international loan imperative. The consul's last major undertaking in Tunisia was to arrange with a Parisian bank for a loan to the government of 35 million francs.

Rome; Roman Empire. The competition between Rome and Carthage over control of the central Mediterranean, begun in the third century B.C.E., ended with Rome's destruction of its rival after the Third Punic War (q.v.) in 146 B.C.E. The Roman province of Africa roughly corresponded with the territory previously controlled by Carthage. A few wealthy Romans acquired large agricultural estates there, but not until a century later did serious efforts at systematic colonization begin. In 46 B.C.E., Julius Caesar awarded plots of land to soldiers in the army that defeated Juba, the Numidian king who had allied with Pompey in the civil wars. By the end of the republic in 27 B.C.E., Roman rule had expanded to encompass virtually all of modern Tunisia north of the desert.

Early in the imperial era, the reconstruction of Carthage and the proliferation of new towns in the Sahil and the Majarda valley signaled the revival of the region and made Africa Proconsularis one of the most highly urbanized parts of the empire. Settlers in these communities fully exploited the agricultural possibilities of the land, garnering for it the title "granary of Rome." The expansion of cultivation and the emergence of an agricultural economy occurred at the expense of nomadic Berbers, whose grazing lands the colonists expropriated. Rome, far more than Carthage, had both the ability and the will to push the Berbers to the social and economic, if not the physical, fringes of the province. Those who attempted to participate in the new economy found their prospects limited to working the least desirable parcels of land themselves or laboring on the increasingly numerous large estates. In the cities and towns, by contrast, a class of Romanized Africans emerged, although few of them ever fully assimilated Roman culture.

Heavy imperial taxes sparked a revolt in Africa's major cities in 238 C.E. Its bloody repression devastated many of them, however, and Africa's economic center of gravity shifted to the smaller communities of the interior, which had been spared the worst of the revolt. The heavy hand of imperial rule soon engendered an animosity frequently expressing itself in antagonism between the Berbers and the Romans or their Romanized protégés.

The appearance and rapid spread of Christianity in Africa in the late first and early second centuries further complicated an already unstable situation. Many Berbers converted to the new faith less from religious conviction than from a desire to challenge the Roman regime. Nor was this the last instance of Christianity serving as a vehicle for dissent in Africa. Early in the fourth century, the Donatist schism (q.v.) split the Christians in the province. Donatus and his followers asserted that clergymen who had not vigorously stood up against imperial persecution forfeited their rights to administer the sacraments. The mainstream church hierarchy, at which these criticisms were directed, naturally rejected them. Donatist support came primarily from rural Berber Christians whose attitude reflected political discontent with the more affluent and powerful Roman and Romanized segments of the population more than theological conviction. For more than a century afterward, revolts flared up in Berber areas under the banner of Donatism.

In Africa, as in Europe, however, Germanic tribes constituted the most serious challenge for the declining empire. Meeting little resistance from the divided population of Africa Proconsularis, the Vandals (q.v.) conquered the entire province, except for Carthage, in 429. The city's fall a decade later dashed any hopes of negotiating an alliance with the Vandals and brought to an ignominious conclusion more than six centuries of Roman rule in Africa.

Rommel, Erwin (1891–1944). German general and World War II commander of the Afrika Korps. After his defeat at the Battle of al-Alamein in October 1942, Rommel retreated westward across Libya and into Tunisia. There his troops were caught between the pursuing British and the Anglo-American forces that had invaded North Africa in Operation Torch (q.v.). Rommel was recalled from Tunisia in March 1943, a few months prior to the surrender of the Afrika Korps. Implicated in a plot against Hitler, he committed suicide at home in Germany in 1944.

-S-

al-Sabah. Arabic-language paper established by the Neo-Dustur in 1951. Most of its staff were pan-Arabists who tended to side with the Ben Yusuf (q.v.) wing of the party in the political controversies immediately before and after independence. As a result, the paper was proscribed in 1957 and 1958. When publication resumed, *al-Sabah* continued to express pan-Arab views with greater enthusiasm than did most Neo-Dustur leaders, although in other respects it adhered to the views of the mainstream party line. In 1963, government efforts to minimize criticism by more tightly controlling the press caused *al-Sabah* to distance itself from the party and assume the status of an independent daily. It has a circulation of approximately 50,000.

Sadiqi College. Tunis secondary school founded by Khair al-Din al-Tunsi (q.v.) in 1875. Its pupils pursued an eight-year course of study that included both a traditional Islamic segment taught in Arabic and a European-style curriculum centering on the sciences, mathematics, and western languages. The purpose of these secular subjects was to prepare Sadiqi graduates for positions in the government previously monopolized by young men from the Zaituna Mosque-University (q.v.) who had little or no knowledge of the world beyond Tunisia. The school continued under the French protectorate, most of whose officials looked favorably on it as a vehicle for acculturating Tunisian youth. The Young Tunisian (q.v.) movement developed around Sadiqi graduates; many leaders of the Dustur and Neo-Dustur parties were also educated there. Sadiqi College remains one of the most prestigious secondary schools in the country.

Sahib al-Tabi. Literally, the master of the seal. An important dignitary in the Husainid (q.v.) bureaucracy, he not only affixed the royal seal to documents but also served as an intermediary between the bey and other officials. Owing to his proximity to the ruler, the sahib al-tabi often acted as the bey's prime minister.

Sahil. The coastal plain between Tunis and Sfax. As deep as 40 kilometers (25 miles) in some places, the Sahil's good soil, abundant underground water, and rainfall averaging up to 500 millimeters (20 inches) annually make it one of the country's most densely populated and intensively farmed regions. The heart of the Sahil is the area between Sousse and Sfax in which Tunisia's olive production is concentrated. Served by good ports and lacking any natural barriers to the penetration of the interior, the Sahil has always been the Tunisian region most susceptible to outside influences. Historically it has served as a conduit for the entry into the country of new people and their cultures.

Sahnun, Imam Abu Said Abd al-Salam (776–854). Legal scholar of Kairouan whose book *al-Mudawwana al-kubra* ranks behind only the writing of Malik ibn Anas himself as a source for the principles of the Maliki madhhab (q.v.). The study is a legal commentary based on information Sahnun obtained directly from a protégé of Malik ibn Anas. One of the most important segments of *al-Mudawwana* discusses the role of religious law in commerce. Imam Sahnun's prominence helped make Kairouan an early center of the Maliki madhhab.

Saint, Lucien (1867–1938). French resident general from 1921 to 1929. His utter rejection of nationalist aspirations and stern demeanor earned him a reputation as a tough, uncompromising colonial administrator. In 1922, Nasir Bey (q.v.) threatened to abdicate if the resident general did not comply with a list of Dustur demands. The ruler relented, however, when Saint, accompanied by an ostentatious escort of armed troops, appeared at the palace to assure the bey that he would not respond to such pressures. Saint believed that a representative assembly and a government responsible to it were incompatible with the protectorate. Instead, he oversaw a series of reforms that the Dustur regarded as mere window dressing. He muzzled renewed criticisms with decrees that restricted the press and defined illegal political activities very broadly, thereby considerably weakening the party. Saint's obdurate approach ensured a surface calm, but latent antagonism toward the French grew steadily during his years in office. After leaving Tunisia, Saint served as the resident general of Morocco, where he employed similar hard-line tactics against the nationalists.

Salafiyya Movement. Deriving its name from the Arabic word for "ancestors" (salaf), this late nineteenth- and early twentieth-century ideology won adherents throughout the Muslim world with its call to restore traditional Islamic values that had been either corrupted or completely abandoned during the centuries since the inception of the religion. Salafiyya activists maintained that only such a renewal would endow the Muslim community with the strength needed to ward off the mounting political and economic pressures coming from the European world. At the same time, however, many Salafiyya leaders also acknowledged their admiration for the technological and scientific achievements of the West, urging that they be adapted to their own societies. Such thinking found a particularly receptive audience among the Young Tunisians (q.v.), whose enthusiasm for the Salafiyya movement was heightened by visits to Tunis in 1885 and 1903 by Muhammad Abduh, one of its most famous leaders.

Sanhaja Confederation. Berber tribal coalition of central Maghribi origin closely linked to the Fatimid dynasty (q.v.). The Kutama tribe (q.v.), a key element in the confederation, was instrumental in bringing the Fatimids to power and, along with other Sanhaja tribes, fought to extend Fatimid rule into the central and western Maghrib during the tenth century. The Zirids (q.v.), whom the Fatimids designated as their successors when they left Ifriqiya for Egypt, were also Sanhaja Berbers.

Saqiyat Sidi Yusuf. Town on the Algerian border some 35 kilometers (21 miles) west of Le Kef. During Algeria's war for independence, the Tunisian government allowed FLN soldiers to launch operations from its territory. Such attacks sometimes occasioned retaliations, as when French warplanes bombed Saqiyat Sidi Yusuf on February 8, 1958, destroying the town and causing at least 80 civilian deaths. In response to this raid, Tunisia placed severe restrictions on the French forces allowed to remain in the country after independence and began negotiations that resulted in the departure of all French troops from Tunisia except for those at the Bizerte naval base and a few posts in the Sahara.

Sayah, Muhammad (1933–). Neo-Dustur party activist. He was secretary-general of the Union Générale des Etudiants Tunisiens (UGET; q.v.) from 1960 to 1962, editor of *L'Action* (q.v.) from 1962 to 1964, director of the Parti Socialiste Dusturien from 1964 to 1969, and a member of the party's political bureau from 1964 until 1987. He held a variety of ministerial-level appointments in the 1970s and 1980s. In 1969, Sayah replaced Chedli Klibi (q.v.) as editor of the *Histoire du Mouvement National Tunisien,* the official account of the Neo-Dustur Party. Over the next decade, he oversaw the completion of this 15-volume series and the beginning of its translation into Arabic. A close adviser to Habib Bourguiba (q.v.) during his last months in office, Sayah urged the president to adopt a policy of uncompromising rejection of domestic opposition groups. Particularly opposed to such Islamist organizations as the Mouvement de la Tendance Islamique (MTI; q.v.), he sanctioned the organization of squads of young toughs who disrupted meetings of the party's political opponents and occasionally assaulted critics of the regime. Sayah and several of his associates were arrested when Zine el-Abidine Ben Ali (q.v.) replaced Bourguiba in November 1987. Released after only a few months in detention, Sayah withdrew from politics.

Sbaitla. The ancient Roman city of Sufetula, it was the capital of the exarch (governor) Gregory (q.v.) at the time of the Arab invasion in

647. The Arabs, under the command of Ibn Saad, defeated Gregory's army near Sbaitla. Unable to conquer the well-defended coastal cities, they imposed an indemnity and then withdrew.

Scipio Africanus (236–184 B.C.E.). Roman commander whose invasion of Africa during the Second Punic War (q.v.) forced Carthage to surrender in 203 B.C.E. In the following year, Scipio defeated the Carthaginian general Hannibal (q.v.) at the Battle of Zama (q.v.), ending the war. These victories over Carthage won him the epithet "Africanus."

Service des Affaires Indigènes. *See* **Service des Renseignements**

Service des Renseignements. Military agency created by protectorate officials in 1882 to oversee the administration of the tribes. Because many Service des Renseignements officers had previously worked in Algeria, they favored a policy of direct rule that minimized the powers of local shaikhs. This tendency contradicted the stated theory of the protectorate and caused friction between the soldier-administrators and successive residents general, all of whom tried to bring the Service des Renseignements firmly under their management. Beginning in 1884, contrôleurs civils (q.v.) under the supervision of the resident general (q.v.) gradually replaced the Service des Renseignements officers throughout central and northern Tunisia. In 1900, at a time when only the desert areas of the south and a few other remote regions remained under military control, the agency's name was changed to Service des Affaires Indigènes. Its officers continued their administrative work until World War I. During the war, they focused most of their attention on military affairs, particularly the maintenance of security along the frontier with Ottoman Libya. At the end of the war, the army relinquished its tribal administrative functions and disbanded the organization.

Sfar, Bashir (1865–1917). A leader of the Young Tunisian movement (q.v.). He advocated extensive education in European languages, such as he himself had received both at Sadiqi College (q.v.) and in France. In keeping with early protectorate officials' thinking that young men such as Sfar could help them bridge the gap between the French and the Arab communities, he received an appointment in the bureaucracy and eventually rose to head the Habus Administration (q.v.). Sfar took the lead in establishing the Khalduniyya educational society (q.v.) in 1896 and was also instrumental in the creation of the Association des Anciens Elèves du Collège Sadiqi (q.v.), a group with similar objectives, in 1903. In 1898, he fell out with the French authorities over their decision to make habus (q.v.) lands available for sale to Europeans. In 1905 and 1906 he again criticized the French administration, this time for allowing colon pressure to force a retreat from French willingness to improve Tunisian education. He was appointed governor of Sousse in 1908, in an effort to stifle his criticisms. His exile from Tunis diminished his influence among the Young Tunisians, and other activists, most notably Ali Bash Hamba (q.v.), rose to leadership positions in the group.

Sfar, Tahar (1903–1942). Lawyer and founding member of the Neo-Dustur Party. Highly critical of the ulama, whom he considered dogmatic and reactionary, he called for a separation of the religious and the secular spheres of life. But he was careful to underscore his respect for the Quran and the traditions of Muhammad. Along with other Neo-Dustur leaders, Sfar was imprisoned in 1934 and 1938. Disagreeing with Bourguiba's insistence on pursuing intransigent tactics, he abandoned his political career in 1938. His *Journal d'un Exilé, Zarzis, 1935,* an account of his participation in the nationalist movement, was posthumously published in Tunis in 1960.

Sfax. Second-largest city in Tunisia, with a population of roughly 250,000. The Sfax region is a major olive (q.v.) producing area, while the city itself is the most important industrial and commercial center in the south. The ancient city of Taparura (near whose ruins Sfax lies) had already earned a reputation for the high quality of its olive oil in the pre-Christian era. The agrarian resources of the district permitted Sfax to function briefly as an independent city-state following the invasion of the Banu Hilal (q.v.). Like most of the coast of Ifriqiya, Sfax experienced a period of Norman (q.v.) control in the mid-twelfth century. Thereafter, growing commercial contacts with Europe increased the city's prosperity. In 1864, angered by economic hardships that they blamed on the central government's incompetence, the citizens of Sfax joined in the revolt that swept the country. The reprisals that followed this rebellion further damaged the city's fortunes. The inability of the bey's forces to halt the French invasion in 1881 occasioned another revolt in Sfax, but heavy French naval bombardment ended the city's resistance to the occupation. The development of phosphate (q.v.) mines around Gafsa led the French to make substantial improvements in the harbor at Sfax, the nearest seaport, in the 1890s. The export of Tunisia's phosphates and phosphate by-products remained concentrated at Sfax until the 1980s, when the ports of Gabès and La Skirra also began shipping ore, fertilizers, and chemicals abroad.

Sfez, Batto. Jew whose 1857 execution opened an era of externally imposed reforms culminating in the Constitution of 1861 (q.v.). Sfez was involved in an accident that took the life of a Tunisian child. In an altercation following the mishap, he made derogatory remarks about Islam and was subsequently found guilty of blasphemy. With the approval of Muhammad Bey (q.v.), Sfez was hastily put to death. As a result of European protests about the case, the bey issued the Ahd al-aman (q.v.), guaranteeing the rights of his subjects and committing his government to enact further changes in the judicial system.

al-Shabbi, Abu'l-Qasim (1909–1934). Poet who stressed the dignity of the common people and the importance of traditional values. The writings of the French Romantics and of the Lebanese poet Gibran Khalil Gibran exerted a considerable influence on the youthful al-Shabbi. His own poetry first appeared in a 1928 anthology of contemporary Tunisian literature, but several more widely circulated Egyptian literary reviews also published his work in the early 1930s, while he was still a student at the Zaituna Mosque-University (q.v.). al-Shabbi gained very little recognition during his lifetime and the only collection of his poetry, *Aghani al-Haya* (1955), was issued posthumously. For many Tunisians of the postwar and independence generations, however, his themes, along with the fact that he wrote only in Arabic, made him a symbol of national pride and their country's Arabo-Islamic heritage. al-Shabbi's premature death resulted from a chronic heart condition.

Sharia. Muslim law, rooted in the Quran and the traditions of the prophet Muhammad. Since these sources did not provide explicit guidance for every case coming before Muslim jurists, the practice of drawing analogies between their cases and similar situations in the Quran or the traditions also assumed the force of law, as did a consensus of scholarly legal opinion on a given issue. By the ninth century, four major schools of legal interpretation, called madhahib (singular, madhhab; q.v.), had developed and gained acceptance throughout the Muslim community. The most important of these in Tunisia have been the Hanafi (q.v.) and Maliki (q.v.) schools.

Shashiyya. Brimless red-felt cap traditionally worn by male Tunisian Muslims. Until the early nineteenth century, the shashiyya industry produced not only for the local market but also for export to the Middle East. However, the rising cost of imported raw materials needed in the manufacturing process, combined with the ability of European competitors to produce a virtually identical item more cheaply, ultimately ruined the industry. Symptomatic of the commercial decline generally characterizing late eighteenth- and early nineteenth-century Tunisia, the collapse of the long-established shashiyya trade sent shock waves throughout the economy.

Shii Islam; Shii Muslims. Branch of Islam whose adherents (Shiis or Shii Muslims) believe that only direct descendants of Ali, the prophet Muhammad's cousin and son-in-law, are acceptable leaders of the Muslim community. After Ali's death in 661, the Shiis refused to accept the authority of the Umayyad and Abbasid caliphs (q.v.) or their representatives, all of whom lacked this pedigree. Whenever they could, Shii agents actively sought to bring down these regimes. In Ifriqiya, the Shii propagandist Abu Abdallah's (q.v.) skillful manipulation of Berber political and social grievances led to the replacement of the Aghlabids (q.v.), who had originally come to Ifriqiya as Abbasid governors, by the Shii Fatimids (q.v.). Despite this success, Shia Islam never sank deep roots in North Africa. After the Fatimid departure for Egypt in 973, it was never again a significant factor in the region.

Sicily. Contacts between Tunisia and Sicily date from Carthaginian times. After making several unsuccessful attempts, Carthage gained control over the western part of the island in the fourth century B.C.E. The Carthaginians' interest in Sicily had been based in their fear of Greek expansion, but Greek power had waned by the time they had achieved their goals on the island. The rise of Rome, whose leaders grasped the strategic and commercial importance of Sicily, confronted Carthage with a new and more powerful rival for the island. This competition incited the First Punic War (q.v.), which resulted in Carthage withdrawing totally from Sicily in 241 B.C.E. Rome (and the Byzantine Empire) ruled the island for the next millennium.

The fear that Byzantine naval forces would use Sicily as a base for attacks on Ifriqiya led the Aghlabids (q.v.) to undertake a campaign to conquer the island in the ninth century. Ziyadat Allah I (q.v.) invaded in 827 in response to a plea for help from Sicilian rebels. For the rest of the century, his successors extended their sway over Sicily, culminating in the capture of Palermo in 900. Aghlabid domination of Sicily's agrarian and commercial assets, coupled with their use of the island as a point of departure for raids on the Italian mainland, brought new wealth to Ifriqiya and helped finance the elaborate public-works projects that characterized the Aghlabid period.

The Fatimids (q.v.) and the Zirids (q.v.) paid less attention to Sicily, although the island's Muslims continued to look to Ifriqiya for guidance and support, especially in times of crisis. The Zirids' inability to avert the eleventh-century Norman (q.v.) seizure of Sicily, which came at a time of serious domestic problems for the dynasty, contributed to the erosion of its prestige. Norman rule ended the island's Muslim era, but many points of contact with the Maghrib continued. The Normans, for example, forced Ifriqiya's rulers to pay tribute to protect their shipping. Although this practice died out as Hafsid (q.v.)

power grew, the desire to renew it was the ostensible reason behind King Louis IX's (q.v.) invasion of Tunisia in 1270.

In 1284, Aragon captured Sicily, which was later ruled by Spain and Austria before becoming part of Italy. The island's most important modern links with Tunisia have been demographic. Many Sicilian peasants and laborers emigrated to Tunisia during the nineteenth century. The Allied invasion of Sicily in July 1943, which paved the way for the September assault on the Italian mainland, was launched from North African ports, including Bizerte, and utilized troops who were veterans of Operation Torch (q.v.).

La Skirra. Petroleum export center, located between Sfax and Gabès. Pipelines deliver oil to its port from the Tunisian Sahara and from fields in southern Algeria.

Slam. Unsound business practice adopted by some eighteenth and nineteenth century beys as a means of securing ready cash. Its application to olive cultivation by Husain Bey (q.v.) in the 1820s proved particularly damaging. In this instance, the bey monopolized the olive crop and simultaneously imposed on the trees' owners a tax in kind to be paid in olive oil, the country's most valuable export commodity. Well before the harvest, the bey purchased the entire crop's yield of oil and contracted with foreign merchants to buy the same oil from him at a much higher rate. If individual farmers could not supply the amount of oil the bey's agents demanded, they were obliged to make up the difference through expensive purchases on the open market. If nationwide shortages developed, however, as they did in 1828, catastrophic results ensued. Unable to meet his contractual obligations to foreign businessmen, the bey had to buy substantial quantities of oil on the international market, incurring in the process an enormous debt that disrupted the entire economy.

Société des Hôtels Tunisiens Touristiques (SHTT)/Tunisian Tourist Hotels Company. Public corporation established in the 1960s to build and manage high quality hotels that would attract European tourists to Tunisia's Mediterranean beaches and Saharan oases. Economic planners correctly assumed that the significant government investment in tourism (q.v.) symbolized by the SHTT would encourage similar private ventures. In less than a decade, many major international hotel chains had opened properties in areas first developed by the Société, making tourism a crucial part of the country's economy.

Sousse. City in the heart of the Sahil located on the site of Hadrumetum, a Phoenician trading center dating from the ninth century B.C.E. Its abundant production of olives and other crops made Hadrumetum one of the most important communities of Roman Africa, eventually becoming the capital of the province of Byzacenia. In the sixth century C.E., its Byzantine rulers renamed it Justinianapolis. The Arab conquerors of Ifriqiya made the city, which they called Susa, part of the chain of coastal fortifications designed to ward off Christian attacks. The combined military and religious roles of Sousse were underscored when the army of the Aghlabid ruler Ziyadat Allah I (q.v.) embarked on the conquest of Sicily from its port in 827. In the modern era, the construction of scores of world-class hotels on the beaches around Sousse has made tourism (q.v.) the mainstay of the city's economy, supplanting agriculture.

Spanish Umayyads (756–1031). Muslim rulers of much of the Iberian Peninsula from the late eighth to the eleventh centuries. Abd al-Rahman, an Umayyad prince who fled Damascus when the Abbasids (q.v.) ousted his family from the caliphate and attempted to revive Umayyad fortunes in Spain, establishing himself in Cordoba in 756. Later Spanish Umayyads attempted to profit from the trans-Saharan trade by gaining control over important commercial centers in the western Maghrib. Their actions sparked conflicts with the Fatimids (q.v.) in the tenth century, as Ifriqiya's rulers sought to extend their own influence westward. Both sides relied heavily on Berber allies, the Umayyads employing the Zanata confederation (q.v.) and the Fatimids making use of the Sanhaja (q.v.) tribes. The rivalry continued under the Fatimids' Zirid (q.v.) successors, but by the early eleventh century domestic problems that would ultimately prove fatal forced the Spanish Umayyads to abandon their African enterprises.

-T-

Tabarqa. Northwestern coastal city founded by the Phoenicians in the fifth century B.C.E. and known in Roman times as Thabraca. It served both as a commercial center for the surrounding area and a port for Mediterranean trade. In 1540, Khair al-Din Barbarossa (q.v.) ceded an offshore island, also called Tabarqa, to Genoa as ransom for the corsair Darghut (q.v.). The Genoese fortified the island and held it for the next two centuries. It became a center for coral fishing and an important market for Genoese-Tunisian trade. In 1741, Ali Pasha (q.v.), fearful that France was about to acquire the island from Genoa, seized it and expelled its European residents.

al-Tajdid. *See* **Parti Communiste Tunisien**

Tell. Region of rolling hills and low mountains extending north of the Dorsal (q.v.) from the Algerian border to the coast. Characterized by rich soils and good rainfall, and watered by the Majarda River, the Tell is a major agricultural area, especially for cereals.

Testour. Town on the Majarda River, some 80 kilometers (50 miles) west of Tunis. Muslim refugees from Andalusia in the sixteenth and seventeenth centuries established Testour on the site of a community known in antiquity as Tichilla. Even more than in other similar settlements, the people of Testour retained customs and traditions associated with their Spanish heritage. As a result, the town has a distinctive character and appearance, discernible especially in its main mosque, many of whose features suggest the influence of Christian church architecture.

Thaalbi, Abd al-Aziz (ca. 1875–1944). A graduate of the Zaituna Mosque-University (q.v.), a member of the Young Tunisians (q.v.), and an adherent of the Salafiyya (q.v.) movement, he founded the Dustur Party in 1920. Thaalbi first achieved notoriety in 1903, when he was imprisoned as the result of a dispute with prominent traditional religious leaders. In the following year he coauthored, along with al-Hadi Sabai and César Benattar (the latter a Tunisian Jew), *L'Esprit Libérale du Coran* (*The Liberal Spirit of the Quran*). Also appearing in an Arabic edition (*al-Ruh al-hurra li'l-Qur'an*), this work criticized the religious establishment and urged Franco-Tunisian cooperation. Like many other Young Tunisians, Thaalbi was exiled after the Jallaz Cemetery incident (q.v.) in 1911.

By the end of World War I, he had returned to Tunisia and joined a delegation of former Young Tunisians that went to Versailles to petition the Allies for a relaxation of French control. Frustrated by France's unwillingness to make concessions, Thaalbi wrote, while still in France, *La Tunisie Martyre* (*Tunisia Martyred;* q.v.), in which he argued that the protectorate had undermined Tunisian development and demanded the restoration of the Constitution of 1861 (q.v.). He was arrested and sent back to Tunisia, but was then released. In 1920, he assumed the leadership of the middle-class merchants, artisans, and lower-level ulama, many of them formerly affiliated with the Young Tunisians, that evolved into the Dustur Party.

In response to Dustur demands for greater participation in the political process, France offered a series of limited reforms in 1922. Thaalbi guided the Dustur's rejection of this proposal, maintaining that it fell too far short of Tunisian requirements to merit consideration. The 1923 death of Nasir Bey (q.v.), who had sympathized with the Dustur, and the protectorate authorities' growing impatience with the party convinced Thaalbi that his political activism would not be tolerated for long. He fled the country in the same year.

He returned in 1937, when the Popular Front (q.v.) government had created an atmosphere that tolerated the expression of nationalist grievances. By then, however, the remnants of Thaalbi's Dustur had given way before the Neo-Dustur, whose secular, dynamic young leaders had little use for either Thaalbi's timid tactics or the traditional Arabo-Islamic values he stressed. Finding support among only a small segment of the population and encountering opposition from Neo-Dustur militants who disrupted his public appearances, Thaalbi's efforts to revive the Dustur failed miserably, although the party survived in moribund form until his death in 1944.

Thameur, Habib (?–1949). Neo-Dustur activist who directed the party's clandestine operations after its proscription and the arrest of its first echelon of leadership in 1938. As a result of his efforts to secure the release from prison of Habib Bourguiba (q.v.) and other Neo-Dustur militants, Thameur served a brief jail term in 1940. His increasingly strident criticisms of France made him a prime target in a police roundup of nationalist agitators in 1941, and he was arrested as he was preparing to cross the border into Axis-controlled Tripolitania. He was tried and again incarcerated. His willingness to seek the help of Germany and Italy ran counter to Bourguiba's desire that the Neo-Dustur cooperate with France in the war effort. From his French prison, Bourguiba wrote to Thameur in August 1942, instructing him to communicate these wishes to the party faithful. Vichy Resident General Esteva released Thameur and other political prisoners late in 1942. In early 1943 Thameur held the post of minister of the interior in a cabinet serving Munsif Bey (q.v.). Despite Bourguiba's counsel, Thameur fled Tunisia after the Allied victory in the spring of 1943, living in Rome and Berlin until the defeat of the Axis. After the war, he participated in the work of the Comité de la Libération du Maghreb Arabe (q.v.) in Cairo. At the time of his death in a plane crash in Pakistan, he was the Tunisian representative to the Islamic Congress.

Thuburbo Majus. Founded in 27 B.C.E. as a colony for Roman veterans, this city on the Miliana River some 65 kilometers (40 miles) southwest of Tunis was a major urban center of Roman Africa for more than three centuries. Already beginning to decline at the time of the Vandal invasions, Thuburbo Majus completely vanished early in the Muslim era. Its ruins were rediscovered only in 1875 by Charles Tissot, a French historian and archeologist.

Thugga. *See* **Dougga**

Tourism. Tourism is an important facet of the Tunisian national economy, accounting for approximately 7 percent of gross domestic product in the mid-1990s. Tunisia's mild climate, its beaches, oases, and cities with their traditional quarters, and its long and varied history, much of it exemplified in well preserved monuments, have combined to make the country an attractive tourist destination.

The tourist industry dates from the 1960s, when the state-owned Société des Hôtels Tunisiens Touristiques (SHTT; q.v.) opened resort hotels on the Mediterranean near Hammamet and Sousse and on the island of Jerba. Within a decade, tourism had become Tunisia's main source of foreign currency, although the escalation of oil prices pushed petroleum exports to the forefront in 1973. Revenues generated by the sale of oil abroad declined substantially in the latter half of the 1980s, but tourism did not regain its primacy. It remained in second place, outstripped by the earnings of textile exports. In addition to providing valuable foreign exchange, the tourist industry is also a major nationwide employer, directly providing jobs for more than 60,000 workers and indirectly supporting another 200,000.

There are, however, serious problems inherent in the industry. Many of its employees, particularly in hotels, perform menial labor, which places them in a subservient relationship to foreigners that is sometimes painfully reminiscent of the colonial era. Moreover, many of the best jobs in hotel management are held by foreigners working for the multinational corporations that own many of the large hotels. Other negative aspects of tourism are that hotel construction has taken agricultural land out of production and has displaced small farmers without providing them with adequate new opportunities, while the concentration of tourism in a few coastal areas has intensified long-standing economic disparities between the coast and the interior. One potential danger of Tunisia's steadily growing tourist industry is its ecological impact. The commercial exploitation of Mediterranean beaches in southern Europe has often upset the fragile coastal ecology there. While there is as yet little evidence of similar damage in Tunisia, the environmental threat remains real, not only on the beaches but also in the deserts and oases of the south where the invasion of tourists has inevitably altered natural balances.

Another drawback to reliance on tourism is that its success or failure depends to a very high degree on circumstances that neither the Tunisian government nor private entrepreneurs can control. Economic slumps in Europe (home of more than half the tourists) or political unrest that creates a feeling of uneasiness about travel in the Arab world can, for example, dramatically affect the number of visitors to the country. In 1991, the year that opened with the war to drive Iraq from Kuwait, the number of European tourists declined by about a third. Only the fact that vacationers from the other Maghrib countries increased by some 50 percent in the same year averted a serious blow to the national economy.

The more usual situation, in which as many as three-fifths of the tourists are Europeans; roughly one-third are Maghribis; and the remainder come from North America, the Middle East, Africa, and elsewhere, returned in 1992 and has prevailed since, despite the concurrent persistence of civil unrest in neighboring Algeria.

Internal politics also affect tourism. The generally stable condition of the country in the 1960s and much of the 1970s contributed to its attractiveness as a tourist destination. Aware of the importance of tourism to the state, Islamist extremists (who also took offense at the comportment and dress of many western tourists) planted bombs in the summer of 1987 at resort hotels in Sousse and Monastir in an attempt to frighten off visitors, thereby crippling the economy and forcing the government to address their demands. The need to protect this vital pillar of the economy led President Habib Bourguiba (q.v.) to take strong measures to curb terrorism. At the same time, however, he demonized the entire Islamist opposition in a way that contributed to his being removed from office a few months later. By preventing the reappearance of such activity, the government of Zine el-Abidine Ben Ali (q.v.) has assured potential visitors of their safety. As a result, the annual number of tourists entering Tunisia in the 1990s consistently exceeded 3 million and approached a record 4 million in 1994.

Trade and Commerce (International). Textiles make up the principal exports of Tunisia. They include, in order of value, clothing and fashion accessories; mechanical and electrical products; agricultural goods; petroleum (q.v.) and its by-products; and ore, fertilizers, and chemicals derived from phosphate (q.v.).

Food products were Tunisia's most valuable export until the development of the petroleum industry. Olive oil (q.v.) has normally been the largest and most remunerative of these, with fish and mollusks, citrus fruits, dates, and wine also figuring prominently. In the first half of the 1990s, agricultural commodities had dropped to fourth place in the total export market although they could produce over 400 million dinars in export revenues in good years. Instead, the Tunisian textile industry had become the mainstay of the export economy, earning in excess of 2 billion dinars from foreign sales in 1994. The bulk of this came from the export of clothing (more than 1.8 billion dinars), hosiery (approximately 270 million dinars), and cotton material (63 million dinars).

From the mid-1970s until the mid-1980s, crude oil and petroleum by-products constituted the nation's most valuable exports. Their peak year came in 1980, when they generated 665 million dinars in foreign earnings. The collapse of world oil prices in 1986 drove down the value of petroleum-related exports to just over 340 million dinars, but the following year witnessed a recovery to a figure in excess of 418 million dinars. Twice in the early 1990s, the export value of hydrocarbons approached or exceeded 600 million dinars (598 million in 1990; 604 million in 1992). Thereafter, however, as domestic demand rose steadily, export earnings again fell, dipping to between 430 million and 440 million dinars in 1993 and 1994.

Phosphate ore had already become an important export in the nineteenth century. More recently, however, in response to its declining value on world markets, such by-products as phosphoric acid, triple superphosphate, and phosphatic fertilizers have become more valuable sources of export revenue than the ore itself. Export earnings from the industry as a whole fluctuated between 335 million and 460 million dinars between 1990 and 1994, less than 10 percent of which derived from the sale of crude phosphate.

The countries of the European Union (EU; q.v.) provide the most accessible and lucrative markets for exports. France, whose purchases of Tunisian goods surpassed 1.2 billion dinars in 1994 and have continued to climb since then, has consistently been Tunisia's best customer since the end of the protectorate. Other important European buyers of Tunisian products in 1994 included Italy (907 million dinars), Germany (730 million dinars), and Belgium (304 million dinars). At the same time, sales to the United States totaled only about 55 million dinars. Exports to fellow members of the Union du Maghreb Arabe (UMA; q.v.) amounted to slightly more than 285 million dinars, the preponderance of which (188 million dinars) went to Libya. Other Arab countries' purchases from Tunisia were relatively insignificant. Syria, which purchased 24 million dinars worth of Tunisian goods, supplanted Iraq, whose annual spending prior to the 1991 war reached as much as 45 million dinars, as Tunisia's best Arab customer outside the Maghrib.

The EU is also the main source of Tunisia's imports, which consist of machinery, motor vehicles, petroleum products (and, since 1993, crude oil), iron and steel, medical and pharmaceutical materials, foodstuffs such as sugar, wheat, and vegetable oils, and raw cotton. As they had since independence, Tunisian imports in 1994 came primarily from France (which supplied more than 1.8 billion dinars worth of goods), Italy (more than 1 billion dinars), and Germany (more than 800 million dinars). Tunisia's fourth-largest source of imports was the United States, which sold commodities valued at just over 300 million dinars.

In 1994 the ratio of exports to imports was 70 percent, a figure nearing the high end of the range over which this statistic has fluctuated since independence. Until the recent expansion of the textile industry, Tunisia relied heavily on mineral exports, whose value hinged on world market factors beyond its control, and on agricultural commodities that were subject to equally unpredictable environmental conditions to cover the high cost of imported goods for which demand rose steadily. This situation saddled the country with a serious trade deficit that customarily exceeded 1 billion dinars annually after 1984 and surpassed 2 billion dinars in 1990, 1992, and 1993, reaching a high of 2.4 billion dinars in the latter year. A 1995 treaty with the European Union, whose members account for roughly three-quarters of Tunisia's import and export commerce, provided for the creation, over a 12-year period, of a free-trade zone with the potential to alleviate the most serious of the country's foreign trade problems.

Tunis. The country's capital and largest city, lying on the western bank of the Lake of Tunis, a shallow lagoon linked to the Mediterranean Sea by a narrow channel. A settlement already existed on this site when Carthage was founded, which the Phoenicians quickly annexed. The commanders of several invading armies, including Scipio Africanus (q.v.) during the Second Punic War (q.v.), used Tunis as their headquarters for assaults on Carthage, located some ten miles away on the coast. With Rome's victory in the Third Punic War in 146 B.C.E., Tunis, like Carthage, was destroyed. It was reconstructed before Carthage, but it assumed little importance until Carthage was revived early in the Christian era. Even then, however, Tunis existed very much in the shadow of its more famous neighbor.

The earliest Arab invaders to enter Africa avoided the environs of Carthage, focusing their attention on the less well defended steppe and desert regions where they built the garrison city of Kairouan. Later in the seventh century, however, the campaigns of the Umayyad commander Hassan ibn Numan (q.v.) extended and strengthened Muslim control throughout Ifriqiya. After Ibn Numan captured Carthage in 698, the city was neglected in favor of Tunis, a site less susceptible to the seaborne Byzantine counterattacks that the Arabs anticipated. In the Umayyad and Aghlabid (q.v.) eras, Tunis was unchallenged as the second city of Ifriqiya and even served briefly as its capital during the reign of the Aghlabid amir Ibrahim II (q.v.) late in the ninth century. Under the Fatimids (q.v.) and Zirids (q.v.), Tunis again reverted to secondary importance, but was one of the few coastal communities to ward off the Norman (q.v.) raiders of the twelfth century.

Ifriqiya's growing orientation toward the Mediterranean influenced the al-Muwahhid leaders' decision to make Tunis their regional capital in 1160, but it was the Hafsid dynasty (q.v.), coming to power half a century later, that elevated Tunis to the ranks of the most important Mediterranean urban centers. The Hafsids lavished vast sums, generated by a flourishing maritime and trans-Saharan commerce, on the city's physical appearance and cultural atmosphere. They erected mosques, schools, fortresses, and government offices, but also patronized learning and the arts, fostering a golden age. The centrality of Tunis is reflected in the increasing use of the word *Tunisia,* rather than *Ifriqiya,* to designate the territory under Hafsid control.

The deterioration of the dynasty in the sixteenth century exposed Tunis to external pressures. In 1534, the corsair captain Khair al-Din Barbarossa (q.v.) seized the fortress guarding the entrance to the Lake of Tunis at La Goulette, only to be ousted in the following year by Charles V (q.v.), whose victory inaugurated a Hapsburg (q.v.) protectorate over Tunis and its vicinity. The Turkish ruler of Algiers, Ilj Ali (q.v.), occupied the city in 1569, but failed to dislodge the Spanish garrison at La Goulette. This facilitated Spain's recapture of Tunis four years later, but in 1574 Turkish troops drove out the Spaniards for the last time.

Direct Ottoman rule over Tunis lasted only until 1591, when a military coup supplanted Istanbul's governor with a succession of officers from the janissary corps (q.v.)—the deys (q.v.). Their inability to exercise control beyond Tunis and a few other urban centers enabled the beys (q.v.), soldiers responsible for the security of the countryside, to seize power. Well aware of the political and economic importance of Tunis, Murad Bey (q.v.) and his descendants made the city their headquarters and carefully cultivated links with its most prominent families. Rivalries within the Muradid family led to a civil war in which one faction appealed to Algeria's Turkish rulers for support. As a result of these political maneuvers, Tunis experienced a brief Algerian occupation in 1686 and a somewhat longer one between 1694 and 1695. Algerian intervention in Muradid family squabbles stemmed, in large part, from envy of the prosperity of Tunis. Until the middle of the seventeenth century, the city thrived on the corsair (q.v.) raiding that had become a mainstay of its economy in Hafsid times and had contributed greatly to the financial resources of the deys and the beys. Even when the mercantilist philosophy of the European powers prompted them to take steps to limit such activities in the latter half of the century, Tunis' entrepreneurs, both private and governmental, compensated by increasing their participation in legitimate, if not always equally remunerative, commerce.

The Husainid beys' (q.v.) toleration of a revival in corsair activity during the Napoleonic Wars precipitated a British naval bombardment of Tunis in 1816 that put an end to maritime raids launched from the city. For the remainder of the nineteenth century, European businessmen invariably held the upper hand in commercial transactions with Tunisians, while European influences in Tunis became increasingly apparent with the proliferation of western commercial and political institutions. European speculators also promoted infrastructural development projects that included the construction of railway and telegraph lines to expedite contacts between Tunis and Europe.

French troops entered the city in May 1881, formally inaugurating the protectorate. But France's policy of maintaining an appearance of continuity with the precolonial regime enabled Tunis to hold its position as the country's political and economic center of gravity. In the years that followed, the city underwent considerable physical expansion, as the mile or so of marshland between its walls and the lake was reclaimed to become the site of European residential and commercial neighborhoods.

The 1994 national census placed the population of Tunis and the neighboring governorates of Ariana and Ben Arous, which include the city's suburbs, at just over 1.8 million, representing more than a fifth of the country's total population. Sfax, the next largest urban conglomeration, has less than half the population of the Tunis region. Such figures suggest that the capital remains the overwhelmingly dominant urban center of the country and that official efforts to promote the growth and development of other regions, which date from the onset of serious economic planning in the 1960s, have not been entirely successful. Industrialization has concentrated in and around Tunis because the best educated and most highly skilled members of the workforce live there. Its easy access to European markets offers another valuable asset. The potential benefits of this process have been blunted by the city's magnet effect on the unemployed and underemployed elsewhere in Tunisia. Internal migration to Tunis has placed a great strain on the city's infrastructure, particularly in terms of housing and essential public services. While less acute than in many cities of the developing world, these issues nonetheless pose a serious challenge.

The temporary location in Tunis of several regional political organizations raised the international profile of the city in the 1980s. To protest Egypt's peace treaty with Israel, the Arab League (q.v.) moved its secretariat from Cairo to Tunis in 1979. Its offices remained there until Egypt was reintegrated into the Arab world, making a return to Cairo feasible in 1990. When the 1982 Israeli invasion of Lebanon drove the Palestine Liberation Organization (PLO; q.v.) out of Beirut, the Tunisian government, at the urging of the United States, proposed its capital as the new site of the PLO's headquarters. In the years that followed, Tunis became the center of Palestinian political and diplomatic activity and the home of several thousand PLO officials and their families. Pursuant to the terms of the 1993 peace treaty between the PLO and Israel, the Palestinian Authority was formed to administer the Gaza Strip and the West Bank city of Jericho in 1994. Thereafter, a steady stream of PLO administrators, led by Yasser Arafat, left

Tunis to take up residence in Palestine. Although a few PLO departments remained behind, the Palestinian presence in the city dwindled to only a few hundred by mid-1995.

La Tunisie Française. Daily newspaper founded in 1892 to represent the views of French colons. Until it was absorbed by the more liberal *La Presse de Tunisie* (q.v.) shortly after World War II, *La Tunisie Française* was the most outspoken journalistic advocate of colon interests and made the most vehement attacks on Tunisian nationalism.

La Tunisie Martyre. Book published in Paris by Abd al-Aziz Thaalbi (q.v.) in 1920 after a Tunisian delegation to the Versailles Peace Conference failed to win support for self-determination. *La Tunisie Martyre* presented a romanticized view of the preprotectorate era. In it, Thaalbi argued that reforms enacted in the 1860s and 1870s demonstrated the country's progressive inclination, which European meddling and the imposition of the protectorate had derailed. He capped his assertion that Tunisian interests had systematically been sacrificed to those of France by noting the 45,000 Tunisians killed or wounded in World War I. Thaalbi was briefly imprisoned after the appearance of *La Tunisie Martyre*.

The book's insistence on the restoration of the Constitution of 1861 (q.v.; *dustur* in Arabic), which Thaalbi depicted as epitomizing the golden age of the nineteenth century, furnished the name for the Dustur Party, which Thaalbi formed after his release from detention.

Le Tunisien. Published under the direction of the Young Tunisian (q.v.) leader Ali Bash Hamba (q.v.) between 1907 and 1911, *Le Tunisien* was the first French-language newspaper issued by Tunisians. It appeared in that language in order to achieve a wider readership than had been possible with previous Young Tunisian publications, such as *al-Hadira* (q.v.). To maintain contact with sympathizers not literate in French, however, Abd al-Aziz Thaalbi (q.v.) edited an Arabic section within *Le Tunisien* after 1909. In keeping with the Young Tunisians' principles, the paper emphasized the importance of education and advocated equality for all within the protectorate framework. The imposition of a state of emergency following the unrest of 1911, coupled with the arrest or exiling of many Young Tunisians, resulted in the collapse of *Le Tunisien*.

-U-

Ubaidallah (r. 909–934). Founder of the Fatimid dynasty (q.v.). After Abu Abdallah (q.v.) had won over many of Ifriqiya's Berbers with his Shii (q.v.) propaganda against the Aghlabids (q.v.), he introduced

Ubaidallah to the tribes. Stressing the newcomer's descent from Ismail (q.v.), whom militant Shiis recognized as the seventh imam (q.v.), Abu Abdallah hailed him as the mahdi (q.v.) who would inaugurate an era of justice and prosperity for his followers. Fighting in Ubaidallah's name, Abu Abdallah led his Berber forces in the campaign that toppled the Aghlabids in 909, paving the way for the mahdi to assume power in Ifriqiya.

Ubaidallah planned to use Ifriqiya as a launching pad for the extension of Shii rule. He articulated the Fatimid challenge to the Sunni establishment by laying claim to the title of caliph (q.v.) and by dispatching exploratory expeditions into Egypt soon after establishing himself in Ifriqiya. But the heavy taxes necessitated by the mahdi's ambitious plans irritated his supporters, and Abu Abdallah's criticisms of the regime resulted in his execution in 911. In part to ease this unrest, but also to guarantee that he would face no threat from the west, Ubaidallah employed the Berber tribes in military operations in the central and western Maghrib that expanded the Fatimid domain as far as what is now Morocco. Popular disillusion with the new dynasty was a major factor in Ubaidallah's decision to leave Kairouan in 912 and build a new capital at Mahdiyya, a site that had the advantage of orienting the Fatimids toward the eastern lands they coveted. Until his death in 934, the mahdi continued to channel the activism of Ifriqiya's Berbers into wars of conquest in the west, while simultaneously laying the groundwork for an eventual thrust into the heartlands of Islam.

Ulama. *See* **Alim**

Umayyads; Umayyad Dynasty (661–750). Descendants of the Umayyad clan, one of the most prominent merchant families of pre-Islamic Mecca, held the office of caliph (q.v.) from 661 until 750. From their capital in Damascus, they presided over a wave of expansion that established a permanent Arab Muslim presence in Ifriqiya that was most clearly symbolized by the foundation of Kairouan in 670. The Umayyad caliphs promoted the settlement of some Arab tribesmen in their western territories, but the Berbers, many of whom converted to Islam, continued to constitute the majority of the population. In Ifriqiya, as in other parts of their domain, the Umayyads were rarely willing to share political power with non-Arabs, including those who had chosen to become Muslims. This attitude inspired a spirit of resistance that manifested itself in Ifriqiya in the form of Kharajism (q.v.) and sparked serious Berber uprisings in the 730s and 740s. Similar and simultaneous unrest in other areas under Umayyad control resulted in the dynasty's overthrow at the hands of the Abbasids (q.v.), whose governors then replaced Umayyad appointees in Ifriqiya.

Union Démocratique Unioniste (UDU)/Democratic Unionist Union
Political party accorded legal recognition in 1988. Its core ideology is
Arab unity. In keeping with this conviction, the UDU has supported the
Union du Maghreb Arabe (UMA; q.v.) since its inception in 1989. It en-
dorses an active Tunisian role in extending the political and economic
cooperation embodied in the UMA throughout the Arab world. In
Tunisia's first multiparty parliamentary elections in 1989, the UDU
entered candidates in only six of the 25 electoral districts. Capturing
only about 0.25 percent of the total votes cast nationwide, the UDU, like
all the other opposition parties, failed to win a seat in the legislature. The
1994 elections, in which the UDU put forward 130 candidates and presented lists in all but two constituencies, demonstrated Secretary-
General Abderrahmane Tlili's success in creating, over the intervening
five years, a national infrastructure for the party. Although the UDU
share of the total vote did not increase significantly (it received roughly
9,000 ballots of some 2.9 million cast), revised electoral laws gave the
party three of the 19 seats allocated to the opposition. The party publishes a weekly newspaper, *al-Watan* (*The Homeland*).

**Union Générale des Etudiants Tunisiens (UGET)/General Union of
Tunisian Students.** National organization of postsecondary students.
The Neo-Dustur Party (q.v.) played a major role in establishing the
UGET in 1953 and effectively controlled it. Through the UGET, party
leaders orchestrated anticolonial student demonstrations and protests
in the final years of the protectorate and used it, as they did other similar interest groups, to mobilize Tunisian public behind their policies
after independence. That the Neo-Dustur regarded the UGET as little
more than an appendage of the party became evident in 1957. Its
secretary-general publicly endorsed the socialist vision of Ahmad Ben
Salah (q.v.), head of the Union Générale des Travailleurs Tunisiens
(UGTT; q.v.). Ben Salah's program accorded with the essentially leftist orientation of most Tunisian students, but President Habib Bourguiba (q.v.) had not yet approved it. As a result, the secretary-general
was ousted by party loyalists.

Although some of its members continued their efforts to secure
UGET autonomy, the 1960 election of longtime Neo-Dustur stalwart
Muhammad Sayah (q.v.) as secretary-general, along with Bourguiba's
appointment of the rehabilitated Ben Salah as minister of planning in
the following year, brought the student organization into closer conformity with the party. UGET students, for example, joined Neo-Dustur
militants in the confrontation with the French at Bizerte (q.v.) in 1961.
Even after the Neo-Dustur was renamed the Parti Socialiste Dusturien
(PSD; q.v.) in 1964, however, the UGET remained more committed to

socialist policies than did the party and remained more detached from the party than did most other groups affiliated with the PSD.

The 1969 dismissal and arrest of Ben Salah constituted a severe setback to relations between the party and the UGET. At the latter's 1972 congress, with students sympathetic to Ben Salah and hostile to the PSD playing an increasingly influential role, the party intervened to orchestrate the election of a UGET executive bureau loyal to the party. This governmental show of force and intolerance, combined with the malaise fostered in many students by the economic policies of Prime Minister Hadi Nouira (q.v.) and other political leaders of the 1970s, reduced the UGET to a shell of party sympathizers who did not genuinely reflect the interests or concerns of the nation's students. UGET leaders disillusioned by this process were among the earliest supporters of Ben Salah's Mouvement d'Unité Populaire (MUP; q.v.).

At the same time, the emergence of Islamist organizations, spawned by similar feelings of dissatisfaction with the country's social and political environment, provided an outlet for the activism of growing numbers of university students. In 1985, the Mouvement de la Tendance Islamique (MTI; q.v.), which had attracted a significant student following since its crystallization at the end of the 1970s, backed the formation of the Union Générale Tunisienne des Etudiants (UGTE; q.v.). Its popularity quickly surpassed that of the virtually moribund UGET but, like other Islamist groups in the closing days of the Bourguiba era, its activities were closely monitored and controlled by the government.

Following Bourguiba's removal, the government of President Zine el-Abidine Ben Ali (q.v.) endeavored to regain student confidence by sanctioning, for the first time since 1972, UGET activity. Nevertheless, the organization, which had drifted increasingly to the left, proved unable to mount a credible challenge to the UGTE or to entice significant numbers of its members to switch their allegiance. Indeed, not even the banning of the UGTE in 1991 improved the fortunes of the UGET. Although it continued to exist, it exerted only minimal impact on the national political scene.

Union Générale des Travailleurs Tunisiens (UGTT)/General Union of Tunisian Workers). Umbrella labor organization created by Farhat Hached (q.v.) in 1946. In the last decade of the colonial era, the UGTT and the Neo-Dustur (q.v.) closely collaborated in the pursuit of common political, economic, and social goals. An early indication of the union's influence came when it engineered a spate of strikes protesting French opposition to modifications in the protectorate's political structure. In 1950 and 1951, the UGTT was affiliated with the communist-oriented

World Federation of Trade Unions (WFTU), but left it to join the opposing International Confederation of Free Trade Unions (ICFTU). This linkage provided an international forum for the expression of UGTT aspirations in political, economic, and social matters. Many of the contacts made by the UGTT leadership with labor organizers around the world blossomed into overseas backing for the union and, by virtue of the union's close relationship with the Neo-Dustur, for the party's political goals.

Ahmad Ben Salah (q.v.) became secretary-general of the UGTT in 1952, following Hached's assassination by right-wing colons. Ben Salah's support for Habib Bourguiba (q.v.) when Salah Ben Yusuf (q.v.) sought to gain control of the Neo-Dustur in 1955 reflected the union's loyalty to the party leader. Several veteran UGTT officials headed ministries in the first independent government. The UGTT lobbied vigorously for the introduction of a planned socialist economy. When Bourguiba declined to embark on such a course, Ben Salah protested by tendering his resignation. Lest the UGTT then develop into a rival power locus, Bourguiba moved quickly to bring it under Neo-Dustur control. Although the union retained a semblance of autonomy during the next fifteen years, it failed to champion workers' interests effectively when they ran counter to those of the party. Such a course of action naturally discredited the UGTT in the eyes of many of its members.

In the early 1970s, as the economic policies of Prime Minister Hadi Nouira (q.v.) took an increasing social and financial toll on the nation's working class, independent union activity revived. The proliferation of wildcat strikes, even after a government ban on all work stoppages in 1973, suggested a loosening of the party's grip on the UGTT. The union's secretary-general during this period was the longtime labor organizer Habib Achour (q.v.), who also sat on the political bureau of the party, now renamed the Parti Socialiste Dusturien (PSD; q.v.). Seeking to balance conflicting pressures from the government and his labor constituents, he led the UGTT into a 1977 pact with the government intended to improve working conditions and redress the most serious grievances. When few improvements occurred, union agitation continued and Achour left the political bureau. Apprehensive that the government was ready to dissolve the UGTT, its leaders scheduled the first general strike since independence for January 26, 1978. Violent demonstrations accompanied the strike and Achour was arrested, along with hundreds of other UGTT members. The union's new leaders, installed at the behest of the PSD, proved unable to control the organization, and unauthorized strikes and demonstrations persisted.

As a good-will gesture and an indication of the more open political atmosphere he claimed to seek, Muhammad Mzali (q.v.), Nouira's successor as prime minister, pardoned many UGTT activists, including Achour, who resumed his post as secretary-general in 1982. As it had during periods of good relations in the past, the union again cooperated with the party in waging the 1981 electoral campaign. Nevertheless, lingering economic difficulties, occasioned by rising oil prices and a decline in tourism and in remittances from abroad, convinced union leaders of the need to continue pressing for the redress of workers' grievances. As wages stagnated and living conditions failed to improve, the relationship between the union and the government again became adversarial. In 1985, after sanctioning the closure of the UGTT's headquarters, Prime Minister Mzali ordered Achour arrested again. An internal struggle for the control of the union ensued, with Abd al-Aziz Bouraoui, a competitor of Achour who had created the rival Union Nationale Tunisienne du Travail (UNTT; q.v.) in 1983, winning the post of secretary-general in elections at the end of 1986. Hoping to restore union confidence in the party, Bourguiba attended a special UGTT congress shortly thereafter. Despite Bouraoui's pledge of support and the subsequent release of Achour, resentment of government policies persisted among the UGTT's rank and file.

Following Bourguiba's replacement by Zine el-Abidine Ben Ali (q.v.), the new president prevailed upon both Achour and Bouraoui to renounce their claims to the leadership of the union in order to reconcile its contentious factions. In 1989, the UGTT elected as secretary-general Ali Sabahni, a relative newcomer to the organized labor scene. Although Sabahni and his executive bureau did not hesitate to criticize the process of privatization, as well as other government economic policies which they perceived as detrimental to their constituents, the UGTT's direct participation in national politics diminished in the Ben Ali era.

Union Générale Tunisienne des Etudiants (UGTE)/General Tunisian Union of Students. Student organization created by the Mouvement de la Tendance Islamique (MTI; q.v.) in 1985 to mobilize the post-secondary student population, which had been without an effective group to promote its interests since the ruling Parti Socialiste Dusturien (PSD; q.v.) had rendered the Union Générale des Etudiants Tunisiens (UGET; q.v.) virtually impotent in 1972. Until President Habib Bourguiba (q.v.) was replaced by Zine el-Abidine Ben Ali (q.v.) in 1987, the UGTE, like other groups affiliated with the Islamist movement, had to contend with official disapproval.

Impressive victories by UGTE candidates in 1988 university council elections persuaded the new government to sanction the organization and prompted its leaders to call, without success, for a merger of the two unions. With the transformation of the MTI into al-Nahda (q.v.) in the following year, the UGTE, while remaining nominally independent, became the party's auxiliary in the universities and also began extending its influence into secondary schools. Union activists organized protests at several university campuses in 1990. Some of them were directed specifically against educational policies, while others were linked to al-Nahda's conclusion that there were no circumstances under which it would be permitted to participate in the political process. Embedded in the violent antigovernment campaign initiated by al-Nahda extremists early in 1991 were renewed demonstrations and disorders on university campuses across the country, resulting in the detention of many UGTE leaders and the imposition of a ban on the organization.

Union du Maghreb Arabe (UMA)/Arab Maghrib Union. Regional organization established in 1989 by Tunisia, Libya, Algeria, Morocco, and Mauritania to promote political, economic, cultural, and security cooperation within North Africa and to facilitate the formulation of coordinated policies toward states outside the Maghrib. The most important components of the UMA include a council of heads of state, a council of ministers of foreign affairs, and a consultative council comprised of 30 delegates from each of the five member countries. Other commissions and agencies oversee the implementation of specific UMA programs. Mohamed Amamou, a Tunisian, has served as the organization's secretary-general since 1991.

Although the Maghrib states shared comparable heritages before and during the colonial era, and although postindependence leaders made recurrent appeals for Maghrib unity, it was the decision of the European Economic Community (EEC; q.v.) to form a single market early in the 1990s that stimulated the emergence of a regional body. With the EEC accounting for two-thirds of the Maghrib's foreign trade at the start of the decade, North African governments recognized that cooperation would maximize the benefits each could derive from an economically unified Europe while also enabling them to cope most effectively with the challenges posed by the new situation that materialized in 1993. In addition to UMA summit meetings at both the head-of-state and ministerial levels, ministers from its five members frequently meet with their European counterparts to exchange information and discuss questions of mutual interest. Initially focused on economic issues, these meetings turned increasingly toward security matters in 1994 and 1995, as political violence in Algeria threatened to undermine the stability of its UMA neighbors and also to spill over into Europe.

UMA summits have produced strategies for creating a North African customs union, improving transportation and communication networks, enhancing food security, and addressing numerous other topics of regional concern, but relatively few of these goals have been achieved. Within two years of the organization's founding, and for several years thereafter, disagreements over foreign policies obstructed the implementation of cooperative measures. UMA members were not able, for example, to take a common stand in the wake of the Iraqi invasion of Kuwait in 1990. Morocco contributed troops to the multinational force that defended Saudi Arabia and ultimately liberated Kuwait, but its UMA partners were generally critical of that operation. Moroccan views on the Western Sahara have often been at odds with those of other members of the UMA, and there have also been disagreements about the propriety of enforcing the sanctions imposed on Libya by the United Nations in 1992. Despite these stumbling blocks, the UMA has maintained its schedule of regular summit meetings, has rotated the chairmanship of the council of heads of state every six months, and has continued to plan, if not yet widely to implement, an impressive array of regional development programs.

Union Nationale Tunisienne du Travail (UNTT)/National Tunisian Union of Labor. Labor organization established in 1983 as an alternative to the Union Générale des Travailleurs Tunisiens (UGTT; q.v.) by Abd al-Aziz Bouraoui and six other UGTT executives expelled from the union for their vigorous support of the Parti Socialiste Dusturien (PSD; q.v.). The UNTT rejoined its parent organization in 1986, following the ouster of Habib Achour (q.v.) and the restoration of party control over the UGTT. Less than a year later, Bouraoui was elected secretary-general of the UGTT.

United States. The first contacts between the United States and Tunisia occurred when Tunisian corsairs (q.v.) seized American merchant vessels in the mid-1780s. In 1797, the United States signed a treaty with Hamuda Bey (q.v.) that insured American shipping against attack in return for a payment of just over $100,000. Periodic payments to the Husainids continued until 1815, when an American fleet forced them, along with other North African rulers, to accept a treaty that included the renunciation of corsair activities.

Events in Tunisia did not again impinge upon the United States until World War II. American soldiers saw combat in Tunisia from February to May 1943, sustaining especially heavy casualties in a massive German offensive at the Kasserine pass (q.v.). In the decade between the end of the war and Tunisian independence, Habib Bourguiba (q.v.) visited the United States in an attempt to marshall support for the nationalist movement. Despite the existence of some helpful links between American labor organizations and the Union Générale des Travailleurs Tunisiens (UGTT) (q.v.), Bourguiba found the American government's opposition to colonialism diluted by a desire not to alienate France and Great Britain, key components in the emerging Atlantic alliance.

Once the protectorate ended, however, the United States bolstered the pro-western and strategically located country with generous amounts of assistance. In the first three decades of independence, Tunisia received more than $1 billion from the United States, its largest aid donor. Until the 1970s, American funds were earmarked primarily for development projects. The abortive Tunisian-Libyan union of 1974, fears that Libya would seek to capitalize on Tunisian political and economic unrest in the late 1970s, the 1980 raid on Gafsa (q.v.), and the frequently bitter disputes between the two neighbors all heightened American concerns about the Libyan regime's intentions toward Tunisia and led to a new emphasis on military rather than economic aid.

Despite Bourguiba's enthusiasm for it, the Tunisian-American connection provoked criticism from several quarters in the closing years of his presidency. Some antagonists faulted the United States for its tolerance of human rights abuses by the Tunisian government, especially in its dealings with alleged members of the Mouvement de la Tendance Islamique (MTI; q.v.) and other Islamist organizations. The dangers of too close an affiliation with any superpower worried some of Bourguiba's opponents, while still others argued that the money spent on purchasing American weaponry would have been better allocated to development needs. The first anti-American demonstrations followed the failure of the United States to condemn a destructive 1985 Israeli air raid on a Palestine Liberation Organization (PLO; q.v.) compound in the suburbs of Tunis that claimed Tunisian as well as Palestinian lives. Two additional factors contributed to the Tunisian sense of outrage over this incident. The United States had pressured Bourguiba to allow the PLO to relocate its headquarters in Tunis after Israel had driven it from Beirut in 1982 and had only recently provided the president with assurances of support in the event of an external attack on his country (which, at the time, Washington assumed would come from Libya).

After Bourguiba's removal in 1987, President Zine el-Abidine Ben Ali (q.v.) sought to continue the good relationship that Bourguiba had cultivated with the United States by securing the Reagan administration's endorsement of the political reforms he introduced during his first months in office. Less than a year later, however, Israeli commandos murdered Khalil al-Wazir (Abu Jihad), a high-ranking PLO official, in his home outside Tunis. Many Tunisians believed that the United States had known of (if it had not given its approval to) this foray, and some even suspected their own government of complicity in the attack, stimulating widespread discontent.

Ben Ali denounced the dispatch of the U.S. led multinational military force to the Arabian peninsula in the wake of the Iraqi invasion of Kuwait in the summer of 1990. His government made no effort to prevent anti-American demonstrations in Tunis and elsewhere in the country. United States economic assistance to Tunisia plummeted from $31 million annually at the beginning of the decade to a mere $1 million in 1992. Military aid was eliminated altogether. Nevertheless, in light of Tunisia's geostrategic importance and Ben Ali's overall propensity toward good relations with the West, the United States recognized the danger of undermining his government by withholding much-needed aid, particularly at a time when neighboring Algeria was torn by a civil war with potentially disastrous consequences for the stability of the entire Maghrib. As a result, aid disbursements returned to their prewar levels in 1993, and a good working relationship was restored.

Tunisian dissidents, however, continued to voice the concern that U.S. support facilitated the government's exclusion of Islamist groups (and other critics) from the political process. An official State Department report in 1994 cited human rights abuses and restrictions on the freedom of the press in Tunisia, but under the circumstances the Clinton administration hesitated to take punitive action against a government that portrayed itself as liberal and opposed only to religious extremism.

Uqba ibn Nafi (fl. 670–683). Commander of the Arab army that entered Ifriqiya in 670. Following a practice dating from the earliest Arab expansion outside the Arabian peninsula, he established Kairouan as the region's first administrative center and as a garrison city for his bedouin troops. Uqba encountered stiff opposition from Kusaila (q.v.), the leader of the Berber resistance to the Arabs, and died in an ambush laid by the Berber chieftain in 683.

al-Urbus, Battle of. Confrontation in 909 between the Aghlabid (q.v.) army and dissident Berber tribes led by Abu Abdallah (q.v.). The crushing defeat sustained by the Aghlabids at al-Urbus, some 25 kilometers (15 miles) southeast of present-day Le Kef, prompted Ziyadat Allah III (q.v.) to flee to Egypt, signaling the dynasty's collapse.

Utica. Phoenician city approximately 35 kilometers (20 miles) northwest of Carthage, with which it was allied during the Punic Wars (q.v.). Utica served as the capital of the Roman province of Africa after the destruction of Carthage in 146 B.C.E. and remained the principal city of the region until Carthage was revived early in the Christian era.

-V-

Vandals. Germanic tribe that entered North Africa from Spain early in the fifth century. They overran the Roman province of Africa Proconsularis in 429, with only the city of Carthage withstanding their onslaught. Its capture a decade later by Genseric (q.v.) confirmed the Vandals' supremacy in Africa and forced Rome to recognize their sovereignty. For the remainder of the century, the Vandals successfully resisted all efforts to curtail their raids throughout the central Mediterranean, which included the sack of Rome itself in 455.

By and large, the Vandals did not try to impose new customs or practices on their African subjects. They ruled as an alien elite, maintaining only limited contacts with the indigenous population. Beyond their racial distinctiveness, the Vandals were Arians and vigorously persecuted adherents of other Christian sects. Harassment of this kind diminished only in the 520s under the leadership of Hilderic (q.v.). Hilderic was more concerned with the threat posed to his kingdom by Berber tribes resentful of foreign domination and he mobilized his forces to contain them. Nevertheless, they defeated him in 530. When his rivals in the Vandal nobility deposed him, the Byzantine emperor Justinian, with whom Hilderic had forged an alliance, intervened. A Byzantine army vanquished Gelimer, Hilderic's successor, south of Carthage in 533. The victors enslaved their prisoners and seized the lands of the aristocracy, effectively terminating the Vandal presence in Africa.

Les Vieux Turbans. Literally, the "Old Turbans." Name derisively applied by the Young Tunisians (q.v.) to members of the religious establishment who resisted their introduction of European concepts and practices, particularly in education. As the Young Tunisians expressed their demands more stridently after 1906, Les Vieux Turbans succeeded in convincing many protectorate officials of the movement's dangers. A policy of placating the conservative, traditional religious establishment replaced one of supporting the progressive ideas of the Young Tunisians.

La Voix du Tunisien. Newspaper published by the Dustur Party beginning in 1930. Its editor was Habib Bourguiba (q.v.). The decision to publish in French was an attempt to circumvent the government's stringent regulation of the Arabic-language press, but also reflected the growing number of young, French-educated Tunisians involved in the party. *La Voix du Tunisien* became the principal outlet for the ideas of this new generation of Dustur members. Disturbed by the party leadership's lack of initiative, Bourguiba and his associates hoped to use the paper to galvanize a more effective opposition to the protectorate. In 1933, however, the government placed French-language newspapers under restrictions similar to those imposed on the Arabic press, leading to the suspension of *La Voix du Tunisien.*

Voizard, Pierre (1896–1982). French resident general of Tunisia from 1953 to 1954. At the outset of his term, Voizard released many Neo-Dustur militants from prison. He then opened negotiations with individuals not affiliated with the Neo-Dustur, hoping to reach with them a political settlement avoiding the most extreme of the nationalists' demands. His strategy failed, however, since the Neo-Dustur had sufficient influence to sway public opinion against any arrangement it had not concluded or at least sanctioned. Voizard's efforts to sidestep the mainstream nationalist movement contributed to a wave of violence requiring the presence of additional French military forces. With the resident general unable to control the deteriorating political situation in the summer of 1954, the government in Paris agreed to begin talks that led, almost a year later, to the internal autonomy accord presaging complete independence.

-W-

Waqf. In Islamic law, a form of unalienable property set aside as a pious trust. In Tunisia (and elsewhere in North Africa) the more commonly used term for such property is *habus* (q.v.).

Women. A few outspoken individuals, among them the Islamic reformer Tahar Haddad (q.v.), criticized the traditional status and role of women in Tunisian society as early as the 1930s. Haddad's views struck a responsive chord with many of the western-educated leaders of the Neo-Dustur party (q.v.), including Habib Bourguiba (q.v.). Convinced that the nation could not squander the half of its human resources that its female population represented, Bourguiba initiated a campaign, almost immediately after independence in 1956, to enable women to contribute more fully to Tunisia's development by enhancing their status and encouraging them to participate actively in the nation's life.

The centerpiece of this program was the Personal Status Code of 1956 (q.v.), a bold attack on many literal and traditional interpretations of Islam affecting women. The code abolished polygyny, established a minimum age for marriage, required the woman's consent to any marriage arranged by her family, and lifted existing restrictions on interfaith marriages. By giving the courts the sole power to terminate marriages and by allowing either spouse to initiate divorce proceedings, the code deprived men of their traditional right to dissolve a marriage unilaterally by oral declaration. Finally, the code increased women's shares of inheritances.

Although the government had the power to alter the laws readily, it could not so readily dictate adjustments in personal attitudes. The code quickly came under attack by religious leaders and other conservatives. Many older, more traditional women, who knew only the social organization that is outlined in the Quran, were also uncomfortable with the changes.

Bourguiba refused to retreat, although he did come to appreciate the limitations of a purely legislative approach to social change, as had been the case with the Personal Status Code. After the enactment of this sweeping legislation, he tended to rely on persuading Tunisians to accept change rather than imposing it. To assist in this process, the Neo-Dustur organized the Union Nationale des Femmes Tunisiennes (UNFT) to promote women's interests. Education, however, was the most effective weapon in the government's arsenal.

Families were encouraged to send their daughters to school to acquaint young women with modern values and to inspire them to reconsider traditional practices. The long-term success of this appeal is reflected in school-enrollment statistics for the 1992–1993 school year. More than 900,000 females were in school, as opposed to 84,400 at independence in 1956. They accounted for 46 percent of all primary-school pupils, 43 percent of those in secondary school, and 50 percent of all university students. As Bourguiba had predicted, better education brought Tunisian women into the workforce in considerable numbers. In the mid-1990s, almost half a million (494,000) worked outside the home, comprising a fifth of the total workforce. In 1956, working women numbered only 37,540.

A campaign against traditional dress, especially the practice of veiling, followed the passage of the Personal Status Code. No articles of clothing were banned outright, but women were forbidden to wear the veil, which Bourguiba criticized as regressive, demeaning, and impractical, in school. For many years, the percentage of young women opting for a western style of dress grew in proportion to female education. Older women, particularly those from rural regions where the impact of Europe had never been as pronounced as in the cities, found it wrenching to give up traditional garments that had lifelong associations with modesty and appropriate behavior.

Family planning was one area concerning women in which government objectives fell short of the mark. In an effort to curb population growth, the Personal Status Code limited government subsidies to a family's first four children and also legalized abortions for women with five or more children. In 1973, all women were made eligible for abortions, regardless of family size, although the government stressed that it did not view abortion as a satisfactory solution to Tunisia's demographic problems.

Systematic programs promoting birth control, begun in 1964, have invariably encountered opposition. Much of it is rooted in traditional beliefs, or circumstances that no longer prevail (such as the once high infant mortality rate), the need to have children who can help work the land and care for parents in their old age, and male attitudes about virility. Although Islam does not explicitly forbid birth control, opposition from religious leaders has occasionally hampered family-planning projects, as have shortages of trained medical and technical personnel needed for their effective implementation. Nevertheless, a combination of the more widespread practice of birth control, the acceptance of the desirability of smaller families, and the older average age at which young women were marrying (over 25 in the 1990s, as opposed to only 19 in the 1950s) caused the average number of children per woman in the childbearing years to drop steadily from 7.1 in the early 1960s to just under 5 in the mid-1980s to 2.9 in 1994. The greater absolute number of women in that category, however, has prevented the crude birth rate of about 2.3 percent a year from declining as dramatically.

The Mouvement de la Tendance Islamique (MTI; q.v.) and other Islamist groups that emerged in the 1970s and 1980s demanded the reversal of many of the changes that had affected Tunisian women since independence. Their spokesmen attacked the Personal Status Code, much of which they viewed as contradicting the Quran, called for the revival of traditional practices limiting contacts between the sexes, and urged women to return to traditional clothing, including the veil, to symbolize their rejection of foreign influences and their emphasis on indigenous Tunisian values. Numerous young women, frustrated with the inability of Bourguiba's secular government to resolve the country's serious social and economic problems, and disillusioned by the pervasiveness of western culture in Tunisia, joined one or another of the Islamist organizations.

After becoming president in November 1987, Zine el-Abidine Ben Ali (q.v.) agreed to some of the demands of the Islamic groups, but not those pertaining to the status of women. On the contrary, his public assertions of opposition to any abridgement of the provisions of the Personal Status Code were reinforced by the establishment of a Ministry of Women and Family Affairs. In 1992, supplements to the code expanded women's rights further by guaranteeing their control over their personal affairs after marriage and by establishing a state fund to provide support for divorced women whose husbands defaulted on alimony payments. Other social legislation in the 1990s made it possible for women to gain custody of children following a divorce, while a 1994 labor law explicitly noted women's right to work, as well as their rights to equal pay and equal training.

Wood, Richard (1806–1900). British consul general in Tunis from 1855 to 1879. His efforts to promote British investments and strengthen the beys' ties with the Ottoman Empire made the years of his service in Tunisia an era of intense Anglo-French rivalry. He believed that substantial infusions of European capital would expedite the development of Tunisia's resources and would shore up the country's depleted treasury, while earning handsome profits for investors. Wood's carefully cultivated friendship with Prime Minister Mustafa Khaznadar (q.v.) facilitated the formation of the Anglo-Tunisian Bank (q.v.) in 1857 and guaranteed a sympathetic hearing for British proposals to augment Tunisia's infrastructure with the construction of railway and telegraph lines. In order to ensure the security of such ventures, Wood joined his French counterpart, Léon Roches (q.v.), in urging Muhammad Bey (q.v.) to enact the Ahd al-aman (q.v.) and the Constitution of 1861 (q.v.). The consul further solidified the British position in Tunisia by negotiating in 1863 an Anglo-Tunisian convention (q.v.) giving British businessmen certain advantages in return for their adherence to Tunisian law. The establishment of the International Finance Commission (q.v.) did little to impede the relationship between Wood and Khaznadar. Indeed, Khaznadar continued to award lucrative concessions to British subjects in the hope that Great Britain would support him in his rivalry with the commission's chairman, the reform-minded Khair al-Din al-Tunsi (q.v.), and his French patrons. Wood's endorsement of Khaznadar could not, however, insulate the prime minister from the wrath of the French and Italian members of the commission, who demanded that the bey dismiss him in 1873. The opportunistic Wood lost no time in opening lines of communication with his successor, Khair al-Din. The new prime minister's interest in a good relationship with the Ottoman Empire, combined with his desire not to become wholly dependent on France, enabled the British consul to continue to exert some influence over Tunisian affairs, at least until Great Britain's Mediterranean policy, particularly its commitment to the integrity of the Ottoman Empire, shifted during the 1870s. Wood, finding his superiors in the Foreign Office less and less interested in his plans for augmenting British influence in Tunisia, distanced himself from Khair al-Din. French investors stepped into the breach with a vigor that alarmed the prime minister. This British reversal, by depriving Khair al-Din of a strong European ally, doomed his efforts to temper French ambitions and he was driven from office in 1877. Thus, despite Wood's twenty-year struggle, the prospect of Tunisia's entering the French orbit was a near certainty by the time of his departure from the country in 1879.

-Y-

Yahya ibn Ghaniyya (?–1238). Brother of Ali ibn Ghaniyya (q.v.) and a commander in his army during its assault on al-Muwahhid territories in the Maghrib in the 1180s. Yahya continued the campaign after Ali died in the Jarid, hoping that a conclusive defeat of the al-Muwahhids would result in a restoration of the al-Murabits, to whom his family had remained loyal. Capitalizing on the resentment many residents of Ifriqiya harbored toward the al-Muwahhids, Yahya forged a coalition of Arab and Berber tribes that captured Tunis in 1203. The al-Muwahhid general Abd al-Wahid ibn Abi Hafs (q.v.) retook the city two years later, but Yahya continued to harass the al-Muwahhids and their Hafsid (q.v.) successors until his death in 1238.

Young Tunisians. Small group of loosely organized political reformers active in the late nineteenth and early twentieth centuries. Virtually all the Young Tunisians shared a commitment to Salafiyya (q.v.) principles and at least some exposure to nontraditional education, often at Sadiqi College (q.v.). While they insisted on the need to protect their Arabo-Islamic heritage, they did not seek to terminate the protectorate, for they believed that Tunisia could benefit from a relationship with France if it were based on the equality of Frenchmen and Tunisians. Consequently, they called upon the French authorities to liberalize the protectorate regime and to guarantee Tunisians the same rights accorded to Frenchmen.

The Young Tunisians' backgrounds persuaded them that they were in a unique position to facilitate their country's integration into the modern world. Convinced that they understood both groups, the Young Tunisians envisioned a role for themselves as explicators of western culture to less sophisticated Tunisians and as interpreters of Tunisia's Arabo-Islamic culture to the French. As early as 1888, partisans of the Salafiyya movement began to publish a newspaper, *al-Hadira* (q.v.), stressing the need for social change within an Islamic context while also urging the selective adaptation of western ideas. Many of those involved in the *al-Hadira* venture formed the core of the movement. In 1896, Bashir Sfar (q.v.) organized the Khalduniyya (q.v.), an educational society offering Arabic-language instruction in a variety of modern subjects to students in traditional institutions, particularly the Zaituna Mosque-University (q.v.). The resident general backed Sfar's effort, which he exerted with a view to mediating between the two cultures.

The Young Tunisians' efforts to straddle the cultural divide elicited criticisms from both European and Tunisian opponents. Conservative Tunisians attacked their enthusiasm for western ideals and practices, while the colons, especially those at the bottom of the socioeconomic ladder, feared the inevitable long-term implications of the equitable relationship the Young Tunisians advocated. In 1907, Ali Bash Hamba, an activist in the movement, began publishing *Le Tunisien* (q.v.), a newspaper designed to disseminate accurate information about the Young Tunisians' goals to French readers. *Le Tunisien* especially sought to appeal to liberal segments of the French community whose support, it was hoped, would offset the antagonism of the colons.

The limited success enjoyed by the paper in this endeavor merely served to heighten the anxiety of the colons, who sabotaged any expansion of modern educational facilities for Tunisians and insisted that protectorate officials concentrate the resources available for Tunisian education almost exclusively on vocational training. The implementation of this policy severely restricted Tunisians' social, economic, and political opportunities, creating acute frustrations. As the Young Tunisians grew correspondingly more strident, they alienated those protectorate officials who, despite colon apprehensions, had continued to regard them as potential links between the two cultures.

At roughly the same time, the reformers' increasing estrangement from the traditional religious establishment culminated in a bitter battle triggered by Young Tunisian criticisms of the Zaituna Mosque-University curriculum as hopelessly outmoded. Contrary to the accusations of their Muslim opponents, the Young Tunisians sought to reform, not abandon, Islamic traditions. They amply demonstrated their commitment to Islam both in their active support for Tripolitanian Muslims during the Italian invasion of 1911 and in their opposition to the desecration of the Jallaz Cemetery (q.v.) in the same year.

Shortly afterward, the Young Tunisians embarked on a collision course with the government. Following an accident in which an Italian tram driver ran down a Tunisian child, the movement's leaders launched a boycott of the trams. As conditions for ending the boycott, they demanded the removal of all Italian workers from the tram lines and a pledge that French and Tunisian workers on the lines would receive equal pay for equal work. When the Young Tunisians ignored the government's order to end the boycott, their leaders were arrested and many of them exiled from the country. Given the small, tightly knit nature of the movement, this crackdown and the government's subsequent declaration of a state of emergency, which remained in effect through the First World War, precluded the revival of Young Tunisian activities. A number of former Young Tunisians did, however, reappear on the political scene after the war to play an important role in the creation of the Dustur Party.

-Z-

Zaituna Mosque-University. Main mosque of Tunis, founded by the Umayyad (q.v.) governor Ubaidallah ibn al-Habbab in 732. In addition to its function as a place of worship, it served as one of the major institutions in North Africa for the education of religious scholars. In the premodern era, the vast majority of Tunisian ulama were trained at Zaituna, but students also came from throughout the Maghrib, the eastern Arab world, and sub-Saharan Africa.

Beginning in the nineteenth century, the nature of the training given to Zaituna students aroused controversy. This was because recipients of a Zaituna education customarily filled not only positions in the religious establishment but also important offices in the government bureaucracy. As contacts with Europe intensified, such prominent individuals as Khair al-Din al-Tunsi (q.v.) stressed the relevance of instruction in modern subjects in tandem with the traditional Islamic curriculum. After 1881, Zaituna came under the supervision of the French-administered Directorate of Public Education. Its officials recognized the possible repercussions if they, as non-Muslims, tried to impose curriculum revisions on the Zaituna faculty and thus made no such attempts. The leaders of the Young Tunisians (q.v.) did voice vociferous demands for modifications in the university course of study, but few changes occurred during the protectorate. After World War I, Tunisians with secular, western educations increasingly assumed roles of political leadership, and Tunisia's ulama, along with their schools, were relegated to the background.

Soon after attaining independence in 1956, the government placed all religious educational institutions, including Zaituna, under the control of the Ministry of Education. In 1961, the University of Tunis was established and shortly afterward the mosque-university was linked to it as a faculty of theology and religious sciences. Although Zaituna's amalgamation with the state university somewhat blurred its identity, it retained many of its institutional characteristics as well as its traditional conservatism. In the early 1970s, students and faculty at the Zaituna, distressed by what they perceived as a deterioration of the country's moral climate, played instrumental roles in the formation of such organizations as the Association pour la Sauvegarde du Coran (q.v.). Similarly, it was from within the Zaituna that the Mouvement de la Tendance Islamique (MTI; q.v.) and other Islamist groups that emerged at the end of the 1970s and in the early years of the next decade drew many of their most dedicated adherents.

A series of higher education reforms in 1986 and 1987 divided the faculties of the University of Tunis into a number of separate universities, one of which was Zaituna. It thus regained its identity as a distinct institution, although it, like the other new units, continued under the supervision of the Ministry of Higher Education. The enrollment at the Zaituna University in 1992 stood at just over 2,000 students.

Zama, Battle of. Engagement in which Scipio Africanus (q.v.) defeated the Carthaginian army under Hannibal (q.v.) in 202 B.C.E. Fought near the contemporary city of Maktar, the battle crushed Carthaginian hopes of expelling the Romans from North Africa and ended the Second Punic War (q.v.).

Zanata Confederation. League of Berber tribes from the western Maghrib. Their alliance with the Spanish Umayyads (q.v.) in the tenth century made them a potentially serious threat to the Fatimids (q.v.). Zanata hostility toward Ifriqiya was heightened by the close ties between the Sanhaja Berbers (q.v.), their traditional rivals, and the Fatimids. After that dynasty relocated in Egypt, its Zirid (q.v.) successors divided its lands, with Hammad ibn Buluggin (q.v.) establishing a state in the central Maghrib that served as a buffer against Zanata forays into Ifriqiya.

Zarruk, Ahmad (?–1881). Mamluk (q.v.), protégé of Mustafa Khaznadar (q.v.), and brother-in-law of the beys Muhammad (q.v.) and Muhammad al-Sadiq (q.v.). Appointed governor of the Jarid in the early 1860s, he gained notoriety for his brutal repression of the 1864 rebellion in the Sahil. Zarruk afterward served as minister of war from 1865 until 1870 and as minister of the navy from 1877 until 1881.

Zarruk, Muhammad Larbi (?–1822). One of the few native Tunisians (as opposed to mamluks; q.v.) to wield significant political authority under the Husainid beys (q.v.). Raised at the Bardo Palace (q.v.), where his father was a member of the ruler's entourage, he developed close ties with many of his contemporaries in the royal family. In 1815, he became the bey's chief minister after conspiring in the assassination of the incumbent. Zarruk's thirst for power earned him many enemies and ultimately kindled suspicions that he was plotting against the royal family itself. Mahmud Bey (q.v.) ordered his arrest and execution in 1822.

Zirids; Zirid Dynasty (973–1148). At first vassals of the Fatimids (q.v.), the Zirids ruled Ifriqiya themselves from 973 until 1148. When the Fatimids left the Maghrib, they appointed Buluggin ibn Ziri (q.v.), a Berber ally of longstanding, as their viceroy, giving him the title of amir, or prince. His death in 984 led to the division of his domains among his heirs, but a civil war three decades later resulted in the emergence of two distinct entities, a principality ruled by Hammad ibn Buluggin (q.v.) in the central Maghrib and a Zirid state within Ifriqiya itself.

Prior to the civil war, the Zirids had wavered between maintaining the loyalty to the Fatimids, on which their legitimacy theoretically rested, and pursuing policies independent of their Egyptian overlords. After it, the dynasty increasingly distanced itself from the Fatimids. In contrast with their Shii (q.v.) predecessors, the Sunni Zirids cultivated the Maliki (q.v.) religious leadership and lavished attention on traditionally Sunni mosques. Amir al-Muizz (q.v.) went so far as to acquiesce in the massacre of many Shii Muslims when he assumed power in 1016. Later in his reign, al-Muizz recognized the spiritual leadership of the Abbasid caliph (q.v.), further dissolving the dynasty's ties with the Fatimids.

Nevertheless, it was deteriorating economic conditions at least as much as religious convictions and dynastic political aspirations that precipitated the final Fatimid-Zirid split in 1049. Control of the caravan routes from sub-Saharan Africa to the Mediterranean had greatly contributed to Fatimid and early Zirid prosperity. By the mid-eleventh century, however, those routes were shifting toward termini in Egypt, the Fatimid political center of gravity, and toward the western Maghrib, where the rise of the al-Murabits was creating new economic hubs. Kairouan, the Zirid capital and a traditional caravan entrepôt, experienced severe economic setbacks that had an impact throughout the province. Widespread disorders erupted, and al-Muizz became convinced that only a break with Egypt, ending Ifriqiya's status as a Fatimid backwater, would quell the rampant turmoil and enable him to restore a measure of stability to his domains.

The Fatimids responded to this mutiny by sending to Ifriqiya a band of Arab nomadic tribes, the Banu Hilal (q.v.), that had proven disruptive in the Nile valley. The Zirids did not at first understand the potential danger of this "Hilalian invasion." Rather than repulsing its vanguard, they tried to use the tribes to police rural regions. The Zirids were, however, quickly overwhelmed by the nomads, who defeated their army at Haidaran (q.v.) in 1052 and sacked Kairouan in 1057, forcing them to evacuate the capital and take up residence in Mahdiyya. Scholars have long debated the magnitude of the nomads' impact on Ifriqiya. The Banu Hilal were not responsible for the province's economic decline, which had begun before their arrival, but the increase in nomadism and its debilitating effects on agriculture aggravated an already disintegrating situation. A more significant consequence of these migrations was the growth of a substantial Arab population in Ifriqiya, leading to a process of Arabization that intensified with the subsequent appearance of a similar Arab nomadic group, the Banu Sulaim (q.v.).

The Zirids' flight to Mahdiyya instilled in the amirs a new interest in the Mediterranean basin, which they demonstrated by initiating maritime raids on the commerce of the emerging Italian city-states and the recently established Norman (q.v.) dominions in Sicily. But the Berber rulers never fully mastered this new environment. In 1087, a European coalition captured Mahdiyya, which the Zirids recovered only after paying a ransom. Both Arab nomads and Normans continued to hem in the Zirids, and later amirs sought help from the al-Murabits. But the Christians' unwillingness to countenance a strong Muslim force in Ifriqiya prompted them to strengthen their own hand there, precluding such intervention. By the 1130s, the dynasty had become so debilitated that it was forced to turn to the Normans for protection against its other enemies. The Normans took advantage of this situation to seize the entire coast of Ifriqiya except for Tunis in 1148. The reigning Zirid amir took refuge with his Hammadid kinsmen, and the family's rule came to an end.

Ziyadat Allah I (r. 817–838). Third Aghlabid (q.v.) ruler. Like his predecessors, he faced opposition from the many Arabs in the army who resented the Aghlabid family's accession to power and its subsequent efforts to assert its authority over all the institutions of the state, including the military. In 824, however, Ziyadat Allah I repressed the most serious revolt that had yet arisen. He initiated a series of campaigns against Byzantine Sicily in 827, in part to provide an outlet for the militancy of the Arab tribes, but also to win the support of Ifriqiya's religious leadership by establishing his credentials as a ruler committed to Islamic values and the expansion of the faith. By the time of his death, much of the island had been brought under Aghlabid control. The income derived from Sicily helped assuage the Arab soldiery, as did an amnesty to the leaders of the rebellion, which Ziyadat Allah I granted in 829. He bequeathed prosperity and stability to his successors, enabling them to consolidate their power and to indulge in building projects, both in Ifriqiya proper and in Sicily, that subsequently characterized the dynasty.

Ziyadat Allah III (r. 903–909). Last Aghlabid (q.v.) ruler. His accession, secured by murdering rival claimants, reinforced the image of Aghlabid immorality and unscrupulousness that Abu Abdallah (q.v.) had already begun to stress among the Berber tribes and thus to undermine the dynasty. A steady stream of defeats at the hands of Abu Abdallah marked his reign. After the last and most devastating of these setbacks, the Battle of al-Urbus (q.v.) in 909, Ziyadat Allah III fled to Egypt and the dynasty collapsed.

Selected Twentieth-Century Bibliography: Introduction

For many years, research and writing on Tunisian topics were largely the preserve of French scholars. Although other historians and social scientists, including many from the English-speaking world, have taken a considerable interest in the country since its independence in 1956, it nevertheless remains true, forty years later, that the majority of material published on Tunisia continues to appear in French. French researchers still produce many of these studies but more and more frequently they are the products of Tunisian scholars. Another significant trend in the study of Tunisia is the growing volume of material written in Arabic by Tunisians and others. This bibliography does not include Arabic titles, but its extensive citation of French and English books and articles, along with a smattering of publications in such other European languages as Spanish, Italian, German, and Dutch, does accurately reflect the nature of twentieth-century scholarship on Tunisia.

Several genres of writing have been excluded from this bibliography. Despite their relative abundance, travelers' accounts have been omitted, except for occasional examples that provide significant insights to the society or are among a limited number of sources available on a specific time period or a specific event. For the most part, these items tell more about the observer than about the observed. Such information can be extremely useful, but it does not directly enhance (and may well impede) the reader's understanding of Tunisian history or society. Tourist guides, of which there are many, a number of them in English, have also been excluded. In keeping with the dictionary's historical emphasis, modern novels, poetry, short stories, literary anthologies, and essays on literary criticism have not generally been listed. This should not, however, be construed as suggestive of a Tunisian deficiency in belles lettres. On the contrary, Tunisian authors publish prolifically. Many are widely read and critically acclaimed in European and Arab circles. Dictionary entries on several prominent literary figures of the modern era include references to their best-known works.

The bibliography begins with a list of general works on Tunisia that encompasses surveys of the country and items dealing with primary source materials. A section enumerating books and articles on geographical topics follows. The remainder of the bibliography is presented chronologically. The first portion, on pre-Islamic Tunisia, lists only a representative sampling of general books and articles on the Carthaginian, Roman, Vandal, and Byzantine eras. Subsequent segments bring together articles and books on the history, politics, economy, and culture of periods identified as "Early Arab Rule" (670–973); "The Berber Dynasties" (973–1574); "The Ottomans and the Deys" (1574–1705); "The Husainid Era" (until 1881); and "The Protectorate Era" (1881–1956). Overlapping the time frame of the last section is a topical category devoted to "Nationalism" and recording material on the country's nationalist movement from the late nineteenth century until independence.

For the years since 1956, entries are also divided thematically. Books and articles on domestic and international politics make up one section; economic matters are the subject of a second; and a third focuses on sociocultural issues broadly defined.

Finally, four periodicals that are especially helpful in keeping abreast of contemporary developments in, as well as contemporary scholarship on, Tunisia deserve mention. *Jeune Afrique* is a weekly newsmagazine published in Paris. Its scope extends well beyond Tunisia with an emphasis on the African and Arab worlds, but *Jeune Afrique* closely follows Tunisian events. The *Annuaire de l'Afrique du Nord* is an annual survey of all the Maghrib countries published under the auspices of the Centre National de Recherche Scientifique (CNRS) in Paris. In addition to scholarly articles, often constructed around a single theme, the *Annuaire* contains an extensive chronology and a detailed bibliography of new publications in European languages and in Arabic that lists books, articles from scholarly journals, relevant items from the popular press, government publications, and dissertations. Owing to the magnitude of this undertaking, each *Annuaire* comes out only several years after the year which it covers, but it is an indispensable reference work for any serious examination of modern Tunisia.

A second chronology and bibliography, although only of recently published works in French, appears quarterly in *Monde Arabe. Maghreb-Machrek* is a journal published under the auspices of the French government's Direction de la Documentation Française. Unquestionably the most detailed bibliography devoted specifically to Tunisia is the one compiled by the *Revue de l'Institut des Belles Lettres Arabes (IBLA)*. Each issue of this Tunisian scholarly journal contains a list of new books (frequently with synopses) and articles on the country in all languages and in virtually every field of the humanities and social sciences, making it an excellent starting point for research on the country.

Reference Works and General Studies

Abid, Mounir. "Notes sur l'organisation médicale dans la Tunisie du XIXè siècle: une analyse préliminaire des documents de santé publique et de médecine d'après les registres des archives nationales de Tunisie." *Revue d'Histoire Maghrébine* 21, nos. 79–80 (1995): 475–79.

Archives Générales de la Présidence du Conseil du Gouvernement Tunisien. *Inventaire des documents d'archives turcs du Dar El-Bey (Tunis)*. Paris: Presses Universitaires de France, 1961.

Attal, Robert, and Joseph Avivi. *Registres matrimoniaux de la communauté juive portugaise de Tunis aux XVIIIème et XIXème siècles*. Jerusalem: Ben Zvi Institute, 1989.

Bachrouch, Taoufik. "L'historiographie tunisienne de 1968 à 1985: l'époque moderne." *Revue de l'Institut des Belles Lettres Arabes* 50, no. 159 (1987): 75–90.

Belaid, Habib, and Kmar Mechri-Bendana. "Les archives microfilmées de la commission des sources de l'histoire tunisienne en France." *Revue Tunisienne de Communication* 12 (1987): 37–56.

———. "Archives, recherche historique et informatique: une expérience tunisienne." *Annuaire de l'Afrique du Nord* 25 (1986): 597–602.

Ben Ali, M., Miguel de Epalza, and Abdelhakim Gafsi. *Bibliographie tunisienne concernant l'histoire de l'Espagne, 1956–1973*. Tunis: Institut National d'Archéologie et d'Art, 1975.

Bendana-Mechri, Kmar. "L'Institut supérieur d'histoire du mouvement national tunisien: naissance et orientations." *Africa* [Rome] 46, no. 1 (1991): 135–36.

Ben Hamida, Abdesslem. "L'apport de Béchir Tlili à l'historiographie tunisienne." *Cahiers de Tunisie* 36, nos. 143–44 (1988): 101–8.

Ben Tahar, Jamel. "Note sur les sources relatives à l'histoire des souks ruraux de la Tunisie au XIXè siècle." *Revue de l'Institut des Belles Lettres Arabes* 53, no. 165 (1990): 39–57.

Ben Younes, Habib. "Trente années d'archéologie et d'histoire ancienne en Tunisie, 1956–1986. Les faits—les idées." *Revue de l'Institut des Belles Lettres Arabes* 50, no. 159 (1987): 11–59.

Bibliothèque Nationale de Tunis. *La Tunisie à travers les ouvrages anglais déposés à la Bibliothèque Nationale, 1632–1975*. Tunis: Service Documentaire, 1978.

Borruso, A. "Il carteggio fra gli arabisti Nallino e Griffini con lo storico tunisino Hasan Husny al-Wahhab." *Levante/al-Mashriq* 28 (1986): 17–24.

Bouhdiba, Abdelwahab. "National Primary Socio-Economic Data Structures. II: Tunisia." *International Social Science Journal* 30 (1978): 119–45.

Buonocore, Ferdinando. *La Reggenza di Tunisi dal 1834 al 1839 in alcune fonti dell'Archivio di Stato di Napoli*. Naples: Fonti e Studi per la storia dell'Africa, 1990.

Camau, Michel. *La Tunisie*. Paris: Presses Universitaires de France, 1989.

"Le Centre des Hautes Etudes d'Administration Musulmane (CHEAM): un fonds, une histoire." *Watha'iq* 10 (1988): 21–71.

"Centre d'Etudes et de Recherches Ottomanes, Morisques, de Documentation et d'Information (CERMODI)." *Studies in Turkish-Arab Relations* 2 (1987): 185–92.

Chabbi, Lahbib. "La Khroumirie dans les archives historiques du Ministère de la Défense (Chateau de Vincennes)." *Africa* [Tunis] 10 (1988): 117–34.

Chadli, A., and Christian Capape. "Les archives de l'Institut Pasteur de Tunis: historique, bilan et perspectives." *Revue Tunisienne de Communication* 10 (1986): 33–44.

Chérif, Mohamed Hédi. "L'histoire du XXème siècle tunisien: sources et études." *Revue de l'Institut des Belles Lettres Arabes* 50, no. 159 (1987): 91–114.

Clancy-Smith, Julia. "Research Facilities in Tunisia. Part II." *Middle East Studies Association Bulletin* 18 (1984), 31–34.

Dar al-Kutab al-Qawmiyah [National Library]. *Bibliographie nationale: publications non-officielles, 1956–1968.* Tunis: Service Documentaire, 1974.

Dellagi, Moncef. "Bibliographie de l'histoire du Mouvement national tunisien." *Revue d'Histoire Maghrébine* 6, nos. 13–14 (1979): 27–49.

Denizet, J. "L'histoire navale de la Tunisie de 1815 à 1888 aux Archives de la Marine." *Cahiers de Tunisie* 4 (1956): 409–12.

Dumas, Lucy. "Points de repère pour une histoire du mouvement ouvrier tunisien." *Revue d'Histoire Maghrébine* 3, no. 6 (1976), 208–19.

Faure, Edgar, and François Poli. *Tunisie, héritière de Carthage.* Paris: Editions Jeunes Afriques, 1979.

"Le fonds microfilmé: Etat et prospection." *Watha'iq* 10 (1988): 7–17.

France. Armée. Etat-major. Service Historique. Section Outre-Mer. *Répertoire du fonds Tunisie, 1831–1920.* Paris: Service Historique de l'Armée, 1968.

Gafsi, Abdelhakim. *Monuments andalous de Tunisie.* Tunis: Agence Nationale du Patrimoine, 1993.

———. "Analyse des Archives générales du Gouvernement tunisien quant aux Andalous de la région de Bizerte." *Cahiers de Tunisie* 26, nos. 103–4 (1978), 109–21.

Ghezzi, Carla. "Un seminario sulla documentazione a Tunisi." *Africa* [Rome] 44 (1989): 139–42.

Hunter, Robert F. "Recent Tunisian Historical Writing on State and Society in Modern Tunisia." *Middle East Studies Association Bulletin* 20 (1986): 23–28.

Jerfel, Kamal. "Les archives des tribunaux de Sousse: description, contenu et valeur documentaire." *Revue d'Histoire Maghrébine* 18, nos. 61–62 (1991): 169–83.

Kraiem, Mustapha. "La recherche historique en Tunisie." *Revue d'Histoire Maghrébine* 4, no. 9 (1977): 334–39.

Ladjili, Jeanne. "Intérêt des sources de l'histoire de l'Eglise Catholique en Tunisie." *Revue d'Histoire Maghrébine* 6, nos. 15–16 (1979): 117–29.

Landau, Jacob M. "Soviet Works on Tunisia." *Middle Eastern Studies* 16 (1980): 267–70.

Larguèche, Abdelhamid. *L'Abolition de l'esclavage en Tunsie à travers les archives, 1841–1846.* Tunis: Société Tunisienne d'Etude du XVIIIè Siècle, 1990.

Larguèche, Dalenda, and Abdelhamid Larguèche. "Les sources de la démographie historique dans la Tunisie moderne." In *La démographie historique en Tunisie et dans le monde arabe,* edited by Dalenda and Abdelhamid Larguèche, 13–33. Tunis: Centre d'Etudes et de Recherches Economiques et Sociales (CERES), 1993.

Lenci, Marco. "Il Maghreb Barbaresco in alcune raccolte di avvisi manoscritti della biblioteca nazionale centrale di Firenze." *Africa* [Rome] 46, no. 12 (1991): 241–61.

Ling, Dwight. *Morocco and Tunisia: A Comparative History.* Washington, D.C.: University Press of America, 1979.

———. *Tunisia from Protectorate to Republic.* Bloomington: Indiana University Press, 1967.

Lipinski, Edouard, ed. *Dictionnaire de la civilisation phénicienne et punique.* Turnhout, Belgium: Brépols, 1992.

Mahfoudh, Dorra. "Bibliographie de sociologie, ethnologie et anthropologie de la Tunisie à l'époque coloniale." *Hespéris-Tamuda* 26–27 (1988/1989): 265–76.

al-Maktabah al-Qawmiyah [National Library]. *Bibliographie historique sur la Tunisie, 1881–1955: livres se trouvant à la Bibliothèque Nationale, Tunis.* Tunis, La Bibliothèque, 1970.

"Matériaux pour une histoire du Sud de la Tunisie." In *Images du Sud tunisien,* 49–85. Tunis: Institut Supérieur d'Histoire du Mouvement National, 1992.

Mechri, Kmar, and Habib Belaid. "Les archives microfilmées du Protectorat: origine, état du fonds, perspectives." *Cahiers de Tunisie* 36, nos. 143–44 (1988): 33–42.

Muller, M., and M. Strohl. "Commission des Sources de l'Histoire Tunisienne en France: une base de données historiques." *ADPA* 4 (1984): 71–82.

Nelson, Harold D., ed. *Tunisia, A Country Study.* 3d ed. Washington, D.C.: United States Government Printing Office, 1987.

Pavy, Auguste. *Histoire de la Tunisie.* 2d ed. Tunis: Editions Bouslama, 1977.

Perkins, Kenneth J. *Tunisia: Crossroads of the Islamic and European Worlds.* Boulder, Colo.: Westview, 1986.

Poncet, Jean, and André Raymond. *La Tunisie*. Paris: Presses Universitaires de France, 1971.

"Présentation des documents: la propagande française en Tunisie dans l'après-guerre." *Watha'iq* 11 (1989): 35–93.

Quilès, J., Danièl Bruchet, M. Burgat, M. Codron, and Jean-Pierre Dahdah. *Le monde arabe et musulman au miroir de l'Université française: répertoire des thèses soutenues dans les Universitaires françaises, en sciences de l'Homme et de la Société, sur le monde arabe et musulman (1973–1987)*. Thesam II: *Algérie-Tunisie-Libye*. Aix-en Provence: Institut de Recherches et d'Etudes sur le Monde Arabe et Musulman, 1990.

Temimi, Abdeljelil. "Pour une histoire sociale de la minorité africaine noire en Tunisie: sources et perspectives." *Revue d'Histoire Maghrébine* 14, nos. 45–46 (1987): 102–9.

Tlili, Béchir. "La recherche historique en Tunisie: bilan et perspectives." *Cahiers de Tunisie* 20 (1972), 125–33.

Turbet-Delof, Guy. "Bibliographie critique des travaux de Jean Pignon sur l'histaire de la Tunisie." *Revue d'Histoire Maghrébine* 6, nos. 13–14 (1979): 187–94.

Wansbrough, John. "The Decolonization of North African History." *Journal of African History* 9 (1968): 643–50.

Witkam, J. J. "Modern Arabic Manuscripts in the National Library of Tunis: A Selection." *Manuscripts of the Middle East* 4 (1989): 56–66.

Yalaoui, Mohamed. "Les recherches sur la Tunisie médiévale au cours des trente dernières années." *Revue de l'Institut des Belles Lettres Arabes* 50, no. 159 (1987): 61–72.

Zghal, Abdelkader, and Hachmi Karoui. "Decolonization and Social Science Research: The Case of Tunisia." *Middle East Studies Association Bulletin* 7 (1973): 11–27.

Geography

Abaab, Ali. "Mutations socio-économiques de la Jeffara orientale (sud tunisien)." *Revue de l'Occident Musulman et de la Méditerranée* 41–42 (1986): 327–38.

Abaab, Ali, and Mokhtar Lamary. "Désertification et projets d'aménagement dans les régions arides du sud tunisien." *Les Cahiers du CREA* 4 (1984): 57–132.

Amami, Slaheddine el-. "Changing Concepts of Water Management in Tunisia." *Impact of Science on Society* (1983): 57–64.

Bachrouch, Taoufik. "Le Sahel: essai de définition d'un espace citadin." *Cahiers de Tunisie* 34, nos. 137–38 (1986): 209–66.

Baduel, Andrée, and Pierre Baduel. "Le pouvoir de l'eau dans le Sud-Tunisien." *Revue de l'Occident Musulman et de la Méditerranée* 30 (1980): 101–34.

Barrion, G. "Contribution à l'étude de la question forestière en Tunisie." *Revue Tunisienne* (1906): 554–71; (1907): 37–50.

Bédoucha, Geneviève. *L'eau, l'amie du puissant: une communauté oasienne du Sud-tunisien.* Montreux: Editions des Archives Contemporaines, 1987.

Belhedi, Amor. "Les facteurs d'organisation de l'espace national tunisien." *Espace Géographique* 22 (1993): 113–24.

Bel Khiria, T. "De la culture de l'olivier dans le Sahel." *Revue Tunisienne* (1919): 384–89.

Bernard, Auguste. "La région du Haut Tell Tunisien." *Annales de Géographie* 23 (1914): 172–75.

Berthon, Louis. "Les forages artésiens en Tunisie." *Revue Tunisienne* (1919): 120–24, 193–215, 320–46.

———. "Notes sur les lignites tertiaires en Tunisie." *Revue Tunisienne* (1916): 125–42, 224–34, 344–47.

———. "Note sur le forage de Bir-Pistor." *Revue Tunisienne* (1916): 3–16.

———. "Note sur l'utilité d'un forage à grande profondeur en Tunisie." *Revue Tunisienne* (1912): 231–40.

———. "Note sur quelques manifestations et suintenements de substances hydrocarburées en Tunisie." *Revue Tunisienne* (1911): 205–12.

Bignens, L. "Utilisation de l'eau de la Medjerda." *Revue Tunisienne* (1909): 116–23.

Bonnenfant, Paul. "Béja de la conquête musulmane à 1881." *Revue de l'Institut des Belles Lettres Arabes* 34, no. 127 (1971): 3–33.

Bonnenfant, Paul, and P. Landy. "Gammouda: essor d'un centre urbain dans la steppe tunisienne." *Revue de l'Institut des Belles Lettres Arabes* 35 (1972): 305–44.

Bonniard, F. "Bizerte et sa région." *Annales de Géographie* 34 (1925): 133–45.

———. "Les Lacs de Bizerte. Etude de géographie physique." *Revue Tunisienne* (1934): 93–143.

Bourgou, Mongi. "L'impact des mutations socio-économiques récentes à Jerba sur le milieu naturel." *Revue Tunisienne de Géographie* 23–24 (1993): 69–86.

Bourial, Hatem. *Répertoire de l'environnement en Tunisie 1992.* Tunis: Editions La Nef, 1992.

Brunet, R. "Un centre minier de Tunisie: Redeyef." *Annales de Géographie* 67 (1958): 430–46.

Bugeat, L. "L'irrigation dans le centre de la Tunisie." *Cahiers de Tunisie* 5 (1957): 63–74.

Bursaux, Paul Auguste. "L'oasis d'El-Guettar, ses ressources, sa décadence." *Revue Tunisienne* (1910): 364–73.

Buthaud, E. "De l'utilisation des documents cadastraux en Tunisie pour l'étude du paysage rural. (Vers une géographie des institutions foncières et des structures agraires)." *Revue de l'Institut des Belles Lettres Arabes* 13, no. 50 (1950): 153–92.

Canal, Joseph. "Le Kef. Etude historique et géographique." *Revue Tunisienne* (1919): 267–77, 453–60, 514–20; (1920): 59–63; (1921): 252–58; (1923): 176–82.

Carton, Dr. "Le reboisement de la Tunisie." *Revue Tunisienne* (1906): 572–90.

Cattan, A.A. "En fôret de Kroumire." *Revue Tunisienne* (1920): 29–43.

Chaabouni, A. "Exploitation des aquifères profondes du Sahara septentrional algéro-tunisien." *Water Supply* 5 (1987): 131–35.

Chauvin, P. "L'irrigation à El-Alem par les eaux de l'Oued Nebana." *Cahiers de Tunisie* 5 (1957): 75–78.

Combet, C. "Les eaux de Korbous à l'Institut de Carthage." *Revue Tunisienne* (1910): 389–408.

Contencin, A. "L'ilot de Sebkhet Kredma el Kebira." *Revue Tunisienne* (1939): 63–65.

Darghouth, S. "Problèmes des périmètres publics irrigués en Tunisie." *Revue Tunisienne de Géographie* 2 (1979): 5–27.

Deglin, Christian, and A. Poitrineau. "Un teroir de la zone côtière du Nord: El Aousdja." *Cahiers de Tunisie* 2 (1954): 254–64.

Despois, Jean. "Le Djebel Ousselat, les Ousseltiya et les Kooub." *Cahiers de Tunisie* 7 (1959): 407–27.

———. "Essai sur l'habitat rural du Sahel tunisienne." *Annales de Géographie* 40 (1931): 259–74.

———. "Les iles Kerkena et leurs bancs. Etude géographique." *Revue Tunisienne* (1937): 3–60.

———. "Régions naturelles et régions humaines en Tunisie." *Annales de Géographie* 51 (1942): 112–28.

Destanne de Bernis, Gérard. "Problèmes économiques concernant l'utilisation de l'eau en périmètre irrigué. (Esquisse d'un plan de travail)." *Cahiers de Tunisie* 5 (1957): 97–111.

Dlala, Habib. "L'aménagement du territoire en Tunisie." *Revue Tunisienne de Géographie* 1 (1978): 99–111.

Fahem, A. "Fonction régionale de la ville de Sousse." *Cahiers de Tunisie* 8 (1960): 157–62.

Faivre-Dupaigre, J. P. "L'irrigation traditionnelle dans l'oasis de Gabès." *Cahiers de Tunisie* 5 (1957): 23–37.

Fakhfakh, Mohamed. *Atlas de Tunisie*. Paris: Editions Jeune Afrique, 1979.

———. *Sfax et sa région: étude de géographie humaine et économique*. Tunis: Salammbo, 1986.

———. "Une nouvelle spéculation dans un pays d'arboriculture sèche: l'élevage laitier à Sfax." *Revue Tunisienne de Sciences Sociales* 6 (1969): 89–125.

Floret, Christian, Edouard Le Floc'h, and Roger Pontanier. "Le désertisation en Tunisie présaharienne." *Revue de l'Occident Musulman et de la Méditerranée* 41–42 (1986): 291–326.

Floret, Christian, Houcine Khattali, Edouard Le Floc'h, and Roger Pontanier. "Le risque de désertisation en Tunisie présaharienne: sa limitation par l'aménagement agro-pastoral." In *Le risque en agriculture,* edited by M. Eldin and P. Milleville, 291–309. Paris: Orstom, 1989.

Frih, A., M. Benaicha, and A. Chaabouni. "Transport d'eau sur de longues distances: conception, dimensionnement et problèmes spécifiques: application à l'adduction du Sahel à partir du Canal des eaux du Nord." *Water Supply* 2 (1984): B193–B199.

Gaillard, Capitaine. "Quelques aspects du problème de l'eau dans les oasis." *Cahiers de Tunisie* 5 (1957): 7–21.

Gendre, F. "La carte de Tunisie." *Revue Tunisienne* (1908): 314–29.

―――. "De Gabès à Nefta (le Nefzaoua et le Djerid)." *Revue Tunisienne* (1908): 383–411, 499–520.

―――. "L'Ile de Djerba." *Revue Tunisienne* (1907): 504–22; (1908): 60–79.

Ginestous, G., and P. Penet. "L'hydraulique agricole dans la Tunisie Méridionale." *Revue Tunisienne* (1913): 556–63.

Gribaudi, P. "Le risorse minerali della Tunisia." *Bulletino della Reale Società Geografica Italiana* 77 (1940): 546–59.

Hannezo, Cyr Gustave. "Mahdia (Tunisie)." *Revue Tunisienne* (1907): 227–36, 340–49, 438–43, 532–35; (1908): 46–59, 149–59, 244–52, 365–69, 413–27.

―――. "Tabarca. Monographie." *Revue Tunisienne* (1916): 239–65, 365–92; (1917): 12–29, 123–37.

Hayder, Adnane. *L'industrialisation à Gabès et ses conséquences: étude de géographie urbaine et économique.* Tunis: Faculté des Lettres et Sciences Humaines, 1986.

Henia, Latifa. "Le sirocco et les types de circulation à sirocco en Tunisie." *Revue Tunisienne de Géographie* 5 (1980): 61–87.

Hollis, G. E., et al. "Implications of Climatic Changes in the Mediterranean Basin: Garaet El Ichkeul abd Lac de Bizerte, Tunisia." In *Climatic Change and the Mediterranean: Environmental and Societal Impacts of Climatic Change and Sea-Level Rise in the Mediterranean Region,* edited by L. Jeftic, John D. Milliman, and Giuliano Sestini, 602–65. London: Edward Arnold, 1992.

Isnard, Hildebert. "La répartition saisonnière des pluies en Tunisie." *Annales de Géographie* 61 (1952): 357–62.

Kassab, Ahmed. "Les Basses terrasses de la Medjerda dans la plaine de Testour-Slouguia." *Revue Tunisienne de Sciences Sociales* 7 (1970): 119–57.

————. "L'irrigation dans les plaines de la moyenne Medjerda." *Cahiers de Tunisie* 26, nos. 101–2 (1978): 133–65.

Kassab, Ahmed, and Hafedh Séthom. *Géographie de la Tunisie: le pays et les hommes*. Tunis: Université de Tunis, 1980.

Kress, Hans-Joachim. "Eléments structuraux 'andalous' dans le genèse de la géographie culturelle de la Tunisie." *Revue de l'Institut des Belles Lettres Arabes* 43, no. 145 (1980): 3–45.

Laitman, Leon. "Le marché et la production de l'huile d'olive en Tunisie." *Annales de Géographie* 62 (1953): 271–86.

Laugerun, D. M. "Les Oasis des montagnes du Sud tunisien: Tamerga, Midis, Chebika." *La Géographie* 37 (1922): 509–26.

Loustalet, F. "La fonction régionale de la ville de Sfax." *Acta Geographica* 67 (1967): 7–19.

Marbeau, V., and R. Garenne. "Djerba. Aperçus sur les paysages et la vie d'une île méditerranéenne." *Acta Geographica* 43 (1962): 2–9.

Marthelot, Pierre. "Problèmes de la steppe tunisienne." *Cahiers de Tunisie* 2 (1954): 17–27.

Masmoudi, Abdelkader. *Mahdia: étude de géographie urbaine*. Tunis: Université de Tunis, 1984.

Miossec, Jean-Marie. "Croissance et environnement à Jerba (Tunisie)." *Bulletin de l'Association des Géographes Français* 53 (1976): 203–8.

Miossec, Jean-Marie, and Pierre Signoles. "Les réseaux de transport en Tunisie." *Cahiers d'Outre-Mer* 29 (1976): 151–94.

Monchicourt, Charles. "Etudes Kairouanaises." *Revue Tunisienne* (1931): 309–38; (1932): 79–91, 307–43; (1933): 57–92, 285–319; (1934): 33–58; (1936): 187–221, 425–50.

Moreau, Pierre. "Des lacs de sel aux chaos de sable. Le pays de Nefzaouas." *Revue de l'Institut des Belles Lettres Arabes* 10, no. 37 (1947): 19–47.

Musset, R. "La culture du blé en Tunisie." *Annales de Géographie* 42 (1933): 540–43.

Mzabi, Hassouna. *La Tunisie du Sud-Est. Géographie d'une région fragile, marginale et dépendante*. Tunis: Faculté des Sciences Humaines et Sociales, 1993.

————. "Frontière et croissance urbaine: le cas de Ben Gardane dans le Sud tunisien." *Revue Tunisienne de Géographie* 25 (1994): 119–37.

Paskoff, Roland. "L'évolution de la lagune littorale de Ghar el Melh, delta de la Medjerda, Tunisie nord-orientale." *Bulletin de la Société Languedocienne de Géographie* 15 (1981): 49–57.

Pauthier, J. "Ain-Draham, station estivale." *Revue Tunisienne* (1916): 337–43.

La pêche en Tunisie: pêche côtière et environnement. Tunis: Centre d'Etudes et de Recherches Economiques et Sociales, 1993.

Perennes, Jean-Jacques. "La politique de l'eau en Tunisie." *Maghreb Machrek* 110 (1988): 23–41.

Pissaloux, Robert. "Les cartes d'occupation du sol en Tunisie. Le cas du Cap Bon." *Cahiers de Tunisie* 2 (1954): 265–306.

Poncet, Jean. "La Géographie et la lutte contre le sous-développement: Mezzogiorno et Tunisie." *Annales de Géographie* 419 (1968): 64–86.

———. "Quelques problèmes actuels des campagnes tunisiennes." *Annales de Géographie* 60 (1951): 255–69.

———. "Vestiges de cadastration antique et histoire des sols en Tunisie." *Cahiers de Tunisie* 1 (1953): 323–29.

Prost, G. "Utilisation de la terre et production dans le Sud tunisien: Matmata et Ouderna." *Cahiers de Tunisie* 2 (1954): 28–66.

Rectenwald, Georges. "Etude sur le cadastre en Tunisie." *Revue Tunisienne* (1927): 14–26.

Rober-Raynaud, . "La question des vins tunisiens." *Renseignements Coloniaux* (1926): 145–49.

Saad, Thameur. "Typologie d'un espace urbain en pays en voie de développement: l'exemple de Nabeul (Tunisie)." *Espace Géographique* 11 (1982): 134–42.

Sethom, Hafedh. "Les rapports entre les modes d'exploitation agricole et l'érosion des sols en Tunisie." *Cahiers de Tunisie* 11 (1963): 85–95.

———. "La vie rurale de la Tunisie contemporaine. Etude historique et géographique." *Cahiers de Tunisie* 14 (1966): 187–212.

Sghaier, Mongi. "Winds of Change and the Threat of Desertification: Case Study from the Tunisian Sahara." *GeoJournal* 31 (1993): 95–99.

Surin, R. "Le cadastre de la haute vallée de la Medjerda." *Cahiers de Tunisie* 1 (1953): 261–319.

Taieb, J. "Une banlieue de Tunis. L'Ariana." *Cahiers de Tunisie* 8 (1960): 33–76.

Tag-Eldeen, Mustafa, and L. Y. Nilsson. "Planning Processes in Disaster Prone Areas with Reference to Floods in Tunisia." *Disasters* 3 (1979): 89–93.

Tlatli, Salah-Eddine. "L'île de Djerba." *Revue Tunisienne* (1941): 1–79; (1942): 1–124.

Pre-Islamic Tunisia

Albertini, Eugène. *L'Afrique romaine.* 2d ed. Algiers: Imprimerie Officielle, 1955.

Ben Baaziz, Sadok. "Les huileries de la Tunisie antique." *Cahiers de Tunisie* 39, nos. 155–56 (1991): 39–64.

Beschaouch, Azedine. *La légende de Carthage.* Paris: Gallimard, 1993.

Blomqvist, Jerker. "Reflections of Carthaginian Commercial Activity in Hanno's Periplus." *Orientalia Suecana* 33–35 (1984/1986): 51–62.

Briselance, Marie-France. *Massinissa le berbère.* Paris: La Table Ronde, 1990.

Broughton, T. Robert S. *The Romanization of Africa Proconsularis.* Baltimore: Johns Hopkins University Press, 1929.

Cagnat, René Louis Victor. *L'Armée romaine d'Afrique et l'occupation militaire de l'Afrique sous les empereurs.* 2 vols. Paris: Leroux, 1913.

Camps, Gabriel. "Massinissa ou les débuts de l'histoire (Aux origines de la Berbérie)." *Libyca* 8 (1960): 1–320.

Camps-Fabrer, Henriette. *L'Olivier et l'huile dans l'Afrique romaine.* Algiers: Imprimerie Officielle, 1953.

Charles-Picard, Gilbert. *La Civilisation de l'Afrique romaine.* Paris: Plon, 1959.

———. *Le Monde de Carthage.* Paris: Editions Corrêa Buchet/Chastel, 1956.

Charles-Picard, Gilbert, and Colette Charles-Picard. *Daily Life in Carthage at the Time of Hannibal.* London: Allen, 1961.

Courtois, Christian. *Les Vandales et l'Afrique.* Paris: Arts et Métiers Graphiques, 1955.

———. "De Rome à l'Islam." *Revue Africaine* 86 (1942): 25–55.

Decret, François. *Carthage ou l'empire de la mer.* Paris: Editions du Seuil, 1977.

Diehl, Charles. *L'Afrique byzantine; histoire de la domination byzantine en Afrique (533–709).* 2 vols. 1896. Reprint, New York: Franklin, Burt, 1959.

Dorey, Thomas A., and Donald R. Dudley. *Rome against Carthage.* London: Secker and Warburg, 1971.

Fantar, Mhamed Hassine. *Carthage: les lettres et les arts.* Tunis: Alif, 1991.

———. *Kerkouane, une cité punique au Cap Bon.* Tunis: Maison Tunisienne d'Edition, 1987.

———. "Survivances de la civilisation punique en Afrique du Nord." *Africa Romana* 7 (1990): 53–72.

Fendri, Mohamed. "Cités antiques et villas romaines de la région sfaxienne." *Africa* [Tunis] 9 (1985): 151–208.

Ferchiou, Naide. "L'occupation du sud de la province romaine d'Afrique au 1er siècle après J.C.: la petite Syrte et le Djérid." *Cahiers de Tunisie* 41–42, nos. 155–56 (1991): 65–104.

Ferjaoui, Ahmed. *Recherches sur les relations entre l'Orient phénicien et Carthage.* Carthage: Bayt al-Hikma, 1992.

Frend, W. H. C. *The Donatist Church: A Movement of Protest in Roman North Africa.* Oxford: The Clarendon Press, 1952.

Gautier, Emile Félix. *Le Passé de l'Afrique du Nord. Les siècles obscurs.* Paris: Payot, 1937.

Gragueb, Abderrazak, and Ali Mtimet. *La préhistoire en Tunisie et au Maghreb.* Tunis: Alif, 1989.

Gsell, Stéphane. *Histoire ancienne de l'Afrique du Nord.* 8 vols. Paris: Hachette, 1914–1928.

Haywood, Richard M. "Roman Africa." In *An Economic Survey of Ancient Rome,* edited by Tenney Frank, 4: 1–119. Baltimore: Johns Hopkins University Press, 1938.

Hours-Miéden, Madeleine. *Carthage.* 3d ed. Paris: Presses Universitaires de France, 1964.

Jaidi, Houcine. *L'Afrique et le blé de Rome au IVème et Vème siècles.* Tunis: Publications de l'Université de Tunis I, 1990.

Jobert, Michel. *Vandales.* Paris: Albin Michel, 1990.

Lancel, Serge. *Carthage: A History.* Translated by Antonia Nevill. Oxford: Blackwell Publishers, 1995.

Lloyd, Alan. *Destroy Carthage: The Death Throes of an Ancient Culture.* London: Souvenir Press, 1977.

Mahjoubi, Ammar. "Les allogènes en Tunisie à l'époque romaine." In *La démographie historique en Tunisie et dans le monde arabe,* edited by Dalenda and Abdelhamid Larguèche, 35–48. Tunis: Centre d'Etudes et de Recherches Economiques et Sociales (CERES), 1993.

Moderan, Yves. "La découverte des Maures. Réflexions sur la 'Reconquête' byzantine de l'Afrique en 533." *Cahiers de Tunisie* 41–42, nos. 155–56 (1991): 211–40.

Pedley, John Griffiths, ed. *New Light on Ancient Carthage.* Ann Arbor: University of Michigan Press, 1980.

Rachet, Marguerite. *Rome et les Berbères: un problème militaire d'Auguste à Dioclétien.* Brussels: Latomus, 1970.

Saumagne, Charles. *La Numidie et Rome. Masinissa et Jugurtha. Essai.* Paris: Presses Universitaires de France, 1966.

Scullard, Howard H. *Scipio Africanus and the Second Punic War.* Cambridge: Cambridge University Press, 1930.

Slim, Hédi. *Histoire de la Tunisie: l'Antiquité.* Tunis: Société Tunisienne de Diffusion, 1968.

Tissot, Charles. *Exploration scientifique de la Tunisie: géographie comparée de la province romaine d'Afrique.* 2 vols. and atlas. Paris: Imprimerie Nationale, 1888.

Tlatli, Salah-eddine. *La Carthage punique: étude urbaine: la ville, ses fonctions, son rayonnement.* Paris: J. Maisonneuve, 1978.

Van Nostrand, John James. *The Imperial Domains of Africa Proconsularis: An Epigraphical Study.* Berkeley: University of California Press, 1925.

Warmington, Brian. *Carthage.* London: Hale, 1960.

———. *The North African Provinces from Diocletian to the Vandal Conquest.* 1954. Reprint, Westport, Conn.: Greenwood Press, 1971.

Early Arab Rule, 670–973

Abdul-Wahab, Hasn Husni. "Sur l'emplacement de Qairouan." *Revue Tunisienne* (1940): 51–53.

————. "Un tournant de l'histoire Aghlabite." *Revue Tunisienne* (1937): 343–52; (1938): 55.

Brett, Michael. "The Fatimid Revolution (861–973) and Its Aftermath in North Africa." *Cambridge History of Africa*. Cambridge: Cambridge University Press, 1978, 2: 589–636.

Brunschvig, Robert. "Ibn Abdal-hakam et la conquête de l'Afrique du Nord par les Arabes." *Annales de l'Institut des Etudes Orientales* 6 (1942/1947): 108–55.

Cahen, Claude. "Un traité de droit commercial maritime du IVè/Xè siècle Ifriqiyen." *Journal of the Economic and Social History of the Orient* 31 (1988): 304–5.

Cambuzat, Paul-Louis. *L'évolution des cités du Tell en Ifrikiya du VIIIè au XIè siécle*. 2 vols. Algiers: Office des Publications Universitaires, 1986.

Canard, Marius. "L'autobiographie d'un chambellain du Mahdi Obeidallah le Fatimide." *Hespéris* 39 (1952): 279–329.

Castano, José. *La Princesse berbère. (La Kahéna)*. Montpellier: Imprimerie Dehan, 1984.

Chowdhury, Habibur Rahman. "Abd Allah b. Saad b. Abi Sarh and his Conquest of North Africa." *Journal of the Asiatic Society of Bangladesh* 21 (1977): 121–47.

Dachraoui, Farhat. "Contribution à l'histoire des Fatimides en Ifriqiya." *Arabica* 8 (1961): 189–203.

————. "La Crète dans la conflit entre Byzance et al-Muizz." *Cahiers de Tunisie* 7 (1959): 307–18.

Despois, Jean. "L'emplacement et les origines de Kairouan." *Revue Tunisienne* (1927): 33–40.

————. "Kairouan. Origine et évolution d'une ancienne capitale musulmane." *Annales de Géographie* (1930): 159–77.

Djait, Hisham. "L'Afrique arabe au VIIIè siècle (86–184 A.H./705–800)." *Annales Economies, Sociétés, Civilisations* 28 (1973): 601–21.

————. "La Wilaya d'Ifriqiya au IIè/IIIè siècle: étude institutionnelle." *Studia Islamica* 27 (1967): 77–122; 28 (1968): 79–107.

Epalza, Mikel de. "La disparition du christianisme au Maghreb et en Andalus." In *Mélanges offerts à Mohamed Talbi à l'occasion de son 70è anniversaire,* 69–80. La Manouba: Faculté des Lettres, 1993.

Fantar, Mhamed Hassine. "La Kahina, reine des Berbères." *Revue des Etudes Phéniciennes-puniques et des Antiquités Libyques* 3 (1987): 169–84.

Gateau, Albert. "Ibn Abd al-Hakam et les sources arabes relatives à la conquête de l'Afrique du Nord et de l'Espagne." *Revue Tunisienne* (1938): 37–54; (1939): 203–19.

————. "Ibn Abd al-Hakam. La conquête de l'Afrique du Nord et de l'Espagne." *Revue Tunisienne* (1931): 233–60; (1932): 71–78; (1935): 247–70; (1936): 57–83; (1937): 63–88.

————. "La *Sirat* Jaafar al-Hajib, contribution à l'histoire des Fatimides." *Hespéris* 34 (1947): 375–96.

Ghrab, Saad. *Ibn Arafa et le Malikisme en Ifriqiya au VIIIè-XIVè siècle.* 2 vols. Manouba: Faculté des Lettres, 1992.

Golvin, Lucien. "Mahdiya à l'époque fatimide." *Revue de l'Occident Musulman et de la Méditerranée* 27 (1979): 75–97.

Guiramand, Simone. *Kahena: drame historique en quatre actes.* Tunis: Maison tunisienne de l'édition, 1977.

Habib, Muhammad al-, and Jean Magnin. "Les femmes de l'époque Aghlabide: Fadhl affranchie de Abou Ayyoub al Qayrawani; texte en arabe, traduction par J. Magnin." *Revue de l'Institut des Belles Lettres Arabes* 12 (1949): 365–72.

Hrbek, Ivan. "The Emergence of the Fatimids." In *General History of Africa.* Vol. 3, *Africa from the Seventh to the Eleventh Century,* edited by M. El Fasi, 314–35. Berkeley: University of California Press, 1988.

Idris, Hady Roger. "Commerce maritime et kirad en Berbérie orientale. D'aprés un recueil inédit de Fatwas médiévales." *Journal of the Economic and Social History of the Orient* 4 (1961): 225–39.

————. "Contribution à l'histoire de l'Ifriqiya. Tableau de la vie intellectuelle et administrative à Kairouan sous les Aghlabites et les Fatimites (4 premiers siècles de l'Hégire) d'aprés le Riyad En Nufus de Abu Bakr al Maliki." *Revue des Etudes Islamiques* 9 (1935): 105–78, 273–305; 10 (1936): 45–104.

————. "D'al-Dabbag, hagiographe et chroniqueur kairouanais de XIIIè siècle et de son jugement sur les Fatimides." *Bulletin d'Etudes Orientales* 29 (1977): 243–49.

————. "Examen critique des récits d'al-Maliki et Ibn Idhari sur la conquête de l'Ifriqiya." *Arabica* 11 (1964): 5–18.

————. "L'Occident musulmane (Ifriqiya et al-Andalus) à l'avènement des Abbasides d'après le chroniqueur ziride al-Raqiq." In *Actes du Vè Congrès International d'Arabisants et d'Islamisants,* 275–83. N.p., 1970.

————. "Problématique de l'épopée sanhadjienne en Berbérie Orientale (X-XIIè siècles)." *Annales de l'Institut des Etudes Orientales* 17 (1959): 243–55.

————. "Le recit d'al-Maliki sur la conquête de l'Ifriqiya, traduction annotée et examen critique." *Revue des Etudes Islamiques* 37 (1969): 117–49.

Le Tourneau, Roger. "La révolte d'Abu-Yazid au Xème siècle." *Cahiers de Tunisie* 1 (1953): 103–25.

Lévi-Provençal, Evariste. "Arabica occidentalia. i. Un nouveau récit de la conquête de l'Afrique du Nord par les Arabes. (ii. Le *zagal* hispanique dans la *Mugrib* d'Ibn Said.)." *Arabica* 1 (1954): 17–52.

Mahfoudh, Faouzi. "Aspects de la démographie de la ville de Sfax au moyen âge (IX-XIIème siècles)." In *La démographie historique en*

Tunisie et dans le monde arabe, edited by Dalenda and Abdelhamid Larguèche, 73–82. Tunis: Centre d'Etudes et de Recherches Economiques et Sociales, 1993.

———. "Les installations hydrauliques de Sfax au moyen âge." *Revue de l'Institut des Belles Lettres Arabes* 54 (1991): 13–29.

Marçais, Georges. "Comment l'Afrique du Nord a été arabisée." *Annales de l'Institut des Etudes Orientales* 4 (1938): 1–22.

———. "Sidi Uqba, Abu l-Muhajir et Kusaila." *Cahiers de Tunisie* 1 (1953): 11–17.

Massé, Henri. "La chronique d'Ibn Atham et la conquête de l'Ifriqiya." In *Mélanges Gaudefroy-Demombynes,* 85–90. Cairo: Imprimerie de l'Institut Français d'Archéologie Orientale, 1935–1945.

Monès, H. "Le Malékisme et l'échec des Fatimides en Ifriqiya." *Etudes d'orientalisme Lévi-Provençal* 1 (1961): 197–220.

Muranyi, M. "Notas sobre la transmisión escrita de la *Mudawwana* en Ifriqiya según algunos manuscritos recientemente descubiertos." *al-Qantara* 10 (1989): 215–31.

Poncet, Jean. "Prospérité et décadence ifrikiyennes (aux sources de l'histoire nord-africaine)." *Cahiers de Tunisie* 9 (1961): 221–43.

Rizzitano, Umberto. "Asad ibn al-Furat, *faqih* et *qadi* d'Ifriqiyah." *Rivista degli Studi Orientali* 36 (1961): 225–43.

Roth, Norman. "The Kahina: Legendary Material in the Accounts of the 'Jewish Berber Queen.'" *Maghreb Review* 7, nos. 5–6 (1982): 122–25.

Sebag, Paul. "Les travaux maritimes de Hassan ibn Numan." *Revue de l'Institut des Belles Lettres Arabes* 33 (1970): 41–55.

Talbi, Mohamed. *L'Emirat aghlabide, 800–909: historique politique.* Paris: Adrien-Maisonneuve, 1966.

———. "Les coutiers en vêtements en Ifriqiya au IXè-Xè siècle d'après les *Masail al-samasira* d'al-Ibyani." *Journal of the Economic and Social History of the Orient* 5 (1962): 160–94.

———. "Deux passages peu connus de la *hulla* d'Ibn al-Abbar relatifs à la grande rebellion du Djund sous Ziyadat Allah 1er." *Cahiers de Tunisie* 14 (1966): 19–29.

———. "Law and Economy in Ifriqiya (Tunisia) in the Third Islamic Century: Agriculture and the Role of Slaves in the Country's Economy." In *The Islamic Middle East, 700–1900: Studies in Economic and Social History,* edited by Avram Udovitch, 209–49. Princeton: Darwin Press, 1981.

———. "Rapports de l'Ifriqiya et de l'Orient au VIIIé siécle." *Cahiers de Tunisie* 7 (1959): 299–305.

Yalaoui, Mohamed. "Les recherches sur la Tunisie médievale au cours des trente dernières années." *Revue de l'Institut des Belles Lettres Arabes* 50 (1987): 61–72.

———. "Les relations entre Fatimides d'Ifriqiya et Omeyyades d'Espagne à travers le Diwan d'Ibn Hani." In *Actas del II Coloquio Hispano-Tunecino de Estudios Historicos,* 13–30. Madrid: Instituto Hispano-árabe de Cultura, 1973.

———. "Sur un possible régence du prince fatimide Abdallah b. Muizz en Ifriqiya au IVè/Xè siècle." *Cahiers de Tunisie* 22 (1974): 7–22.

Young, M. J. L. "Abu'l-Arab al-Qayrawani and his Biographical Dictionary of the Scholars of Qayrawan." *al-Masaq* 6 (1993): 57–75.

The Berber Dynasties, 973–1574

Abulafia, David. "A Tyrrhenian Triangle: Tuscany, Sicily, Tunis, 1276–1300." In *Studi di storia economica toscana nel Medioevo e nel Rinascimento in memoria di F. Melis,* 53–75. Pisa: Pacini, 1987.

Abdul-Wahab, Hasn Husni. "Les steppes tunisiennes (région de Grammouda) pendant le Moyen-Age." *Cahiers de Tunisie* 2 (1954): 5–16.

———. "Villes arabes disparues." In *Mélanges W. Marcais,* 1–15. Paris: G.-P. Maisonneuve, 1950.

Akkari-Weriemmi, J. "La mosquée Harmal: étude et travaux de restauration." *Africa* [Tunis] 10 (1988): 293–316.

Alvarez Rubiano, Pablo. "La politica imperial española y su relacion con los hafsies tunecinos. Nuevos datos para su estudio." *Hispania* 1 (1941): 32–46.

Arribas Palau, Mariano. "Une lettre de Martin l'Humain à Abou Faris de Tunis (Contribution à l'étude de l'histoire de la Tunisie)." *Revue de l'Institut des Belles Lettres Arabes* 18, no. 71 (1955): 349–56.

Bacaicoa Arnaiz, Dora. "Subditos aragoneses cautivos en Túnez en tiempos de Juan I el Cazador." *Tamuda* 4 (1956): 239–40.

Balard, Michel. "Notes sur le commerce génois en Tunisie au XIIIè siècle." *Cahiers de Tunisie* 41–42, nos. 155–56 (1991): 369–86.

Bel, Alfred. *Les Banou Ghaniya, derniers représentants de l'empire almoravide et leur lutte contre l'empire almohade.* Paris: Leroux, 1903.

Belkhodja, K. "Les Normandes de Sicile en Ifriqiya." *Cahiers de Tunisie* 47–48 (1964): 37–40.

———. "Roger II en Ifriqiya." *Africa* [Tunis] 1 (1969): 111–17.

Ben Sliman, Ferid. "Despotisme et violence sous les Hafsides." *Revue de l'Institut des Belles Lettres Arabes* 54, no. 168 (1991): 255–62.

———. "Entre Ibn al-Imam le Tudélien (mort en 996) et Ibn al-Rami le Tunisois (mort après 1333)." *Sharq al-Andalus* 8 (1991): 109–12.

Bouaita, Hédi. "Note sur le fort d'Espagne de Bizerte." *Revue de l'Institut des Belles Lettres Arabes* 52, no. 163 (1989): 69–80.

Brett Michael. "Ibn Khaldun and the Arabisation of North Africa." *Maghreb Review* 4 (1979): 9–16.

————. "Ifriqiya as a Market for Saharan Trade from the Tenth to the Twelfth Century." *Journal of African History* 10 (1969): 347–64.

————. "The Military Interest of the Battle of Haydaran." In *War, Technology, and Society in the Middle East,* edited by V. J. Parry and M. E. Yapp, 78–88. New York: Oxford University Press, 1975.

————. "Muslim Justice under Infidel Rule. The Normans in Ifriqiya, 517–555 A.H./1123–1160 A.D." *Cahiers de Tunisie* 41–42, nos. 155–56 (1991): 325–68.

Brunschvig, Robert. *La Berbérie orientale sous les Hafsides des origines à la fin du XVè siècle.* 2 vols. Paris: Adrien-Maisonneuve, 1940, 1947.

————. "A propos d'un toponyme tunisien du moyen age." *Revue Tunisienne* (1935): 149–55.

————. "Un Calife hafside méconnu." *Revue Tunisienne* (1930): 38–48.

————. "Un document sur une princesse hafside de la fin du XVIè siècle." *Revue Africaine* 80 (1937): 81–92.

————. "Ibn as-Samma, historien hafside." *Annales de l'Institut des Etudes Orientales* 1 (1934/1935): 193–212.

————. "Une lettre du calife hafside Uthman au Duc de Milan (1476)." *Cahiers de Tunisie* 26 (1978): 27–34.

————. "Mesures de capacité de la Tunisie médiévale." *Revue Africaine* 77 (1935): 86–96.

————. "Note sur un traité conclu entre Tunis et l'Empéreur Frédéric II." *Revue Tunisienne* (1932): 153–60.

————. "Un voyageur flamand en Tunisie au XVè siècle." *Revue Africaine* 76 (1935): 291.

Cahen, Claude. "Quelques notes sur les Hilaliens et le nomadisme." *Journal of the Economic and Social History of the Orient* 11 (1968): 130–33.

Chelli, Zouhir. *La Tunisie au rythme des estampes du XVè au XIXè siècle.* Tunis: Tunis-Carthage, 1987.

Courtois, Christian. "Remarques sur le commerce maritime en Afrique au XIè siècle." In *Mélanges d'histoire et d'archéologie de l'Occident musulman. Hommage à Georges Marçais,* 51–59. Algiers: Imprimerie Officielle, 1957.

Cowdrey, Herbert Edward John. "The Mahdia Campaign of 1087." *English Historical Review* 92 (1977): 1–30.

Daoulatli, Abd al-Aziz. *Tunis sous les hafsides: évolution urbaine et activité architecturale.* Tunis: Institut National d'Archéologie et d'Art, 1976.

————. "L'alimentation en eau de Tunis sous la règne des Hafçides." *al-Manar* 1 (1993): 37–50.

————. "L'eau à Tunis au temps des Hafsides (XIIIè-XVIè siècles)." In *L'eau et le Maghreb,* edited by Elda Sortino, 123–30. Paris: Programme des Nations Unies pour le Développement, 1988.

————. "Les relations entre le sultan Qalaun et l'Ifriqiya: d'après deux documents égyptiens (680Hg/1281 J.C.–689 Hg/1290 J.C.)." *Revue de l'Occident Musulman et de la Méditerranée* 17 (1974): 43–62.

Djait, Hicham, et al. *Histoire de la Tunisie: le Moyen Age.* Tunis: Société tunisienne de diffusion, 1976.

Doumerc, Bernard. "Le consulat vénitien de Tunis (1470–1473)." *Cahiers de Tunisie* 41–42, nos. 155–56 (1991): 447–78.

————. "Le corail d'Ifriqiya à la fin du Moyen-Âge." *Bulletin Archéologique du Comité des Travaux Historiques et Scientifiques. Afique du nord* 19 (1983): 479–82.

————. "Venise et la dynastie hafside à la fin du XVè siécle." *Cahiers de Tunisie* 29 (1981): 573–81.

————. "La ville et la mer: Tunis au XVème siècle." *Cahiers de Tunisie* 34 (1986): 111–30.

Dufourcq, Charles Emmanuel. "La Couronne d'Aragonne et les Hafsides au XIIIè siècle (1229–1301)." *Analecta sacra tarraconensia* 25 (1952): 51–113.

Ehrensvärd, U. "Die Belagerung von Djerba im Jahre 1560: zu einer Zeichnung in der Königlichen Bibliothek, Stockholm." In *Turcica et Orientalia: Studies in Honor of Gunnar Jarring on his Eightieth Birthday, 12 October 1987,* 19–36. Stockholm: Swedish Research Institute in Istanbul, 1988.

Epalza, Mikel de. "L'auteur de la 'tuhfa al-arib' Anselm Turmeda (Abdallah al-Turjuman)." *Revue de l'Institut des Belles Lettres Arabes* 28, no. 111 (1965): 261–90.

————. "Deux récits bilingues (arabe et espagnol) de voyageurs vers l'Orient qui passent par Tunis (XVè et XVIè siècles)." *Cahiers de Tunisie* 26 (1978): 35–52.

————. "Recherches d'histoire des morisques en Tunisie." *al-Masaq* 2 (1989): 41–42.

————. "La situación urbanística de la tumba de Anselm Turmeda en Túnez." In *Studia in honorem prof. M. de Riquer,* 637–41. Barcelona: Quaderns Crema, 1987.

Fabris, Antonio. "Disavventure di mercanti in margine alle imprese del Barbarossa." *Quaderni di Studi Arabi* 7 (1989): 191–97.

Gafsi, Abdel Hakim al-. "Algunas observaciones sobre el agua en las mezquitas de los pueblos andaluses de Túnez." In *Agua y poblamiento musulmán,* edited by Mikel de Epalza, 55–58. Benissa: Ajuntament de Benissa, 1988.

————. "L'andalou Ibn al-Abbar, 595/1199–658/1260, victime de repression." In *Ibn al-Abbar, politic i escriptor àrab valencià (1199–1260),* 131–42. Valencia: Generalitat Valenciana, Conselleria de Cultura, Educació i Cinéncia, 1990.

————. "La medersa des moriscos andalous à Tunis." *Sharq al-Andalus* 5 (1988): 169–80.

————. "Note sur les cimetières en Tunisie." *Sharq al-Andalus* 6 (1989): 173–83.

————. "Una princesa hafsi de origen español en Túnez en tiempos de Ibn al-Abbar." *Sharq al-Andalus* 6 (1989): 193–94, 261.

Gautier, Emile. "Un passage d'Ibn Khaldoun et du Bayan." *Hespéris* 4 (1924): 305–12.

Ghrab, Saad. *Ibn Arafa et le Malikisme en Ifriqiya au VIIIè-XIVè siècle.* 2 vols. Manouba: Faculté des Lettres, 1992.

Giraldo, Z. "Martin I of Aragon and Negotiations for Peace and Prisoner Exchange with Tunis (1398–1410)." *Journal of the Faculty of Arts of the University of Malta* 6 (1977): 82–95.

Goitein, Shlomo D. "La Tunisie du XIè siècle à la lumière des documents de la *Geniza* du Caire." *Etudes d'Orientalisme Lévi-Provençal* 2 (1962): 559–79.

Gragueb, Abderrazak. "Notes sur le voyage de Tijani dans le Sud tunisien." *Cahiers de Tunisie* 24 (1976): 25–44.

Grandchamp, Pierre. "Documents divers relatifs à la croisade de Saint Louis contre Tunis." *Revue Tunisienne* (1912): 384–94, 447–70; (1913): 480–81.

Guemara, Raoudha. "Les immigrés dans les sources médiévales italiennes." In *La démographie historique en Tunisie et dans le monde arabe,* edited by Dalenda and Abdelhamid Larguèche, 57–71. Tunis: Centre d'Etudes et de Recherches Economiques et Sociales, 1993.

Guéry, Roger. "Survivance de la vie sédentaire pendant les invasions arabes en Tunsie centrale: l'exemple de Rougga." *Bulletin Archéologique du Comité des Travaux Historiques et Scientifiques. Bulletin Afrique du Nord* 19 (1985): 399–410.

Habib, Muhammad al-, and Jean Magnin. "Pages oubliées d'histoire tunisienne. Les Banou Al-Khalaf de Nefta (715–777 A.H.)." *Revue de l'Institut des Belles Lettres Arabes* 12, no. 48 (1949): 347–58.

Hopkins, J. "Sousse et la Tunisie orientale mediévales vues par les géographes arabes." *Cahiers de Tunisie* 8 (1960): 83–95.

Idris, Roger. *La Berbérie orientale sous les Zirides, Xè–XIIè siècles.* 2 vols. Paris: Adrien-Maisonneuve, 1962.

————. "Contribution à l'histoire de la vie religieuse en Ifriqiya ziride." In *Mélanges Louis Massignon* 2, 327–59. Paris: Université de Paris, 1957.

————. "De la réalité de la catastrophe hilalienne." *Annales Economies, Sociétés, Civilisations* 23 (1968): 390–94.

————. "Deux maitres de l'école juridique kairouanaise sous les Zirides (XIè siècle): Abu Bakr b. Abd al-Rahman et Abu Imran al-Fasi." *Annales de l'Institut des Etudes Orientales* 13 (1955): 30–60.

————. "Fêtes chrétiennes célébrées en Ifriqiya à l'époque ziride. (IVé siècle de l'Hégire/Xè siècle après J.-C.)." *Revue Africaine* 98 (1954): 261–76.

――――. "Glanes sur les Zirides d'Ifriqiya dans le manuscrit d'Istanbul de l'*Itti'az al-hunafa'*." *Arabica* 11 (1964): 286–305.

――――. "L'invasion hilalienne et ses conséquences." *Cahiers de Civilisation Médiévale* 11 (1968): 353–69.

――――. "Al-Muizz ben Badis, grandeur et décadence de la 'civilisation kairouanaise.'" *Les Africains, sous la direction de Ch.-A. Julien et al.* 12 (1978): 223–51.

――――. "Sur le retour des Zirides à l'obédience fatimide." *Annales de l'Institut des Etudes Orientales* 11 (1953): 25–39.

――――. "La vie intellectuelle en Ifriqiya méridionale sous les Zirides (XIè siècle) d'après Ibn Al-Chabbat.'" In *Mélanges d'histoire et d'archéologie de l'Occident musulman. Hommage à Georges Marçais*, 95–106. Algiers: Imprimerie Officielle, 1957.

Jehel, Georges. "Catalogue analytique et chronologique des actes du notaire Petrus Batifolius rédigés à Tunis du 20 décembre 1288 au 24 juin 1289." *Cahiers de Tunisie* 25 (1977): 69–137.

Las Cagigas, Isidro de. "Un traité de paix entre le roi Pierre IV d'Aragon et le sultan de Tunis Abu Ishak II (1360)." *Hespéris* 19 (1934): 65–77.

Lavajo, J. C. "Tunis e o primeiro *studium arabicum* hispánico do século XIII: problemática do capitulo dominicano de Toledo de 1250." In *Islão e Arabismo na peninsula ibérica: Actas do XI Congresso da União Europeia de Arabistas e Islamólogos*, edited by Adel Sidarus, 225–52. Évora: Universidade de Évora, 1986.

Limam, Rashid. "Ibn al-Abbar y su época en Túnez." In *Ibn al-Abbar, politic i escriptor àrab valencià (1199–1260)*, 107–30. Valencia: Generalitat Valenciana, Conselleria de Cultura, Educació i Cinéncia, 1990.

Lubienski-Bodenham, H. "The Interpreter or Interpreters in Froissart's Account of the Siege of Mahdia (1390)." *Romanische Forschungen* 90 (1978): 254–59.

Magnin, Jean-Gabriel. "Coutumes des fêtes à Tunis au XIè-XVIIè siècle d'après Ibn Abi Dinar." *Revue de l'Institut des Belles Lettres Arabes* 15, no. 60 (1952): 387–421.

Mahfoudh, Faouzi. "A propos d'une inscription arabe découverte à Bab al-Gibli (Sfax)." *Revue de l'Institut des Belles Lettres Arabes* 52, no. 166 (1990): 237–47.

――――. "Aspects de la démographie de la ville de Sfax au moyen âge (IX–XIIème siècles)." In *La démographie historique en Tunisie et dans le monde arabe*, edited by Dalenda and Abdelhamid Larguèche, 73–82. Tunis: Centre d'Etudes et de Recherches Economiques et Sociales, 1993.

――――. "Aspects de la fortification de la côte ifriqyenne: les défenses de Sfax." *Bulletin Archéologique du Comité des Travaux Historiques et Scientifiques: Afrique du nord* 22 (1992): 235–50.

————. "Les relations entre l'Ifriqiya et le califat fatimide à la fin du Xè siècle après J. C. d'après les documents épigraphiques." *Cahiers de Tunisie* 41–42, nos. 155–56 (1991): 313–24.

Mahjoubi, Ammar. "Nouveau témoignage épigraphique sur la communauté chrétienne de Kairouan au XIè siécle." *Cahiers de Tunisie* 12 (1964): 159–62.

Mami, Ridha. "La obra de un morisco expulsado en Túnez." In *L'expulsió del moriscos: conseqüències en el món islàmic i el món cristià,* edited by Mikel de Epalza, 361–68. Barcelona: Generalitat de Catalunya, 1994.

Marçais, Georges. *La Berbérie musulmane et l'Orient au moyen age.* Paris: Editions Montaigne, 1946.

————. "Les Hafçides d'après un livre récent." *Revue Africaine* 93 (1949): 25–37.

Mazouz-Benachour, Heger. "Aux origines de la ferme du Dar al-gild: Hypothèse sur la mise en place des structures et les Andalous en Tunisie." *Sharq al-Andalus* 7 (1990): 11–14.

Mirot, L. "Une expédition française en Tunisie au XIVè siècle. Le siège de Mahdia (1390)." *Revue des Etudes Historiques* 97 (1931): 357–406.

Monti, Gennaro Maria. "Tunisia, Italia meridionale e Sicilia nel medio evo." *Nuova Antologia* 401 (1939): 305–14.

Motylinski, A. de C. "Expédition de Pedro de Navarre et de Garcia de Tolède contre Djerba (1510) d'après les sources abadhites." In *Recueil de mémoires orientaux.* [14th International Orientalists' Congress], 133–59. Paris: E. Leroux, 1905.

Noel, C. "Un manuscrit du XIVè siècle relatif à une Ambassade auprès du 'roy de Thunis.'" *Revue Tunisienne* (1920): 93–100.

Pignon, Jean. "Une ville européenne à Tunis au XVIè siècle." *Cahiers de Tunisie* 9 (1961): 97–108.

Pistarino, G. *Notai genovesi in Oltremare: atti rogati a Tunisi da Pietro Battifoglio (1288–1289).* Genoa: Università di Genova, Instituto di Medievistica, 1986.

Poncet, Jean. "Encore à propos des hilaliens." *Annales Economies, Sociétés, Civilisations* 23 (1968): 660–62.

————. "L'évolution des 'genres de vie' en Tunisie. Autour d'une phrase d'Ibn Khaldoun." *Cahiers de Tunisie* 2 (1954): 315–23.

————. "Le Mythe de la 'catastrophe' hilalienne." *Annales Economies, Sociétés, Civilisations* 22 (1967): 1099–1120.

Ribera, J. "Tratado de paz o tregua entre Fernando I el bastardo, Rey de Nàpoles, y Abuamer Otman, rey de Tunez." *Centenario Amari* 2 (1910): 373–86.

Rodriguez Joulia, Carlos. "Carta de Fernando I de Aragon à Abu Faris de Tunez." *Tamuda* 3 (1955): 124–28.

Rubiera Mata, Maria Jesus. "Un aspecto de las relaciones entre la Ifriqiya hafsi y la Granada nasri: la presencia tunecina en las tariqat misticas granadinas." *Cahiers de Tunisie* 26 (1978): 165–72.

Sacerdoti, Albert. "Il consolato veneziano del regno Hafsida di Tunisi (1274–1518)." *Studi Veneziani* 11 (1969): 531–35.

————. "Venezia e il regno hafsida di Tunisi. Trattati e relazione diplomatiche (1231–1534). *Studi Veneziani* 8 (1966): 303–46.

Sayous, E. A. *Le Commerce des européens à Tunis depuis le XIIè siècle jusqu'a la fin du XVIè siècle.* Paris: Société d'Editions Géographiques, Maritimes, et Coloniales, 1929.

————. "Le commerce européen en Tunisie au moyen âge et au début de l'ère moderne." *Revue de l'Histoire des Colonies Françaises* 17 (1929): 225–50.

Sehili, Chedli. "La Tunisie et l'Afrique sub-saharienne." *Revue d'Histoire Maghrébine* 13, nos. 41–42 (1986): 169–71.

Souidi, D. "Problèmes de succession dans la dynastie ziride." *Lybica* 32–34 (1984/1986): 283–95.

Stillman, Norman. "Un témoignage contemporain de l'histoire de la Tunisie ziride." *Hespéris Tamuda* 13 (1972): 37–59.

Talbi, Mohamed. "Les contacts culturels entre l'Ifriqiya hafside (1230–1569) et le sultanat nasride d'Espagne (1232–1492)." In *Actas del II Coloquio Hispano-Tunecino de Estudios Historicos,* 63–90. Madrid: Instituto Hispano-Arabe de Cultura, 1973.

————. "Opérations bancaires en Ifriqiya à l'époque d'al-Mazari (453–536/1061–1141). Crédit et paiement par chèque." In *Recherches d'islamologie. Recueil d'articles offert à G. Anawati et L. Gardet par leurs collègues et amis,* 307–19. Louvain: Editions Peeters, 1977.

Turki, Mohamed. "Les Andalous-Morisques en Tunisie à la recherche d'un univers mythique et religieux." *Revue d'Histoire Maghrébine* 16, nos. 55–56 (1989): 59–74.

Udina Martorell, Federico. "Documents relatifs à la Tunisie dans les Archives de la Couronne d'Aragon." *Cahiers de Tunisie* 18 (1970): 107–16.

————. "Las relaciones entre Túnez y la Corona de Aragón en el segundo tercio del siglo XIV hasta 1360." *Anuario de Estudios Medievales* 10 (1980): 337–40.

————. "Sur les rapports entre la Tunisie et l'Aragon entre 1360–1379." In *Actas del II Coloquio Hispano-Tunecino de Estudios Historicos,* 49–62. Madrid: Instituto Hispano-Arabe de Cultura, 1973.

Vera Aparici, J. "La Goleta: comienzos de una fortaleza." *Sharq al-Andalus* 8 (1991): 235–41.

Vilar, Juan Bautista. "L'occupation de Tunis par l'Espagne en 1573 d'après deux lettres de Don Juan d'Autriche à Guzman de Silva, ambassadeur espagnol à Venise." *Revue d'Histoire Maghrébine* 21, no. 74 (1994): 149–51.

Zbiss, Slimane-Mostafa. "Brillante carrière en Tunisie de deux grands savants valenciens: Abu al-Mutarrif Ibn Amira et Muhammad Ibn al-Abbar." In *Ibn al-Abbar, politic i escriptor àrab valencià (1199–1260),*

99–106. Valencia: Generalitat Valenciana, Conselleria de Cultura, Educació i Cinéncia, 1990.

The Ottomans and the Deys, 1574–1705

Abun-Nasr, Jamil. "The Beylicate in Seventeenth Century Tunisia." *International Journal of Middle East Studies* 6 (1975): 70–93.

Anselme des Arcs, Révérend Père. "Mémoires pour servir à l'histoire de la mission des Capuchins dans la Régence de Tunis (1624–1865). Revus et publiés par le R. P. Apollinaire de Valence (Rome 1889). Présenté et commenté par Pierre Soumille." *Revue d'Histoire Maghrébine* 11, nos. 33–34 (1984): 164–82; 11, nos. 35–36 (1984): 229–52; 13, nos. 41–42 (1986): 175–204.

Aouani, Muhammed el-. "A la recherche des influences andalouses dans les campagnes tunisiennes: essai de mise au point." In *Recueil d'études sur les moriscos andalous en Tunisie,* edited by Mikel de Epalza and Ramon Petit, 374–77. Madrid: Dirección General de Relaciones Culturales, Instituto Hispano-Arabe, 1973.

Arnoulet, François. "Fiumara Sallatta, un comptoir commercial en Tunisie au XVIème et XVIIème siècle." *Revue d'Histoire Maghrébine* 4, nos. 7–8 (1977): 33–40.

Arogundade, J. S. "The Effect of the Decline of the Ottoman Empire in the 17th and 18th Centuries on the Politics of the Ottoman Provinces in North Africa." *The African Historian* 31 (1969): 10–15.

Bachrouch, Taoufik. *Formation sociale barbaresque et pouvoir à Tunis au XVIè siècle.* Tunis: Université de Tunis, 1977.

———. "Les Barbaresques de Tunisie au XVIIè siècle: mythes et interprétations." *Revue d'Histoire Maghrébine* 10, nos. 31–32 (1983): 85–99.

———. "Sur la fiscalité muradite. Présentation d'une source et de premiers résultats d'une enquête en cours." *Cahiers de Tunisie* 20 (1972): 125–46.

Bacquencourt, M. de and Pierre Grandchamp. "Documents divers concernant Don Philippe d'Afrique, prince tunisien, deux fois renégat (1646–1686)." *Revue Tunisienne* (1938): 55–77, 289–311.

Ben Smail, Mohamed, and Lucette Valensi. "Le règne de Hammouda Pacha dans la chronique d'Ibn Abi-d-Diyaf." *Cahiers de Tunisie* 19 (1971): 87–108.

Beranger, Nicolas. *La Régence de Tunis à la fin du XVIIè siècle.* [Edited by Paul Sebag.] Paris: L'Harmattan, 1993.

Bono, Salvatore. *I corsari barbareschi.* Turin: ERI, 1964.

———. "Documenti inediti e rari sulla storia della Tunisia negli anni 1573–1574." *Studi Maghrebini* 1 (1966): 91–101.

———. "L'occupazione spagnola e la riconquista musulmana di Tunisi (1573–1574). *Africa* [Rome] 33 (1978): 351–82.

————. "La politica nord-africana di Carlo V." *Africa* [Rome] 20 (1965): 56–59.

———— "Tunisi e La Goletta negli anni 1573–1574." *Africa* [Rome] 31 (1976): 1–39.

Bouali, Mahmoud. *La sédition permanente en Tunisie.* Tunis: Maison Tunisienne de l'Edition, 1972.

Boubaker, Sadok. *La Régence de Tunis au XVIIème siècle: ses relations commerciales avec les ports de l'Europe méditerranéenne, Marseille et Livourne.* Zaghouan: Centre d'Etudes et de Recherches Ottomanes et Morisco-Andalouses, 1987.

————. "Poids et mesures dans la Régence de Tunis au XVIIè siècle: le *ritl,* le *qafiz* de blé et le *mtar* d'huile." *Turcica* 16 (1984): 157–72.

Bouzgarrou-Larguèche, Dalenda. *Watan al-Munastir: fiscalité et société (1676–1856).* Tunis: Publications de la Faculté des Lettres de la Manouba, Université de Tunis I, 1993.

Brahimi, Denise. "Quelques jugements sur les maures andalous dans les régences turques au XVIIè siècle." In *Recueil d'études sur les moriscos andalous en Tunisie,* edited by Mikel de Epalza and Ramon Petit, 135–49. Madrid: Dirección General de Relaciones Culturales, Instituto Hispano-Arabe de Cultura, 1973.

Brunschvig, Robert. "Sur les mesures tunisiennes de capacité au commencement du XVIIè siècle." *Annales de l'Institut des Etudes Orientales* 3 (1937): 74–88.

Canal, Joseph. "Le canon 'le Saint-Paul' de la Goulette." *Revue Tunisienne* (1927): 116–17.

Chater, Khalifa. "Le fait ottoman en Tunisie: mythe et réalité." *Revue d'Histoire Maghrébine* 10, nos. 31–32 (1983): 141–48.

————. "La perception tunisienne de l'état ottoman." In *Actes du VIème Congrès du CIEPO: Les provinces arabes à l'époque ottomane,* edited by Abdeljelil Temimi, 87–93. Zaghouan: Centre d'Etudes et de Recherches Ottomanes et Morisco-Andalouses, 1987.

Chelli, Zouhir. *La Tunisie au rythme des estampes du XVè au XIXè siècle.* Tunis: Tunis-Carthage, 1987.

Chérif, Mohammed. "La 'déturqisation' du pouvoir en Tunisie: classes dirigeantes et société tunisienne de la fin du XVIè siècle à 1881." *Cahiers de Tunisie* 29, nos. 117–18 (1981): 177–97.

————. "Fermage (lizma) et fermiers d'impôts (lazzam) dans la Tunisie des XVIIè–XVIIIè siècles." *Cahiers de la Méditerranée* 41 (1990): 19–29.

————. "Introduction de la piastre espagnole ('ryal') dans la Régence de Tunis au début du XVIIè siècle." *Cahiers de Tunisie* 16, nos. 61–64 (1968): 45–55.

————. "Témoignages du 'mufti' Qasim Azzum sur les rapports entre Turcs et autochtones dans la Tunisie de la fin du XVIè siècle." *Cahiers de Tunisie* 20, nos. 77–78 (1972): 39–50.

Conor, M. "Les exploits d'Alonso de Contreras, aventurier espagnol en Tunisie (1601–1611)." *Revue Tunisienne* (1913): 597–611.

Daouletli, Abdelaziz. "Les influences ottomanes dans l'architecture tunisienne." In *La vie économique des provinces arabes et leurs sources documentaires à l'époque ottomane,* edited by Abdeljelil Temimi, 276–80. Zaghouan: Centre d'Etudes et de Recherches sur les Provinces Arabes à l'Epoque Ottomane, 1986.

Debbasch, Yvan. *La Nation française en Tunisie, 1577–1835.* Paris: Sirey, 1957.

Djait, Hisham. "Influences ottomanes sur les institutions, la civilisation et la culture tunisiennes du XVIè au XIXè siècle." *Revue d'Histoire Maghrébine* 3, no. 6 (1976): 150–56.

Djelloul, Néji. "Les fortifications de Bizerte à l'époque ottomane." *Arab Historical Review for Ottoman Studies* 7–8 (1993): 163–204.

———. "Remarques sur les fortifications des côtes tunisiennes à l'époque ottomane." *Revue de l'Institut des Belles Lettres Arabes* 56, no. 171 (1993): 3–38.

Dolot, Général. "La prise de Tunis par Charles Quint." *Revue Tunisienne* (1913): 497–98.

Emerit, Marcel. "L'essai d'une marine marchande barbaresque au XVI-IIè siècle." *Cahiers de Tunisie* 3 (1955): 363–70.

———. "La révolution tunisienne de 1864 et le secret de l'empéreur." *Revue Tunisienne* (1939): 221–39.

Epalza, Mikel de. "Moriscos y andalusíes en Túnez durante el siglo XVII. *al-Andalus* 24 (1969): 247–327.

———. "Morisques et andalous en Tunisie au XVIIè siècle." In *Recueil d'études sur les moriscos andalous en Tunisie,* edited by Mikel de Epalza and Ramon Petit, 150–86. Madrid: Dirección General de Relaciones Culturales, Instituto Hispano-Arabe de Cultura, 1973.

———. "Trabajos actuales sobre la comunidad de moriscos refugiados en Túnez, desde el siglo XVII a nuestros dias." In *Actas del Coloquio internacional sobre literatura aljamiada y morisca,* edited by Departamento di Filologia Romanica de la Facultad de Filosofia y Letras de la Universidad de Oviedo, 427–45. Madrid: Gredos, 1978.

Esin, Emel. "La géographie tunisienne de Piri Reis, à la lumière des sources turques du Xè/XVIè siècle." *Cahiers de Tunisie* 29, nos. 117–18 (1981): 585–605.

Fabris, Antonio. "Un caso di pirateria veneziana: la cattura della galea del Bey di Gerba (21 ottobre 1584)." *Quaderni di Studi Arabi* 8 (1990): 91–112.

———. "Note sul mappamondo cordiforme di Haci Ahmed di Tunisi." *Quaderni di Studi Arabi* 7 (1989): 3–17.

———. "The Ottoman mappa mundi of Hajji Ahmed of Tunis." *Arab Historical Review for Ottoman Studies* 7–8 (1993): 31–37.

Filesi, Teobaldo. "Un principe tunisino tra Islam e Christianesimo. (1646–1686)." *Africa* [Rome] 25 (1970): 25–48.

Gandolphe, M. "Notes inédites sur un canon de La Goulette." *Revue Tunisienne* (1919): 216–19, 410.

García-Arenal, Mercedes. "Nota a las traducciones manuscritas de F. Ximénez en la Real Academia de la Historia." *al-Qantara* 6 (1985): 525–33.

Gleizes, R. "La France en Tunisie. Le Consul Le Vacher." *Revue des Questions Historiques* 109 (1928): 81–100.

———. "Saint Vincent de Paul, esclave à Tunis." *Revue Tunisienne* (1920): 208–16, 296–304.

Gonzalez Castrillo, Ricardo. "La perdida de la Goleta y Tunez en 1574, y otros sucesos de historia otomana, narrados por un testigo presencial: Alonso de Salamanca." *Anaquel de Estudios Arabes* 3 (1992): 247–86.

Grandchamp, Pierre. *Etudes d'histoire tunisienne, XVIIè–XXè siècles.* Paris: Presses Universitaires de France, 1966.

———. *La France en Tunisie au XVIIè siècle (1651–1660).* Tunis: Imprimerie Rapide, 1928.

———. "Les beys mouradites (161?–1702)." *Revue Tunisienne* (1941): 227–32.

———. "Documents turcs relatifs aux relations entre Tunis et la Toscane (1626–1703)." *Revue Tunisienne* (1940): 109–14.

———. "Etablissement en 1692 d'une auberge dans le fondouk de la nation française. Sa suppression en 1778." *Revue Tunisienne* (1918): 226–32.

———. "Le Fondouk des Français." *Cahiers de Tunisie* 13 (1965): 37–40.

———. "La maison de campagne de Don Philippe (1659–1669)." *Revue Tunisienne* (1942): 256–58.

———. "Nicholas Béranger et sa correspondance." *Cahiers de Tunisie* 13 (1965): 85–117.

———. "Notables français à Tunis de 1592 à 1881." *Revue Tunisienne* (1942): 201–41.

———. "Pages d'histoire tunisienne: désignation d'un Vice-Consul de France pour Sousse, Monastir, Sfax et Djerba en février 1686." *Revue Tunisienne* (1918): 44–46.

———. "La Prétendue captivité de Saint Vincent de Paul à Tunis." *Cahiers de Tunisie* 13 (1965): 57–83.

Guellouz, Suzanne. "A propos de la Bataille de Tunis: contribution à une recherche sur la fonction des nouvelles intercalées dans le Quichotte." *Cahiers de Tunisie* 30, nos. 119–20 (1982): 199–211.

Henia, Abdelhamid. *Le Grid: ses rapports avec le beylik de Tunis (1676–1840).* Tunis: Université de Tunis, 1980.

————. "Circulation des biens et liens de parenté à Tunis (XVIIè–début XXè siècle)." In *Hasab wa nasab—Parenté, alliance et patrimoine en Tunisie,* edited by Sophie Ferchiou, 217–50. Paris: Centre National de la Recherche Scientifique, 1992.

————. "Fiscalités et politique fiscale dans la Régence de Tunis aux débuts de la conquête ottomane." In *Actes du VIème Congrès du CIEPO: Les provinces arabes à l'époque ottomane,* edited by Abdeljelil Temimi, 139–52. Zaghouan: Centre d'Etudes et de Recherches Ottomanes et Morisco-Andalouses, 1987.

————. "Mémoire d'origine d'un lignage dominant le pouvoir local à Tozeur (16è–19è siècles)." In *Mélanges offerts à Mohamed Talbi à l'occasion de son 70è anniversaire,* 125–48. La Manouba: Faculté des Lettres, 1993.

Heywood, Colin. "A Letter from Cerrah Mustafa Pasha, *Vali* of Tunis, to Sir William Trumbull (A.H. 1099/A.D. 1688)." *British Library Journal* 19, no. 2 (1993): 218–29.

Hopkins, Nicholas. "Notes sur l'histoire de Testour." *Revue d'Histoire Maghrébine* 4, no. 9 (1977): 294–313.

Hubac, Pierre. *Les Barbaresques.* Paris: Berger-Levrault, 1949.

Kassab, Ahmed. "L'évolution d'un village 'andalous': Testour." In *Recueil d'études sur les moriscos andalous en Tunisie,* edited by Mikel de Epalza and Ramon Petit, 359–68. Madrid: Dirección General de Relaciones Culturales, Instituto Hispano-Arabe de Cultura, 1973.

Kassab, Ahmed, and Fatima Kassab. "Técnicas de control del agua en Túnez y sus alrededores en época pre-colonial." In *Agua y poblamiento musulmán,* edited by Mikel de Epalza, 93–102. Benissa: Ajuntament de Benissa, 1988.

Krieken, Gérard van. "Trois représentants hollandais à Tunis (1616–1628)." *Revue de l'Institut des Belles Lettres Arabes* 39, no. 137 (1976): 41–71.

La Motte, Père de. "Voyages en Tunisie au XVIIème siècle: la mission du Père de La Motte (2 juin–26 juin 1700). Présentation et notes de Paul Sebag." *Revue de l'Institut des Belles Lettres Arabes* 53, no. 165 (1990): 3–37; 53, no. 166 (1990): 219–36.

Latham, John D. "Muçtafa de Càrdenas et l'apport des 'Morisques' à la société tunisienne du XVIIè siècle." *Les Africains, sous la direction de Charles-André Julien et al.* 7 (1977): 197–229.

————. "Towards a Study of Andalusian Immigration and its Place in Tunisian History." *Cahiers de Tunisie* 5 (1957): 203–52.

Louis, André, and Léon Verplancke. "La Tunisie au XVIIè siècle d'après la 'Description de l'Afrique' du Dr. C. Dapper." *Revue de l'Institut des Belles Lettres Arabes* 29, nos. 114–15 (1966): 143–213.

Magnin, Jean-Gabriel. "Coutumes des fêtes à Tunis au XIè–XVIIè siécle d'après Ibn Abi Dinar." *Revue de l'Institut des Belles Lettres Arabes* 15, no. 60 (1952): 387–421.

Magnin, Jean-Gabriel, ed. and trans. "Ibn Abi Dinar. Description de Tunis." *Revue de l'Institut des Belles Lettres Arabes* 14, no. 54 (1951): 150–82.

Mantran, Robert. "La description des côtes de la Tunisie dans le Kitabi Bahriye de Piri Reis." *Revue de l'Occident Musulmane et de la Méditerranée* 24 (1977): 223–35.

———. "L'évolution des relations entre la Tunisie et l'Empire Ottoman du XVIè au XIXè siècle." *Cahiers de Tunisie* 7 (1959): 319–33.

Médina, G. "L'expédition de Charles-Quint à Tunis. La légende et la vérité." *Revue Tunisienne* (1906): 185–94, 301–7.

Mesnard, P. "Charles-Quint et les Barbaresques." *Bulletin Hispanique* 61 (1959): 215–35.

Monchicourt, Charles. "A travers l'histoire de la Tunisie: l'insecurité en Mediterranée durant l'été de 1550." *Revue Tunisienne* (1917): 317–24.

———. "Dragut, amiral turn (juin 1551–avril 1558)." *Revue Tunisienne* (1930): 106–18.

———. "Episodes de la carrière tunisienne de Dragut." *Revue Tunisienne* (1918): 35–43, 263–73.

———. "Le voyageur Peysonnel de Kairouan au Kef et à Dougga (Aôut 1724)." *Revue Tunisienne* (1916): 266–77, 356–64.

Monlau, Jean. *Les Etats barbaresques.* Paris: Presses Universitaires de France, 1964.

Oueslati, Hedi. "Texto de un exiliado morisco en Túnez (siglo XVII)." *Sharq al-Andalus* 4 (1987): 257–61.

Penella, J. "El sentimiento religioso de los moriscos españoles emigrados: notas para una literatura morisca en Túnez." In *Actas del Coloquio internacional sobre literatura aljamiada y morisca,* 447–73. Madrid: Gredos, 1978.

———. "Le transfert des moriscos espagnols en Afrique du Nord." In *Recueil d'études sur les moriscos andalous en Tunisie,* edited by Mikel de Epalza and Ramon Petit, 77–88. Madrid: Dirección General de Relaciones Culturales, Instituto Hispano-Arabe de Cultura, 1973.

Pieri, Henri. "L'accueil par des tunisiens aux morisques expulsés d'Espagne: un témoignage morisque." *Revue de l'Institut des Belles Lettres Arabes* 31, no. 121 (1968): 63–70.

Pignon, Jean. "Aperçu sur les relations entre Malte et la Côte Orientale de la Tunisie au début du XVIIème siècle. (Quelques documents inédits des Archives de Malte)." *Cahiers de Tunisie* 12 (1964): 59–78.

———. "Dix ans de relations franco-tunisiennes (1606–1616)." *Cahiers de Tunisie* 4 (1956): 199–212.

———. "Un document inédit sur la Tunisie au début du XVIIè siècle." *Cahiers de Tunisie* 9 (1961): 109–219.

———. "L'esclavage en Tunisie de 1590 à 1620." *Revue Tunisienne* (1930): 18–37; (1932): 346–77. [Also in *Cahiers de Tunisie* 24, nos. 93–94 (1976): 145–65].

──────. "La France en Tunisie aux XVIè et XVIIè siècles. Un comptoir français à l'Est du cap Serrat 'La Fumayre Sallatte.'" *Revue Africaine* 76 (1935): 275–79.

──────. "Gênes et Tabarca au XVIIème siècle." *Cahiers de Tunisie* 27, nos. 109–10 (1979): 7–141.

──────. "La milice des janissaires de Tunis au temps des Deys (1590–1650)." *Cahiers de Tunisie* 4 (1956): 301–26.

──────. "Osta Moratto Turcho Genovese, Dey de Tunis." *Cahiers de Tunisie* 3 (1955): 331–62.

──────. "Les relations franco-tunisiennes au début du XVIIè siècle: l'accord de 1606." *Cahiers de Tunisie* 26, nos. 101–2 (1978): 164–79. [Also in *Revue Africaine* 100 (1956): 409–21.

Pignon-Reix, Jean. "Un document inédit sur les relations franco-tunisiennes au début du XVIIè siècle." *Revue de l'Occident Musulmane et de la Méditerranée* 20 (1975): 105–30.

Raymond, André. "Le déplacement des tanneries à Alep, au Caire et à Tunis à l'époque ottomane: un 'indicateur' de croissance urbaine." *Revue du Monde Musulman et de la Méditerranée* 55–56 (1990): 34–43.

──────. "Une liste des deys de Tunis de 1590 à 1832." *Cahiers de Tunisie* 8 (1960): 129–36.

──────. "Les zones de résidence dans les grandes villes arabes à l'époque ottomane: mixité ou ségregation socio-économique? Le cas de Tunis, le Caire et Alep." *Arab Historical Review for Ottoman Studies* 9–10 (1994): 185–95.

Renon, A. "Le chevalier d'Arvieux et sa mission dans la Régence, 1666." *Revue de l'Institut des Belles Lettres Arabes* 3, no. 2 (1939): 227–44.

Revault, Jacques. *Palais, demeures et maisons de plaisance à Tunis et dans ses environs du XVIè au XIXè siècle.* Aix-en-Provence: Edisud, 1984.

Ricard, R. "Ibero-Africana. Le Père Jérôme Gratien de la Mère de Dieu et sa captivité à Tunis (1593–1595)." *Revue Africaine* 89 (1945): 190–200.

Rossi, E. "Relazioni tra i Gran Maestri dell' Ordine di Malta e i Bey di Tunisi dal 1642 al 1756." *Revue Tunisienne* (1932): 193–215.

Rozen, M. "The Leghorn Merchants in Tunis and Their Trade with Marseilles at the End of the 17th Century." In *Les relations intercommunautaires juives en Méditerranée occidentale, XIIIè–XXè siècles: actes du Colloque International de l'Institut d'Histoire des Pays d'Outre-Mer (GIS Méditerranée Aix-en-Provence) et du Centre de Recherches sur les Juifs d'Afrique du Nord (Institut Ben Zvi, Université de Jérusalem),* edited by Jean Miège, 51–59. Paris: Centre Nationale de la Recherche Scientifique, 1984.

Sebag, Paul. *Tunis au XVIIè siècle: une cité barbaresque au temps de la course.* Paris: L'Harmattan, 1989.

————. "Cartes, plans et vues générales de Tunis et de La Goulette aux XVIIè et XVIIIè siècles." In *Etudes maghrébines. Mélanges C. A. Julien,* edited by Pierre Marthelot and André Raymond, 89–101. Paris: Université de Paris, 1964.

————. "La Goulette et sa fortresse de la fin du XVIè siècle à nos jours." *Revue de l'Institut des Belles Lettres Arabes* 30, no. 117 (1967): 13–34.

————. "Les monnaies tunisiennes au XVIIè siècle." *Revue du Monde Musulman et de la Méditerranée* 55–56 (1990), 257–65.

————. "La peste dans la Régence de Tunis aux XVIIè et XVIIIè siècles." *Revue de l'Institut des Belles Lettres Arabes* 28, no. 109 (1965): 35–48.

————. "La régence de Tunis et la France au XVIIè siècle." In *Itinéraires de France en Tunisie du XVIè au XIXè siècle,* 23–30. Marseille: Bibliothèque Municipale, 1995.

————. "Sur une chronique des beys mouradites. Une oeuvre posthume de Guilleragues?" *Revue de l'Institut des Belles Lettres Arabes* 36, no. 131 (1973): 53–78.

————. "Voyages en Tunisie au XVIIè siècle. L'Escale de Jean Thévenot (9 mars 1659–30 mars 1659)." *Revue de l'Institut des Belles Lettres Arabes* 43, no. 145 (1980): 47–78.

————. "Voyages en Tunisie au XVIIè siècle. La négociation de Laurent d'Arvieux (12 juin 1665–15 août 1666)." *Revue de l'Institut des Belles Lettres Arabes* 44, no. 147 (1981): 71–94; 44, no. 148 (1981): 253–86.

Sebag, Paul, ed. *Une relation inédite sur la prise de Tunis par les Turcs en 1574: Sopra la desolatione della Goletta e forte di Tunisi de Bartholomeo Ruffino.* Tunis: Université de Tunis, 1971. [Also in *Cahiers de Tunisie* 17 (1969): 7–250.]

Sethom, Hafedh. "L'apport andalous à la civilisation rurale de la presqu'île du Cap Bon." In *Recueil d'études sur les moriscos andalous en Tunisie,* edited by Mikel de Epalza and Ramon Petit, 369–73. Madrid: Dirección General de Relaciones Culturales, Instituto Hispano-Arabe de Cultura, 1973.

Soucek, Svat. *Tunisia in the Kitab-i Bahriye by Piri Reis.* Lisse: Peter de Ridder, 1976.

————. "The Rise of the Barbarossas in North Afrcia." *Archivium Ottomanicum* 3 (1971): 238–50.

————. "Tunisia in the *Kitab-i bahriye* by Piri Reis." *Archivum Ottomanicum* 5 (1973): 129–296.

Soumille, Pierre, and Jean Peyras. "La mémoire du protestantisme à Tunis d'après les monuments du cimetière anglican de Bab-Carthagène (depuis le milieu du XVIIè siècle jusqu'à la fin du XIXè siècle)." In *Les Monuments et la mémoire,* edited by Jean Peyras, 51–70. Paris: L'Harmattan, 1993.

Temimi, Abdeljalil. "L'arrière plan religieux du duel hispano-ottomane au Maghreb au XVIè siècle." *Revue d'Histoire Maghrébine* 10, nos. 31–32 (1983): 373–82.

———. "Evolution de l'attitude des autorités de la Régence de Tunis face à l'accueil des morisques, à la lumière d'un nouveau firman du sultan ottoman." *Revue d'Histoire Maghrébine* 20, nos. 69–70 (1993): 169–80.

Tenenti, Alberto. "I corsari in Mediterraneo all'inizio del Cinquecento. *Rivista Storica Italiana* 72 (1960): 234–87.

Turbet-Delof, Guy. "Une turquerie tunisienne imprimée à Paris en 1673." *XVIIè Siècle* 27 (1975): 35–41.

Turki, Abdelmajid. "Documents sur le dernier exode des andalous vers la Tunisie." In *Recueil d'études sur les moriscos andalous en Tunisie,* edited by Mikel de Epalza and Ramon Petit, 114–27. Madrid: Dirección General de Relaciones Culturales, Instituto Hispano-Arabe de Cultura, 1973.

Vilar, Juan Bautista. *Mapas, planos y fortificationes hispánicos de Túnez (s. XVI–XIX).* Madrid: Instituto de Cooperación con el Mundo Arabe, 1991.

———. "Cartografia hispanica sobre Tunez (1500–1881)." *Bolletino de la Real Academia de la Historia* 187 (1990): 145–58.

———. "Dos siglos de presencia de España en Tabarka (1535–1741)." *Revue d'Histoire Maghrébine* 20, nos. 77–78 (1995): 163–82.

Vittu, Jean-Pierre. "Un commissionaire marseillais à Tunis et ses affaires de 1684 à 1706: Nicolas Béranger." *Revue d'histoire moderne et contemporaine* 24 (1977): 582–601.

The Husainid Era to 1881

Abdesselem, Ahmed. *Les Historiens tunisiens des XVIIè, XVIIIè, et XIXè siècles.* Tunis: Université de Tunis, 1973.

———. "Ahmad ben Abi-d-Diaf, chroniqueur du beylicat de Tunis." *Les Africains, sous la direction de Ch.-A. Julien et al.* 8 (1977): 13–37.

———. "Contribution à l'étude de la politique et de l'administration d'Ahmad Bey (1837–1855). La délégation de pouvoirs de 1846." *Cahiers de Tunisie* 19 (1971): 109–18.

———. " 'Révolutions barbaresques' et poésie arabe: réflexions sur la vie et l'oeuvre d'un prince-poète tunisien du XVIIIè siècle." *Cahiers de Tunisie* 22 (1964): 35–40.

Abid, Mounir. "Les débuts de la règlementation sanitaire du pélerinage tunisien à la Mecque (1831–1866)." *Revue d'Histoire Maghrébine* 21, nos. 79–80 (1995): 273–78.

Abu-Lughod, Ibrahim. "The Islamic Influence on Khayr al-Din of Tunis." In *Essays on Islamic Civilisation Presented to Niyazi Berkes,* edited by Donald Little, 9–24. Leiden: Brill, 1976.

Abun-Nasr, Jamil. "The *Mashyahat al-Islam* in Tunisia." In *Proceedings of the Ninth Congress of the Union Européenne des Arabisants et Islamisants, Amsterdam, 1978,* edited by R. Peters, 1–14. Leiden: Brill, 1981.

———. "Religion and Politics in Eighteenth Century Tunisia." *XIX Deutscher Orientalistentag* (1975): 295–318.

———. "The Tunisian State in the 18th Century." *Revue de l'Occident Musulman et de la Méditerranée* 33 (1982): 33–66.

Ammairia, Hafnaoui. "Doléances et résistance dans le chant populaire de la région de Gafsa (1860–1885)." *Revue du Monde Musulman et de la Méditerranée* 51 (1989): 127–36.

Anderson, Lisa. *The State and Social Transformation in Tunisia and Libya, 1830–1930.* Princeton: Princeton University Press, 1986.

Anselme des Arcs, Révérend Père. "Mémoires pour servir à l'histoire de la mission des Capuchins dans la Régence de Tunis (1624–1865). Revus et publiés par le R. P. Apollinaire de Valence (Rome 1889). Présenté et commenté par P. Soumille. Troisième Partie." *Revue d'Histoire Maghrébine* 11, nos. 33–34 (1984): 164–82; 11, nos. 35–36 (1984): 229–52; 13, nos. 41–42 (1986): 175–204.

Arnoulet, François. "L'activité diplomatique française en Tunisie à l'époque de l'expédition d'Alger (1828–1831)." *Revue de l'Institut des Belles Lettres Arabes* 39, no. 138 (1976): 243–75.

———. "Conception de l'assistance sanitaire en Tunisie au XIXème siècle." *Revue d'Histoire Maghrébine* 17, nos. 59–60 (1990): 17–22.

———. "Les explorations tunisiennes de 1802 à 1881." *Revue de l'Institut des Belles Lettres Arabes* 10, no. 38 (1947): 167–80.

———. "Les français en Tunisie pendant la révolution française (1789–1802)." In *La Révolution française et le monde arabo-musulman,* edited by Hédia Khadhar, 27–60. Tunis: Alif, 1991.

———. "Les installations du comptoir corailleur du cap Négro au XVIIIè siècle." *Revue d'Histoire Maghrébine* 9, nos. 25–26 (1982): 7–16.

———. "D'Ogier Sorhaindre et Mathieu de Lesseps: deux conceptions du système consulaire français." *Revue d'Histoire Maghrébine* 16, nos. 53–54 (1989): 13–28.

———. "Participation tunisienne à la guerre de Crimée (1854–1856)." *Cahiers de Tunisie* 20 (1972): 269–84.

———. "La pénétration intellectuelle en Tunisie avant le Protectorat." *Revue Africaine* 98 (1954): 140–82.

———. "Les rapports tuniso-ottomans de 1848 à 1881 d'après les documents diplomatiques." *Revue de l'Occident Musulman et de la Méditerranée* 47 (1988): 143–52.

———. "Structure urbaine et essai démographique de Tripoli de Barbarie, Tunis et Alger au XVIIIè siècle." *Arab Historical Review for Ottoman Studies* 9–10 (1994): 17–22.

Arnoulet, François, C. Matrat, and Jean Louis Miège. *Etudes d'histoire contemporaine tunisienne (1846–1871)*. Aix-en-Provence: Institut d'Histoire des Pays d'Outre-Mer, 1973.

"Autour du premier voyage effectué en France par un Souverain de la dynastie husseinite, Ahmed Bey." *Revue Tunisienne* (1923): 161–66.

Bachrouch, Taoufik. "Les Sadikiens de la première heure ou la tentation de l'ouverture." *Cahiers de Tunisie* 36, nos. 143–44 (1988): 167–82.

Bardin, Pierre. *Algériens et tunisiens dans l'Empire ottoman de 1848 à 1914*. Paris: Centre Nationale de Recherche Scientifique, 1979.

Bashrush [Bachrouch], Tawfiq. *Le Saint et le prince en Tunisie. Les élites tunisiennes du pouvoir et de la dévotion. Contribution à l'étude des groupes sociaux dominants (1782–1881)*. Tunis: Publications de l'Université de Tunis I, 1989.

Bdira, Mezri. *Relations internationales et sous-développement: la Tunisie 1857–1864*. Stockholm: Almqvist and Wiksell, 1978.

———. "Développement arabe et conflits internationaux: l'exemple de la Tunisie, 1815–1855 d'après des documents suédois." *Revue Tunisienne des Sciences Sociales* 92–93 (1988): 181–343.

Ben Achour, Mohamed el-Aziz. *Catégories de la société tunisienne dans la deuxième moitié du XIXème siècle*. Tunis: Institut National d'Archéologie et d'Arts, 1989.

———. *Les décorations tunisiennes à l'époque husseinite*. Tunis: Sagittaire, 1993.

———. "Autorités urbaines de l'économie et du commerce de Tunis au XIXème siècle." *Revue de l'Institut des Belles Lettres Arabes* 51, no. 162 (1988): 243–62; 52, no. 163 (1989): 3–21.

———. "Les aylat du corpus: notes historiques." In *Hasab wa nasab— Parenté, alliance et patrimoine en Tunisie*, edited by Sophie Ferchiou, 107–36. Paris: Centre National de la Recherche Scientifique, 1992.

———. "Cadre urbain, habitat et structures sociales à Tunis dans la deuxième moitié du XIXè siècle." *Cahiers de Tunisie* 34, nos. 137–38 (1986): 267–307.

———. "Quelques notes sur l'onomastique tunisienne à l'époque husaynite précoloniale (XVIIIè–XIXè siècles)." *Cahiers d'onomastique arabe* (1979): 21–36.

Benali, Muhiddine. "Un pueblo andalusi en Tunez en el siglo XIX: Soliman." *Miscelanea de Estudios Arabes y Hebraicos* 25 (1976): 97–113.

Bennett, Norman. "Christian and Negro Slavery in Eighteenth-Century North Africa." *Journal of African History* 1 (1960): 65–82.

Ben Tahar, Jamel. "Note sur les sources relatives à l'histoire des souks ruraux de la Tunisie au XIXème siècle." *Revue de l'Institut des Belles Lettres Arabes* 53, no. 165 (1990): 39–57.

Ben Youssef, Mohammed Seghir. *Mechra el melki: chronique tunisi-enne (1705–1771), pour servir à l'histoire des quatre premiers Beys de la famille Husseinite.* Translated by Victor Serres and Mohammed Lasram. 2d ed. Tunis: Editions Bouslama, 1978.

Bercher, L. "En marge du pacte 'fondamental'. Un document inédit." *Revue Tunisienne* (1939): 67–86; (1940): 59–69. [Also in *Cahiers de Tunisie* 20 (1972): 243–60.]

Bergaoui, Sami. "Fortunes tribales dans la Tunisie du milieu du XIXè siècle: le cas des Ben Said (tribu des Beni Zid)." *Cahiers de la Méditerranée* 45 (1992): 5–18.

Berque, Jacques. "Ulémas tunisois de jadis et de naguère. Notes de lecture sur les *Musamarat al-Zarif.*" *Cahiers de Tunisie* 20 (1972): 87–124.

Bono, Salvatore. "'Il Ragguaglio del viaggio compendioso' di Felice Caronni a Tunisi (1804). Un impegno di conoscenza dell'islam." *Islam Storia e Civiltà* 11, no. 40 (1992): 171–77.

Bouali, Mahmoud. *Introduction à l'histoire constitutionelle de la Tunisie.* 2 vols. Tunis: En-Najah, 1963–1964.

———. *La sédition permanente en Tunisie.* Tunis: Maison Tunisienne de l'Edition, 1972.

———. *Le temps de la non-revolté, 1827–1832.* Tunis: Société Tunisienne de Diffusion, 1976.

Boubaker, Sadok. "L'économie de traite dans la Régence de Tunis au début du XVIIIème siècle: le comptoir du Cap-Nègre en 1741." *Revue d'Histoire Maghrébine* 16, nos. 53–54 (1989): 29–86.

———. "Les relations entre Gênes et la Régence de Tunis depuis 1741 jusqu'à la fin du XVIIIème siècle." *Arab Historical Review for Ottoman Studies* 7–8 (1993): 11–29.

———. "Simon Merlet, marchand marseillais dans la Régence de Tunis (1693–1741)." *Provence Historique* 34 (1984): 327–43.

Boudard, René. "Genois et barbaresques dans la deuxième moitié du XVIIIè siècle." *Revue d'Histoire Diplomatique* 74 (1960): 138–56.

Bouhdiba, Abd Ulwahab. "Genèse du concept de nation en Tunisie." *Revue de l'Institut de Sociologie* 40 (1967): 441–56.

Boulanger, Patrick. "Navires provençaux sur les côtes de la Tunisie au XVIIIè siècle." In *Itinéraires de France en Tunisie du XVIè au XIXè siècle,* 31–46. Marseille: Bibliothèque Municipale, 1995.

Bouzgarrou-Larguèche, Dalenda. *Watan al-Munastir: fiscalité et société (1676–1856).* Tunis: Publications de la Faculté des Lettres de la Manouba, Université de Tunis I, 1993.

Brahimi, Denise. "Témoignages sur l'île de Tabarque au XVIIIè siècle." *Revue de l'Occident Musulmane et de la Méditerranée* 7 (1970): 15–35.

Brown, L. Carl. *The Tunisia of Ahmad Bey*. Princeton: Princeton University Press, 1974.

——. "Ahmed Bey, un monarque éclairé à l'aube de la Tunisie moderne." *Les Africains, sous la direction de Ch.-A. Julien et al.* 9 (1978): 13–43.

——. "The Religious Establishment in Husainid Tunisia." In *Scholars, Saints, and Sufis,* edited by Nikki Keddie, 47–91. Berkeley: University of California Press, 1972.

——. "The Tunisian Path to Modernization." In *Society and Political Structure in the Arab World,* edited by Menahem Milson, 183–230. New York: Humanities Press, 1973.

Buccianti, C. "Da Tunisi a Tozeur (1751–1752): viaggio del medico toscano Giuseppe Cei." *Africa* [Rome] 49 (1994): 574–86.

Buonocore, Ferdinando. *Ai margini della peste di Tunisi del 1818–1820*. Casoria: Polisud, 1974.

——. "Due tragici avvenimenti nella Reggenza di Tunisi all'inizio del XIX secolo: visiti attraverso il carteggio del Consolato delle Due Sicile conservato nell' Archivo di Stato di Napoli." *Africa* [Rome] 23 (1968): 165–95.

Burgard, R. "Semilasso en Tunisie." *Revue Tunisienne* (1932): 217–43.

——. "Victor Cherbuliez et la Tunisie." *Revue Tunisienne* (1930): 119–26.

Cannon, Byron, and Mohammed Sufiullah. "The Function of Wakalah in Intra-Ottoman Relations: Egypt and Tunisia in the First Half of the 19th Century." *Arab Historical Review for Ottoman Studies* 5–6 (1992): 11–17.

Chater, Khalifa. *Dépendances et mutations précoloniales: La Régence de Tunis de 1815 à 1857*. Tunis: Université de Tunis, 1984.

——. *Insurrection et repression dans la Tunisie du XIXè siècle: la Mehalla de Zarrouk au Sahel (1864)*. Tunis: Université de Tunis, 1978.

——. "Le commerce caravanier au Maghreb et ses mutations au cours de l'ère précoloniale." *Maghreb Review* 3–4 (1987): 99–104.

——. "Eléments pour une approche de certaines phénomènes de 'açabiya' dans la Tunisie du XIXè siècle (Sahel et Basses Steppes). *Cahiers de Tunisie* 25, nos. 97–98 (1977): 61–73.

——. "Les élites du pouvoir et de l'argent: le cas de la Tunisie aux XIXè–XXè siècle." *Cahiers de la Méditerranée* 46–47 (1993): 155–72.

——. "En marge d'une lecture du chroniqueur Seghir ben Youssef: la situation économique et sociale de la Régence de Tunis au XVIIIème siècle." In *La vie économique des provinces arabes et leurs sources documentaures à l'époque ottomane,* edited by Abdeljelil Temimi,

161–76. Zaghouan: Centre d'Etudes et de Recherches sur les Provinces Arabes à l'Epoque Ottomane, 1986.

————. "Islam et réformes politiques dans la Tunisie du XIXè siècle." *Maghreb Review* 13 (1988): 77–83.

————. "La ville tunisienne au XIXè siècle. Théorie et réalités." *Cahiers de Tunisie* 26, nos. 103–4 (1978): 83–108.

Chelli, Zouhir. *La Tunisie au rythme des estampes du XVè au XIXè siècle*. Tunis: Tunis-Carthage, 1987.

Chenoufi, Ali. *Le ministre Khreddine et ses contemporains—XIXème siècle*. Carthage: Bayt al-Hikma, 1990.

————. *Un savant tunisien du XIXème siècle: Muhammad as-Sanusi, sa vie et son oeuvre*. Tunis: Université de Tunis, 1977.

Chérif, Mohammed. *Pouvoir et société dans la Tunisie de Husayn bin Ali, 1705–1740*. Tunis: Faculté des Lettres et Sciences Humaines, 1986.

————. "La 'déturqisation' du pouvoir en Tunisie: classes dirigeantes et société tunisienne de la fin du XVIè siècle à 1881." *Cahiers de Tunisie* 29, nos. 117–18 (1981): 177–97.

————. "Document relatif à des tribus tunisiennes des débuts du XVIIIè siècle: enseignements démographiques et économiques." *Revue de l'Occident Musulman et de la Méditerranée* 33 (1982): 67–87.

————. "Les documents de Bayt al-Mal dans les archives de l'ancienne direction des Habous (en Tunisie)." In *La vie économique des provinces arabes et leurs sources documentaures à l'époque ottomane*, edited by Abdeljelil Temimi, 209–212. Zaghouan: Centre d'Etudes et de Recherches sur les Provinces Arabes à l'Epoque Ottomane, 1986.

————. "Expansion européenne et difficultés tunisiennes de 1815 à 1830." *Annales Economies, Sociétés, Civilisations* 25 (1961): 714–45.

————. "Fermage (lizma) et fermiers d'impôts (lazzam) dans la Tunisie des XVIIè–XVIIIè siècles." *Cahiers de la Méditerranée* 41 (1990): 19–29.

————. "Hammuda Pacha bey et l'affermissement de l'autonomie tunisienne." *Les Africains, sous la direction de Ch.-A. Julien et al.* 7 (1977): 99–127.

————. "L'histoire économique et sociale de la Tunisie au XVIIIé siècle à travers les sources locales: enseignements et perspectives." In *Les Arabes par leurs archives,* edited by Jacques Berque and Dominique Chevallier, 101–18. Paris: Centre Nationale de Recherche Scientifique, 1976.

————. "Les mouvements paysans dans la Tunisie du XIXè siècle." *Revue de l'Occident Musulman et de la Méditerranée* 30 (1980): 21–55.

————. "Tunis de la fin du XVIIè siècle à 1956. Introduction historique." In *Hasab wa nasab—Parenté, alliance et patrimoine en*

Tunisie, edited by Sophie Ferchiou, 27–50. Paris: Centre National de la Recherche Scientifique, 1992.

Clancy-Smith, Julia. *Rebel and Saint: Muslim Notables, Populist Protest, Colonial Encounters (Algeria and Tunisia, 1800–1904).* Berkeley: University of California Press, 1994.

Cleveland, William. "The Municipal Council of Tunis." *International Journal of Middle Eastern Studies* 9 (1978): 33–61.

Conor, M. "Chateaubriand à Tunis. Janvier-Mars 1807." *Revue Tunisienne* (1918): 337–48.

Conor, M., and Pierre Grandchamp. "Relation du court voyage d'un antiquaire amateur (F. Caroni) surpris par les corsaires, conduit en Barbarie et heureusement rapatrié (1804)." *Revue Tunisienne* (1916): 287–94, 393–403; (1917): 32–54, 96–122.

Dabbab, Mohamed. *La presse arabe de Tunisie, 1860–1914.* Tunis: Société Tunisienne de Diffusion, 1990.

Davies, G. "Greek Slaves at Tunis in 1823." *English Historical Review* 34 (1919): 84–89.

Debbasch, Yvan. *La nation française en Tunisie, 1577–1835.* Paris: Sirey, 1957.

Demeerseman, André. "Aspect humain des réformes de Khéreddine en Tunisie." *Revue de l'Institut des Belles Lettres Arabes* 20, no. 80 (1957): 317–50.

———. "Au berceau des premières réformes démocratiques en Tunisie." *Revue de l'Institut des Belles Lettres Arabes* 20, no. 77 (1957): 1–12.

———. "Catégories familiales et judicature tunisienne de la fin du XVIIIè à la seconde moitié du XIXè siècles." *Revue de l'Institut des Belles Lettres Arabes* 43, no. 146 (1980): 245–77; 44, no. 147 (1981): 95–125.

———. "Catégories sociales en Tunisie au XIXè siècle d'après la chronique de A. Ibn Ali al Diyaf." *Revue de l'Institut des Belles Lettres Arabes* 32, no. 123 (1969): 17–36; 32, no. 124 (1969): 241–72; 23, no. 125 (1970): 69–101.

———. "Doctrine de Khéreddine en matière de politique extérieure." *Revue de l'Institut des Belles Lettres Arabes* 21, no. 81 (1958): 13–29.

———. "La fonction de Cheikh al-islam en Tunisie de la fin du XVIIIème au début du XXème siècles." *Revue de l'Institut des Belles Lettres Arabes* 42, no. 142 (1978): 215–70.

———. "Fondation de la première zawiya qadiriyya tunisienne à la fin du XVIIIè siècle, d'après al-Sayh al-Amin al-Kilani." *Revue de l'Institut des Belles Lettres Arabes* 49, no. 158 (1986): 321–26.

———. "Formulations de l'idée de patrie en Tunisie (1837–1872)." *Revue de l'Institut des Belles Lettres Arabes* 29, nos. 114–15 (1966): 109–42.

————. "Formulations de l'idée de patrie en Tunisie (1837–1872). Analyse des données linguistiques." *Revue de l'Institut des Belles Lettres Arabes* 29, no. 113 (1966): 35–71.

————. "Un grand témoin des premières idées modernisantes en Tunisie (Khéreddine)." *Revue de l'Institut des Belles Lettres Arabes* 19, no. 76 (1956): 349–73.

————. "Idéal politique de Khéreddine. Sa valeur morale." *Revue de l'Institut des Belles Lettres Arabes* 20, no. 79 (1957): 179–215.

————. "Indépendance de la Tunisie et politique extérieure de Khéreddine." *Revue de l'Institut des Belles Lettres Arabes* 21, no. 83 (1958): 229–77.

————. "Licences d'exportation d'huile tunisienne (1816–1823)." *Revue de l'Institut des Belles Lettres Arabes* 39, no. 137 (1976): 73–119.

————. "Une mission tunisienne en France dans la première moitié du XIXè siècle." *Revue de l'Institut des Belles Lettres Arabes* 34, no. 127 (1971): 63–92.

————. "Note sur les inter-relations des ulémas au XIXème siècle d'après Ibn Abi D-Diyaf." *Revue de l'Institut des Belles Lettres Arabes* 42 (1978): 345–48.

Demeerseman, André, trans. "Inventaire des biens d'un Caid en 1826: Bakkar Djellouli." *Revue de l'Institut des Belles Lettres Arabes* 45, no. 150 (1982): 281–302.

Denizet, J. "L'histoire navale de la Tunisie de 1815 à 1888 aux Archives de la Marine." *Cahiers de Tunisie* 4 (1956): 409–12.

Desfeuilles, Paul. "Scandinaves et Barbaresques à la fin de l'Ancien Régime." *Cahiers de Tunisie* 4 (1956): 327–49.

Djait, Hisham. "Influences ottomanes sur les institutions, la civilisation et la culture tunisiennes du XVIè au XIXè siècle." *Revue d'Histoire Maghrébine* 3, no. 6 (1976): 150–56.

Emerit, Marcel. "Les crises des finances tunisiennes et les origines du Protectorat." *Revue Africaine* 93 (1949): 249–76.

————. "La pénétration industrielle et commerciale en Tunisie et les origines du Protectorat." *Revue Africaine* 96 (1952): 196–219.

Epalza, Mikel de. "Autour d'un centenaire: le voyageur espagnol Domingo Badia (Ali Bey el-Abbasi, 1767–1818) en Tunisie." *Revue de l'Institut des Belles Lettres Arabes* 31, no. 121 (1968): 51–61.

————. "Nota sobre consecuencias hispano-magrebies de la Revolución Francesa." *Awraq* 11 (1990): 171–74.

————. "Nouveaux documents sur les Andalous en Tunisie au début du XVIIIème siècle." *Revue d'Histoire Maghrébine* 7, nos. 17–18 (1980): 78–108.

Epalza, Mikel de, and Abdelhakim Gafsi. "Relations tuniso-espagnoles au XIXè siècle: documents et synthèse." *Cahiers de Tunisie* 26, nos. 101–2 (1978): 183–216.

Fendri, Mounir. *Heinrich Barth's briefe aus Tunesien (1845–1846)*. Tunis: Beit al-Hikma, 1987.

———. "L'audience du 9 mai 1835: le Prince de Pückler-Muskau chez Hussein Bey." *Cahiers de Tunisie* 30, nos. 121–22 (1982): 187–231.

———. "Kheireddine et *Aqwam al-masalik* dans l'opinion d'un contemporain étranger: Le baron Heinrich von Maltzan." *Revue d'Histoire Maghrébine* 19, nos. 67–68 (1992): 247–51.

———. "Trois voyageurs allemands en Tunisie au XVIIIème siècle. III—August von Einsiedel (1785)." *Revue d'Histoire Maghrébine* 13, nos. 41–42 (1986): 47–85.

Filesi, Teobaldo. "Napoli e Tunisi nel 1833." *Annali della Facolta di Scienze Politiche (Università di Cagliari)* 9 (1983): 369–92.

———. "Un sorrentino alla corte tunisina: Mariano Stinca segretario di Mauda Bey (1789–1814)." *Islam: Storia e Civiltà* 3 (1984): 33–43.

Fozzard, A. "Tribes and the State: The Experience of Southern Tunisia (1850–1950)." In *BRISMES: Proceedings of the 1988 Conference on Middle Eastern Studies,* 158–66. Oxford: British Society for Middle Eastern Studies, 1988.

Froidevaux, Henri. "La tribulation de Jacques Devoize à Tunis en 1796." *Revue de l'Histoire des Colonies Françaises* 10 (1922): 116–26.

Gafsi, Abdelhakim. "Conséquence de l'expulsion des *moriscos:* la régénération de la culture des oliviers à Tebourba en 1726." In *L'expulsió dels moriscos: conseqüènces en el món islàmic i el mon cristià. 380è aniversari de l'expulsió del moriscos,* edited by Mikel de Epalza, 147–57. Barcelona: Generalitat de Catalunya, 1994.

———. "Estudio económico-social de un pueblo andalusí tunecino: Kalat al-Andalus de 1847 a 1881." *Almenara* 9 (1976): 83–93.

———. Une famille des monétaires sous les Husseinites: les Kastalli." In *Monnaies tunisiennes depuis l'époque punique jusqu'à nos jours,* 23–40. Tunis: Banque Centrale de Tunisie, 1993.

Gallagher, Nancy. "The Arab Medical Organization in Nineteenth Century Tunisia." *Revue d'Histoire Maghrébine* 2, no. 4 (1975): 145–49.

———. "Toward an Evaluation of the Population of the Nineteenth-Century Regency of Tunis." *Revue d'Histoire Maghrébine* 5, no. 12 (1978): 303–7.

Gallico, Augusto. *Tunis et les consuls sardes (1816–1834)*. Translated by Lina and Mohamed Yalaoui. Beirut: Dar al-Gharb al-Islami, 1992.

Gandolphe, M. "Chronique d'histoire tunisienne. La tragique aventure d'Andrea Poggi." *Revue Tunisienne* (1927): 41–58.

———. "Les événements de 1864 dans le Sahel et principalement à Sousse d'après des lettres inédites." *Revue Tunisienne* (1918): 138–53.

———. "Extraits de l'ouvrage 'Documenti sulla storia di Tunis' da G. Niculy detto Limberi." *Revue Tunisienne* (1919): 507–13.

―――. "La Goulette avant l'occupation française." *Revue Tunisienne* (1912): 200–211.

―――. "Lettres sur l'histoire politique de la Tunisie de 1728 à 1740." *Revue Tunisienne* (1924): 209–30, 287–303; (1926): 352–67, 457–83.

―――. "Note inédite sur Testour et sur une famille hispano-juive habitant le village en 1746." *Revue Tunisienne* (1918): 47–48.

―――. "Notes inédites sur Tunis en 1786." *Revue Tunisienne* (1918): 210–21.

―――. "Une page de la révolte de 1864." *Revue Tunisienne* (1923): 142–51.

Ganiage, Jean, ed. *Une entreprise italienne de Tunisie au milieu du XIXè siècle: correspondance commerciale de la thonaire de Sidi Daoud.* Paris: Presses Universitaires de France, 1960.

―――. *Les Origines du protectorat français en Tunisie (1861–1881).* Paris: Presses Universitaires de France, 1959.

―――. "La crise des finances tunisiennes et l'ascension des Juifs de Tunis (1860–1880)." *Revue Africaine* 99 (1955): 153–73.

―――. "Les Européens en Tunisie au milieu du XIXè siècle (1840–1870)." *Cahiers de Tunisie* 3 (1955): 388–421.

―――. "La population de Monastir vers 1860." *Cahiers de Tunisie* 24, nos. 95–96 (1976): 345–46.

―――. "La population de la Tunisie vers 1860. Essai d'évaluation d'après les registres fiscaux." *Population* 21 (1965): 857–86. [Also in *Etudes maghrébines: Mélanges C. A. Julien,* edited by Pierre Marthelot and André Raymond. Paris: Université de Paris, 1964.]

Gehring, Gilbert. *Les Relations entre la Tunisie et l'Allemagne avant le Protectorat français.* Tunis: Université de Tunis, 1971. [Also in *Cahiers de Tunisie* 18 (1970): 7–155.]

Ghalloussi, Béchir. "Archives du Sahel au XIXè siècle." *Cahiers de Tunisie* 8 (1960): 97–108.

Gharbi, Mohamed Lazhar. *Impérialisme et réformisme au Maghreb: Histoire d'un chemin de fer algéro-tunisien.* Tunis: Centre d'Etudes et de Recherches Economiques et Sociales, 1994.

Ghoul, Faisal al-. "Histoire d'une rumeur: la peste de Tunis de 1792." *Cahiers de Tunisie* 36, nos. 143–44 (1988): 77–84.

Goldzeiguer, Annie Rey. "La vision de "l'AUTRE" dans l'élite intellectuelle tunisienne de la seconde moitié du XIXè siècle." In *Gli interscambi culturali e socio-economici fra l'Africa settentrionale e l'Europa mediterranea,* edited by Luigi Serra, 2: 693–718. Naples: Instituto Universitario Orientale, 1986.

Grandchamp, Pierre. *Etudes d'histoire tunisienne, XVIIè–XXè siècles.* Paris: Presses Universitaires de France, 1966.

―――. "A propos du séjour à Tunis de Caroline de Brunswick, princesse de Galles (4–22 avril 1816)." *Revue Tunisienne* (1934): 59–71.

————. "Arbre généalogique de la famille hassinite (1705–1944)." *Revue Tunisienne* (1941): 233. [Also in *Cahiers de Tunisie* 13 (1965): 133.]

————. "Le baiseman des Consuls à la cour des Beys de Tunis." *Revue Africaine* 89 (1945): 291–92.

————. "Le différend tuniso-sarde de 1843–1844." *Revue Tunisienne* (1933): 127–213.

————. "Les Différends de 1832–1833 entre la Régence de Tunis et les Royaumes de Sardaigne et des Deux Siciles." *Revue Tunisienne* (1931): 1–96. [Also in *Cahiers de Tunisie* 13 (1965): 119–32.]

————. "Dix mémoires en italien sur le procès Vandori (1869–1879)." *Revue Tunisienne* (1919): 347–49.

————. "Documents concernant la course dans la Régence de Tunis de 1764 à 1769 et de 1783 à 1843." *Cahiers de Tunisie* 5 (1957): 269–340.

————. "Le Duc de Montpensier à Tunis (20–25 juin 1845)." *Revue Tunisienne* (1940): 318–24.

————. "Etablissement en 1692 d'une auberge dans le fondouk de la nation française. Sa suppression en 1778." *Revue Tunisienne* (1918): 226–32.

————. "Fixation du statut des sujets toscans israélites dans la Régence de Tunis (1822–1847)." *Revue Tunisienne* (1938): 155–79, 323–42.

————. "Francesco Crispi: 'Questioni Internazionali.'" *Revue Tunisienne* (1913): 464–79, 520–51, 658–75.

————. "Un incident entre le consul de Hollande et le consul d'Angleterre à Tunis en mars 1714." *Revue Tunisienne* (1942): 243–50.

————. "Un Mameluk tunisien d'origine française: le Colonel Selim Corso, alias Joseph Merini." *Cahiers de Tunisie* 13 (1965): 133–39.

————. "Une mission tunisienne à Paris en 1743." *Revue Tunisienne* (1931): 339–403.

————. "Pages d'histoire tunisienne. Antoine Michel, Consul de France à Tunis." *Revue Tunisienne* (1918): 118–23.

————. "Pages d'histoire tunisienne: l'incident du 'Guérin-Mesquin' (26 mai 1804)." *Revue Tunisienne* (1917): 325–37.

————. "La rédemption des captives de Sicile." *Revue Tunisienne* (1931): 287–93.

————. "Un sarde comte tunisien? Jean Porcile, comte de Saint-Antioche." *Revue Tunisienne* (1941): 223–26.

————. "Suppression du baise-main des consuls à la cour du Bey de Tunis." *Revue Africaine* 62 (1921): 335–39.

————. "Les tempêtes de 1821 et de 1859 sur les côtes de Tunis." *Revue Tunisienne* (1941): 285–315.

Grandchamp, Pierre, and B. Mokaddem. "Une mission tunisienne à Paris (février-mai, 1853)." *Revue Africaine* 90 (1946): 59–98.

Green, Arnold. "Political Attitudes and Activities of the Ulama in the Liberal Age: Tunisia as an Exceptional Case." *International Journal of Middle East Studies* 7 (1976): 209–41.

———. "A Tunisian Reply to a Wahhabi Proclamation: Texts and Contexts." In *In Quest of an Islamic Humanism: Arabic and Islamic Studies in Memory of Mohamed al-Nowaihi,* edited by Arnold Green, 155–77. Cairo: American University in Cairo Press, 1984.

Hagege, Claude. "Communautés juives de Tunisie à la veille du Protectorat français." *Le Mouvement Social* 110 (1980): 35–50.

Hamza, Raouf. "Les pêcheurs saisonniers italiens à Mahdia (1871–1945)." In *Etre marginal au Maghreb,* edited by Fanny Colonna and Zakya Daoud, 155–60. Paris: Centre National de la Recherche Scientifique, 1993.

Henia, Abdelhamid. *Le Grid: ses rapports avec le beylik de Tunis (1676–1840).* Tunis: Université de Tunis, 1980.

———. "Circulation des biens et liens de parenté à Tunis (XVIIè–début XXè siècle)." In *Hasab wa nasab—Parenté, alliance et patrimoine en Tunisie,* edited by Sophie Ferchiou, 217–50. Paris: Centre National de la Recherche Scientifique, 1992.

———. "Mécanismes d'articulation des communautés oasiennes du Jérid avec le pouvoir central de Tunisie au cours du XVIIIème et de la première moitié du XIXème siècle." In *Le Maghreb: approches des mécanismes d'articulation,* edited by Rahma Bourquia and Nicholas Hopkins, 153–72. Casablanca: Editions al-Kalam, 1991.

———. "Mémoire d'origine d'un lignage dominant le pouvoir local à Tozeur (16è–19è siècles)." In *Mélanges offerts à Mohamed Talbi à l'occasion de son 70è anniversaire,* 125–48. La Manouba: Faculté des Lettres, 1993.

Hopkins, Nicholas. "Testour au XIXè siècle." *Revue d'Histoire Maghrébine* 7, nos. 17–18 (1980): 19–31.

Huard, Pierre, and Jacqueline Sonolet. "La derrière maladie et la mort de Sidi Mohamed Ben Kassem (1811–59), Bey de Tunis." *Ouest-Médicale* 25 (1972): 479–84.

Hugon, Henri. "Une ambassade tunisienne à Paris en 1825." *Revue Tunisienne* (1933): 93–126.

———. "Un document numismatique du voyage d'Ahmed Bey à Paris (1846)." *Revue de l'Histoire des Colonies Françaises* 10 (1922): 107–14.

———. "Les instructeurs français de l'ancienne Armée Beyicale." *Revue Tunisienne* (1923): 152–60.

———. "La mission du Commandant Guy à Tunis (1831)." *Revue Tunisienne* (1937): 393–407.

———. "Un singulier diplomate. Le Comte De Vandoni, agent et consul général du Bey Mohammed es Sadok." *Revue Tunisienne* (1918): 349–62.

————. "Un souvenir tunisien de la proclamation de l'unité italienne (1861)." *Revue Tunisienne* (1921): 77–79.

Hunter, Robert. "Capital Appreciation and Provincial Power in Pre-Protectorate Tunisia (1850–1881): Notes from the Tunis Archives." *Middle Eastern Studies* 23 (1987): 108–15.

————. "The Comparative History of Tunisia and Egypt in the Nineteenth Century: A Reexamination." *Arab Historical Review for Ottoman Studies* 7–8 (1993): 59–70.

————. "Notes on the Comparative Political Evolution of Tunisia and Egypt under Ahmad Bey and Muhammad Ali." *Revue d'Histoire Maghrébine* 13, nos. 43–44 (1986): 43–48.

Jdey, Ahmed. "Espace et démographie dans la Tunisie moderne: le cas des Fraichiches (1861–1881)." *Arab Historical Review for Ottoman Studies* 9–10 (1994): 81–94.

Jegham, Hachemi. *La Constitution tunisienne de 1861*. Tunis: Editions CHEMS, 1989.

Julien, Charles-André. *L'affaire tunisienne, 1878–1881*. Tunis: Dar el-Amal, 1981.

Kahl, O. "A Letter from Ahmad Bey of Tunisia to Queen Victoria of England." *Journal of Semitic Studies* 31 (1986): 187–94.

————. "Zwei Briefe des Ahmad Bey von Tunis an König Louis Philippe von Frankreich." *Welt des Islams* 32 (1992): 99–106.

Karoui, Abdeljelil. *Tunisie et son image dans la littérature française du 19ème siècle et de la 1ère moitié du 20ème*. Tunis: Société Tunisienne de Diffusion, 1975.

————. "Considérations sur la Tunisie vue par quelques observateurs étrangers du Siècle des Lumières et de la Révolution." In *La Révolution française et le monde arabo-musulman,* edited by Hédia Khadhar, 297–306. Tunis: Alif, 1991.

Karpat, Kemal. "Notes and Documents on Tunisian and Algerian Relations with the Porte: The Provision of Tunisian Military Units for the Russian War of 1877–1878 and the French Interference in Algeria." *Arab Historical Review for Ottoman Studies* 1–2 (1990): 141–43.

Kerrou, Mohamed, and Moncef Mhalla. "La prostitution dans la médina de Tunis au XIXè et au XXè siècles." In *Etre marginal au Maghreb,* edited by Fanny Colonna and Zakya Daoud, 201–24. Paris: Centre National de la Recherche Scientifique, 1993.

Khadhar, Hédia. "La Révolution française, le Pacte Fondamental et la Constitution tunisienne de 1861." *Revue du Monde Musulman et de la Méditerranée* 52–53 (1989): 132–37.

Khayr al-Din al-Tunsi. *Essai sur les réformes nécessaires aux états musulmans*. Edited and annotated by Magali Morsy. Aix-en-Provence: Edisud, 1987.

————. *The Surest Path*. Translated with an introduction by L. Carl Brown. Cambridge: Harvard University Press, 1967.

Kraiem, Abdelmajid, and Hédi Jellab. *Le mouvement réformiste en Tunisie, 1815–1920.* Tunis: Institut Supérieur d'Histoire du Mouvement National, 1994.

Krieken, Gérard S. van. *Khayr al-Din et la Tunisie (1850–1881).* Leiden: Brill, 1976.

———. "Hammuda Basha et le port de la Goulette." *Revue de l'Institut des Belles Lettres Arabes,* 51, no. 162 (1988): 221–42.

Ladjili, Jeanne. "La Paroisse de Tunis au XVIIIème siècle d'après les registres de Catholicité." *Revue de l'Institut des Belles Lettres Arabes* 37, no. 134 (1974): 227–77.

Lakhdar-Ghoul, Latifa. "Dar al-Jawad: Approche préliminaire d'une prison domestique." *Revue de l'Institut des Belles Lettres Arabes* 56, no. 171 (1993): 49–64.

Largueche, Abdelhamid. "La minorité noire de Tunis au XIXè siècle." In *Etre marginal au Maghreb,* edited by Fanny Colonna and Zakya Daoud, 135–54. Paris: Centre National de la Recherche Scientifique, 1993.

———. "Le mouvement intellectuel tunisien et le choc de la modernité au XIXème siècle." *Revue d'Histoire Maghrébine* 17, nos. 59–60 (1990): 113–15.

Largueche, Abdelhamid, and Dalenda Largueche. *Marginales en terre d'islam.* Tunis: Centre d'Etudes et de Recherches Economiques et Sociales, 1992.

Largueche, Dalenda. "Dar joued ou l'oubli dans la mémoire." In *Etre marginal au Maghreb,* edited by Fanny Colonna and Zakya Daoud, 177–90. Paris: Centre National de la Recherche Scientifique, 1993.

Lenci, Marco. "Un curioso carteggio tra Tunisi e San Marino, 1863–1870." *Africa* [Rome] 49 (1994): 445–50.

"Léon Roches et la chapelle de Sainte-Eugénie (1862)." *Revue Africaine* 94 (1950): 426–28.

Leone, E. de. "Un ligure alla corte del Bey di Tunisi: Giuseppe Maria Raffo." *Annali della Facolta di Scienze Politiche (Università di Cagliari)* 9 (1983): 293–302.

———. "L'opera riformatrice di un Piemontese in Tunisia." In *Atti del II Convegno su la presenza culturale italiana nei paesi arabi: storia e prospettivi,* 417–20. Rome: Instituto per l'Oriente, 1984.

Limam, Haifa Malouf. "Ports tunisiens et défense côtière (1705–1814)." *Revue Tunisienne des Sciences Sociales* 84–87 (1986): 511–59.

Loth, Gaston. "Arnoldo Soler, Chargé d'Affaires d'Espagne à Tunis et sa correspondance 1808–1810." *Revue Tunisienne* (1906): 45–50, 142–61.

Mabrouk, Mohieddine. "Administration et personnel administratif de la Tunisie précoloniale." *Revue Juridique et Politique, Indépendance et Coopération* 26 (1972): 175–200.

Magnin, Jean-Gabriel. "Urbanisme, constructions et hôtellerie à Tunis vers 1880." *Revue de l'Institut des Belles Lettres Arabes* 24, no. 93 (1961): 23–37.

Mahfoudh, Faouzi. "Le quartier franc de Sfax du XVIIIème au XIXème siècle." *Revue d'Histoire Maghrébine* 18, nos. 63–64 (1991): 325–32.

Mahjoub, Azzam. "Analyse historique du sous-développement en Tunisie." *Annuaire de l'Afrique du Nord* 18 (1979): 443–56.

―――. "Economie et société: la formation du 'sous-développement.' L'évolution socio-économique de la Tunisie pré-coloniale." In *Tunisie au présent. Une modernité au-dessus de tout soupçon?*, edited by Michel Camau and Jellal Abdelkefi, 97–117. Paris: Centre National de la Recherche Scientifique, 1987.

Manca, Bruno. "Gebel Rassas: le vicende di una miniera tunisina dal primo decreto (amr) di concessione (1828–1898)." *Annali della Facolta di Scienze Politiche (Università di Cagliari)* 1 (1976): 115–54.

Mantran, Robert. "Documents turcs relatifs à l'armée tunisienne." *Cahiers de Tunisie* 4 (1956): 359–72.

―――. "L'évolution des relations entre la Tunisie et l'Empire Ottoman du XVIè au XIXè siècle." *Cahiers de Tunisie* 7 (1959): 319–33.

―――. "Une relation inédite d'un voyage en Tunisie au milieu du 19ème siècle." *Cahiers de Tunisie* 3 (1955): 474–80.

―――. "La titulaire des Beys de Tunis au XIXè siècle d'après les documents d'archives turcs du Dar el-Bey (Tunis)." *Cahiers de Tunisie* 5 (1957): 341–48.

Marsden, Arthur. *British Diplomacy and Tunis, 1875–1902.* Edinburgh: Scottish Academic Press, 1971.

Martel, André. *Luis Arnold et Joseph Allegro, consuls du Bey de Tunis à Bône.* Paris: Presses Universitaires de France, 1967.

―――. "L'armée d'Ahmed Bey d'après un instructeur français." *Cahiers de Tunisie* 4 (1956): 373–407.

―――. "Note autobiographique. Les origines d'un vice-consul de France à Sfax, A. d'Espina (1819–1867)." *Cahiers de Tunisie* 7 (1959): 511–15.

―――. "Pouvoirs étatiques et sociétés bédouines: l'équilibre des çoffs et la non-émergence des élites tribales dans le Maghreb oriental au XIXè siècle." In *Elites et pouvoir dans le monde arabe pendant la période moderne et contemporaine,* 197–207. Tunis: Centre d'Etudes et de Recherches Economiques et Sociales, 1992.

―――. "Sources inédites de l'histoire tunisienne. Les Papiers Nyssen aux Archives Nationales." *Cahiers de Tunisie* 5 (1957): 349–80.

Marty, Paul. "Historique de la mission militaire française en Tunisie (1827–1882)." *Revue Tunisienne* (1935): 171–207, 309–46.

Marzouki, Afifa. "Les Sidiennes ou 'comment peut-on être tunisien en 1825'?" *Revue Tunisiennes des Langues Vivantes* 2 (1987): 1–24.

Masi, C. "Chroniques de l'ancien temps (1815–1859)." *Revue Tunisienne* (1935): 83–122.

Masson, Paul. *Histoire des établissements et du commerce français dans l'Afrique barbaresque (1560–1793)*. Paris: Hachette, 1903.

Mathiex, J. "Sur la marine marchande barbaresque au XVIIIè siècle." *Annales Economies, Sociétés, Civilisations* 13 (1958): 87–93.

Mizouri, Laroussi. "La naissance de la franc-maçonnerie dans la Tunisie pré-coloniale." *Revue de l'Institut des Belles Lettres Arabes* 57, no. 173 (1994): 69–80.

————. "La pénétration de l'enseignement européen dans la Tunisie précoloniale: origine et répercussions." *Cahiers de Tunisie* 44, nos. 157–58 (1991): 177–96.

Monchicourt, Charles, "Un autre texte du 'Mémoire sur Tunis' publié par Chateaubriand." *Revue de l'Histoire des Colonies Françaises* 11 (1923): 67–104.

————. "La Mahalla d'Ahmed Zarroug dans le Sahel (1864)." *Revue Tunisienne* (1917): 3–11.

————. "Notice sur Tunez et biographie du Bach Mamelouk Hassine par Louis Calligaris." *Revue de l'Histoire des Colonies Françaises* 16 (1928): 525–88.

M. S. Z. "Tahar Pacha Kheireddine: Stratège et homme d'état." *Revue de l'Institut des Belles Lettres Arabes* 10, no. 40 (1947): 425–36.

Mzali, Mohamed Saleh. *Les Beys de Tunis et le roi des Français*. Algiers: Maison Tunisienne de l'Edition, 1976.

————. *L'Hérédité dans la dynastie husseinite: évolution et violations.* Tunis: Maison Tunisienne de l'Edition, 1969.

————. "L'exercice de l'autorité suprême en Tunisie durant le voyage d'Ahmed-Bey en France (5 Novembre–30 Décembre 1846)." *Revue Tunisienne* (1918): 274–84.

Mzali, Mohamed Saleh, ed. *La situation en Tunisie à la veille du protectorat d'après les lettres de Conti à Khéreddine et d'autres documents inédits.* Tunis: Maison Tunisienne de l'Edition, 1969.

Mzali, Mohamed Saleh, and Jean Pignon. *Khéréddine, homme d'état: documents historiques annotés.* Tunis: Maison Tunisienne de l'Edition, 1971.

————. "Documents sur Khéréddine." *Revue Tunisienne* (1938): 79–153; (1940): 71–107, 251–302.

Nallino, Carlo A. "Venezia e Sfax nel secolo xviii secondo il cronista arabo Maqdisi." *Centenario Amari* 1 (1910): 306–56.

Panzac, Daniel. "La régence de Tunis et la mer à l'époque d'Hammouda Pacha Bey (1782–1814)." *Cahiers de Tunisie* 46, no. 165 (1993): 65–84.

————. "La Tunisie et la mer à l'époque d'Hammuda Pacha Bey, 1782–1814." In *Itinéraires de France en Tunisie du XVIè au XIXè siècle,* 47–60. Marseille: Bibliothèque Municipale, 1995.

Pätzold, Mathias. "Auf verlorenem Posten: zur Reformspolitik Hair al-Dins in Tunesien." In *Entwicklung durch Reforms: Asien und Afrika im 19 Jahrhundert,* edited by G. Höpp, 133–39. Berlin: Akademie Verlag, 1991.

Perkins, Kenneth J. " 'The Masses Look Ardently to Istanbul': Tunisia, Islam, and the Ottoman Empire, 1837–1931." In *Islamism and Secularism in North Africa,* edited by John Ruedy, 23–36. New York: St. Martin's Press, 1994.

Peysonnel, Jean-André. *Voyages dans les régences de Tunis et d'Alger.* Edited by Lucette Valensi. Paris: La Découverte, 1987.

Piano, Lorenzo del. *La penetrazione italiana in Tunisia, 1861–1881.* Padua: CEDAM, 1964.

Pignon, Jean and Mohamed Mzali. "Documents sur Khéreddine." *Revue Tunisienne* (1934): 177–225, 347–96; (1935): 50–80, 209–33, 289–307; (1936): 223–54; (1937): 209–52, 409–32.

Poncet, Jean. "Note sur la situation de la Tunisie à la suite des événements de 1864–1868." *Cahiers de Tunisie* 2 (1954): 324–28.

———. "Un problème d'histoire rurale: le habous Aziza Othmana, au Sahel." *Cahiers de Tunisie* 8 (1960): 137–56.

Puaux, Gabriel. "Une croisière de l'Archiduc Louis-Salvator sur les côtes de Tunisie, en 1873." *Revue Tunisienne* (1918): 253–62.

Raymond, André. *Ibn Abi Diyaf: Présent aux hommes de notre temps. Chronique des rois de Tunis et du Pacte Fondamental, Chapitres IV et V.* Tunis: Alif, 1994.

———. "La France, la Grande-Bretagne et le problème de la réforme à Tunis (1855–1857)." In *Etudes maghrébines. Mélanges C.A. Julien,* edited by Pierre Marthelot and André Raymond, 137–64. Paris: Université de Paris, 1964.

———. "Une liste des deys de Tunis de 1590 à 1832." *Cahiers de Tunisie* 8 (1960): 129–36.

———. "Les relations franco-tunisiennes de 1830 à 1861." In *Itinéraires de France en Tunisie du XVIè au XIXè siècle,* 61–72. Marseille: Bibliothèque Municipale, 1995.

———. "Salisbury and the Tunisian Question, 1878–1880." *St. Antony's Papers* 11 (1961): 101–38.

———. "Les tentatives anglaises de pénétration économique en Tunisie (1856–1877)." *Revue Historique* 214 (1955): 48–67.

Regaya, Mourad. "Essai d'évaluation de la population de Kairouan en 1280 H./1863–1864, d'après le registre de l'iana no. 929: approche démographique, sociologique, et fiscale." *Revue d'Histoire Maghrébine* 16, nos. 53–54 (1989): 205–9.

———. "Migrations intérieures dans la Tunisie du XIXème siècle: Cas des insulaires jerbiens." *Revue de l'Institut des Belles Lettres Arabes* 56, no. 171 (1993): 39–47.

—————. "Profil et niveaux de fortune chez les Hanafia de Mahdia en 1284/1867 d'après le registre de capitation no. 971." *Arab Historical Review for Ottoman Studies* 5–6 (1992): 179–86.

Les relations franco-tunisiennes au miroir des élites XVIIIè, XIXè, XXè siècles. Tunis: Archives Nationales, 1994.

Revault, Jacques. *Palais, demeures et maisons de plaisance à Tunis et dans ses environs du XVIè au XIXè siècle*. Aix-en-Provence: Edisud, 1984.

Riggio, Achille. "Cronaca tabarchina dal 1750 ai primordi dell'ottocento ricavata dai registri parrochiali di Santa Croce in Tunisi." *Revue Tunisienne* (1937): 353–91.

—————. "Notizie sul cimitero di Sant' Antonio abate e gli schiavi cristiani in Tunisi nel secolo xviii." *Oriente Moderno* 31 (1951): 38–47.

—————. "Origini della guerra veneto-tunisina (1784–1792)." *Oriente Moderno* 29 (1949): 75–82.

—————. "Relazioni della Toscana granducale con la Reggenza di Tunisi (1818–1823)." *Oriente Moderno* 20 (1940): 93–124.

—————. "Tunisi e il Regno di Napoli nei primordi del secolo XIX." *Oriente Moderno* 27 (1947): 1–23.

Rossi, Ettore. "Relazioni tra i Gran Maestri dell' Ordine di Malta e i Bey di Tunisi dal 1642 al 1756." *Revue Tunisienne* (1932): 193–215.

Sacerdoti, Albert. "Venise et les Régences d'Alger, Tunis, et Tripoli (1699–1764)." *Revue Africaine* 101 (1957): 273–97.

Sebag, Paul. "Cartes, plans et vues générales de Tunis et de La Goulette aux XVIIè et XVIIIè siècles." In *Etudes maghrébines. Mélanges C. A. Julien,* edited by Pierre Marthelot and André Raymond, 89–101. Paris: Université de Paris, 1964.

—————. "Une description de Tunis au XIXè siècle." *Cahiers de Tunisie* 6 (1958): 161–81.

—————. "L'Hôpital des Trinitaires espagnols (1720–1818)." *Revue de l'Institut des Belles Lettres Arabes* 57, no. 174 (1994): 203–18.

—————. "Les Juifs de Tunisie au XIXè siècle d'après J.-J. Benjamin II." *Cahiers de Tunisie* 7 (1959): 489–92.

—————. "La peste dans la Régence de Tunis aux XVIIè et XVIIIè siècles." *Revue de l'Institut de Belles Lettres Arabes* 28, no. 109 (1965): 35–48.

Sghair, Noureddine. "En marge d'une lecture du chroniqueur Mahmud ben Said Magdish: les relations culturelles Mashreq-Maghreb et les ulama de Sfax." *Revue d'Histoire Maghrébine* 13, nos. 43–44 (1986): 83–101.

Slama, Bice. "L'insurrection de 1280–1864 dans le Sahel." *Cahiers de Tunisie* 8 (1960): 109–36.

Smida, Mongi. *Consuls et consulats de Tunisie au XIXè siècle*. Tunis: Imprimerie de l'Orient, 1991.

Soudan, Fédérique. "al-Mahdiyya et son histoire, d'après le récit de voyage d'al-Tijani. Traduction annotée." *Revue des Etudes Islamiques* 63 (1990): 135–88.

Soumille, Pierre. "Une correspondance inédite entre Ahmed Bey et le Pape Pie IX (1849–1851)." *Revue d'Histoire Maghrébine* 2, no. 3 (1975): 95–99.

———. "Les multiples activités d'un prêtre français au Maghreb: l'Abbé François Bourgade en Algérie et en Tunisie de 1838 à 1858." *Histoire d'Outre-Mer* 1 (1992): 233–72.

Soumille, Pierre, and Jean Peyras. "Un aspect des relations austro-tunisiennes au dix-huitième siècle." *Revue de l'Instiut des Belles Lettres Arabes* 35 (1972): 1–31.

———. "La mémoire du protestantisme à Tunis d'après les monuments du cimetière anglican de Bab-Carthagène (depuis le milieu du XVIIè siècle jusqu'à la fin du XIXè siècle)." In *Les Monuments et la mémoire*, edited by Jean Peyras, 51–70. Paris: L'Harmattan, 1993.

Speziale, Salvatore. "La Reggenza di Tunisi e le crisi epidemiche nel XVIII e XIX secolo." *Incontri Meridionali* 3, no. 3 (1989): 75–97.

Sraieb, Noureddine. "Khéréddine et l'enseignement: une nouvelle conception du savoir en Tunisie." *Revue du Monde Musulman et de la Méditerranée* 63–64 (1992): 203–10.

———. "Poésie populaire et résistance en Tunisie." *Revue du Monde Musulman et de la Méditerranée* 51 (1989): 143–49.

Temimi, Abdeljelil. "Affranchissement des esclaves et leurs recensements au milieu du XIXème siècle dans la Régence de Tunis." In *La vie économique des provinces arabes et leurs sources documentaures à l'époque ottomane*, edited by Abdeljelil Temimi, 213–18. Zaghouan: Centre d'Etudes et de Recherches sur les Provinces Arabes à l'Epoque Ottomane, 1986.

———. "Considérations nouvelles sur la révolution d'Ali ben Gadehem." *Revue de l'Occident Musulmane et de la Méditerranée* 7 (1970): 171–85.

———. "Impact de l'information sur la politique de Hammouda Pacha (1810–1813) et problématiques d'histoire maghrébine." *Revue d'Histoire Maghrébine* 16, nos. 55–56 (1989): 53–58.

———. "Pour une histoire sociale de la minorité africaine noire en Tunisie: sources et perspectives." *Revue d'Histoire Maghrébine* 14, nos. 45–46 (1987): 102–9.

———. "La thèse de M. Béchir Tlili ou la décadence du métier d'historien. (Les rapports culturels et idéologiques entre l'Orient et l'Occident, en Tunisie au XIXè siècle, 1830–1880)." *Revue d'Histoire Maghrébine* 2, no. 4 (1975): 205–8.

———. "Le traité de paix entre la régence de Tunis et Venise du mois de mai 1792." *Revue d'Histoire Maghrébine* 21, nos. 77–78 (1995): 223–46.

Thouvenot, R. "Notes d'un espagnol sur un voyage qu'il fit en Tunisie (1724)." *Revue Tunisienne* (1938): 313–22.

Tlili, Béchir. *Les Rapports culturels et idéologiques entre l'Orient et l'Occident en Tunisie au XIXème siècle (1830–1880).* Tunis: Université de Tunis, 1974.

———. "A l'aube du mouvement de réformes à Tunis: un important document de Ahmed ibn abi ad-Diyaf sur le féminisme (1856)." *Ethnies* 2 (1972): 167–230.

———. "Contribution à l'élucidation de la pensée réformiste tunisienne moderne et contemporaine (1830–1930)." *Africa* [Rome] 30 (1975): 317–45.

———. "Contribution à l'étude de la pensée sociale et politique de Bayram V (1840–1889). *Revue de l'Occident Musulmane et de la Méditerranée* 15–16 (1973): 327–43.

———. "Eléments pour une approche de la pensée socio-économiques de Khreddine (1810–1889)." *Revue de l'Occident Musulmane et de la Méditerranée* 9 (1971): 119–52.

———. "L'idée d'un bon gouvernement ottoman dans la pensée de Bayram V (1840–1889)." *Cahiers de Tunisie* 20 (1972): 147–70.

———. "Khérédine, réformateur et homme d'état, tunisien et ottoman." *Les Africains, sous la direction de Ch.-A. Julien et al.* 8 (1977): 133–67.

———. "Note sur la notion d'état dans la pensée de Ahmad ibn Abi Addiyaf, réformateur tunisien du XIXè siècle (1804/5–1874)." *Revue de l'Occident Musulmane et de la Méditerranée* 8 (1970): 141–70.

———. "La notion d'umran dans la pensée tunisienne précoloniale." *Revue de l'Occident Musulmane et de la Méditerranée* 12 (1972): 131–51.

Triulzi, Alessandro. "Una fonte ignorata per la storia della Tunisia: i dispacci dei consoli americani a Tunis, 1797–1867." *Oriente Moderno* 51 (1971): 653–78.

———. "Italian-Speaking Communities in Early Nineteenth Century Tunis." *Revue de l'Occident Musulmane et de la Méditerranée* 9 (1971): 153–84.

Valensi, Lucette. *Fellahs tunisiens: l'économie rurale et la vie des compagnes aux 18è et 19è siècles.* Paris and The Hague: Mouton, 1977.

———. *On the Eve of Colonialism: North Africa before the French Conquest.* Translated by Kenneth J. Perkins. New York: Africana Publishing Company, 1977.

———. *Tunisian Peasants in the Eighteenth and Nineteenth Centuries.* Translated by B. Archer. Cambridge: Cambridge University Press, 1985.

———. "La conjoncture agraire en Tunisie aux XVIIIè et XIXè siècles." *Revue Historique* 243 (1968): 321–36.

———. "Le Djebel Ousselat au XVIIIème siècle." *Cahiers de Tunisie* 12 (1964): 89–97.

———. "Esclaves chrétiens et esclaves noirs à Tunis au XVIIIè siècle." *Annales Economies, Sociétés, Civilisations* 22 (1967): 1267–88.

————. "Islam et capitalisme, production et commerce des chéchias en Tunisie et en France aux XVIIè et XIXè siècles." *Revue d'Histoire Moderne et Contemporaine* 16 (1969): 376–400.

————. "The Tunisian Fellaheen in the Eighteenth and Nineteenth Centuries." In *The Islamic Middle East, 700–1900: Studies in Economic and Social History,* edited by Avram Udovitch, 709–24. Princeton: Darwin Press, 1981.

————. "La Tunisie des XVIIIè et XIXè siècles: des archives générales du gouvernement à l'histoire sociale." In *Les Arabes par leurs archives,* edited by Jacques Berque and Dominique Chevallier, 119–23. Paris: Centre Nationale de Recherche Scientifique, 1976.

Venture de Paradis, Jean-Michel. *Tunis et Alger au XVIIIè siècle: Mémoires et observations.* Paris: Sindbad, 1983.

La Véronne, Chantal de. "Commerce et ressources de la Régence de Tunis, d'après l'histoire de Barbarie et de ses corsaires de R. P. P. Dan." In *La vie économique des provinces arabes et leurs sources documentaures à l'époque ottomane,* edited by Abdeljelil Temimi, 41–47. Zaghouan: Centre d'Etudes et de Recherches sur les Provinces Arabes à l'Epoque Ottomane, 1986.

Verplancke, Léon. "Mohamed Es-Sadok Pacha Bey, Chevalier de l'ordre de la Toison d'Or (31 octobre 1870)." *Revue de l'Institut des Belles Lettres Arabes* 28, no. 111 (1965): 321–38.

Vilar, Juan-Bautista. *Mapas, planos y fortificationes hispànicos de Túnez (s. XVI–XIX).* Madrid: Instituto de Cooperación con el Mundo Arabe, 1991.

————. "Dos siglos de presencia de España en Tabarka (1535–1741)." *Revue d'Histoire Maghrébine* 20, nos. 77–78 (1995): 163–82.

Zecca, G. "L'emigrazione italiana in Tunisia." *Africa* [Rome] 18 (1963): 55–62.

Zouari, Ali. *Les relations commerciales entre Sfax et le Levant aux XVIIIème et XIXème siècles.* Tunis: Institut National d'Archéologie et d'Art, 1990.

————. "Un établissement économique du XVIIIè siècle à Sfax: le fondouk des forgerons." In *Les Villes dans l'empire ottoman: activités et sociétés,* edited by Daniel Panzac, 237–79. Paris: Centre National de la Recherche Scientifique, 1994.

Protectorate Era, 1881–1956

Abd al-Haq. *Au temps de la colonisation. I. Des hommes et leurs comportements.* Tunis: Maison Tunisienne d'Edition, 1989.

Abdelmoula, Mahmoud. *Jihad et colonialisme. La Tunisie et la Tripolitaine (1914–1918).* Tunis: Editions Tiers-Monde, 1987.

Abdessamad, Hichem. "La Résidence face à la question de la réforme de l'enseignement zaytounien 1930–1933." In *Les mouvements poli-*

tiques et sociaux dans la Tunisie des années trente, edited by Moncef Chenoufi, 799–816. Tunis: Ministère de l'Education, de l'Enseignement et de la Recherche Scientifique, 1987.

Ageron, Robert. "La commission d'enquête du Front populaire sur les colonies et la question tunisienne." In *Les mouvements politiques et sociaux dans la Tunisie des années trente,* edited by Moncef Chenoufi, 103–26. Tunis: Ministère de l'Education, de l'Enseignement et de la Recherche Scientifique.

———. "Le 'parti colonial' français face à la question tunisienne." In *Le Monde arabe au regard des sciences sociales,* edited by Anne-Marie Planel, 1: 29–37. Tunis: Centre de Documentation Tunisie-Maghreb, 1989. [Also in *La Tunisie de l'après-guerre,* 183–208. Tunis: Institut Supérieur d'Histoire du Mouvement National, 1991.]

Ammairia, Hafnaoui. "Doléances et résistance dans le chant populaire de la région de Gafsa (1865–1885). *Revue du Monde Musulman et de la Méditerranée* 51 (1989): 127–36.

Anderson, Lisa. *The State and Social Transformation in Tunisia and Libya, 1830–1930.* Princeton: Princeton University Press, 1986.

Annabi, Hassen al-. "Alfa et alfatiers en Tunisie pendant les années trente." In *Les mouvements politiques et sociaux dans la Tunisie des années trente,* edited by Moncef Chenoufi, 485–524. Tunis: Ministère de l'Education, de l'Enseignement et de la Recherche Scientifique.

———. "Réorganisation du notariat musulman de Tunisie et mouvement zitounien au sortir des années 1920." *Cahiers de Tunisie* 36, nos. 143–44 (1989): 85–100.

Arnoulet, François. *Tunisie 1881 . . . L'aboutissement d'un long périple.* Marseille: Calendal, 1985.

———. "Analyse de deux documents d'archives relatifs aux périodes conflictuelles entre le bey et le Résident Général." *Revue d'Histoire Maghrébine* 21, no. 74 (1994): 135–41.

———. "Le Cardinal Lavigerie et le clergé italien en Tunisie, 1881–1891." *Revue d'Histoire Maghrébine* 20, nos. 71–72 (1993): 375–86.

———. "En marge de l'expedition française en Tunisie: De Billing, un diplomate français subversif." *Revue d'Histoire Maghrébine* 13, nos. 41–42 (1986): 5–14.

———. "Interférences diplomatiques et préoccupations politiques à l'occasion du Congrès Eucharistique de Carthage (mai 1930)." *Revue d'Histoire Maghrébine* 18, nos. 61–62 (1991): 7–21.

———. "Le journal d'un officier du service de renseignements durant l'expédition militaire en Tunisie (avril–décembre 1881)." *Revue d'Histoire Maghrébine* 7, nos. 19–20 (1980): 149–56.

———. "L'oeuvre hospitalière des Trinitaires et des Capuchins dans la Régence du Tunis." *Cahiers de Tunisie* 26, nos. 105–6 (1978): 35–47.

————. "La presse française et algérienne lors des événements de 1881 en Tunisie." *Revue Tunisienne de Communication* 12 (1987): 57–70.

————. "Les problèmes de l'enseignement au début du protectorat français en Tunisie (1881–1900)." *Revue de l'Institut des Belles Lettres Arabes* 54, no. 167 (1991): 31–61.

Attal, Robert. "Polémique autour la désignation d'un grand rabbin de Tunisie en 1928." *Revue des Etudes Juives* 151, nos. 1–2 (1992): 95–140.

Ayachi, Mokhtar. "Le mouvement zitouien dans le contexte de la Seconde Guerre Mondiale." In *La Tunisie de 1939 à 1945,* edited by Centre National Universitaire de Documentation Scientifique et Technique and Ministère de l'Education, de l'Enseignement et de la Recherche Scientifique, 271–310. Tunis: Imprimerie Officielle, 1989.

————. "La politique coloniale et la question zaytounienne dans les années trente." In *Les mouvements politiques et sociaux dans la Tunisie des années trente,* edited by Moncef Chenoufi, 817–36. Tunis: Ministère de l'Education, de l'Enseignement et de la Recherche Scientifique, 1987.

————. "Pour une histoire des mouvements de jeunes en Tunisie: la jeunesse scolaire avant la genèse de l'UGTT." *Cahiers de Tunisie* 46, nos. 162–63 (1992/1993): 167–88.

Ayadi, Taoufik. "Der Sfaxer Widerstand gegen die koloniale Besetzung im Jahre 1881." *Wuquf* 2 (1987): 289–344.

Bachrouch, Taoufik. "Les Sadikiens de la première heure ou la tentation de l'ouverture." *Cahiers de Tunisie* 36, nos. 143–44 (1989): 167–82.

Baduel, Pierre-Robert. "Politique tunisienne de développement hydro-agricole (1881–1943)." In *L'homme et l'eau en Méditerranée et au Proche-Orient,* edited by Pierre Louis, Jean Metral, Françoise Metral, and Paul Sanlaville, 147–74. Lyon: Presses Universitaires de Lyon, 1987.

Bakalti, Souad. "L'enseignement féminin dans le primaire au temps de la Tunisie coloniale." *Revue de l'Institut des Belles Lettres Arabes* 53, no. 166 (1990): 249–73.

————. "La scolarisation des tunisiennes et leur entrée dans la vie publique dans la Tunisie coloniale." *Peuples Méditerranéens* 48–49 (1989): 45–57, 329–30.

Bardin, Pierre. "Les débuts difficiles du protectorat tunisien (mai 1881–avril 1882)." *Revue d'Histoire Diplomatique* 85 (1971): 17–64.

Belaid, Habib. "Aperçu sur les mouvements de la jeunesse tunisienne pendant la Deuxième Guerre Mondiale." In *La Tunisie de 1939 à 1945,* edited by Centre National Universitaire de Documentation Scientifique et Technique and Ministère de l'Education, de l'Enseignement et de la Recherche Scientifique, 311–36. Tunis: Imprimerie Officielle, 1989.

————. "Espace urbain et mouvements sociaux à la fin des années 1940." In *La Tunisie de l'après-guerre,* 57–75. Tunis: Institut Supérieur d'Histoire du Mouvement National, 1991.

————. "Les mouvements scouts en Tunisie dans les années 1930." In *Les mouvements politiques et sociaux dans la Tunisie des années trente,* edited by Moncef Chenoufi, 713–42. Tunis: Ministère de l'Education, de l'Enseignement et de la Recherche Scientifique, 1987.

————. "La révolte de 1915–1916 dans le Sud Tunisien à travers les archives du protectorat." In *Révolte et Société,* 176–84. Paris: Histoire au Présent, 1989.

Ben Achour, Mohamed el-Aziz. "L'autobiographie d'un lettré tunisien au début du XXème siècle." *Revue d'Histoire Maghrébine* 17, nos. 59–60 (1990): 27–34.

————. "Les signes extérieurs de la notabilité citadine au début du siècle à Tunis." *Cahiers de la Méditerranée* 45 (1992): 105–16.

Bendana-Mechri, Kmar. "Les missions scientifiques françaises en Tunisie dans la deuxième moitié du XIXè siècle." *Cahiers de Tunisie* 44, nos. 157–58 (1991): 197–208.

————. "La révolte à travers les archives françaises du protectorat en Tunisie: une lecture de quelques cas." In *Révolte et Société,* 163–72. Paris: Histoire au Présent, 1989.

Ben Halima, Hamadi. *Un demi siècle de théâtre arabe en Tunisie (1907–1957).* Tunis: Publications de l'Université de Tunis, 1974.

Ben Hamida, Abdesslam. "Les bourgeois tunisiens face à la crise de 1929." *Cahiers de la Méditerranée* 45 (1992): 129–36.

————. "Comment devient-on notable et grand bourgeois? Le cas d'Ali Mheni." *Cahiers de la Méditerranée* 46–47 (1993): 191–202.

————— [Ibn Hamida]. "L'impact de la colonisation sur les échanges commerciaux de Djerba." *Cahiers de la Méditerranée* 48 (1994): 49–58.

————. "Syndicats, affinités et solidarités de type traditionnel dans la Tunisie coloniale (1924–1956)." *Cahiers de la Méditerranée* nos. 24–25 (1982): 91–114.

Bennoune, Mahfoud. "Primary Capital Accumulation in Colonial Tunisia." *Dialectical Anthropology* 4 (1979): 83–100.

Ben Said Cherni, Zeineb. *Les dérapages de l'histoire chez Tahar Haddad. Les travailleurs, dieu et la femme.* Tunis: Ben Abdallah, 1993.

Bergaoui, Sami. "Rente foncière et prix agricoles en Tunisie (1920–1945)." *Revue de l'Institut des Belles Lettres Arabes* 49, no. 158 (1986): 297–319.

Bessis, Juliette. *La Méditerranée fasciste: l'Italie mussolinienne et la Tunisie.* Paris: Editions Karthala, 1981.

————. "A propos de la question des naturalisations." In *Les mouvements politiques et sociaux dans la Tunisie des années trente,* edited by Moncef Chenoufi, 605–10. Tunis: Ministère de l'Education, de l'Enseignement et de la Recherche Scientifique, 1987.

———. "La crise de l'autonomie et de l'indépendance tunisienne, classe politique et pays réel." In *Mouvement ouvrier, communisme et nationalismes dans le monde arabe,* edited by René Gallissot, 265–92. Paris: Les Editions Ouvrières, 1978.

———. "Les Etats-Unis et le protectorat tunisien dans la Deuxième Guerre Mondiale." In *La Tunisie de 1939 à 1945,* edited by Centre National Universitaire de Documentation Scientifique et Technique and Ministère de l'Education, de l'Enseignement et de la Recherche Scientifique, 197–214. Tunis: Imprimerie Officielle, 1989.

Binsberger, Wim M. J. van. "Popular and Formal Islam and Supra-local Relations: The Highlands of North-western Tunisia, 1800–1970." *Middle East Studies* 16 (1980): 71–91.

Boukraa, Ridha. "Humour et idéologie dans la presse d'avant l'indépendance: essai de sociologie culturelle." *Cahiers de Tunisie* 25, nos. 99–100 (1977): 223–41.

Bournizeau, J. "Les tirailleurs tunisiens dans la guerre du Rif." *Revue Historique des Armées* 166 (1987): 33–41.

Bouyahia, Salem. "Les relations entre travailleurs tunisiens et égyptiens de 1945 à 1958." *Revue d'Histoire Maghrébine* 16, nos. 53–54 (1989): 204.

Brondino, Michele. "Le pouvoir colonial et l'élite des réformistes: le cas de la *Revue du Maghreb*." In *Elites et pouvoir dans le monde arabe pendant la période moderne et contemporaine,* 31–43. Tunis: Centre d'Etudes et de Recherches Economiques et Sociales, 1992.

———. "Préliminaires pour une étude de la presse en langue italienne en Tunisie (1945–1950)." In *La Tunisie de l'après-guerre,* 171–82. Tunis: Institut Supérieur d'Histoire du Mouvement National, 1991.

Burgard, R. "Julius von Eckardt, Consul Général d'Allemagne à Tunis (1885–1889)." *Revue Tunisienne* (1931): 121–34.

"La campagne de Kroumirie d'après la correspondance inédite du Comte de Villebois-Mareuil." *Cahiers de Tunisie* 4 (1956): 413–17.

"Campagne de Tunisie." *Revue Historique de l'Armée* 39 (1983): 4–51.

Canal, Joseph. "Pages d'histoire de la Tunisie. Une figure qui disparait: Monsieur Roy, sécretaire général du Gouvernement Tunisien." *Revue Tunisienne* (1919): 367–72.

Cannon, Byron. "Administrative and Economic Regionalism in Tunisian Oleiculture: The Idarat al-Ghabah Experiment, 1870–1914." *International Journal of African Historical Studies* 11 (1978): 585–628.

———. "The Beylical Habous Council and Suburban Development: Tunis, 1881–1914." *Maghreb Review* 7 (1982): 32–40.

———. "Experimental Joint Stock Cooperatives in the Tunisian *Madinah,* 1900–1914." *Journal of South Asian and Middle Eastern Studies* 2 (1978): 27–41.

———. "Le marché de location des habous en Tunisie: dialectique du développement agricole, 1875–1902." In *Terroirs et Sociétés au Maghreb et au Moyen Orient,* edited by Byron Cannon, 79–108. Lyon: Maison de l'Orient, 1988.

———. "Socio-governmental Intermediaries in Tunisia under the Early Protectorate: A Case Study of the Amin al-Suq." *Revue d'Histoire Maghrébine* 4, nos. 7–8 (1977): 80–90.

———. "Tunisian Money Adjustments and the Union Latine, 1872–1894." *Revue d'Histoire Maghrébine* 1, no. 2 (1974): 107–15.

Chaibi, Mohamed Lotfi. "La politique coloniale du Front populaire en Tunisie (1936–1938)." In *Les mouvements politiques et sociaux dans la Tunisie des années trente,* edited by Moncef Chenoufi, 549–67. Tunis: Ministère de l'Education, de l'Enseignement et de la Recherche Scientifique, 1987.

Charni, Zeineb. "Rapports homme-femme au sein du couple et devenir social chez Tahar El Haddad." In *Les relations interpersonnelles dans la famille maghrébine,* 109–18. Tunis: Centre d'Etudes et de Recherches Economiques et Sociales, 1988.

Chater, Khelifa. "Les elites du pouvoir et de l'argent: le cas de la Tunisie aux XIXè–XXè siècle." *Cahiers de la Méditerranée* 46–47 (1993): 155–72.

———. "Les notables citadins en Tunisie au cours de l'ère coloniale: le concept de beldi et ses mutations." *Cahiers de la Méditerranée* 45 (1992): 117–27.

Chérif, Mohamed Hédi. "Composition sociale des mouvements de rue en Tunisie dans les années trente." In *Les mouvements politiques et sociaux dans la Tunisie des années trente,* edited by Moncef Chenoufi, 611–22. Tunis: Ministère de l'Education, de l'Enseignement et de la Recherche Scientifique, 1987.

———. "L'incident des Khmir de 1881, d'après les sources tunisiennes." *Cahiers de Tunisie* 45, nos. 162–63 (1992/1993): 149–55.

———. "Mouvement national et occupation germano-italienne de la Tunisie (novembre 1942–mai 1943)." In *La Tunisie de 1939 à 1945,* edited by Centre National Universitaire de Documentation Scientifique et Technique and Ministère de l'Education, de l'Enseignement et de la Recherche Scientifique, 157–84. Tunis: Imprimerie Officielle, 1989.

———. "Les mouvements paysans dans la Tunisie du XIXè siècle." *Revue de l'Occident Musulman et de la Méditerranée* 30 (1980): 21–55.

———. "Tunis de la fin du XVIIè siècle à 1956. Introduction historique." In *Hasab wa nasab—Parenté, alliance et patrimoine en Tunisie,* edited by Sophie Ferchiou, 27–50. Paris: Centre National de la Recherche Scientifique, 1992.

Chtioui, Hachemi. "La croissance de la population et des ressources en Tunisie pendant la période coloniale." *Revue Tunisienne de Sciences Sociales* 6 (1969): 53–64.

Clancy-Smith, Julia. *Rebel and Saint. Muslim Notables, Populist Protest, Colonial Encounters (Algeria and Tunisia, 1800–1904)*. Berkeley: University of California Press, 1994.

Cohen-Hadira, Elie. *Du protectorat français à l'indépendance tunisienne: souvenirs d'un témoin socialiste*. Nice: Centre de la Méditerranée moderne et contemporaine, 1976.

———. "Les juifs francophones dans la vie intellectuelle et politique de la Tunisie entre les deux guerres." In *Judaisme d'Afrique du Nord aux XIXè–XXè siècles,* edited by M. Abitbol, 49–66. Jerusalem: Ben-Zvi Institute, 1980.

Colacicchi, Paolo. *L'ultimo fronte d'Africa—Tunisia: novembre 1942–maggio 1943*. Milan: Mursia, 1977.

Compagnon, Jean. "La campagne de Tunisie et la Légion étrangère." *Mondes et Cultures* 2 (1988): 127–54.

———. "La Légion étrangère dans la campagne de Tunisie, 1942–1943." *Revue Historique de l'Armée* 37 (1981): 185–216.

Dabbab, Mohamed. *La presse arabe de Tunisie de 1860 à la veille de la première guerre mondiale. Le rôle de la presse dans le développement de la conscience nationale*. Tunis: Société Tunisienne de Diffusion, 1990.

Daillier, Pierre. *Terre d'affrontements. Le Sud-Tunisien. La ligne Mareth et son étrange destin*. Paris: Nouvelles Editions Latines, 1985.

Dammak, Abdesselem. "Méthodologie pour l'étude de la crise des années trente en Tunisie: à propos de l'étude de M. Mahjoub sur le développement du sous-développement." In *Les mouvements politiques et sociaux dans la Tunisie des années trente,* edited by Moncef Chenoufi, 403–10. Tunis: Ministère de l'Education, de l'Enseignement et de la Recherche Scientifique, 1987.

Darghouth, Abdelkebir. *Du pacha à son descendant*. Tunis: Imprimerie Les Nouvelles Presses, 1977.

Debernardi, Laurent. "Le premier chemin de fer tunisien, le TGM (1870–1898)." *Revue Française d'Histoire d'Outre-Mer* 40 (1963): 197–226.

Dellagi, Moncef. "Une campagne sur l'insécurité des colons de Tunisie en 1898." *Revue d'Histoire Maghrébine* 4, nos. 7–8 (1977): 99–106.

Demeerseman, André. "Soixante ans de pensée tunisienne à travers les revues de langue arabe." *Revue de l'Institut des Belles Lettres Arabes* 16, no. 62 (1953): 113–201.

———. "Tahar Haddad et le concept d'efficacité." *Revue de l'Institut des Belles Lettres Arabes* 39, no. 138 (1976): 277–81.

Dor, M.-J., and J. Fisset. "Los padres blancos y las hermanas blancas en Túnez y Argelia." *El cristianismo en el Norte de Africa,* edited by Henri Teissier and Ramon Lourido Diaz, 207–25. Madrid: MAPFRE, 1993.

Dougui, Nourredine. "La construction et l'exploitation du reseau de chemin de fer de Sfax-Gafsa (1897–1914)." *Cahiers de Tunisie* 31, nos. 123–24 (1983): 13–46.

———. "Dépression économique et mouvement ouvrier dans les mines du sud-ouest tunisien." In *Les mouvements politiques et sociaux dans la Tunisie des années trente,* edited by Moncef Chenoufi, 411–30. Tunis: Ministère de l'Education, de l'Enseignement et de la Recherche Scientifique, 1987.

———. "La naissance d'une grande entreprise coloniale: la Compagnie des Phosphates et du Chemin de Fer de Gafsa." *Cahiers de Tunisie* 30, nos. 119–20 (1982): 123–64.

Douib, Abdelmajid. "La région de Zarzis. II. Contact européen et exploitation du sol de 1881 à 1959." *Cahiers de Tunisie* 20 (1972): 171–78.

Driss, Rachid. "Le mouvement de jeunesse en Tunisie entre les deux guerres." In *Les mouvements politiques et sociaux dans la Tunisie des années trente,* edited by Moncef Chenoufi, 697–712. Tunis: Ministère de l'Education, de l'Enseignement et de la Recherche Scientifique, 1987.

———. "Souvenirs des années 1934–1939." *Cahiers de Tunisie* 26, nos. 105–6 (1978): 287–302.

———. "La Tunisie au début de la seconde guerre mondiale (1939–1940)." *Cahiers de Tunisie* 27, nos. 107–8 (1979): 213–75.

———. "La Tunisie sous l'occupation allemande, novembre 1942–mai 1943." *Cahiers de Tunisie* 27, nos. 109–10 (1979): 455–84.

Driss, Rachid, and J. Driss. "L'établissement du protectorat français en Tunisie vu par la presse américaine (1ére partie)." *Revue d'Histoire Maghrébine* 8, nos. 21–22 (1981): 103–16.

Ducroquet, P. "La crise économique de 1897 au Sahel Tunisien." *Revue Tunisienne* (1908): 124–30, 377–82, 491–98; (1909): 220–26, 313–38, 386–93; (1910): 7–17, 104–17.

———. "Georges Pavillier, Directeur Général des travaux publics de la Régence (1893–1903)." *Revue Tunisienne* (1917): 205–14.

Emerit, Marcel. "Aux origines de la colonisation française en Tunisie. L'affaire de Sidi Tabet." *Revue Africaine* 89 (1945): 201–35.

Faroua, Mahmoud. "L'affaire des pêcheurs italiens de Gabès (juin 1889–avril 1890)." *Revue d'Histoire Maghrébine* 16, nos. 55–56 (1989): 11–17.

———. "Le commerce caravanier de la Tunisie après la première guerre mondiale." *Revue d'Histoire Maghrébine* 16, nos. 55–56 (1989): 19–32.

Fendri, Mounir. "Les ressortissants allemands à Tunis au déclenchement de la 1ère guerre mondiale: un témoinage de l'écrivain Lion Feuchtwanger." *Revue d'Histoire Maghrébine* 21, no. 74 (1994): 47–52.

Fozzard, A. "Tribes and the State: The Experience of Southern Tunisia (1850–1950)." In *BRISMES: Proceedings of the 1988 Conference on Middle Eastern Studies,* 158–66. Oxford: British Society for Middle Eastern Studies, 1988.

Francolini, B. "La Tunisia e il lavoro italiano." *Bulletino della Reale Società Geografica Italiana* 76 (1939): 255–72.

Gafsi, Abdel-Hakim el-. "La situación de los refugiados españoles en Túnez, entre el 4 de febrero de 1939 y el 18 de julio 1940 según unos documentos de archivos del gobierno tunecino." *Almenara* 10 (1976/1977): 91–108.

Gallissot, René. "Les thèses du 'socialisme colonial' en Tunisie: colonisation socialiste et formation d'une nouvelle patrie par le mélange des races. Le discours de J. Durel au Conseil national du parti socialiste S.F.I.O. de juillet 1928." *Pluriel* 12 (1977): 53–59.

Ganiage, Jean. "Une affaire tunisienne, l'affaire d'Enfida (1880–1882)." *Revue Africaine* 99 (1955): 341–78.

Garnault, J. "La prise de Sfax et Gabès (15 juillet–24 juillet 1881). Une page trop oubliée de nos fastes maritimes." *Revue des Questions Historiques* 67 (1939): 105–29.

Gaumer, Benoît. "Aspect épidémiologique de l'histoire de la lèpre en Tunisie à l'époque contemporaine." *Revue de l'Institut des Belles Lettres Arabes* 52, no. 163 (1989): 23–38.

———. "Esquisse d'une histoire de l'administration de la santé publique en Tunisie de la fin du XIXè siècle à l'indépendance." *Revue de l'Institut des Belles Lettres Arabes* 51, no. 161 (1988): 37–57.

Gharbi, Mohamed Lazhar. *Impérialisme et réformisme au Maghreb: Histoire d'un chemin de fer algéro-tunisien.* Tunis: Centre d'Etudes et de Recherches Economiques et Sociales, 1994.

———. "L'affaire de l'Ouenza, 1900–1914." *Revue d'Histoire Maghrébine* 18, nos. 63–64 (1991): 259–79.

———. "La Compagnie du Bône-Guelma et son réseau minier tunisien (1900–1914)." *Revue de l'Institut des Belles Lettres Arabes* 52, no. 164 (1989): 227–54.

———. "La politique financière de la France en Tunisie au lendemain de la deuxième guerre: contraintes mondiales et exigences nationalistes." In *La Tunisie de l'après-guerre,* 11–43. Tunis: Institut Supérieur d'Histoire du Mouvement National, 1991.

Ghoul, Fayçal el-. "La pêche des éponges et la rivalité franco-italienne dans le golfe de Gabès, 1900–1914." *Cahiers de Tunisie* 46, no. 165 (1993): 85–100.

Ghoul, Yahya el-. "Antisémitisme en milieu colonial: l'affaire Bonan à Nabeul (1895–1898)." *Cahiers de Tunisie* 46, no. 164 (1993): 57–83.

———. "Colonisation et vie municipale. La fiscalité et les recettes municipales à Nabeul à la fin du XIXè siècle." *Revue de l'Institut des Belles Lettres Arabes* 58, no. 176 (1995): 261–88.

———. "La commission municipale de Nabeul (1887–1898)." *Cahiers de Tunisie* 45, nos. 159–60 (1992): 25–45.

Gourg, Jean. "Etienne Burnet et l'émigration russe en Tunisie." *Cahiers de Tunisie* 29, nos. 115–16 (1981): 221–35.

———. "La Tunisie de Pierre Mac Orlan." *Cahiers de Tunisie* 27, nos. 109–10 (1979): 345–58.

Grandchamp, Pierre. *Etudes d'histoire tunisienne, XVIIè–XXè siècles.* Paris: Presses Universitaires de France, 1966.

Grazzini, F. "La Iglesia en Túnez durante el protectorado." In *El cristianismo en el Norte de Africa,* edited by Henri Teissier and Ramon Lourido Diaz, 135–38. Madrid: MAPFRE, 1993.

Green, Arnold. *The Tunisian Ulama, 1873–1915. Social Structure and Response to Ideological Currents.* Leiden: Brill, 1978.

———. "French Islamic Policy in Tunisia, 1881–1918: A Preliminary Inquiry." *Revue d'Histoire Maghrébine* 2, no. 3 (1975): 5–17.

———. "On Identifying and Delimiting the Corps of Tunisian Ulama." *Revue d'Histoire Maghrébine* 4, nos. 7–8 (1977): 150–64.

———. "Taqwimat as a Source for the History of Modern Tunisia." *Revue d'Histoire Maghrébine* 15, nos. 49–50 (1988): 7–24.

———. "The Tunisian Ulama and the Establishment of the French Protectorate, 1881–1882." *Revue d'Histoire Maghrébine* 1, no. 1 (1974): 14–25.

Haddad de Paz, Charles. *Juifs et arabes au pays de Bourguiba.* Aix-en-Provence: P. Roubaud, 1977.

Hadhri, Mohieddine. "Compétitions et rivalités entre les puissances européennes en Méditerranée: l'enjeu tunisien 1935–1939." In *Les mouvements politiques et sociaux dans la Tunisie des années trente,* edited by Moncef Chenoufi, 333–50. Tunis: Ministère de l'Education, de l'Enseignement et de la Recherche Scientifique, 1987.

Hahn, Lorna. "Tunisia: A Challenge to American Foreign Policy." *Middle Eastern Affairs* 5 (1954): 159–67.

Hamdane, Mohamed. "Panorama historique de la presse rurale en Tunisie (1881–1981)." *Revue de l'Institut des Belles Lettres Arabes* 49, no. 157 (1986): 75–86.

Hamza, Raouf. "Les Etats-Unis et la question tunisienne (1939–1943): à la recherche d'une politique." In *La Tunisie de 1939 à 1945,* edited by Centre National Universitaire de Documentation Scientifique et Technique and Ministère de l'Education, de l'Enseignement et de la Recherche Scientifique, 215–48. Tunis: Imprimerie Officielle, 1989.

———. "Les pêcheurs saisonniers italiens à Mahdia (1871–1945)." In *Etre marginal au Maghreb,* edited by Fanny Colonna and Zakya Daoud, 155–60. Paris: Centre National de la Recherche Scientifique, 1993.

Hanna, Sami. "Abu Al-Qasim Ash-Shabbi, A Modern Tunisian Poet." *Maghreb Review* 6 (1981): 100–104.

Hannezo, Cyr-Gustave. "Mateur, 1881–1882." *Revue Tunisienne* (1906): 109–16.

Harber, Charles C. "Tunisian Land Tenure in the Early Protectorate." *Muslim World* 63 (1973): 307–15.

Hedi, Timoumi. "Origines et avatars du syndicalisme patronal autotochtone de Tunisie (1947–1948)." *Cahiers de Tunisie* 29, nos. 117–18 (1981): 413–33.

Heffernan, Michael J. "Bringing the Desert to Bloom: French Ambitions in the Sahara Desert during the Late Nineteenth Century—The Strange Case of 'La Mer Intérieure'." In *Water, Engineering and Landscape: Water Control and Landscape Transformation in the Modern Period,* edited by D. Cosgrove and G. Petts, 94–114. London: Belhaven, 1990.

Henia, Abdelhamid. "Circulation des biens et liens de parenté à Tunis (XVIIè–début XXè siècle)." In *Hasab wa nasab—Parenté, alliance et patrimoine en Tunisie,* edited by Sophie Ferchiou, 217–50. Paris: Centre National de la Recherche Scientifique, 1992.

Jerad, Mustapha. "La politique fiscale du gouvernement de la Régence de Tunisie et la crise des années trente." *Revue d'Histoire Maghrébine* 18, nos. 63–64 (1991): 289–94.

Karoui, Abdeljelil. *Tunisie et son image dans la littérature française du 19ème siècle et de la 1ère moitié du 20ème, 1801–1945.* Tunis: Société Tunisienne de Diffusion, 1975.

Karoui, Hachemi. "La résistance populaire à l'occupation française (1881) chez les élites tunisiennes: désaveu et oubli." In *Connaissances du Maghreb: Sciences sociales et colonisation,* edited by Jean-Claude Vatin, 401–21. Paris: Centre National de la Recherche Scientifique, 1984.

Karoui, Naima. "Les femmes dans le domaine agricole dans la Tunisie coloniale." *Revue Tunisienne des Sciences Sociales* 98–99 (1989): 129–51.

Kassab, Ahmed. *Histoire de la Tunisie. L'époque contemporaine.* Tunis: Société Tunisienne de Diffusion, 1976.

———. "La communauté israélite de Tunisie entre la francisation et le sionisme (1930–1940)." In *Les mouvements politiques et sociaux dans la Tunisie des années trente,* edited by Moncef Chenoufi, 525–48. Tunis: Ministère de l'Education, de l'Enseignement et de la Recherche Scientifique, 1987.

Kazdaghli, Habib, ed. *Mémoire des femmes tunisiennes dans la vie publique, 1920–1960.* Tunis: Credif, 1993.

———. "L'évolution de la politique du parti communiste pendant la Deuxième Guerre Mondiale (septembre 1939–mai 1943)." In *La Tunisie de 1939 à 1945,* edited by Centre National Universitaire de Documentation Scientifique et Technique et Ministère de l'Education, de l'Enseignement et de la Recherche Scientifique, 185–93. Tunis: Imprimerie Officielle, 1989.

————. "L'évolution organisationnelle du mouvement communiste en Tunisie (1926–1939)." In *Les mouvements politiques et sociaux dans la Tunisie des années trente,* edited by Moncef Chenoufi, 203–20. Tunis: Ministère de l'Education, de l'Enseignement et de la Recherche Scientifique, 1987.

Kerrou, Mohamed, and Moncef Mhalla. "La prostitution dans la médina de Tunis au XIXè et au XXè siècles." In *Etre marginal au Maghreb,* edited by Fanny Colonna and Zakya Daoud, 201–24. Paris: Centre National de la Recherche Scientifique, 1993.

Khaddar Zangar, Salwa. "Nabuel: de la domination coloniale à la libértaion nationale (1881–1954)." *Revue d'Histoire Maghrébine* 15, nos. 49–50 (1988): 47–70.

Kologlu, Orhan. "Les Jeunes Turcs et la Tunisie avant 1908." *Revue d'Histoire Maghrébine* 18, nos. 63–64 (1991): 315–23.

Kossentini, Karray. "La pensée réformiste au lendemain du départ de l'Axe de la Tunisie (mai–décembre 1943)." In *La Tunisie de 1939 à 1945,* edited by Centre National Universitaire de Documentation Scientifique et Technique and Ministère de l'Education, de l'Enseignement et de la Recherche Scientifique, 114–16. Tunis: Imprimerie Officielle, 1989.

————. "Quelques données sur les ouvriers agricoles occasionnels dans le nord de la Tunisie (1936–1939)." In *Les mouvements politiques et sociaux dans la Tunisie des années trente,* edited by Moncef Chenoufi, 431–84. Tunis: Ministère de l'Education, de l'Enseignement et de la Recherche Scientifique, 1987.

Kraiem, Abdelmajid. "L'échec de la politique de naturalisation en Tunisie (1933–1937)." In *Les mouvements politiques et sociaux dans la Tunisie des années trente,* edited by Moncef Chenoufi, 623–54. Tunis: Ministère de l'Education, de l'Enseignement et de la Recherche Scientifique, 1987.

————. "La résistance de Gabès à l'occupation française en 1881." *Cahiers de Tunisie* 36, nos. 143–44 (1988): 121–56.

Kraiem, Abdelmajid, and Hédi Jellab. *Le mouvement réformiste en Tunisie, 1815–1920.* Tunis: Institut Supérieur du Mouvement National, 1994.

Kraiem, Mustapha. *Le Fascisme et les italiens de Tunisie (1918–1939).* Tunis: Centre d'Etudes et de Recherches Economiques et Sociales, 1987.

————. *Le Mouvement sociale en Tunisie dans les années trente.* Tunis: Centre d'Etudes et de Recherche Economique et Sociale, 1984.

————. "L'adhésion de l'U.G.T.T. à la Fédération syndicale mondiale." *Revue d'Histoire Maghrébine* 1, no. 1 (1974): 26–34.

————. "Le mouvement associatif en Tunisie dans les années trente." *Revue Tunisienne des Sciences Sociales* 92–93 (1988): 11–61.

————. "Aux origines du Parti Communiste Tunisien, 1919–1929." *Revue d'Histoire Maghrébine* 1, no. 2 (1974): 116–37.

————. "Le parti communiste tunisien dans les années trente." *Revue d'Histoire Maghrébine* 8, nos. 21–22 (1981): 7–23.

————. "La question de l'unité syndicale entre l'U.G.T.T. et l'U.S.T.T." *Revue d'Histoire Maghrébine* 5, no. 12 (1978): 272–85.

————. "La question du droit syndical en Tunisie (1881–1932). *Revue d'Histoire Maghrébine* 2, no. 3 (1975): 27–44.

Labidi, Lilia. "Circulation des femmes musulmanes dans l'espace publique et politique formel: le cas de la Tunisie en période coloniale." In *Participation des femmes à la vie publique,* edited by Lilia Labidi, 44–62. Tunis: Centre de Recherche et de Formation Pédagogique, 1990.

Lamourette, Charles. "Polémique autour du statut de la femme musulmane en Tunisie en 1930." *Bulletin d'Etudes Orientales* 30 (1978): 11–31.

Langer, William L. "The European Powers and the French Occupation of Tunis, 1878–1881." *American Historical Review* 31 (1925/1926): 55–78, 251–65.

Laskier, Michael M. "The Evolution of Zionist Activity in the Jewish Communities of Morocco, Tunisia, and Algeria: 1897–1947." *Studies in Zionism* 8 (1983): 205–36.

Le Boeuf, Jules. "Historique de la conqûete pacifique des territoires militaires de Tunisie." *Revue Tunisienne* (1907): 112–28, 244–67.

Liauzu, Claude. *Salariat et mouvement ouvrier en Tunisie: crises et mutations, 1931–1939.* Paris: Editions du Centre National de la Recherche Scientifique, 1978.

————. "Un aspect de la crise en Tunisie: la naissance des bidonvilles." *Revue Française d'Histoire d'Outre-Mer* 63 (1976): 607–21.

————. "Cheminots majorés et cheminots guenillards en Tunisie jusqu'en 1938." *Revue de l'Occident Musulmane et de la Méditerranée* 24 (1977): 171–205.

————. "La pêche et les pêcheurs de thon en Tunisie dans les années 1930." *Revue de l'Occident Musulman et de la Méditerranée* 12 (1972): 69–91.

————. "Les pêcheurs tunisiens à la veille de la deuxième guerre mondiale." *Revue de l'Institut des Belles Lettres Arabes* 34, no. 128 (1971): 295–332.

————. "Des précurseurs du mouvement ouvrier: les libertaires en Tunisie à la fin du XIXè siècle." *Cahiers de Tunisie* 21, nos. 81–82 (1973): 153–82.

————. "Situation coloniale et opinion publique: petits blancs et socialistes pendant trente ans de luttes électorales." *Cahiers de Tunisie* 22, nos. 87–88 (1974): 41–91.

————. "Les syndicats en Tunisie au temps du Cinquantenaire." *Annuaire de l'Afrique du Nord* 12 (1973): 1031–44.

———. "Les traminots de Tunis du début de siècle à la deuxième guerre mondiale." *Cahiers de Tunisie* 23, nos. 89–90 (1975): 141–90; 23, nos. 91–92 (1975): 235–81.

Mahjoub, Azzam. "Analyse historique du sous-développement en Tunisie, 2è partie: Le capitalisme colonial, du Protectorat à la crise des années 30 ou la deuxième forme historique du sous-développement." *Annuaire de l'Afrique du Nord* 20 (1981): 509–22.

———. "La crise des années trente ou le développement du sous-développement en Tunisie." In *Les mouvements politiques et sociaux dans la Tunisie des années trente,* edited by Moncef Chenoufi, 387–402. Tunis: Ministère de l'Education, de l'Enseignement et de la Recherche Scientifique, 1987.

Mahjoubi, Ali. *L'établissement du Protectorat français en Tunisie.* Tunis: Université de Tunisie, 1977.

Mahjoubi, Ali, and Hachemi Karoui. *Quand le soleil s'est levé à l'ouest: Tunisie 1881. Impérialisme et résistance.* Tunis: Cérès Productions, 1983.

Majed, Jaafar. *La presse littéraire en Tunisie de 1904 à 1955.* Tunis: Université de Tunis, 1979.

Marsden, Arthur. *Britain and the End of the Tunis Treaties, 1894–1897.* London: Longmans, 1965.

———. "Britain and her Conventional Rights in Tunis, 1888–1892." *Actes du IIème Congrès International d'Etudes Nord-Africaines.* In *Revue de l'Occident Musulman et de la Méditerranée,* special issue (1970): 163–73.

———. "Britain and the 'Tunis Base,' 1894–1899." *English Historical Review* 79 (1964): 67–96.

Martel, André. *Les Confins Saharo-Tripolitains de la Tunisie (1881–1911).* 2 vols. Paris: Presses Universitaires de France, 1965.

———. "Le commerce maritime du Sud-Tunisien 1885–1910." *Cahiers de Tunisie* 12 (1964): 109–45.

———. "Le Makhzen du Sud Tunisien (1881–1910)." *Cahiers de Tunisie* 8 (1960): 7–30; 11 (1963): 63–70; 14 (1966): 88–142.

———. "Préoccupations sahariennes à Tunis (1911)." *Cahiers de Tunisie* 7 (1959): 517–18.

———. "Une razzia touareg dans le Nefzaoua tunisien (1887)." *Travaux de l'Institut de Recherches Sahariennes* 17 (1958): 207–12.

Marzouki, Ilhem. "Le voile des colonisées (Tunisie 1924–1936)." *Revue de l'Institut des Belles Lettres Arabes* 51, no. 161 (1988): 59–89.

Mechri-Bendana, Kmar. "L'Institut des Hautes Etudes de Tunis, 1945–1950." In *La Tunisie de l'après-guerre,* 119–34. Tunis: Institut Supérieur d'Histoire du Mouvement National, 1991.

———. "Revues françaises publiées à Tunis pendant la Deuxième Guerre Mondiale. Présentation et essai d'interprétation idéologique."

In *La Tunisie de 1939 à 1945,* edited by Centre National Universitaire de Documentation Scientifique et Technique and Ministère de l'Education, de l'Enseignement et de la Recherche Scientifique, 337–54. Tunis: Imprimerie Officielle, 1989.

Medici, Anna-Maria. "L'occupazione francese di Sfax e la communità italiana." *Africa* [Rome] 46 (1991): 262–73.

Mejri, Abdelkrim. "La colonie maltaise en Tunisie et ses préoccupations à la veille de la Deuxième Guerre Mondiale." *Cahiers de Tunisie* 36, nos. 143–44 (1988): 109–20.

Messenger, Charles. *The Tunisian Campaign.* London: I. Allan, 1982.

Mizouri, Laroussi. "La loge 'Travail, Liberté et Progrès, Orient de Tunis.' " *Revue de l'Institut des Belles Lettres Arabes* 58, no. 175 (1995): 3–14.

M. S. Z. "Taher Pacha Kheireddine: Stratège et homme d'état." *Revue de l'Institut des Belles Lettres Arabes* 10, no. 40 (1947): 425–36.

Nagy, Laszlo J. "Les évènements des années 1881–1882 en Tunisie et en Egypte vus par la presse hongroise." *Arab Historical Review for Ottoman Studies* 1–2 (1990): 135–40.

Nouschi, André. "Un Débat: la colonisation de la Tunisie: des terres ou des capitaux." *Cahiers de Tunisie* 14 (1966): 171–85.

O'Donnell, J. Dean. *Lavigerie in Tunisia: The Interplay of Imperialist and Missionary.* Athens, Ga.: University of Georgia Press, 1979.

Ouled Mohammed, L. "Notes à propos des enquêtes coloniales sur la religion populaire en Tunisie de 1886 à 1934." *Cahiers de la Méditerranée* 20–21 (1980): 81–99.

Passamonti, Eugenio. "La questione tunisina il domani del trattato del Bardo e la politica europa contemporanea." *Rivista Storica Italiana,* 4th ser., 52 (1936): 48–126.

Payre, G. "Les origines et le rôle du contrôle civil dans la Régence de Tunis (1881–1956): une institution conforme à l'esprit des traités." *Revue d'Histoire Diplomatique* 98 (1984): 266–88.

Pellegrin, René. *La Phalange africaine: la L.V.F. en Tunisie, 1942–1943: Une page cachée de l'histoire de la Deuxième Guerre mondiale.* Paris: N.p., 1973.

Périllier, Louis. *La conquête de l'indépendance tunisienne. Souvenirs et témoignages.* Paris: Robert Lafont, 1979.

Perkins, Kenneth J. " 'The Masses Look Ardently to Istanbul': Tunisia, Islam, and the Ottoman Empire, 1837–1931." In *Islamism and Secularism in North Africa,* edited by John Ruedy, 23–36. New York: St. Martin's Press, 1994.

———. "The Transformation of Bizerte, 1881–1914: The Razing of a Traditional Tunisian Community and the Raising of a Modern French Naval Base." *Revue d'Histoire Maghrébine* 21, no. 74 (1994): 53–70.

Peyras, Jean, and Pierre Soumille. "Les souvenirs d'un soldat Bas-Alpin sur la conquête de la Tunisie." *Revue de l'Occident Musulman et de la Méditerranée* 34 (1982): 63–79.

Poncet, Jean. *La Colonisation et l'agricultre européennes en Tunisie depuis 1881.* Paris and The Hague: Mouton, 1962.

———. "La crise des années 30 et ses répercussions sur la colonisation française en Tunisie." *Revue Française d'Histoire d'Outre-Mer* 63 (1976): 622–27.

Porcet, Charles. "La Franc-maçconnerie tunisienne et l'héritage révolutionnaire: la loge Nouvelle Carthage, 1885–1936, et les autres." In *La Révolution française et le monde arabo-musulman,* edited by Hédia Khadhar, 321–35. Tunis: Alif, 1991.

Pouillon, François. "Du savoir malgré tout: la connaissance coloniale de l'extrême-sud tunisien." In *Connaissances du Maghreb: Sciences sociales et colonisation,* edited by Jean-Claude Vatin, 79–93. Paris: Centre National de la Recherche Scientifique, 1984.

Pradel de Lamase, Martial de. "La station navale français de Tunis." *Cahiers de Tunisie* 4 (1956): 351–57.

Rainero, Romain. *La rivendicazione fascista sulla Tunisia.* Milan: Marzorati, 1978.

———. "L'Italie et la Question Tunisienne dans l'après-guerre: du dépassement des revendications à une politique d'amitié." In *La Tunisie de l'après-guerre,* 369–83. Tunis: Institut Supérieur d'Histoire du Mouvement National, 1991.

———. "Pépinières d'agitateurs ou centres de culture? Observations sur les écoles italiennes en Tunisie dans les années 1938–1940." *Cahiers de la Méditerranée* no. 27 (1983): 171–93.

———. "La politique fasciste à l'égard de l'Afrique du Nord: l'épee de l'Islam et la revendication sur la Tunisie." *Revue Française d'Histoire d'Outre-Mer* 64 (1977): 498–515.

———. "Réactions italiennes en Tunisie après la déclaration de Ciano du 30 novembre 1938." *Mondes et Cultures* 38 (1978): 447–57.

Raymond, André. "Les libéraux anglais et la question tunisienne (1880–1881)." *Cahiers de Tunisie* 3 (1955): 422–65.

Rectenwald, Georges. "Les assemblées élues du protectorat française en Tunisie." *Renseignements Coloniaux* 33 (1923): 186–211.

———. "La Tunisie agricole et rurale et l'oeuvre de la France." *Revue Africaine* 83 (1939): 84–96.

Regaya, Mourad. "Aperçu sur la période insurrectionnelle sur le territoire de Sousse en 1881–1882." *Revue d'Histoire Maghrébine* 18, nos. 63–64 (1991): 393–96.

Les relations franco-tunisiennes au miroir des élites XVIIIè, XIXè, XXè siècles. Tunis: Archives Nationales, 1994.

Rendu, Christian. *La saga des pionniers. Lyon et la Tunisie (1880–1914).* Oullins: Editions Chantoiseau, 1995.

Rey-Goldzeiguer, Annie. "L'opinion publique tunisienne (1940–1944)." In *La Tunisie de 1939 à 1945,* edited by Centre National Universitaire de Documentation Scientifique et Technique and Ministère de l'Education, de l'Enseignement et de la Recherche Scientifique, 133–56. Tunis: Imprimerie Officielle, 1989.

Sammoud, Hamadi. "Souci de spécificité chez un intellectuel tunisien, Tahar Haddad." *Revue de l'Institut des Belles Lettres Arabes* 37, no. 133 (1974): 45–67.

Sammut, Carmel. "L'installation du Protectorat français et la réforme du système monétaire tunisien (d'après les Archives du Quai d'Orsay, Paris)." *Revue d'Histoire Maghrébine* 2, no. 4 (1975): 184–94.

———. "Régime des terres collectives de tribus: une lettre inédite datée du 27 janvier 1900 et adressée par le Résident Général à Tunis . . . au Ministre des affaires étrangères . . ." *Revue d'Histoire Maghrébine* 3, no. 6 (1976): 195–202.

———. "La situation du prolétariat dans une entreprise coloniale française en Tunisie: la Compagnie des chemins de fer et phosphates de Gafsa." *Revue d'Histoire Maghrébine* 4, no. 9 (1977): 350–59.

Sangmuah, Egya. "Interest Groups and Decolonization: American Business and Organized Labor in French North Africa, 1948–1956." *Maghreb Review* 13 (1988): 161–74.

Saumagne, Charles. *Journal et écrits: Tunisie, 1947–1957.* Nice: Centre de la Méditerranée Moderne et Contemporaine, 1979.

Sayah, Mohamed. *Le Néo-Destour face à la troisième épreuve, 1952–1956: textes réunis et commentés.* 3 vols. Tunis: Dar al-Amal, n.d. [1979].

Senoussi, Mohamed Larbi. "La presse judéo-arabe parue en Tunisie entre 1884–1897." *Cahiers de Tunisie* 36, nos. 143–44 (1988): 183–220.

Serra, E. "L'accordo italo-francese de 1896 sulla Tunisia." *Rivista Storica Italiana* 73 (1961): 473–512.

Serres, Victor. "La mission française au Hedjaz. Le pélerinage des Tunisiens à la Mecque en 1917 et la nouvelle hôtellerie." *Revue Tunisienne* (1918): 25–34.

Sghair, Amira Aleya. "Contribution à l'étude de l'histoire des institutions religieuses européennes en Tunisie entre 1920 et 1946." *Revue d'Histoire Maghrébine* 20, nos. 69–70 (1993): 49–72.

———. "Contribution à l'étude des associations françaises non-politiques en Tunisie entre 1881 et 1939 (sources bibliographiques et présentation)." *Revue d'Histoire Maghrébine* 21, nos. 75–76 (1994): 271–74.

———. "La Fédération Républicaine, Radicale et Radicale Socialiste de Tunisie entre 1925 et 1945." *Revue d'Histoire Maghrébine* 21, no. 74 (1994): 99–122.

———. "Les questions tunisiennes des années trente dans *l'Afrique Française.*" *Revue d'Histoire Maghrébine* 21, nos. 75–76 (1994): 315–19.

Silvera, Victor. "Le Ministère des affaires marocaines et tunisiennes." *Revue Tunisienne de Droit* 3 (1955): 17–27.

———. "La récente réforme gouvernementale tunisienne." *Revue Juridique et Politique de l'Union Française* 2 (1948): 175–212.

———. "La réforme des assemblées locales en Tunisie. (Conseils municipaux et conseils de caidats.)" *Revue Juridique et Politique de l'Union Française* 7 (1953): 23–105.

———. "Les réformes institutionelles tunisiennes (mars 1954)." *Revue Juridique et Politique de l'Union Française* 8 (1954): 25–103.

———. "Les réformes tunisiennes de février 1951." *Revue Juridique et Politique de l'Union Française* 5 (1951): 1–54.

Slabslab, Ali. "La population tunisoise durant la période coloniale." In *La démographie historique en Tunisie et dans le monde arabe,* edited by Dalenda and Abdelhamid Larguèche, 95–102. Tunis: Centre d'Etudes et de Recherches Economiques et Sociales (CERES), 1993.

Snoussi, Mohamed el-Arbi. "Aux origines du mouvement sioniste en Tunisie à la veille de la grande guerre. Création de l'Aghoudat-Sion et sa première session, 1887–1914." *Cahiers de Tunisie* 44, nos. 157–58 (1991): 225–74.

Soulie, G. Jean-Louis. "Les Djich dans la campagne de Tunisie (1942–1943)." *Revue Historique de l'Armée* 25 (1969): 83–89.

Soumille, Pierre. *Européens de Tunisie et questions religieuses (1892–1901). Etude d'opinion publique.* Aix-en-Provence: Centre National de la Recherche Scientifique, 1975.

———. "Anticléricaux européens et processions catholiques en Tunisie dans les années 1905–1910." *Revue d'Histoire Maghrébine* 4, nos. 7–8 (1977): 221–33.

———. "Le cimetière européen de Bab-el-Khadra à Tunis. Etude historique et sociale." *Cahiers de Tunisie* 19 (1971): 129–82.

———. "Les Européens de Tunisie et les questions religieuses de 1893 à 1901: études d'une opinion publique." *Revue d'Histoire Maghrébine* 2, no. 3 (1975): 56–64.

———. "L'idée de race chez les européens de Tunisie dans les années 1890–1910." *Revue d'Histoire Maghrébine* 3, no. 5 (1976): 59–65.

———. "Lavigerie et les Capuchins italiens en Tunisie de 1875 à 1891." *Bulletin de Littérature Ecclésiastique* 95 (1994): 197–231.

———. "Problèmes religieux des minorités européennes en Tunisie au temps de la colonisation. Méthodologie et sources." *Revue d'Histoire Maghrébine* 6, nos. 13–14 (1979): 119–22.

Soumille, Pierre, and Jean Peyras. "La mémoire du protestantisme à Tunis d'après les monuments du cimetière anglican de Bab-Carthagène (depuis le milieu du XVIIè siècle jusqu'à la fin du XIXè siècle)." In *Les Monuments et la mémoire,* edited by Jean Peyras, 51–70. Paris: L'Harmattan, 1993.

Speziale, Salvatore. "Società e malattia: Tunisi di fronte al colera del 1885." *Africa* [Rome] 49 (1994): 275–98.

Sraieb, Noureddine. *Le Collège Sadiki de Tunis, 1875–1956.* Paris: Centre National de la Recherche Scientifique, 1995.

———. "La Comité Française de Libération nationale: politique scolaire et stratégie politique (1943–1949)." In *La Tunisie de l'après-guerre,* 101–19. Tunis: Institut Supérieur d'Histoire du Mouvement National, 1991.

———. "L'idéologie de l'école en Tunisie coloniale (1881–1945)." *Revue du Monde Musulman et de la Méditerranée* 68–69 (1994): 239–54.

———. "Poésie populaire et résistance en Tunisie." *Revue du Monde Musulman et de la Méditerranée* 51 (1989): 143–49.

———. "Le Problème franco-tunisien et un problème de souveraineté. Traduction et présentation de la lettre de Bourguiba à la Beyye (1953)." *Revue de l'Occident Musulman et de la Méditerranée* 1 (1966): 205–22.

———. "Tahar Haddad, une pensée au service de l'action émancipatrice en Tunisie." *Les Africains, sous la direction de Ch.-A. Julien et al.* 7 (1977): 73–97.

Taieb, Jacques. "Le commerce extérieur de la Tunisie aux premiers temps de la colonisation (1881–1913)." *Revue de l'Institut des Belles Lettres Arabes* 43, no. 145 (1980): 79–115.

———. "Evolution et comportement démographique des juifs de Tunisie sous le protectorat français (1881–1956)." *Population* 4–5 (1982): 952–58.

———. "La Tunisie des premiers temps coloniaux." *Revue de l'Institut des Belles Lettres Arabes* 41, no. 141 (1978): 57–83.

Thiebaut, Claude. "Les manifestations pout le centenaire de la naissance du cardinal Lavigerie (Rome, Alger, Tunis et Paris, 1925)." *Revue Historique* 291, no. 590 (1994): 361–400.

Tlili, Béchir. "Un document inédit de al-Tahir Hayr al-Din, réformateur et ministre de la justice (1875–1937)." *Cahiers de Tunisie* 22, nos. 85–86 (1974): 215–26.

———. "En marge des *Souvenirs* de Cohen-Hadira: un témoignage de Ahmed B. Miled." *Cahiers de Tunisie* 25, nos. 97–98 (1977): 246–47.

———. "La Fédération radicale-socialiste de Tunisie à la veille de la Deuxième guerre mondiale (1937–1938)." *Cahiers de Tunisie* 28, nos. 111–12 (1980): 75–202.

———. "La fédération socialiste de Tunisie (SFIO) et les questions islamiques (1919–1925)." In *Mouvement ouvrier, communisme et nationalisme dans le monde arabe,* edited by René Gallissot, 57–89. Paris: Les Editions Ouvrières, 1978.

—————. "Du front antifasciste et antihitlérien de Tunisie. Le groupement Il Giornale (1939)." *Cahiers de Tunisie* 27, nos. 109–10 (1979): 161–300.

—————. "La Grande Guerre et les questions tunisiennes: le groupement de la *Revue du Maghreb* (1916–1918)." *Cahiers de Tunisie* 26, nos. 101–2 (1978): 31–108.

—————. "Aux origines du syndicalisme tunisien: deux documents relatifs au séjour et aux activités de Muhammad Ali à la veille et au lendemain de la Grande Guerre." *Cahiers de Tunisie* 25, nos. 97–98 (1977): 239–45.

—————. "La réorganisation de la justice tunisienne au sortie de la Grande Guerre (1921–1924): réforme ou réajustement de la souvraineté française?" *Cahiers de Tunisie* 24, nos. 95–96 (1976): 147–86.

—————. "Socialisme libertaire et questions tunisiennes à la veille de la Grande Guerre (1911)." *Etudes Balkaniques* 12 (1976): 79–94.

—————. "Syndicalisme révolutionnaire et questions tunisiennes à la veille de la Grande Guerre: le groupement de *La Bataille* (1911–1912)." *Cahiers de Tunisie* 23, nos. 91–92 (1975): 133–233.

Turki, Mohamed, and Abdelaziz Laroui. *Abdelaziz Laroui*. Paris: Publisud, 1988.

Valensi, Lucette. "Le fait divers, témoin des tensions sociales: Djerba, 1892." *Annales Economies, Sociétés, Civilisations* 38 (1983): 884–910.

Voizard, P. "Paul Bourde et l'olivier de Tunisie." *Comptes Rendus des Séances Trimestriels de l'Académie des Sciences Outre-Mer* 34 (1974): 205–19.

Zangar, Selwa. "Les socialistes et les questions arabes au lendemain de la première guerre mondiale." *Cahiers de Tunisie* 28, nos. 113–14 (1980): 77–114.

—————. "La Tunisie et l'Union Française: Position nationale et position coloniale 1946–1951." *Revue d'Histoire Maghrébine* 19, nos. 67–68 (1992): 295–334.

Zitouna, Mohamed Moncef. *La Médecine en Tunisie, 1881–1994*. Tunis: Simpact, 1994.

Zouari, Taieb. "La grève des carriers de Tunis. Juillet 1936." *Etudes de Sociologie Tunisienne* 1 (1968): 311–15.

Tunisian Nationalism

Achour, Habib. *Ma vie politique et syndicale. Enthousiasme et déception (1944–1981)*. Tunis: Alif, 1989.

Adda, Georges. "Quelques souvenirs et réflexions à propos des événements du 9 avril 1938." Cahiers de Tunisie 37–38, nos. 145–48 (1988/1989): 201–10.

Ahmad, Eqbal, and Stuart Schaar. "Mhamed Ali and the Tunisian Labour Movement." *Race and Class* 19 (1978): 253–76.

———. "Mhamed Ali et les fondements du mouvement syndical tunisien." *Les Africains, sous la direction de Ch.-A.* Julien et al. 11 (1978): 13–45.

———. "Mhamed Ali: Tunisian Labor Organizer." In *Struggle and Survival in the Modern Middle East,* edited by Edmund Burke III, 191–204. Berkeley: University of California Press, 1993.

Anderson, Lisa. *The State and Social Transformation in Tunisia and Libya, 1830–1980.* Princeton: Princeton University Press, 1986.

Ayachi, Mokhtar. "Le Néo-Destour et les étudiants zaytouniens: de l'alliance à l'affrontement." In *La Tunisie de l'après-guerre,* 231–50. Tunis: Institut Supérieur d'Histoire du Mouvement National, 1991.

———. "L'union générale des étudiants de Tunisie (UGET) et le Néo-Destour devenu 'parti-état' (1952)." In *Elites et pouvoir dans le monde arabe pendant la période moderne et contemporaine,* 207–20. Tunis: Centre d'Etudes et de Recherches Economiques et Sociales, 1992.

Ayadi, Taoufik. *Mouvement réformiste et mouvements populaires à Tunis (1906–1912).* Tunis: Université de Tunis, 1986.

———. "Insurrection et religion en Tunisie: l'exemple de Thala-Kasserine (1906) et du Jellaz (1911)." In *Révolte et Société,* 166–75. Paris: Histoire au Présent, 1989.

Azzouz, Azzedine. *L'Histoire ne pardonne pas.* Paris: L'Harmattan, 1988.

Beling, Willard A. "W.F.T.U. and Decolonisation: A Tunisian Case Study." *Journal of Modern African Studies* 2 (1964): 551–64.

Bendana-Mechri, Kmar. "Préliminaires pour une étude de l'AEMNA dans les années trente à travers les archives du Quai d'Orsay." In *Les mouvements politiques et sociales dans la Tunisie des années trente,* edited by Moncef Chenoufi, 317–28. Tunis: Ministère de l'Education, de l'Enseignement et de la Recherche Scientifique, 1987.

Ben Hamida, Abdesselem. *Le syndicalisme tunisien de la deuxième guerre mondiale à l'autonomie interne.* Tunis: Publications de l'Université de Tunis I, 1989.

———. "Pouvoir syndicale et édification d'un état national en Tunisie." *Cahiers de la Méditerranée* 41 (1990): 129–42.

———. "Le rôle du syndicalisme tunisien dans le mouvement de libération nationale (1946–1956)." *Cahiers de Tunisie* 29, nos. 117–18 (1981): 237–50.

Ben Miled, Ahmed. *Mhamed Ali. La naissance du mouvement ouvrier tunisien.* Tunis: Editions Salammbo, 1984.

Bessis, Juliette. "La crise de l'autonomie et de l'indépendance tunisienne, classe politique et pays réel." In *Mouvement ouvrier, communisme et nationalismes dans le monde arabe,* 265–92, edited by René Gallissot. Paris: Les Editions Ouvrières, 1978.

————. "Farhat Hached, héraut d'un syndicalisme national et victime du colonialisme en Tunisie." *Les Africains, sous la direction de Ch.-A. Julien et al.* 5 (1977): 147–75.

Bessis, Sophie, and Souhayr Belhassen. *Bourguiba.* Vol. 1, *A la conquête d'un destin, 1901–1957.* Paris: Jeune Afrique, 1988.

Boulares, Habib, and Charles-Robert Ageron. "Deux grands figures du nationalisme maghrébin: Tahar Ben Ammar et Farhat Abbas." *Maghreb-Machrek* 115 (1987): 71–79.

Bourguiba, Habib. *Articles de presse, 1929–1933.* 3d edition. Tunis: Dar al-Amal, 1982.

————. *Ma vie, mon oeuvre, 1934–1938.* Edited by Mohamed Sayah. Paris: Plon, 1986.

————. *Ma vie, mon oeuvre, 1938–1943.* Edited by Mohamed Sayah. Paris: Plon, 1986.

————. *Ma vie, mon oeuvre, 1944–1951.* Edited by Mohamed Sayah. Paris: Plon, 1987.

————. *Ma vie, mon oeuvre, 1952–1956.* Edited by Mohamed Sayah. Paris: Plon, 1987.

————. *La Tunisie et la France: Vingt-cinq ans de lutte pour une coopération libre.* Paris: Julliard, 1954.

Brondino, Michele. "Le problème de l'indépendance tunisienne et la question nord-africaine dans la presse italienne de 1954 à 1956." *Oriente Moderno* 67 (1987): 25–41.

Brown, Kenneth. "Muhammad Ameur: A Tunisian Comrade." In *Struggle and Survival in the Middle East,* edited by Edmund Burke III, 251–67. Berkeley: University of California Press, 1993.

Brown, S. E. "Modernism, Association, and Pan-Islamism in the Thought of Ali Bash Hanbah." In *Essays on Islamic Civilization Presented to Niyazi Berkes,* edited by Donald Little, 74–88. Leiden: Brill, 1976.

Cannon, Byron. "La constitution ottomane dans la stratégie politique Jeune Tunisienne, 1908–1910." *Cahiers de Tunisie* 29, nos. 117–18 (1981): 279–94.

————. "Rural Social Justice Rhetoric and the Young Tunisian Movement (1907–1912)." *Revue d'Histoire Maghrébine* 17, nos. 59–60 (1990): 63–72.

Carlier, Omar. "Mimétisme et nationalisme: l'interaction algéro-tunisienne; de la polarité tunisoise aux tunisiens de l'Etoile nord-africaine." In *Les mouvements politiques et sociales dans la Tunisie des années trente,* edited by Moncef Chenoufi, 127–202. Tunis: Ministère de l'Education, de l'Enseignement et de la Recherche Scientifique, 1987.

Chabbi-Labidi, Lilia, and Abdelkadir Zghal. *Génération des années 30: la mémoire vivante des sujets de l'histoire.* Tunis: Centre d'Etudes et de Recherche Economique et Sociale, 1985.

Chikhaoui, Tahar. "Les journée d'avril 38 à travers les mémoires de Mahmoud Materi. Mouvance et obliquité." *Cahiers de Tunisie* 37–38, nos. 145–48 (1988/1989): 211–23.

Dabbab, Mohammed. *Les délégations destouriennes à Paris ou la "Question tunisienne" dans les années 1920.* Tunis: Maison Tunisienne de l'Edition, 1980.

―――. *La presse arabe de Tunisie de 1860 à la veille de la première guerre mondiale. Le rôle de la presse dans le développement de la conscience nationale.* Tunis: Société Tunisienne de Diffusion, 1990.

Dellagi, Moncef. "L'activité de Bourguiba à Sfax (22–29 octobre 1943) vue par les autorités françaises." *Revue d'Histoire Maghrébine* 7, nos. 19–20 (1980): 215–31.

―――. "Un débat sur la revendication de l'indépendance au congrès du Néo-Destour de 1937." *Revue d'Histoire Maghrébine* 4, no. 9 (1977): 342–49.

Demeerseman, André. "Soixante ans de pensée tunisienne à travers les revues de langue arabe." *Revue de l'Institut des Belles Lettres Arabes* 16, no. 62 (1953): 113–201.

Dimassi, Ali. *Habib Bourguiba: l'apôtre de la liberté tunisienne.* Sousse: Dimassi, 1979.

Driss, Rachid. "Premières années d'exil, 1943–1946." *Cahiers de Tunisie* 29, nos. 115–16 (1981): 405–29.

―――. "Résistance du Néo-Destour. Contribution de Moncef Bey à l'action nationale (1941–1943)." *Cahiers de Tunisie* 28, nos. 113–14 (1980): 255–88.

―――. "Six mois de résistance, janvier–juillet 1941." *Cahiers de Tunisie* 28, nos. 111–12 (1980): 335–55.

Duvignaud, Jean. "L'idéologie nationale en Tunisie." *Revue de l'Institut de Sociologie* 40 (1967): 431–40.

Gallico, Loris. "Fascismo e movimento nazionale in Tunisia." *Studi storici* 19 (1978): 863–68.

Gallissot, René. "Les conceptions de la nation dans les trois pays du Maghreb. Le point comparatif en 1941–1945." In *La Tunisie de 1939 à 1945,* edited by Centre National Universitaire de Documentation Scientifique et Technique and Ministère de l'Education, de l'Enseignement et de la Recherche Scientifique, 43–113. Tunis: Imprimerie Officielle, 1989.

―――. "La question nationale au Maghreb: une approche comparée Maroc-Algérie-Tunisie." In *Le Monde Arabe au regard des sciences sociales,* edited by Anne-Marie Planel, 1: 11–27. Tunis: Centre de Documentation Tunisie-Maghreb, 1989.

Ganari, Ali el-. *Bourguiba, le combattant suprême.* Paris: Plon, 1985.

Goldstein, Daniel. *Libération ou annexion aux chemins croisés de l'histoire tunisienne (1914–1922).* Tunis: Maison Tunisienne de l'Edition, 1978.

Green, Arnold. "A propos d'un document inédit de Béchir Sfar." *Revue d'Histoire Maghrébine* 3, no. 5 (1976): 87–92.

Guezmir, Khaled. *Jeunes Tunisiens*. Tunis: Alif, 1986.

Hamza, Hassine Raouf. *Communisme et nationalisme en Tunisie de la "Libération" à l'indépendance (1943–1956)*. Tunis: Université de Tunis I, 1994.

————. "Eléments pour une réflexion sur l'histoire du Mouvement national pendant l'entre-deux-guerres: la scission du Destour de mars 1934." In *Les mouvements politiques et sociales dans la Tunisie des années trente*, edited by Moncef Chenoufi, 51–78. Tunis: Ministère de l'Education, de l'Enseignement et de la Recherche Scientifique, 1987.

————. "Les émeutes du 9 avril 1938 à Tunis: Machination policière, complot nationaliste ou mouvement spontané?" In *Révolte et Société*, 185–92. Paris: Histoire au Présent, 1989.

————. "Le mouvement national tunisien de 1945 à 1950: hégémonie et institutionalisation du Néo-Destour." In *La Tunisie de l'après-guerre*, 209–30. Tunis: Institut Supérieur d'Histoire du Mouvement National, 1991.

————. "Le Parti communiste tunisien et la question nationale (1943–1946)." In *Mouvement ouvrier, communisme et nationalismes dans le monde arabe*, edited by René Gallissot, 231–63. Paris: Les Editions Ouvrières, 1978.

————. "Rôle et centralité des enseignants et du syndicalisme enseignant dans le processus de formation du nationalisme et de l'état national tunisien." In *Elites et pouvoir dans le monde arabe pendant la période moderne et contemporaine*, 221–36. Tunis: Centre d'Etudes et de Recherches Economiques et Sociales, 1992.

Hassan, Abdelhamid. "Moncef Bey et le Mouvement moncefiste (1942–1948)." *Revue d'Histoire Maghrébine* 15, nos. 49–50 (1988): 25–46.

Heine, Peter. "Salih Ash-Sharif al-Tunisi, a North African Nationalist in Berlin during the First World War." *Revue de l'Occident Musulman et de la Méditerranée* 33 (1982): 89–96.

Hopwood, Derek. *Habib Bourguiba of Tunisia. The Tragedy of Longevity*. New York: St. Martin's Press, 1992.

Identité culturelle et conscience nationale en Tunisie. Actes du Colloque tenu à Tunis, 18–19 mars 1974. Tunis: Université de Tunis, 1975.

Jones, Richard. "The Naturalization Crisis of 1933: French Analysis and Tunisian Response." *Revue d'Histoire Maghrébine* 4, nos. 7–8 (1977): 165–78.

Julien, Charles-André. *L'Afrique du nord en marche: nationalismes musulmanes et souveraineté français*. Paris: Julliard, 1972.

————. "Colons français et Jeunes Tunisiens (1882–1912)." *Revue Française d'Histoire d'Outre-Mer* 54 (1967): 87–150.

————. "Une lettre de Habib Bourguiba à Andrée Viollis." *Revue d'Histoire Maghrébine* 1, no. 2 (1974): 181–84.

Kassab, Ahmed. *Histoire de la Tunisie. L'époque contemporaine.* Tunis: Société Tunisienne de Diffusion, 1976.

Khairallah, Chedly. "L'extraordinaire destinée d'Habib Bourguiba." *Confluent* 40 (1964): 306–22.

Khayati, Mustapha. "Brèves remarques sur la poème libertaire 'As-Sabr lillah . . .' et son auteur." *Revue du Monde Musulman et de la Méditerranée* 51 (1989): 136–42.

Kraiem, Abdelmajid. "Le premier procès de Abdelaziz Thaalbi (juillet 1904)." *Revue d'Histoire Maghrébine* 13, nos. 41–42 (1986): 101–15.

Kraiem, Mustapha. *Nationalisme et syndicalisme en Tunisie, 1918–1929.* Tunis: Union Générale Tunisienne du Travail, 1976.

————. *Pouvoir colonial et mouvement national. La Tunisie dans les années trente.* Tunis: Alif, 1990.

————. "L'adhésion de l'U.G.T.T. à la Fédération syndicale mondiale." *Revue d'Histoire Maghrébine* 1, no. 1 (1974): 26–34.

————. "Autobiographie et relations avec la Résidence de Tahar Khereddine Pacha, Ministre de la justice de la Régence." *Revue d'Histoire Maghrébine* 1, no. 2 (1974): 185–91.

————. "Contribution à l'étude de l'histoire du mouvement national tunisien pendant la seconde guerre mondiale." *Revue d'Histoire Maghrébine* 5, nos. 10–11 (1978): 25–66.

————. "Destructuration socio-culturelle et émergence du pluralisme politique en Tunisie pendant la période coloniale." In *Pluralisme social, pluralisme politique et démocratie,* 107–24. Tunis: Centre d'Etudes et de Recherches Economiques et Sociales, 1991.

————. "Les élites du mouvement nationaliste tunisien pendant la période de l'entre-deux-guerres." In *Elites et pouvoir dans le monde arabe pendant la période moderne et contemporaine,* 7–30. Tunis: Centre d'Etudes et de Recherches Economiques et Sociales, 1992.

————. "Les événements du 5 août 1947 à Sfax." *Revue d'Histoire Maghrébine* 4, no. 9 (1977): 314–33.

————. "La fédération socialiste de Tunisie et le mouvement national entre les deux guerres." *Revue d'Histoire Maghrébine* 3, no. 5 (1976): 5–26.

————. "Le Néo-Destour: cadres, militants et implantation pendant les années trente." In *Les mouvements politiques et sociales dans la Tunisie des années trente,* edited by Moncef Chenoufi, 17–50. Tunis: Ministère de l'Education, de l'Enseignement et de la Recherche Scientifique, 1987.

————. "Aux origines du Parti Communiste Tunisien, 1919–1929." *Revue d'Histoire Maghrébine* 1, no. 2 (1974): 116–37.

————. "Le parti communiste tunisien dans les années trente." *Revue d'Histoire Maghrébine* 8, nos. 21–22 (1981): 7–23.

————. "Le parti reformiste tunisien (1920–1926)." *Revue d'Histoire Maghrébine* 2, no. 4 (1975): 150–62.

————. "L'U.G.T.T. et le Mouvement Syndical Maghrébin avant l'assassinat de Farhat Hached." *Revue d'Histoire Maghrébine* 7, nos. 17–18 (1980): 33–42.

Kraiem, Mustapha, and Carmel Sammut. "Mouvement national et mouvement ouvrier dans un milieu colonial (ex: la Tunisie)." *Revue d'Histoire Maghrébine* 6, nos. 13–14 (1979): 69–94.

Labidi, Lilia. "L'émergence du sentiment politique chez les féministes dans la première moitié du XXè siècle: le cas de la Tunisie." In *Participation des femmes à la vie publique,* edited by Lilia Labidi, 44–62. Tunis: Centre de Recherche et de Formation Pédagogique, 1990.

Ladgham, Bahi. *Correspondance, 1952–1955. Les années décisives.* Tunis: Cérès Productions, 1990.

Lakhdar, Chedli. "Le Concept de 'Constitution' dans le mouvement nationaliste tunisien." *L'Afrique et l'Asie modernes* no. 158 (1988): 76–93.

Laskier, Michael M. "From Hafsia to Bizerte: Tunisia's Nationalist Struggle and Tunisian Jewry, 1952–1961." *Mediterranean Historical Review* 2, no. 2 (1987): 188–222.

Lejri, Mohamed Salah. *L'Histoire du mouvement national.* 2 vols. Tunis: Maison Tunisienne de l'Edition, 1974.

Le Tourneau, Roger. *L'Evolution politique de l'Afrique du nord musulmane, 1920–1961.* Paris: Armand Colin, 1962.

Liauzu, Claude. "Mouvement ouvrier, mouvement national, mouvements sociaux dans la Tunisie coloniale." *Pluriel* 15 (1978): 61–104.

————. "La naissance d'une presse révolutionnaire tunisienne. Eléments pour une étude des mouvements sociaux et nationaux." *Annuaire de l'Afrique du Nord* 13 (1974): 875–84.

Mahjoubi, Ali. *Les origines du mouvement national en Tunisie (1904–1934).* Tunis: Université de Tunis, 1982.

————. "Le cartel des gauches en France et le mouvement national tunisien." *Cahiers de Tunisie* 24, nos. 95–96 (1976): 187–214.

————. "Le Congrès eucharistique de Carthage et le mouvement national tunisien." *Cahiers de Tunisie* 26, nos. 101–2 (1978): 109–32.

Martel, André. "Un témoin des débuts de l'indépendance tunisienne: l'Action." *Revue de l'Occident Musulman et de la Méditerranée* 15–16 (1973): 175–87.

Martin, J.-F. *La Tunisie de Ferry à Bourguiba.* Paris: L'Harmattan, 1993.

Materi, Mahmoud. *Itinéraire d'un militant (1926–1942).* Tunis: Cérès Productions, 1992.

Mechat, Samia el-. *Tunisie: les chemins vers l'indépendance (1945–1956).* Paris: L'Harmattan, 1992.

————. "La guerre des 'deux Destours' de 1937 à 1939." *Revue d'Histoire Maghrébine* 9, nos. 25–26 (1982): 175–76.

————. "Le Nationalisme tunisien et la Ligue des Etats Arabes de 1945 à 1956." *Revue d'Histoire Maghrébine* 18, nos. 61–62 (1991): 165–68.

Mestiri, Said. *Moncef Bey. Le règne*. Tunis: Arcs, 1988.

Moalla, Mansour. *L'Etat tunisien et l'indépendance*. Tunis: Centre d'Etudes et de Recherches Economiques et Sociales, 1992.

M. Z. M. "Béchir Sfar (1865–1917). Educateur et Grand Commis." *Revue de l'Institut des Belles Lettres Arabes* 14, no. 53 (1951): 101–08.

Nagy, Laszlo. "Les partis politiques dans le mouvement national: le cas de l'Algérie et de la Tunisie." *Cahiers de la Méditerranée* 41 (1990): 77–88.

Nouschi, André. "La Crise de 1930 en Tunisie et les débuts du Néo-Destour." *Revue de l'Occident Musulmane et de la Méditerranée* 8 (1970): 113–23.

Rainero, Romain. "Observations sur les anti-fascistes italiens en Tunisie et la lutte politique du Néo-Destour." In *Les mouvements politiques et sociales dans la Tunisie des années trente,* edited by Moncef Chenoufi, 353–64. Tunis: Ministère de l'Education, de l'Enseignement et de la Recherche Scientifique, 1987.

————. "Une occasion manquée en Tunisie: La courte rencontre entre antifascistes italiens et néo-destouriens à la veille de la guerre." *Cahiers de la Méditerranée* nos. 24–25 (1982): 117–23.

Rivlin, Benjamin, "The Tunisian Nationalist Movement. Four Decades of Evolution." *Middle East Journal* 6 (1952): 167–93.

Romeril, Paul E. A. "Tunisian Nationalism: A Bibliographical Outline." *Middle East Journal* 14 (1960): 206–15.

Rondot, Pierre. "Mhamed Chenik, pionnier de l'indépendance tunisienne (1889–1976)." *L'Afrique et l'Asie modernes* 111 (1976): 37–40.

Salem, Norma. *Habib Bourguiba, Islam, and the Creation of Tunisia*. Dover, N.H.: Croom Helm, 1984.

Sammut, Carmel. *L'Impérialisme capitaliste français et le nationalisme tunisien (1881–1914)*. Paris: Publisud, 1983.

————. "L'expression des symboles nationalistes par les premiers nationalistes tunisiens dans le contexte colonial français." *Revue d'Histoire Maghrébine* 4, nos. 7–8 (1977): 201–20.

————. "La genèse du nationalisme tunisien: le mouvement Jeunes-Tunisiens." *Revue d'Histoire Maghrébine* 1, no. 2 (1974): 151–68.

————. "L'impérialisme capitaliste français et le nationalisme tunisien (1881–1914)." *Revue d'Histoire Maghrébine* 1, no. 1 (1974): 62–66.

Sayah, Mohamed, ed. *Histoire du mouvement national tunisien*. 15 vols. Tunis: Ministry of Information, 1967–1979.

Silvera, Victor. "De l'autonomie interne à l'indépendance de la Tunisie." *Revue Juridique et Politique de l'Union Française* 10 (1956): 687–704.

Snoussi, Mohamed Larbi. "Le Mouvement national tunisien et les régimes totalitaires à la veille de la Deuxième Guerre Mondiale (1934–1939)." In *Les mouvements politiques et sociales dans la Tunisie des années trente,* edited by Moncef Chenoufi, 365–85. Tunis: Ministère de l'Education, de l'Enseignement et de la Recherche Scientifique, 1987.

Sraieb, Noureddine. *Le Collège Sadiki de Tunis, 1875–1956. Enseignement et nationalisme.* Paris: Centre National de la Recherche Scientifique, 1994.

———. "Aux origines du Destour ou un continuité exemplaire." *Revue d'Histoire Maghrébine* 19, nos. 65–66 (1992): 71–79.

———. "Notes sur les dirigeants politiques et syndicalistes tunisiens de 1905 à 1934." *Revue de l'Occident Musulmane et Méditerranée* 9 (1971): 91–118.

Szymanski, Edward. *Le Problème de l'indépendance de la Tunisie après la seconde guerre mondiale.* Warsaw: Panstwowe Wydawn Naukowe, 1962.

Timoumi, Hedi. "Origines et avatars du syndicalisme patronal autotochtone de Tunisie (1947–1948)." *Cahiers de Tunisie* 19, nos. 117–18 (1981): 413–33.

Tlatli, Salah-Eddine. *Ecrits pour l'indépendance, 1946–1956.* Tunis: Alif, 1991.

Tlili, Béchir. *Nationalismes, socialisme et syndicalisme dans le Maghreb des années 1919–1934.* Tunis: Université de Tunis. 1984.

———. "A propos de la formation du fait national et de l'idéologie nationaliste en Tunisie: un colloque sur 'L'identité culturelle et la conscience nationale' (Tunis, mars 1974)." *Cahiers de Tunisie* 22, nos. 87–88 (1974): 237–52.

———. "Contribution à l'élucidation de la pensée réformiste tunisienne moderne et contemporaine (1830–1930)." *Africa* [Rome] 30 (1975): 317–45.

———. La Fédération socialiste et la 'Tunisie-martyre' (1919–1925)." *Cahiers de Tunisie* 25, nos. 99–100 (1977): 139–209.

———. "Aux origines du syndicalisme tunisien: deux documents relatifs au séjour et aux activités de Muhammad Ali à la veille et au lendemain de la Grande Guerre." *Cahiers de Tunisie* 25, nos. 97–98 (1977): 239–45.

———. "Problématique des processus de formation des faits nationaux et des idéolgies nationalistes dans le monde islamo-méditerranéen de l'entre deux-guerres (1919–1930). L'exemple de la Tunisie." *Cahiers de Tunisie* 21, nos. 81–82 (1973): 183–221.

————. "Des rapports entre le Parti Libéral et Constitutionnaliste Tunisien et la Confédération Générale Tunisienne du Travail (1924–1925)." *Cahiers de Tunisie* 28, nos. 113–14 (1980): 115–64.

————. "Au seuil du nationalisme tunisien: documents inédits sur le pan-islamisme au Maghreb (1919–1923)." *Africa* [Rome] 28 (1973): 211–36.

————. "Socialistes et Jeunes-Tunisiens à la veille de la Grande Guerre (1911–1913)." *Cahiers de Tunisie* 22, nos. 85–86 (1974): 47–134.

Toumi, Mohsen. "Le Néo-Destour dans le mouvement national tunisien." *Revue Française d'Etudes Politiques Africaines* 9 (1974): 26–53.

Zangar-Khaddar, Salwa. "Les nationalistes tunisiens au seuil des années trente (1929–1933)." In *Les mouvements politiques et sociales dans la Tunisie des années trente,* edited by Moncef Chenoufi, 79–102. Tunis: Ministère de l'Education, de l'Enseignement et de la Recherche Scientifique, 1987.

Ziadeh, Nicola. *Origins of Nationalism in Tunisia*. Beirut: American University of Beirut, Faculty of Arts and Sciences, 1962.

Government and Politics Since Independence

Domestic Politics

Abdallah, Ridha. "Le Néo-Destour depuis l'indépendance." *Revue Juridique et Politique de l'Outre-Mer* 17 (1963): 573–657.

————. "Structures et évolution du Néo-Destour." *Revue Juridique et Politique de l'Outre-Mer* 17 (1963): 385–428.

Achour, Habib. *Ma vie politique et syndicale. Enthousiasme et déception (1944–1981)*. Tunis: Alif, 1989.

Anderson, Lisa. *The State and Social Transformation in Tunisia and Libya, 1830–1980*. Princeton: Princeton University Press, 1986.

Ashford, Douglas. *National Development and Local Reform: Political Participation in Morocco, Tunisia, and Pakistan*. Princeton: Princeton University Press, 1967.

————. *The Politics of Planning in Morocco and Tunisia*. Syracuse: Syracuse University Press, 1965.

————. "Succession and Social Change in Tunisia." *Revue de l'Occident Musulman et de la Méditerranée* 13–14 (1973): 49–65.

Baccouche, Hachemi. *Décolonisation: grandeurs et servitudes de l'anticolonialisme*. Paris: Nouvelles Editions Latines, 1962.

Baduel, Pierre-Robert. "Gafsa comme enjeu." *Annuaire de l'Afrique du Nord* 19 (1980): 485–511.

Bellin, Eva. "Tunisian Industrialists and the State." In *Tunisia: The Political Economy of Reform,* edited by I. William Zartman, 45–65. Boulder, Colo.: Lynne Rienner, 1991.

Ben Ezzedine, Alia. "La Tunisie à l'heure de l'après-Bourguiba." *Cahiers de l'Orient* 7 (1987): 13–21.

Bessis, Sophie, and Souhayr Belhassen. *Bourguiba.* Vol. 2, *Un si long règne (1957–1989).* Paris: Jeune Afrique, 1989.

Brondino, Michele. "La Tunisia dopo Burghiba." *Oriente Moderno* 69 (1989): 57–82.

Brown, L. Carl. "Tunisia: The Record since Independence." *American-Arab Affairs* 6 (1983): 79–87.

Camau, Michel. "Le discours politique de légitimité des élites tunisiennes." *Annuaire de l'Afrique du Nord* 10 (1971): 25–65.

Camau, Michel, Fadila Amrani, and Rafaa Ben Achour. *Contrôle politique et régulations électorales en Tunisie: les élections législatives du 4 novembre 1979.* Aix-en-Provence: Edisud, 1981.

Chaker, Mustapha. "Les tendances actuelles du contrôle politique de l'administration en Tunisie." *Revue Tunisienne de Droit* 2 (1979): 159–203.

Charfi, Mounir. *Les ministres de Bourguiba.* Paris: L'Harmattan, 1989.

Charrad, Mounira. "Les cadres politiques au niveau local." *Revue Tunisienne de Sciences Sociales* 6 (1969): 53–63.

Damis, John. "Tunisia." In *Yearbook on International Communist Affairs,* edited by Richard F. Staar, 69–70. Stanford, Calif.: Hoover Institute, 1984.

———. "Tunisia." In *Yearbook on International Communist Affairs,* edited by Richard F. Staar, 461–63. Stanford, Calif.: Hoover Institute, 1987.

Debbasch, Charles. "L'Assemblée nationale constituante tunisienne." *Revue Juridique et Politique d'Outre-Mer,* n.s., 13 (1959): 32–54.

———. "La Constitution de la République tunisienne du 1er juin 1959." *Revue Juridique et Politique d'Outre-Mer* 13 (1959): 573–85.

———. "La Constitution de 1er juin 1959 de la République tunisienne à l'épreuve des faits (novembre 1959–décembre 1960). *Revue Juridique et Politique d'Outre-Mer* 15 (1961): 145–55.

———. "Du Néo-Destour au Parti Socialiste Destourien. Le Congrès de Bizerte." *Annuaire de l'Afrique du Nord* 3 (1964): 27–43.

Deeb, Mary-Jane. "Tunisia." In *Political Parties of the Middle East and North Africa,* edited by Frank Tachau, 530–48. London: Mansell, 1994.

Destour Socialist Party. *The Contractual Policy and the Events of January 1978.* Tunis: Editions Dar el Amal, 1978.

Durupty, Michel. "Les élections présidentielles et législatives tunisiennes du 2 Novembre 1969." *Annuaire de l'Afrique du Nord* 8 (1969): 339–57.

Entelis, John. "Ideological Change and an Emerging Counter-Culture in Tunisian Politics." *Journal of Modern African Studies* 12 (1974): 543–68.

Faath, Sigrid. "Rachid Sfar." *Orient* [Opladen] 27 (1986): 354–61.

Ferchiou, Sophie. "Pouvoir, contre-pouvoir et société en mutation: l'exemple tunisien." *Peuples Méditerranéens* 48–49 (1989): 81–92; 330–31.

Gasiorowski, Mark. "The Failure of Reform in Tunisia." *Journal of Democracy* 3 (1992): 85–97.

Germann, Raimund E. "L'administration dans le système politique tunisien." *Annuaire de l'Afrique du Nord* 7 (1968): 139–56.

Hahn, Lorna. "Tunisian Political Reform: Procrastination and Progress." *Middle East Journal* 26 (1972): 405–14.

———. "Tunisia: Pragmatism and Progress." *Middle East Journal* 16 (1962): 18–28.

Hanna, Sami. "Changing Trends in Tunisian Socialism." *Muslim World* 62 (1972): 230–40.

Hermassi, Mohamed Elbaki. "Le système politique tunisien et le 7 novembre." In *Le Maghreb: les années de transition,* edited by Bassma Kodmani-Darwish, 97–106. Paris: Masson, 1990.

Hopwood, Derek. *Habib Bourguiba of Tunisia: The Tragedy of Longevity.* New York: St. Martin's Press, 1992.

Jenayah, Ridha. "Les élections présidentielles et législatives tunisiennes. (A travers le scrutin du 3 novembre 1974)." *Intégration: Revue du C.M.E.R.A.* 10 (1978): 67–122.

Khelil, Hédi. "Habib Bourguiba. Les trois nouveaux enjeux: la télévision, l'ordinateur et la monnaie." In *Nouveaux enjeux culturels au Maghreb,* edited by J.-R. Henry, 299–308. Paris: Centre National de la Recherche Scientifique, 1986. [Also in *Annuaire de l'Afrique du Nord* 23 (1984): 299–308.]

Kraiem, Mustapha. "Systèmes totalitaires et pluralisme en Tunisie (Fondements socio-culturels et évolutions)." In *Elecciones, participation y transiciones politicas en el norte de Africa,* edited by Bernabe Lopez Garcia, Gema Martin Munoz, and Miguel Hernando de Larramedi, 97–120. Madrid: Instituto de Cooperacion con el Mundo Arabe, 1991.

Krichen, Aziz. *Le syndrome Bourguiba.* Tunis: Centre d'Etudes et de Recherches Economiques et Sociales, 1992.

Lacouture, Jean. "Les partis politiques nord-africains. Le Néo-Destour de Ksar-Hellal ou pouvoir sans partage." *Confluent* 28 (1963): 143–52.

Lahmar, Mouldi. "La 'révolte du pain' dans la campagne tunisienne: notables, ouvriers et fellahs." *Esprit* 100 (1985): 9–19.

Lakhoua, Foued. *Le gouvernement Ladgham (7 novembre 1969–2 novembre 1970).* Tunis: Alif, 1990.

Landuré, Jean-Louis. "La Tunisie en quête d'un équilibre politique." *Revue Juridique et Politique de l'Union Française* 25 (1971): 377–400; 26 (1972): 3–46.

Larif-Beatrix, Asma. "L'évolution de l'état tunisien." *Maghreb-Machrek* 116 (1987): 35–44.

Larramendi, Miquel Hernando de. "Frontismo electoral y democratia en Tunez (1956–1989)." In *Elecciones, participation y transiciones politicas en el norte de Africa,* edited by Bernabe Lopez Garcia, Gema Martin Munoz, and Miguel Hernando de Larramedi, 295–319. Madrid: Instituto de Cooperacion con el Mundo Arabe, 1991.

Larson, Barbara K. "Local-National Integration in Tunisia. *Middle Eastern Studies* 20 (1984): 17–26.

———. "National Seeds in Local Soil: Will Development Grow?" In *Local Politics and Development in the Middle East,* edited by Louis J. Cantori and Iliya Harik, 193–211. Boulder, Colo.: Westview Press, 1984.

Ling, Dwight. "Tunisia: Modernization and Moderation." *Muslim World* 60 (1970): 247–53.

Lucas, Paul-Louis. "Les institutions politiques de la Tunisie." *Revue de l'Institut des Belles Lettres Arabes* 24, nos. 95–96 (1961): 373–77.

Mabrouk, Mohieddine. "L'organisation administrative tunisienne depuis l'indépendance." *Annuaire de l'Afrique du Nord* 7 (1968): 157–73.

Marks, Jon. "Tunisia." In *Economic and Political Liberalization in the Middle East,* edited by T. Niblock and E. Murphy, 166–76. London: British Academic Press, 1993.

Micaud, Charles. "Leadership and Development. The Case of Tunisia." *Contemporary Politics* 1 (1968/1969): 468–84.

Moalla, Mansour. *L'Etat tunisien et l'indépendance.* Tunis: Centre d'Etudes et de Recherches Economiques et Sociales, 1992.

Moore, Clement Henry. *Tunisia since Independence.* Berkeley: University of California Press, 1965.

———. "Politics in a Tunisian Village." *Middle East Journal* 17 (1963): 527–40.

———. "Tunisia and Bourguibisme: Twenty Years of Crisis." *Third World Quarterly* 10 (1988): 176–90.

———. "Tunisian Banking: Politics of Adjustment and the Adjustment of Politics." In *Tunisia: The Political Economy of Reform,* edited by I. William Zartman, 67–97. Boulder, Colo.: Lynne Rienner, 1991.

———. "La Tunisie après Bourguiba. Libéralisation ou décadence politique?" *Revue Française des Sciences Politiques* 17 (1967): 645–67.

———. "La Tunisie après vingt ans de crise du succession." *Maghreb-Machrek* 120 (1988): 5–22.

Munchow, K. " 'Schwierigkeiten mit der Demokratie' unter den Bedingungen der Unterentwicklung?!" *Asien, Afrika, Lateinamerika* 20 (1993): 683–98.

Mzali, Muhammad. *Tunisie: quel avenir?* Paris: Publisud, 1991.

Pigasse, Jean-Paul. "Ombres et lumières sur la Tunisie." *Politique Etrangère* 34 (1969): 615–30.

Ravenel, Bernard. "Tunisie: le maillon faible?" *Politique Etrangère* 52 (1987): 935–50.

Rondot, Pierre. "Le 'Tournant Tunisien' de 1963. Causes, caractéristiques et justification des aménagements internes." *Annuaire de l'Afrique du Nord* 2 (1963): 179–98.

Rous, Jean. *Habib Bourguiba*. Paris: Martinsart, 1984.

Rudebeck, Lars. *Party and People: A Study of Political Change in Tunisia*. 2d ed. London: C. Hurst and Company, 1969.

Ruf, Werner. "Le socialisme tunisien: Conséquences d'une expérience avortée." In *Introduction à l'Afrique du Nord Contemporaine,* edited by Werner Ruf et al., 399–411. Paris: Centre Nationale de Recherche Scientifique, 1975.

———. "Tunisia: Contemporary Politics." In *North Africa: Contemporary Politics and Economic Development,* edited by Richard Lawless and Allan Findlay, 101–19. London: Croom Helm, 1984.

Salivarova, M. "L'analyse sociologique du socialisme tunisien." *Asian and African Studies* [Bratislava] 5 (1969): 77–85.

Sayah, Mohamed, ed. *Le nouvel état aux prises avec le complot youssefiste 1956–1958*. Tunis: Dar al-Amal, 1983.

Schaar, Stuart. "Creation of a Mass Political Culture in Tunisia." *Maghreb Review* 18, nos. 1–2 (1993): 2–17.

———. "Le jeu des forces politiques en Tunisie." *Maghreb-Machrek* 78 (1977): 70–73.

Seddon, David. "Riot and Rebellion in North Africa: Political Responses to Economic Crisis in Tunisia, Morocco and Sudan." In *Power and Stability in the Middle East,* edited by Berch Berberoglu, 114–35. London: Zed Press, 1989.

Sfeir, Antoine. "Tunisie ou l'inconnue de l'après-Bourguiba." *Cahiers de l'Orient* 1 (1986): 149–58.

Silvera, Victor. *Les Institutions tunisiennes*. Paris: La Documentation Française, 1966.

———. "La coopération technique et culturelle franco-tunisienne." *Revue Juridique et Politique de l'Outre-Mer* 13 (1959): 197–221.

Stone, Russell. "Tunisia: A Single Party System Holds Change in Abeyance." In *Political Elites in Arab North Africa,* edited by I. William Zartman, 144–76. New York: Longmans, 1982.

Suleiman, Michael. "Political Orientation of Young Tunisians: The Impact of Gender." *Arab Studies Quarterly* 15, no. 1 (1993): 61–80.

Tibi, Bassam. "Trade Unions as an Organizational Form of Political Opposition in Afro-Arab States: The Case of Tunisia." *Orient* [Opladen] 20 (1979): 75–91.

Toumi, Mohsen. *La Tunisie de Bourguiba à Ben Ali*. Paris: Presses Universitaires de France, 1989.

———. *Tunisie. Pouvoirs et luttes*. Paris: Sycamore, 1978.

———. "Le courant ouvriériste et populaire en Tunisie face au pouvoir d'état." *Revue Française des Etudes Politiques Africaines* 148 (1978): 79–102.

————. "Le parti socialiste destourien." *Revue Française des Etudes Politiques Africaines* 111 (1975): 32–68.

Trab Zemzemi, Abdel-Majid. *La Tunisie face à l'imposture. Le Bourguibisme.* Paris: L'Albatros, 1988.

Vandewalle, Dirk. "Bourguiba, Charismatic Leadership and the Tunisian One Party System." *Middle East Journal* 34 (1980): 149–59.

————. "From the New State to the New Era: Toward a Second Republic in Tunisia." *Middle East Journal* 42 (1988): 602–20.

Waltz, Susan. "Clientism and Reform in Ben Ali's Tunisia." In *Tunisia: The Political Economy of Reform,* edited by I. William Zartman, 29–44. Boulder, Colo.: Lynne Rienner, 1991.

————. "Tunisia's League and the Pursuit of Human Rights." *Maghreb Review* 14 (1989): 214–25.

Ware, Lewis B. "Ben Ali's Constitutional Coup in Tunisia." *Middle East Journal* 42 (1988): 587–601.

————. "The Role of the Tunisian Military in the post-Bourguiba Era." *Middle East Journal* 39 (1985): 27–47.

Zamiti, Khalil. "De l'insurrection syndicale à la révolte du pain (janvier 1978–janvier 1984)." *Revue Tunisienne de Sciences Sociales* 104–5 (1991): 41–68.

————. "La société tunisienne: absolutisme et démocratie après la déposition du 'Président à vie'." *Peuples Méditerranéens* 47 (1989): 125–35, 139.

Zartman, I. William. "The Conduct of Political Reform: The Path toward Democracy." In *Tunisia: The Political Economy of Reform,* edited by I. William Zartman, 9–28. Boulder, Colo.: Lynne Rienner, 1991.

Zghal, Abdelkader. "Le concept de la société civile et la transition vers le multipartisme." In *Changements politiques au Maghreb,* edited by Michel Camau, 207–28. Paris: Centre National de la Recherche Scientifique, 1991.

————. "Décolonisation et nouvelle dynamique de la construction nationale en Tunisie." *Revue Tunisienne de Sciences Sociales* 4 (1967): 73–89.

————. "The Reactivation of Tradition in a Post-Traditional Society." *Daedalus* 102 (1973): 225–37.

————. "Le retour du sacré et la nouvelle demande idéologique des jeunes scholarisés: le cas de Tunisie." *Annuaire de l'Afrique du Nord* 18 (1979): 41–64.

Islam and Politics

Ahnaf, M. al-. "Tunisie: Un débat sur les rapports Etat/religion." *Maghreb-Machrek* 126 (1989): 93–108.

Anderson, Lisa. "Tunisia and Libya: Responses to the Islamic Impulse." In *The Iranian Revolution: Its Global Impact,* edited by John Esposito, 157–76. Miami: Florida International University, 1990.

Bannerman, Patrick. "The Mouvement de la Tendance Islamique in Tunisia." In *Islamic Fundamentalism,* edited by R. M. Burrell, 67–74. London: Royal Asiatic Society, 1989.

Boulby, Marion. "The Islamic Challenge: Tunisia since Independence." *Third World Quarterly* 10 (1988): 590–614.

Burgat, François. "L'évolution du mouvement islamiste en Tunisie." In *Les intellectuels et le pouvoir: Syrie, Egypte, Tunisie, Algérie,* edited by G. Delanoue, 139–52. Cairo: Centre d'Etudes et de Documentation Economique, Juridique et Sociale, 1986.

———. "Islamistes en Tunisie: la séconde génération?" *Cahiers de l'Orient* 4 (1986): 49–61.

———. "Aux sources de l'islamisme en Tunisie: entretien avec le Sheikh Hamida Enneifer, directeur de la revue *15/21* (Tunis)." In *Les intellectuels et le pouvoir: Syrie, Egypte, Tunisie, Algérie,* edited by G. Delanoue, 209–21. Cairo: Centre d'Etudes et de Documentation Economique, Juridique et Sociale, 1986.

Camau, Michel. "Religion politique et religion d'Etat en Tunisie." In *Islam et politique au Maghreb,* edited by Ernest Gellner, Jean-Claude Vatin, and Abdallah Hammoudi, 221–30. Paris: Centre National de Recherche Scientifique, 1981.

Dunn, Michael C. "The al-Nahda Movement in Tunisia: From Renaissance to Revolution." In *Islam and Secularism in North Africa,* edited by John Ruedy, 149–65. New York: St. Martin's Press, 1994.

Faath, Sigrid. "Islamistische Agitation und staatliche Reaktion in Tunesien 1987/1988." *Wuquf* 2 (1987): 14–68.

Halliday, Fred. "The Politics of Islamic Fundamentalism: Iran, Tunisia and the Challenge to the Secular State." In *Islam, Globalization and Postmodernity,* edited by Akbar S. Ahmed and H. Donnan, 91–113. London: Routledge, 1993.

Henry, Delphine. "Le Président Ben Ali et les islamistes." *L'Afrique et L'Asie Modernes* 164 (1990): 135–49.

Hermassi, Abdelbaki. "L'Etat tunisien et le mouvement islamiste." In *Changements politiques au Maghreb,* edited by Michel Camau, 297–308. Paris: Centre National de la Recherche Scientifique, 1991.

———. "The Islamist Movement and November 7." In *Tunisia: The Political Economy of Reform,* edited by I. William Zartman, 193–204. Boulder, Colo.: Lynne Rienner, 1991.

———. "La société tunisienne au miroir islamiste." *Maghreb-Machrek* 103 (1984): 39–56.

Keddie, Nikki. "The Islamist Movement in Tunisia." *Maghreb Review* 11 (1986): 26–39.

Magnuson, Douglas K. "Islamic Reform and Contemporary Tunisia: Unity and Diversity." In *Tunisia: The Political Economy of Reform,* edited by I. William Zartman, 169–92. Boulder, Colo.: Lynne Rienner, 1991.

Mahdi, Sadok. "Le mouvement des Frères Musulmans en Tunisie." *Oriente Moderno* 59 (1979): 691–706.

Munson, Henry. "Islamic Revivalism in Morocco and Tunisia." *Muslim World* 76 (1986): 203–18.

Salem, Norma. "Islam and the Politics of Identity in Tunisia." *Journal of Arab Affairs* 2 (1986): 194–216.

Samandi, Zeyneb. "Autorité religieuse et pouvoir politique, tradition et mutation: le cas de la Tunisie." In *Pluralisme sociale, pluralisme politique et démocratie,* 77–84. Tunis: Centre d'Etudes et de Recherches Economiques et Sociales, 1991.

———. "Elite au pouvoir et processus de sécularisation en situation d'Islam sunnite et d'état républicain: le cas de la Tunisie." In *Elites et pouvoir dans le monde arabe pendant la période moderne et contemporaine,* 251–55. Tunis: Centre d'Etudes et de Recherches Economiques et Sociales, 1992.

———. " 'Fondamentalisme'-'Modernisme laic,' sens d'un antagonisme." *Revue Tunisienne des Sciences Sociales* 96–97 (1989): 159–74.

Sfeir, Antoine. "Voyage au sein de l'Islamisme tunisien." *Cahiers de l'Orient* 7 (1987): 23–32.

Tessler, Mark. "Political Change and the Islamic Revival in Tunisia." *Maghreb Review* 5 (1980): 8–19.

Vogt, Kari. "Militant Islam in Algeria and Tunisia in the '80s: A Survey." In *The Middle East Viewed from the North,* edited by Bo Utas and Knut S. Vikør, 149–55. Bergen, Norway: Alma Mater, 1992.

Waltz, Susan. "Islamist Appeal in Tunisia." *Middle East Journal* 40 (1986): 651–70.

Zghal, Abdelkader. "The New Strategy of the Movement of the Islamic Way: Manipulation or Expression of Popular Culture?" In *Tunisia: The Political Economy of Reform,* edited by I. William Zartman, 205–17. Boulder, Colo.: Lynne Rienner, 1991.

———. "Le retour du sacré et la nouvelle demande idéologique des jeunes scholarisés: le cas de Tunisie." *Annuaire de l'Afrique du Nord* 18 (1979): 41–64.

International Relations

Ben Yahia, Habib. "Les grandes lignes de la politique étrangère de la Tunisie." *Etudes Internationales* [Tunis] 42 (1992): 10–23.

———. "Tunisia's Perception of the Conflict in the Middle East." *American-Arab Affairs* 16 (1986): 108–11.

Bilinsky, Yaroslav. "Moderate Realism in an Extremist Environment: Tunisia and the Palestine Question (1965–1970)." *Revue de l'Occident Musulmane et de la Méditerranée* 13–14 (1973): 109–23.

Chater, Khalifa. "Relations inter-arabes et problématiques de la confiance: prélude à une réflexion." *Etudes Internationales* 38 (1991): 8–27.

Deeb, Mary-Jane, and Ellen Laipson. "Tunisian Foreign Policy: Continuity and Change under Bourguiba and Ben Ali." In *Tunisia: The Political Economy of Reform,* edited by I. William Zartman, 221–41. Boulder, Colo.: Lynne Rienner, 1991.

Grimaud, Nicole. *La Tunisie à la recherche de sa sécurité.* Paris: Presses Universitaires de France, 1995.

Hachiche, Abdelwahab. "Conflict and Resolution in Libyan-Tunisian Relations." *Maghreb Review* 14 (1989): 50–69.

Hamada, Rida. "Les origines des relations diplomatiques tuniso-américaines." *Etudes Internationales* 36 (1990): 129–62; 37 (1990): 103–38.

Leveau, Rémy. "La Tunisie du président Ben Ali: équilibre interne et environnement arabe." *Maghreb-Machrek* 124 (1989): 4–17.

Lucchini, Laurent. "Les thèmes de la politique extérieure tunisienne." *Revue Tunisienne de Droit* (1966/1967): 129–54.

Medimegh, Aziza. "L'UMA dans l'opinion publique tunisienne." *Etudes Internationales* [Tunis] 41 (1991): 157–68.

Mejdoub, Noureddine. "Les relations Tunisie-Europe à la veille du Marché Unique Européen." *Etudes Internationales* [Tunis] 42 (1992): 24–29.

Mezerik, Avrahm. *Tunisian-French Dispute: Bizerte, Sahara, UN Action.* New York: International Review Service, 1961.

Mzioudet, Hareth. "La Tunisie et la Monde Arabe. Quelques aspects de la politique étrangère tunisienne." *Etudes Internationales* [Tunis] 31 (1989): 137–51.

Ruf, Werner. "The Bizerte Crisis: A Bourguibist Attempt to Resolve Tunisia's Border Problem." *Middle East Journal* 25 (1971): 201–11.

———. "Le Bourguibisme et la politique étrangère tunisienne." In *Proceedings of the 27th International Congress of Orientalists,* 1967, edited by Denis Sinor, 164. Weisbaden: Otto Harrassowitz, 1971.

Santucci, Robert. "La politique étrangère de la Tunisie." *Maghreb-Machrek Monde Arabe* 91 (1981): 43–58.

Sayah, Mohamed, ed. *La République délivrée de l'occupation étrangère, 1959–1964: textes.* Tunis: Dar al-Amal, 1986.

Sehili, Chedli. "La Tunisie et l'Afrique sub-saharienne." *Revue d'Histoire Maghrébine* 13, nos. 41–42 (1986): 169–71.

Toumi, Mohsen. "La politique africaine de la Tunisie." *Annuaire de l'Afrique du Nord* 17 (1978): 113–69.

Treutenaere, Michel. "La coopération culturelle, scientifique et technique entre la Tunisie et la France: évolution et perspectives." *Annuaire de l'Afrique du Nord* 20 (1981): 498–507.

Economic Issues since Independence

Abdelhafid, Ridha. "L'aide américaine au Tiers-Monde à travers le cas de coopération Tunisie-Etats-Unis." *Etudes Internationales* [Tunis] 7 (1983): 40–51.

Abdi, Nourredine. "Le processus de désétatisation en Algérie et en Tunisie." *Mediterrán Tanulmányok* 5 (1993): 25–39.

Abeele, M. van den. "Considérations sur le tourisme tunisien." *Revue Tunisienne de Sciences Sociales* 5 (1968): 223–29.

Alaya, Hachemi. *L'économie tunisienne: réalités et voies pour l'avenir.* Tunis: Afkar wa Ichhaar, 1989.

Alouane, Youssef. "Attitudes et comportements des coopérateurs dans deux unités de production du Nord." *Etudes de Sociologie Tunisienne* 1 (1968): 81–163.

Aouani, Mohamed el-. "Structure agraire dans un village côtier du nord-est de la Tunisie: Galaat El Andleuss." *Revue Tunisienne de Sciences Sociales* 3 (1965): 71–108.

Apthorpe, Raymond. "Peasants and Planistrators: Rural Co-Operatives in Tunisia." *Maghreb Review* 2 (1977): 1–18.

Ashford, Douglas. "Organization of Cooperatives and Structure of Power in Tunisia." *Journal of Developing Areas* 1 (1966/1967): 317–32.

Attia, Habib. "L'Evolution des structures agraires en Tunisie depuis 1962." *Revue Tunisienne de Sciences Sociales* 3 (1966): 33–58.

———. "Modernisation agricole et structure sociale: exemple des oasis du Djerid." *Revue Tunisienne de Sciences Sociales* 2 (1965): 59–93.

———. "Problématique du développement du nord-ouest tunisien." *Revue de l'Occident Musulman et de la Méditerranée* 41–42 (1986): 264–80.

Aventur, J. "La politique agricole tunisienne depuis l'indépendance." *Annales Africaines* 9 (1962): 305–14.

Ayari, Chedly. "La structure du financement extérieur des investissements en Tunisie, 1960–1968." *Revue Tunisienne de Sciences Sociales* 5 (1968): 11–32.

Azria, Claude. "L'industrialisation de Bizerte." *Confluence* 38 (1964): 148–54.

———. "La Tunisie à l'heure de l'industrialisation." *Confluent* 40 (1964): 351–57.

Azzam, Mahjoub. "Etat, secteur public et privatisation en Tunisie." *Annuaire de l'Afrique du Nord* 26 (1987): 299–315.

Bahroun, Sadok. "Annual Planning in Tunisia." *Journal of Development Planning* 3 (1971): 60–98.

Belhedi, Amor. "L'industrie manufacturière dans l'agglomeration tunisoise: contribution à l'étude d'une évolution (1967–1978). *Revue Tunisienne de Géographie* 5 (1980): 9–39.

Ben Achour, Rafaa. *Le trésor public tunisien: rôle et fonctions.* Tunis: Imprimerie Officielle, 1981.

Ben Romdhane, Mahmoud. "L'Etat, la paysannerie et la dépendance alimentaire en Tunisie." In *L'Agriculture africaine en crise dans ses rapports avec l'état, l'industrialisation et la paysannerie,* edited by

Hamid Ait Amara and Bernard Founou-Tchuigoua, 277–309. Paris: L'Harmattan, 1989.

———. "Fondements et contenu des restructurations face à la crise économique en Tunisie: une analyse critique." *Annuaire de l'Afrique du Nord* 26 (1987): 149–76.

Ben Salah, Ahmed. "Tunisia: Endogenous Development and Structural Transformations." In *Another Development: Approaches and Strategies,* edited by Marc Nerfin, 242–62. Uppsala: The Dag Hammarskjold Foundation, 1977.

Ben Salem, Lilia. *Développement et problème de cadres: le cas de la Tunisie. Un exemple: les cadres supérieurs de l'économie tunisienne.* Tunis: Centre d'études et de recherche économiques et sociales, 1976.

———. "Les cadres de l'économie locale en Tunisie." *Revue Tunisienne de Sciences Sociales* 6 (1969): 21–40.

———. "Centralization and Decentralization of Decision Making in an Experiment in Agricultural Cooperation in Tunisia." In *Popular Participation in Social Change: Cooperatives, Collectives, and Nationalized Industry,* edited by June Nash et al., 271–88. The Hague: Mouton, 1976.

Ben Slama, Moncef. *Relations intersectorelles de croissance.* Tunis: Faculté de Droit et des Sciences Politiques et Economiques, Université de Tunis, 1981.

Bessis, Sophie. "Banque mondiale et FMI en Tunisie: une évolution sur trente ans." *Annuaire de l'Afrique du Nord* 26 (1987): 135–48.

Bouaouaja, Mohammed. "Privatization in Tunisia: Objectives and Limits." In *Privatization and Structural Adjustment in the Arab Countries,* edited by Said al-Naggar, 234–58. Washington: International Monetary Fund, 1989.

Bouchrara, Moncef. "L'industrialisation rampante: ampleur, mécanismes et portée. Le cas de la Tunisie." *Economie et Humanisme* 296 (juillet–août 1987): 37–49.

———. "Sfax: 'capitale' de l'industrialisation rampante." *Revue Tiers-Monde* 30 (1989): 433–40.

Boukraa, Ridha. "Développement national et développement régional en Tunisie." In *Renaissance du monde arabe. Colloque interarbe de Louvain,* edited by Anouar Abdel-Malek, Abdel-Aziz Belal, and Hassan Hanafi, 122–35. Gembloux: Duculot, 1972.

———. "L'entreprise industrielle en milieu rural." *Etudes de Sociologie Tunisienne* 1 (1968): 43–80.

———. "Quelques considérations générales sur la nouvelle organisation du système coopératif dans la région du Kef." *Etudes de Sociologie Tunisienne* 1 (1968): 301–10.

Brugnes-Romieu, Marie-Paule. "Les investissements en Tunisie de 1955 à 1961." *Revue Tunisienne de Sciences Sociales* 3 (1965): 159–66.

Callens, Michel. "Cinq années d'action administrative dans le domaine agricole." *Revue de l'Institut des Belles Lettres Arabes* 25, no. 98 (1962): 111–33; 26, no. 101 (1963): 29–41.

――――. "Développement de la coopération." *Revue de l'Institut des Belles Lettres Arabes* 27 (1964): 72–82.

――――. "Développement des structures coopératives." *Revue de l'Institut des Belles Lettres Arabes* 29 (1966): 371–96.

――――. "La planification tunisienne." *Revue de l'Institut des Belles Lettres Arabes* 26, no. 101 (1963): 63–73.

Camau, Michel. "Etat, espace public et développement: le cas tunisien." *Annuaire de l'Afrique du Nord* 26 (1987): 67–78.

Chabbi, Abdelhafidh. "Population active, revenus et formation dans l'agriculture tunisienne." *Annuaire de l'Afrique du Nord* 19 (1980): 89–103.

Charmes, Jacques. "L'apprentissage sur le tas dans le secteur non-structuré en Tunisie." *Annuaire de l'Afrique du Nord* 19 (1980): 357–95.

Chebil, Mohsen. "Evolution of Land Tenure in Tunisia in Relation to Agricultural Development Programs." In *Land Policy in the Near East,* edited by Mohamad Riad El-Ghonemy, 189–204. Rome: Food and Agriculture Organization, 1967.

Cherel, Jean. "Les Unités Coopératives de Production du Nord Tunisien." *Tiers-Monde* 5 (1964): 235–54.

――――. "Les unités de production du nord-Tunisien." *Tiers-Monde* 12 (1971): 303–50.

Davies, Howard M. "The Role of Surplus in the Process of Development and Its Impact on Urbanism: The Case of Tunisia." *Maghreb Review* 3 (1978): 23–31.

Denieuil, Pierre-Noël. *Les entrepreneurs du développement: l'ethnoindustrialisation en Tunisie: la dynamique de Sfax.* Paris: L'Harmattan, 1992.

Dimassi, Hassine. "La crise économique en Tunisie: une crise de regulation." *Maghreb-Machrek* 103 (1984): 57–69.

――――. Le désengagement de l'état tunisien de la reproduction de la force de travail." *Annuaire de l'Afrique du Nord* 26 (1987): 327–39.

Dlala, Habib. "Développement économique et l'action régionale en Tunisie." *Revue Tunisienne de Géographie* 6 (1980): 67–85.

――――. "Etat et développement industriel en Tunisie: de l'investissement direct au désengagement." *Revue Tunisienne de Géographie* 17 (1989): 33–65.

――――. "Le transfert de technologie et de savoir-faire industriels en Tunisie." *Annales de Géographie* 99 (1990): 441–57.

Dooren, Pierre J. van. "The Co-operative Approach in Implementing Land Reform Programmes, with Special reference to Tunisia and Egypt." In *Co-Operation as an Instrument for Rural Development,* edited by M. Konopnicki and G. Vandewalle, 20–33. London: International Cooperative Alliance, 1978.

Ducruet, J. "Perspectives tunisiennes de développement." *Travaux et Jours* 6 (1962): 41–64.

Dufour, J. "The Problem of Collectively Owned Land in Tunisia." *Land Reform* 1 (1971): 38–51.

Fakhfakh, Mohamed. *La grande exploitation agricole dans la région sfaxienne*. Tunis: Centre d'Etudes et de Recherches Economiques et Sociales, 1976.

———. "Le rôle de l'investissement national à Sfax." *Revue Française des Etudes Politiques Méditerranéennes* 30–31 (1978): 121–26.

Falise. M., and P. Masson. "La politique de développement technologique en Tunisie. Investissements étrangers et sous-traitance internationale." *Annuaire de l'Afrique du Nord* 15 (1976): 161–74.

Ferchiou, Ridha. "The Social Pressure on Economic Development in Tunisia." In *Tunisia: The Political Economy of Reform,* edited by I. William Zartman, 101–8. Boulder, Colo.: Lynne Rienner, 1991.

Ferchiou, Sophie. "Place de la production domestique féminine dans l'économie familiale du Sud tunisien." *Revue de Tiers-Monde* 19 (1978): 831–44.

Findlay, Allan. "Labor Mobility and Manpower Planning in Tunisia." In *Change and Development in the Middle East. Essays in Honour of W. B. Fischer,* edited by John I. Clarke and Howard Bowen-Jones, 242–51. London: Methuen, 1981.

———. "Tunisia: The Vicissitudes of Economic Development." In *North Africa: Contemporary Politics and Economic Development,* edited by Richard Lawless and Allan Findlay, 217–40. London: Croom Helm, 1984.

Gachet, Jean-Paul. "Choix technologiques et formation dans l'agriculture tunisiennes." *Annuaire de l'Afrique du Nord* 19 (1980): 105–30.

Gagnon, Gabriel. *Coopératives ou autogestion: Sénégal, Cuba, Tunisie.* Montreal: Presses de l'Université, 1977.

Genoud, Roger. "La révolution industrielle en Tunisie et le droit à l'industrialisation." *Revue de l'Institut des Belles Lettres Arabes* 24, nos. 95–96 (1961): 309–35.

Glasman, Wladimir. "Entre la disparition et la survie: le métier de 'dallal' à Tunis." *Revue de l'Institut des Belles Lettres Arabes* 45, no. 149 (1982): 3–56.

Granier, Roland. "Les revenus agricoles en Tunisie." *Etudes Internationales* [Quebec] 6 (1975): 255–61.

Grissa, Abdelsatar. "The Tunisian State Enterprises and Privatization Policy." In *Tunisia: The Political Economy of Reform,* edited by I. William Zartman, 109–27. Boulder, Colo.: Lynne Rienner, 1991.

Guen, Moncef. *Les défis de la Tunisie: une analyse économique.* Paris: L'Harmattan, 1988.

Hamdane, Abdelkader. "Conservation artisanale du piment dans la presqu'île du Cap Bon." *Revue de l'Institut des Belles Lettres Arabes* 43, no. 145 (1980): 149–53.

Hamouda, M. Larbi. "Quelques aspects économiques du tourisme en Tunisie." *Revue Tunisienne de Sciences Sociales* 7 (1970): 185–201.

Hamzaoui, Salah. "Non-Capitalist Relations of Production in Capitalist Society: The Khammessat in Southern Tunisia." *Journal of Peasant Studies* 6 (1979): 444–70.

Haouet, Tahar. "L'expérience tunisienne de developpement agricole." In *Problèmes du développement économique dans les pays méditerranéens,* edited by Jean Cuisenier, 65–116. Paris and The Hague: Mouton, 1963.

Haraguhi, Takehiko. "Réforme agraire en Tunisie. Quelques aspects socio-économiques de l'unité de production." *Revue Tunisienne de Sciences Sociales* 5 (1968): 89–120.

Harik, Iliya. "Privatisation et développement en Tunisie." *Maghreb-Machrek* 128 (1990): 5–26. [Also in English in *Privatization and Liberalization in the Middle East,* edited by Iliya Harik and Dennis J. Sullivan, 210–32. Indianapolis: Indiana University Press, 1992.]

Hassainya, Jemaïel. *Irrigation et développement agricole: l'expérience tunisienne.* Montpellier: Centre International de Hautes Etudes Agronomiques Méditerranéennes, 1991.

Hawrylyshyn, Oli, et al. *Planning for Economic Development: The Construction and Use of a Multisectoral Model for Tunisia.* New York: Praeger, 1977.

Hopkins, Nicholas. "Modern Agriculture and Political Centralization: A Case from Tunisia." *Human Organization* 37 (1978): 83–87.

———. "The Political Economy of Two Arab Villages." In *Arab Society: Social Science Perspectives,* edited by Saad Eddin Ibrahim and Nicholas S. Hopkins, 307–21. Cairo: American University in Cairo Press, 1985.

———. "The Small Urban Center in Rural Development: Kita (Mali) and Testour (Tunisia)." *Africa* [London] 49 (1979): 316–28.

———. "Tunisia: An Open and Shut Case." *Social Problems* 28 (1981): 385–93.

Hubert, Anne. *Le Pain et l'olive. Aspects de l'alimentation en Tunisie.* Lyons: Centre National de la Recherche Scientifique, 1984.

Hutchinson, J. "The Industries of Southern Sousse: A Case Study in Tunisian Industrial Development and Planning." In *Field Studies in Tunisia,* edited by R. Harris and R. Lawless, 78–87. Durham: Department of Geography, University of Durham, 1981.

Huxley, Frederick C. "Development in Hammam Sousse, Tunisia: Change, Continuity, and Challenge." In *Anthropology and Development in North Africa and the Middle East,* edited by Muneera Salem-Murdock and Michael M. Horowitz, 126–54. Boulder, Colo.: Westview Press, 1990.

Jedidi, Mohamed. "L'emploi touristique dans la zone de Sousse—Skanes—Monastir." *Revue Tunisienne de Géographie* 2 (1979): 45–92.

————. "L'expansion du tourisme en Tunisie et ses problèmes." *Revue Tunisienne de Géographie* 18 (1990): 149–80.

Jemmali, Slaheddine. *Les souks hebdomadaires du Cap Bon: étude sociale et économique.* Tunis: Maison Tunisienne de l'Edition, 1986.

Kamelgarn, D. "Stratégies de self-reliance et système économique mondial: l'expérience tunisienne des années 1960." *Peuples Méditerranées* 13 (1980): 107–26.

Kassab, Ahmed. "L'agriculture tunisienne sur la voie de l'intensification." *Annales de Géographie* 90 (1981): 55–86.

————. "La crise des grandes cultures dans la Tunisie tellienne: causes naturelles et structurelles." *Revue Tunisienne de Géographie* 1 (1978): 13–39.

————. "L'élevage dans les pays de moyenne Medjerda et du Bled Béja." *Revue Tunisienne de Sciences Sociales* 6 (1969): 127–87.

————. "Quelques données récentes sur les systèmes de production des agro-combinats, fermes-pilotes et U.C.P." *Cahiers de Tunisie* 25, nos. 99–100 (1977): 211–18.

————. "Quelques signes d'évolution de la production de la commercialisation et de la consommation de l'huile en Tunisie." *Revue Tunisienne de Sciences Sociales* 4 (1967): 111–43.

————. "Les secteurs en développement et les secteurs en crise dans l'agriculture tunisienne." In *Le développement en question,* edited by Abdelwahab Bouhdiba, 139–56. Tunis: Centre d'Etudes et de Recherches Economiques et Sociales, 1990.

Kassah, Abdelfettah. "Le secteur dattier en Tunisie." *Revue Tunisienne de Géographie* 18 (1990): 201–36.

Kilani, Monder. "Etat et développement: transformation du système hydraulique du groupe d'oasis de Gafsa (Tunisie)." *Sou'al* 6 (1987): 79–93.

Lahmar, Mouldi. "La réforme agraire dans les années soixante en Tunisie: le PSD contre ses assises rurales." *Revue de l'Institut des Belles Lettres Arabes* 52, no. 163 (1989): 39–68.

Larson, Barbara. "Rural Development in Central Tunisia: Constraints and Coping Strategies." In *Tunisia: The Political Economy of Reform,* edited by I. William Zartman, 143–52. Boulder, Colo.: Lynne Rienner, 1991.

Lasta, Zohra. "Aspects et problèmes du tourisme dans la ville de Tunis." *Revue Tunisienne de Géographie* 21–22 (1992): 120–54.

Laurent, J. "La Tunisie à l'heure multi-nationale." *Revue Africaine de Management* 53 (1973): 111–29.

Le Coz, Jean. "Exemples d'unités coopératives de production en Tunisie." In *Maghreb et Sahara: études géographiques offertes à J.*

Despois, edited by Xavier de Planhol, 247–52. Paris: Société de Géographie, 1973.

Lelong, Michel. "Valeurs traditionelles, idéologies nouvelles dans les perspectives tunisiennes de développement." *Revue de l'Institut des Belles Lettres Arabes* 24, no. 94 (1961): 149–65.

Makhlouf, Ezzedine. "Nouveau dualisme de l'agriculture tunisienne. Coopératives agricoles de production et grandes exploitations privées." *Revue Tunisienne de Sciences Sociales* 4 (1967): 27–56.

——. "Political and Technical Factors in Agricultural Collectivization in Tunisia." In *Popular Participation in Social Change: Cooperatives, Collectives, and Nationalized Industry,* edited by June Nash et al., 381–411. The Hague: Mouton, 1976.

Manoubi, Khaled. "Etat infra-rentier, endettement extérieur et mouvements urbains en Tunisie." *Annuaire de l'Afrique du Nord* 23 (1984): 587–600.

Manoubi, Khaled, and Abdeljelil Bedoui. *Economie tunisienne, état et capital mondial.* Cahiers du CERES: Série Economique, 5. Tunis: Centre d'Etudes et de Recherches Economiques et Sociales, 1987.

Marks, Jon. "Tunisia." In *Economic and Political Liberalization in the Middle East,* edited by T. Niblock and E. Murphy, 166–76. London: British Academic Press, 1993.

Marthelot, Pierre. "De l'empirisme à la planification. Vers une refonte des structures rurales en Tunisie." In *Etudes maghrébines. Mélanges C. A. Julien,* edited by Pierre Marthelot and André Raymond, 245–65. Paris: Université de Paris, 1964.

——. "Juxtaposition d'une économie traditionnelle et d'une économie moderne." *Revue de l'Institut des Belles Lettres Arabes* 18, no. 72 (1955): 481–501.

Mejdoub, Noureddine. "Les relations Tunisie-Europe à la veille du Marché Unique Européen." *Etudes Internationales* 42 (1992): 24–29.

Mezghani, Ali. *Le cadre juridique des rélations commerciales internationales de la Tunisie.* Tunis: Faculté de Droit et des Sciences Politiques et Economiques, Université de Tunis, 1981.

Miladi, Salem. "Economic Reforms and Transformation of the Role of the State: The Case of Tunisia." In *The Role of the State in Development Processes,* edited by C. Auroi, 155–61. EADI Book Series, 15. Geneva: European Association of Development Research and Training Institutes, 1992.

Miossec, Jean-Marie. "L'affirmation de la fonction économique de Tunis." In *Revue Française d'Etudes Politiques Méditerranéennes* 30–31 (1978): 91–120.

Montmarin, A. de, and Gérard Destanne de Bernis. "Industrialisation et plein emploi en Tunisie." *Revue de l'Institut des Belles Lettres Arabes* 18, no. 72 (1955): 395–436.

Moss, F. *Export Instability and its Causes: A Case Study of Tunisia*. Louvain: Catholic University, 1982.

Mzabi, Hassouna. "L'emploi et les investissements touristiques à Jerba." *Revue Tunisienne de Géographie* 2 (1979): 111–34.

———. "Le tourisme en Tunisie." *Cahiers de Tunisie* 26, nos. 101–2 (1978): 217–28.

Naccache, G. "Les coopératives de production du Nord. Commentaires d'une enquête statistique." *Revue Tunisienne de Sciences Sociales* 5 (1968): 141–60.

Nellis, John R. "A Comparative Assessment of the Development Performance of Algeria and Tunisia." *Middle East Journal* 27 (1983): 370–93.

L'oléiculture tunisienne: activités de recherche-développement. Sfax: Institut de l'Olivier, 1986.

Pelletreau, Pamela Day. "Private Sector Development through Public Sector Restructuring? The Cases of the Gafsa Phosphate Company and the Chemical Group." In *Tunisia: The Political Economy of Reform*, edited by I. William Zartman, 129–41. Boulder, Colo.: Lynne Rienner, 1991.

Perez, R. "Capacités et productions. Schémas d'analyses applicables à la Tunisie." *Revue Tunisienne de Sciences Sociales* 5 (1968): 33–69.

Peyrol, Manuèle. "L'expérience des coopératives en Tunisie." *Revue Française d'Etudes Politiques Africaines* 61 (1971): 33–48.

Platt, Kenneth. "An Oasis in the Sea: The Economic Organization of the Kerkennah Islands of Tunisia." *Maghreb Review* 8 (1983): 38–44.

Poirier, Robert and Stephen Wright. "The Political Economy of Tourism in Tunisia." *Journal of Modern African Studies* 31, no. 1 (1993): 149–62.

Poncet, Jean. *Le sous-développement vaincu? La lutte pour le développement en Italie méridionale, en Tunisie, et en Roumanie*. Paris: Editions Sociales, 1970.

———. "Les champs et l'évolution du paysage agraire en Tunisie." *Annales de Géographie* 71 (1962): 620–29.

———. "L'économie tunisienne depuis indépendance." *Annuaire de l'Afrique du Nord* 8 (1969): 93–114.

———. "L'expérience des 'unités coopératives de production' dans la région du Kef." *Tiers-Monde* 7 (1966): 567–80.

———. "La régionalisation en Tunisie." *Tiers-Monde* 14 (1973): 597–614.

———. "Les structures actuelles de l'agriculture tunisienne." *Annuaire de l'Afrique du Nord* 14 (1975): 45–56.

———. "Les structures agraires tunisiennes après l'expérience des 'unités coopératives de production.'" In *Actes du Colloque de géographie agraire*, 167–69. Aix-en-Provence: Centre Géographique d'Etudes et de Recherches Méditerranéennes, 1971.

————. "Tunisie de la dévaluation aux réformes." *Tiers-Monde* 6 (1965): 147–69.

————. "La Tunisie se développe-t-elle?" *Actes du IIème Congrès International d'Etudes Nord-Africaines. Revue de l'Occident Musulman et de la Méditerranée,* special issue (1970): 311–25.

Potter, Christopher S. and Allan T. Showler. "The Desert Locust: Agricultural and Environmental Impacts." In *Tunisia: The Political Economy of Reform,* edited by I. William Zartman, 153–66. Boulder, Colo.: Lynne Rienner, 1991.

Purvis, Malcolm J. "The Status of the Agricultural Economic Profession in North Africa: The Case of Tunis." In *International Training in Agricultural Economic Development,* edited by L. P. Schertz, A. R. Stevenson, and A. M. Weisblat, 72–77. 1976.

Radwan, Samir, Ajit Ghose, and Vali Jamal. *Tunisia: Rural Labor and Structural Transformation.* London: Routledge, 1991.

Raymond, H. "Socialisme et planification en Tunisie." *Confluent* 35 (1963): 890–96.

Rijn, Monique van. *Développement du paysage dans le Sahel nord de Soussa (Tunisie) sous l'aspect particulier des facteurs naturels.* Bremen: Ubersee-Museum, 1980.

Sahli, Mounir. *Le Tourisme en Tunisie.* Tunis: Serviced, 1990.

Sakouti, M. "La structure de l'emploi dans les industries alimentaires." *Revue Tunisienne de Sciences Sociales* 5 (1968): 113–46.

Schliephake, Konrad. *Oil and Regional Development: Examples from Algeria and Tunisia.* Translated by Merrill D. Lyew. New York: Praeger, 1977.

————. "Tunisia and Libya: Diversity of Economic Strategies and Similarities of Geological Constraints." *Maghreb Review* 11 (1986): 124–33.

Sebag, Paul. "L'industrialisation de la Tunisie. Une expérience-pilote dans l'industrie de la chaussure." *Cahiers de Tunisie* 7 (1959): 147–73.

Seddon, David. "Riot and Rebellion in North Africa: Political Responses to Economic Crisis in Tunisia, Morocco and Sudan." In *Power and Stability in the Middle East,* edited by Berch Berberoglu, 114–35. London: Zed Press, 1989.

Seklani, Mahmoud. *Economie et population du Sud-Tunisien.* Paris: Centre Nationale de Recherche Scientifique, 1976.

Sethom, Hafedh. *Pouvoir urbain et paysannerie en Tunisie.* Tunis: Centre d'Etudes et de Recherches Economiques et Sociales, 1992.

————. "L'aggravation de la concurrence entre la ville et la campagne pour le partage de l'eau disponible en Tunisie." *al-Madar* 1 (1993): 125–48.

————. "Agriculture et tourisme dans la région de Nabeul-Hammamet, co-existence féconde ou déséquilibre croissant?" *Cahiers de Tunisie* 24, nos. 93–94 (1976): 101–11.

————. "L'industrie tunisienne: bilan et perspectives." *Revue Tunisienne de Géographie* 19–20 (1991): 181–224.

————. "Liquidation des habous et évolution des campagnes dans la presqu'île du Cap Bon." *Cahiers de Tunisie* 24, nos. 95–96 (1976): 227–42.

————. "Modification des structures agraires et industrialisation. Introduction à une approche du problème en Tunisie." *Revue Tunisienne de Sciences Sociales* 6 (1966): 43–67.

————. "The Tunisian Experience with Service Cooperatives." In *Popular Participation in Social Change: Cooperatives, Collectives, and Nationalized Industry,* edited by June Nash et al, 481–95. The Hague: Mouton, 1976.

Sethom, Noureddine. "L'industrie et le tourisme en Tunisie: problématique de développement." *Revue Tunisienne de Géographie* 18 (1990): 237–60.

Signoles, Pierre. "Les inégalités régionales entre Tunis et la Tunisie." *Revue Française d'Etudes Politiques Méditerranéennes* 30–31 (1978): 49–59.

Silvera, Victor. "L'évolution des rapports financiers et économiques franco-tunisiens." *Revue Juridique et Politique de l'Outre-Mer* 14 (1960): 89–112.

Simmons, John. "Agricultural Cooperatives and Rural Development." *Middle East Journal* 24 (1970): 455–65; 25 (1971): 45–57.

Simon, Gildas. "Les Tunisiens: promotion des investissements et retours." In *L'argent des immigrés: revenues, épargne et transferts de huit nationalités immigrés en France,* edited by Jean-Pierre Garson and G. Tapinos, 219–45. Paris: Presses Universitaires de France, 1981.

Slim, Taieb. "Problems of Development: The Experience of Tunisia." In *Africa: Progress through Cooperation,* edited by J. Karefa-Smart, 54–65. New York: Dodd, Mead, 1966.

Stephenson, David E. "Specialized Labor Migration in Tunisia: Preliminary Conclusions." *Annales Algériennes de Géographies,* special issue (1972): 59–72.

Tajina, Mohamed Aziz. "Le tourisme saharien et son impact sur le développement régional du Sud-Tunisien." In *Actes du IIè Séminaire Universitaire Tuniso-Allemand,* 137–87. Tunis: Centre d'Etudes et de Recherches Economiques et Sociales, 1991.

Weidnitzer, Eva. "Haupttendenzen der Wirtschaftspolitik Tunesiens—Kontinuität und Wechsel." *Asien, Afrika, Lateinamerika* 14 (1986): 836–46.

Younes, E., and G. Berrebi. "Les places respectives de la réforme agraire et de l'industrialisation dans la stratégie du développement économique." In *Studies on Developing Countries,* edited by Ignacy Sachs, 119–72. Warsaw: Panstwowe Wydawn, 1964.

Zamiti, Khalil. "The Reform of Marketing Structures in Tunisia: State Capitalism or Collectivization of the Means of Exchange." In *Popular Participation in Social Change: Cooperatives, Collectives, and Nationalized Industry,* edited by June Nash et al, 459–80. The Hague: Mouton, 1976.

Zaouali, Jeanne. "Aperçu sur la pêche cotière tunisienne." *Revue Tunisienne de Communication* 10 (1986): 61–67.

Zaouche, Abdeljelil. "La condition des métayers indigènes en Tunisie. Moyens d'améliorer cette condition." *Cahiers de Tunisie* 26, nos. 105–6 (1978): 259–76.

Zarka, C. "L'économie tunisienne à l'heure de la planification impérative." *Annuaire de l'Afrique du Nord* 1 (1962): 207–41.

Zarrad, Tahar. *Le développement agro-alimentaire de la Tunisie en question.* Tunis: Cérès Productions, 1994.

Zghal, Abdelkader. "Changement de système politique et réformes des structures agraires en Tunisie." *Revue Tunisienne de Sciences Sociales* 5 (1968): 9–32.

———. "Modernisation de l'agriculture et population semi-nomade." *Revue Tunisienne de Sciences Sociales* 2 (1965): 31–49.

Sociocultural Issues Since Independence

General Studies

Abu Zahra, Nadia. *Sidi Ameur. A Tunisian Village.* London: Ithaca Press, 1982.

Acklam, N. "Problems of Rural Modernization in the Sahel." In *Field Studies in Tunisia,* edited by Ray Harris and Richard Lawless, 35–42. Durham: Department of Geography, University of Durham, 1981.

Anderson, Lisa. *The State and Social Transformation in Tunisia and Libya, 1830–1980.* Princeton: Princeton University Press, 1986.

Aouani, Mohamed el-. "Les populations rurales de la région de Tunis." *Revue Tunisienne de Sciences Sociales* 7 (1970): 39–90.

Baud, Isa. *Jobs and Values: Social Effects of Export-Oriented Industrialization in Tunisia.* Tilburg: Developmenet Research Institute, 1977.

Belgaid, Noureddine. "Motivation et aspiration ouvrière." *Etudes de Sociologie Tunisienne* 1 (1968): 235–57.

Belkacem, Boubaker. "L'organisation sanitaire en Tunisie." *Revue Juridique et Politique, Indépendance et Coopération* 35 (1981): 208–21.

Bouhdiba, Abdelwahab. *A la recherche des normes perdues.* Tunis: Maison Tunisienne d'Edition, 1973.

———. "Mass Tourism and Cultural Traditions." *UNESCO Courier* 34 (1981): 4–8.

Boukraa, Ridha. *Hammamet, le paradis perdu: étude anthropologique et écologique de la métamorphose d'une communauté.* Aix-en-Provence: Centre des Etudes Touristiques, 1993.

――――. "L'entreprise industrielle en milieu rural." *Etudes de Sociologie Tunisienne* 1 (1968): 43–80.

Camau, Michel, Hajer Bahri, and Hédi Zaiem. *Etat de santé: besoin médical et enjeux politiques en Tunisie.* Paris: Centre National de la Recherche Scientifique, 1990.

Demeerseman, André. "Un contraste saisissant: la personnalité actuelle et la personnalité ancienne de la Tunisie." *Confluent,* 23–24 (1962): 503–26.

Djedidi, Tahar Labib. "Culture et société en Tunisie." *Annuaire de l'Afrique du Nord* 12 (1973): 19–27.

Duvignaud, Jean. *Change at Shebika.* New York: Pantheon, 1970.

――――. *Chebika suivi de Retour à Chebika.* Paris: Plon, 1991.

Ennaceur, Mohamed. "La politique sociale de la Tunisie depuis l'indépendance et sa place dans le développement." In *Le développement en question,* edited by Abdelwahab Bouhdiba, 335–92. Tunis: Centre d'Etudes et de Recherches Economiques et Sociales, 1990.

Freund, Wolfgang Slim. "Les jerbiens en Tunisie: réminiscences d'un sociologue allemand devant une recherche inachevée." *Revue de l'Institut des Belles Lettres Arabes* 49, no. 157 (1986): 31–57.

Gachet, Jean-Paul. "Choix technologiques et formation dans l'agriculture tunisiennes." *Annuaire de l'Afrique du Nord* 19 (1980): 105–30.

Ginestous, Paul. "Bizerte et sa région: la vie artisanale." *Revue de l'Institut des Belles Lettres Arabes* 19, no. 73 (1956): 93–114.

Girard, Alain. "Pour une observation en Tunisie des attitudes à l'égard du changement." *Revue Tunisienne de Sciences Sociales* 5 (1966): 95–103.

Hamza, Ali. "Données preliminaires sur l'aménagement intégré dans la Tunisie centrale." *Revue Tunisienne de Géographie* 6 (1980): 87–101.

Hermassi, Abdelbaki. "Elite et société en Tunisie. Intégration et mobilisation." *Revue Tunisienne de Sciences Sociales* 6 (1969): 11–19.

Hopkins, Nicholas. "Les classes moyennes dans une ville moyenne: Testour." In *Les classes moyennes au Maghreb,* edited by Abdelkader Zghal et al., 144–54. Paris: Centre National de Recherche Scientifique, 1980.

――――. "The Emergence of Class in a Tunisian Town." *International Journal of Middle East Studies* 8 (1977): 453–91.

Kassab, Ahmad. *Etudes rurales en Tunisie.* Tunis: Université de Tunis, 1980.

――――. "L'évolution d'un village 'andalous': Testour." In *Recueil d'études sur les moriscos andalous en Tunisie,* edited by M. de Epalza and R. Petit, 359–68. Madrid: Dirección General de Relaciones Culturales, Instituto Hispano-Arabe de Cultura, 1973.

Louis, André. *Nomades d'hier et d'aujourd'hui dans le Sud tunisien.* Aix-en-Provence: Edisud, 1979.

———. *Tunisie du sud: ksars et villages de crêtes.* Paris: Centre Nationale de la Recherche Scientifique, 1975.

———. "Sur un pilon de l'Extrême-Sud, une étrange cité berbère: Douiret." *Revue de l'Institut des Belles Lettres Arabes* 27 (1964): 381–91.

Magnin, Jean-Gabriel. "Problèmes de la santé publique." *Revue de l'Institut des Belles Lettres Arabes* 24, nos. 95–96 (1961): 337–47.

Marzouki, Ilhem. "Pour une étude du changement social dans les tribus berbères: présupposés théoriques." *Revue de l'Institut des Belles Lettres Arabes* 49, no. 158 (1986): 263–96.

O'Reilly, C. "Employment and Social Change in the Sahel: A Case Study of Ksibet el-Mediouni." In *Field Studies in Tunisia,* edited by R. Harris and R. Lawless, 70–77. Durham: Department of Geography, University of Durham, 1981.

Sethom, Hafedh. "Liquidation des habous et évolution des compagnes dans la presqu'île de Cap Bon." *Cahiers de Tunisie* 24, nos. 95–96 (1976): 227–42.

———. "La vie rurale de la Tunisie contemporaine. Etude historique et géographique." *Cahiers de Tunisie* 14 (1966): 187–212.

Stone, Russell, and John Simmons. *Change in Tunisia. Studies in the Social Sciences.* Albany: State University of New York Press, 1976.

Tabone, Bernard. "Aspects socio-culturels de la folie en Tunisie." *Revue de l'Institut des Belles Lettres Arabes* 45, no. 150 (1982): 259–79.

Tessler, Mark, and Linda Hawkins. "Acculturation, Socioeconomic Status, and Attitude Change in Tunisia: Implications for Modernization Theory." In *Political Socialization in the Arab States,* edited by Tawfic E. Farah and Yasumasa Kuroda, 107–27. Boulder, Colo.: Lynne Rienner, 1987.

Toumi, Mohsen. "Le courant ouvriériste et populaire en Tunisie face au pouvoir d'état." *Revue Française d'Etudes Politiques Africaines* 148 (1978): 79–102.

Zamiti-Horchani, Malika. "Les tunisiennes, leurs droits et l'idée qu'on s'en fait." *Peuples Méditerranéens* 22–23 (1983): 181–92, 310.

Zghal, Abdelkader. "Construction nationale et nouvelles classes en Tunisie." *Revue de l'Institut de Sociologie* 40 (1967): 307–20.

———. "L'élite administrative et la paysannerie." *Revue Tunisienne de Sciences Sociales* 6 (1969): 41–52.

———. "The Reactivation of Tradition in a Post-Traditional Society." *Daedalus* 102 (1973): 225–37.

Zussman, Mira. *Development and Disenchantment in Rural Tunisia: The Bourguiba Years.* Boulder, Colo.: Westview Press, 1992.

Demography

Attia, Habib. "Croissance et migrations des populations sahéliennes." In *Maghreb et Sahara: Etudes Géographiques Offertes à J. Despois,* edited by Xavier de Planhol, 29–43. Paris: Société de Géographie, 1973. [Also in *Revue Tunisienne de Sciences Sociales* 7 (1970): 91–117.]

Bchir, Mongi. *La population tunisienne: caractéristiques et évolution récente.* Tunis: Institut Supérieur de l'Education et de la Formation Continue, 1986.

———. "Croissance démographique du gouvernorat de Tunis, 1956–1966." *Revue Tunisienne de Sciences Sociales* 7 (1970): 15–38.

Ben Adjima, M. "Structure des villages et origine de leur population dans le Sahel septentrional." *Cahiers de Tunisie* 12 (1964): 101–8.

Boukhris, Mohamed. *La population en Tunisie. Réalités et perspectives.* Tunis: Office National de la Famille et de la Population, 1992.

Cohen-Hadira, Elie. "La politique démographique de la Tunisie." *Maghreb-Machrek* 71 (1976): 56–60.

Dahmani, Béchir. "Croissance démographique de la population sahelienne." In *La démographie historique en Tunisie et dans le monde arabe,* edited by Dalenda and Abdelhamid Larguèche, 103–12. Tunis: Centre d'Etudes et de Recherches Economiques et Sociales, 1993.

———. "Situation démographique et mortalité infantile dans une région du nord-ouest de la Tunisie: Ain Draham." *Revue de l'Institut des Belles Lettres Arabes* 49, no. 157 (1986): 101–19.

Kassab, Ahmad. "Le phénomène de dispersion de la population rurale dans le Tell septentrionel et le Haut-Tell tunisiens." *Revue Tunisienne de Géographie* 3 (1979): 31–42.

Seklani, Mohamed. *La Population de la Tunisie.* Paris: Committee for International Coordination of National Research in Demography, 1974.

Situation démographique en Tunisie à la fin de l'année 1985. Tunis: Institut de la Statistique, 1986.

Education and Culture

Allman, James. *Social Mobility, Education and Development in Tunisia.* Leiden: Brill, 1977.

———. "Social Mobility and Educational Access in Tunisia." In *Commoners, Climbers, and Notables,* edited by C. A. O. van Nieuwenhuijze, 344–59. Brill: Leiden, 1977.

Amrani, Fadila. "Mutations de la population active et limites du système éducatif: le cas tunisien de 1970 à 1980." *Annuaire de l'Afrique du Nord* 29 (1980): 11–23.

Baldacchino, Georges. "L'Enseignement primaire et sécondaire tunisien en 1976–1977." *Revue de l'Institut des Belles Lettres Arabes* 40, no. 140 (1977): 297–302.

Ben Sedrine, Marie. "Milieu socio-familial et orientation scolaire. Une enquête dans un lycée de Tunis." *Revue de l'Institut des Belles Lettres Arabes* 23 (1970): 297–304.

Ben Slama, Béchir. *La politique culturelle en Tunisie.* Tunis: N.p., 1986.

Kacem, Abdelaziz. "La politique culturelle tunisienne." *Annuaire de l'Afrique du Nord* 12 (1973): 29–44.

Larif-Beatrix, Asma. "Edification étatique et environment culturel en Tunisie." *Arabica* 33 (1986): 295–324.

Lelong, Michel. "Aspects du renouveau culturel en Tunisie." *Revue de l'Institut des Belles Lettres Arabes* 19 (1956): 65–71.

———. "Culture arabe et culture occidentale dans la Tunisie d'aujourd'hui. (Une enquête de la Revue Al-fikr)." *Revue de l'Institut des Belles Lettres Arabes* 19, no. 75 (1956): 313–31.

———. "L'effort tunisien pour la diffusion de la culture. (Comités culturels—Maison de la culture—Maisons du peuple—Bibliothèques)." *Revue de l'Institut des Belles Lettres Arabes* 27 (1964): 43–54.

———. "Le ressurgissement de la culture nationale en Tunisie." *Annuaire de l'Afrique du Nord* 6 (1967): 21–44.

———. "La vie intellectuelle et artistique en Tunisie." *Revue de l'Institut des Belles Lettres Arabes* 20, no. 79 (1957): 239–82; 20, no. 80 (1957): 381–91; 21, no. 81 (1958): 61–75; 22, no. 87 (1959): 325–36.

Maamouri, Mohamed. "Illiteracy in Tunisia: An Evaluation." In *Language in Tunisia,* edited by R. M. Payne, 139–58. Cambridge: Heffer, 1983.

Mami, Mustapha. *Action culturelle et développement: une approche analytique des festivals en Tunisie.* Tunis: Maison Tunisienne de l'Edition, 1986.

Mizouri, Laroussi. "La réforme du système éducatif en Tunisie: analyse du projet de juin 1986." *Revue de l'Institut des Belles Lettres Arabes* 51, no. 161 (1988): 163–77.

Rejeb, Souad, and Samia Hagra Mahjoub. "Les lycéens et l'éducation." *Revue de l'Institut des Belles Lettres Arabes* 55, no. 169 (1992): 31–56; 55, no. 170 (1992): 195–209.

Sraieb, Noureddine. "Laicisation et/ou religiosité dans l'enseignement sécondaire tunisien." In *Islam et politique au Maghreb,* edited by Ernest Gellner, Jean-Claude Vatin, and Abdallah Hammoudi, 231–42. Paris: Centre National de Recherche Scientifique, 1981.

Language

Aboub, Abdesselem. "L'administration tunisienne et le recours au français." In *La Linguistique au Maghreb,* edited by Jochem Pleines, 223–36. Rabat: Okard, 1990.

Ben Letaifa, Said. "Utilisation respective de l'arabe et du français dans quelques administrations tunisiennes." *Revue Tunisienne de Sciences Sociales* 4 (1967): 57–75.

Freund, Wolfgang Slim. "La langue allemande en Tunisie: mythe ou réalité?" *Revue de l'Institut des Belles Lettres Arabes* 51, no. 161 (1988): 151–62.

Garmadi, Salah. "La langue des enseignes de quelques rues importantes de Tunis." In *Language in Tunisia,* edited by R. M. Payne, 177–209. Cambridge: Heffer, 1983. [Also in *Revue Tunisienne de Sciences Sociales* 3 (1966): 59–81.]

———. "Les problèmes du plurilinguisme en Tunisie." In *Renaissance du Monde Arabe. Colloque Interarabe de Louvain,* edited by Anouar Abdel-Malek, Abdel-Aziz Belal, and Hassan Hanafi, 309–22. Gembloux: Duculot, 1972.

———. "La situation linguistique actuelle en Tunisie: problèmes et perspectives." In *Language in Tunisia,* edited by R. M. Payne, 1–9. Cambridge: Heffer, 1983.

Ghachem, Moncef. "Rhaïs Hugo." In *Nouveaux enjeux culturels au Maghreb,* edited by J.-R. Henry, 159–72. Paris: Centre National de la Recherche Scientifique, 1986. [Also in *Annuaire de l'Afrique du Nord* 23 (1984): 159–72.]

Hamzaoui, Rachad. "L'arabisation au Ministère de l'Intérieur: la Brigade de la Circulation de la Garde Nationale." In *Language in Tunisia,* edited by R. M. Payne, 211–60. Cambridge: Heffer, 1983.

Krichen, Aziz. "La fracture de l'intelligentsia. Problèmes de la langue et de la culture nationales." In *Tunisie au Présent: Une modernité au-dessus soupçon?,* edited by Michel Camau and Jellal Abdelkafi, 297–341. Paris: Centre National de la Recherche Scientifique, 1987.

Maamouri, Mohamed. "The Linguistic Situation in Independent Tunisia." In *Language in Tunisia,* edited by R. M. Payne, 11–21. Cambridge: Heffer, 1983. [Also in *American Journal of Arabic Studies* 1 (1973): 50–65.]

Micaud, Charles. "Bilingualism in North Africa: Cultural and Socio-Political Implications." *Western Political Quarterly* 27 (1974): 92–103.

Payne, R. M. "Language Planning in Tunisia." In *Language in Tunisia,* edited by R. M. Payne, 261–71. Cambridge: Heffer, 1983.

Riahi, Zohra. "Le Français parlé par les cadres tunisiens." *Revue Tunisienne de Sciences Sociales* 5 (1968): 195–217.

Riguet, Maurice. "Variations dans l'opinion selon la langue en milieu tunisien." *Revue de l'Institut des Belles Lettres Arabes* 44, no. 148 (1981): 229–52; 45, no. 149 (1982): 57–86.

Souriau, Christiane. "Structuration de la société par le choix de langue en Tunisie." In *Les Classes Moyennes au Maghreb,* edited by Abdelkader Zghal et al., 249–311. Paris: Centre National de Recherche Scientifique, 1980.

Stevens, Paul B. "Ambivalence, Modernisation, and Language Attitudes: French and Arabic in Tunisia." *Journal of Multilingual and
Multicultural Development* 4 (1983): 101–14.

———. "Modernism and Authenticity as Reflected in Language Attitudes: The Case of Tunisia." *Civilisations* 30 (1980): 37–59.

Literature and the Arts

Bachy, Victor. *La Cinéma de Tunisie, 1956–1977*. Tunis: Société Tunisienne de Diffusion, 1978.

Bchir, Badra. *Eléments du fait théâtrale en Tunisie*. Tunis: Centre d'E-
tudes et de Recherches Economiques et Sociales, 1993.

Bekri, Tahar. "On French Language Tunisian Literature." *Research in
African Literatures* 23 (1992): 177–82.

Bencheikh, Naceur. "Mythes, réalités et significations de l'activité pic-
turale en Tunisie." *Annuaire de l'Afrique du Nord* 12 (1973): 151–68.

Boughedir, Férid. "Le cinéma en Tunisie (1966–1986). Vingt ans de
cinéma tunisien: la société tunisienne vue par ses films." *Revue
Tunisienne de Communication* 9 (1986): 88–113.

Boujedra, Rachid. *Naissance du cinéma tunisien*. Paris: Maspéro, 1971.

Chelbi, Mustapha. *Musique et la société en Tunisie*. Tunis: Editions
Salammbo, 1985.

Davis, Ruth. "Modern Trends in the 'Arab-Andalusian' Music of
Tunisia." *Maghreb Review* 11 (1986): 58–63.

Driss, Mohamed Masoud. "L'activité théâtrale en Tunisie, 1970–1980:
Essai de bilan." *Revue de l'Institut des Belles Lettres Arabes* 48, no.
156 (1985): 313–29.

Fontaine, Jean. *Ecrivaines tunisiennes*. Tunis: Le Gai Savoir, 1990.

———. "Arabic Language Tunisian Literature (1956–1990)." *Research
in African Literatures* 23 (1992): 183–93.

———. "La littérature féminine tunisienne (1971–1980) marque-t-elle
un renouveau?" *Cahiers de Tunisie* 29, nos. 115–16 (1981): 269–85.

———. "Le 'Nouveau Théâtre' de Tunis, 1976–1982." *Revue de l'Institut des Belles Lettres Arabes* 46, no. 151 (1983): 123–33.

———. "Nouvelles et romans tunisiens, 1978–1979." *Revue de l'Institut des Belles Lettres Arabes* 43, no. 146 (1980): 323–44.

Goulli, Sophie el-. "Les Arts plastiques en Tunisie." *Europe* 702 (October 1987): 49–56.

Guettat, Mahmoud. "Visages de la musique tunisienne." *Revue de l'Institut des Belles Lettres Arabes* 45, no. 150 (1982): 227–40.

Haffner, Pierre. "Les Cinémas de libération à Tunis." *Peuples Noirs-
Peuples Africains* 44 (April 1985): 73–102; 45 (June 1985): 56–75.

Houssi, Majid El-. *Pour un histoire du théâtre tunisien*. Padua: Francisci,
1982.

Khilfi, Omar. *Histoire du cinéma en Tunisie*. Tunis: Société Nationale d'Edition et de Diffusion, 1970.

Lelong, Michel. "A travers les revues tunisiennes." *Revue de l'Institut des Belles Lettres Arabes* 25 (1962): 49–57.

Naser, Abdelkader Belhaj. *Quelques aspects du roman tunisien*. Tunis: Maison Tunisienne de l'Edition, 1981.

Ogunbiyi, I. A. "The Birth and Growth of the Tunisian Arabic Short Story." *Maghreb Review* 6 (1981): 94–97.

Racy, Ali. "Music of Tunisia: A Contemporary Perspective." *Arabesque* 5, no. 1 (1979): 18–24; 28.

Rassaa, Mohamed Salah. *35 ans de cinéma tunisien*. Tunis: Sahar, 1993.

Sayadi, Salem. "Le Cinéma tunisien, ses moyens, ses problèmes." *Revue de l'Institut des Belles Lettres Arabes* 35, no. 129 (1972): 141–48.

The Media

Chelbi, Mustapha. *Le patrimoine journalistique de Tunisie*. Tunis: Bouslama, 1986.

Faath, Sigrid. "Radio und Politik in Tunesien." *Wuquf* 2 (1987): 171–253.

Hamdane, Mohamed. "Panorama historique de la presse rurale en Tunisie (1881–1981)." *Revue de l'Institut des Belles Lettres Arabes* 49, no. 157 (1986): 75–86.

Houidi, Fethi and Ridha Najar. *Presse, radio, télévision en Tunisie*. Tunis: Maison Tunisienne de l'Edition, 1983.

Kepplinger, Hans-Mathias, Wolfgang Donsbach, Reiner Auer, Mohamed Ali Kembi, Mohamed Hamdane, and Rached Skik. "The Impact of Television on Rural Areas of Tunisia: A Panel Field Experiment on Changes in Social Perception, Attitudes, and Roles after the Introduction of Television." *Revue Tunisienne de Communication* 10 (1986): 107–64.

Malchiodi, M. "L'impatto della televisione italiana (RAI I) sulla società tunisina." *Africa* [Rome] 47 (1992): 595–617.

Tarchouna, Mahmoud. "Moyen et formes d'expression en Tunisie." *Maghreb Review* 11 (1986): 64–68.

Tlili, Hassan. "Notes sur la radio et la population rurale en Tunisie." *Annuaire de l'Afrique du Nord* 20 (1981): 954–57.

Migration (Internal and External)

Baduel, Pierre Robert. "Emigration et transformation des rapports sociaux dans le Sud tunisien." *Peuples Méditerranéens* 17 (1981): 3–22.

———. "Migrations internes et émigration: le cas tunisien." *Annuaire de l'Afrique du Nord* 20 (1981): 169–85.

Belhedi, Amor, Hechmi Labaied, and Azzam Mahjoub. *Analyse des mouvements migratoires dans le sud et le sud-est du bassin méditerranéen en direction de la CEE: le cas de la Tunisie*. Tunis: Centre d'Etudes et de Recherches Economiques et Sociales, 1992.

Ben Ali, Ridha. "L'émigration des Tunisiens." *Revue Juridique et Politique, Indépendance et Coopération* 34 (1980): 249–52.

Bouraoui, Abdelhamid. "Les travailleurs tunisiens en France." In *Actes du Colloque "La migration internationale des travailleurs tunisiens,"* 75–92. Tunis: Centre d'Etudes et de Recherches Economiques et Sociales, 1987.

Damette Group. "Les Migrations dans la région minière du Sud." *Revue Tunisienne de Sciences Sociales* 7 (1970): 175–207.

Di Comite, Luigi. "L'immigration tunisienne en Italie: quelques données censitaires." In *Actes du Colloque "La migration internationale des travailleurs tunisiens,"* 187–202. Tunis: Centre d'Etudes et de Recherches Economiques et Sociales, 1987.

Drira, M. "Les migrations internes en Tunisie." In *La démographie historique en Tunisie et dans le monde arabe,* edited by Dalenda and Abdelhamid Larguèche, 113–31. Tunis: Centre d'Etudes et de Recherches Economiques et Sociales, 1993.

Findlay, Allan. "Migration Planning: The Case for Tunisia." *Applied Geography* 2 (1982): 221–30.

Findlay, Allan, Ann Findlay, and Richard Lawless. "New Directions in Tunisian Emigration: Windfall or Pitfall?" *Maghreb Review* 4 (1979): 78–81.

Karoui, Hachimi. "Mateur . . . lieu d'immigration." *Revue Tunisienne de Sciences Sociales* 7 (1970): 119–42.

Lamine, R., and H. Boubakri. "Modifications des champs migratoires internes dans le Sahel et immigration dans la ville de Sousse." *Revue Tunisienne de Géographie* 21–22 (1992): 97–119.

Pitie, Jean. "L'exode rural dans les pays du Maghreb, esquisse de bibliographie annotée." In *Hommage à Gérard Maurer,* 433–52. Poitiers: Centre Interuniversitaire d'Etudes Méditerranéennes, 1987.

Seklani, Mohamed. "La mobilité intérieure dans le Sud Tunisien." *Revue Tunisienne de Sciences Sociales* 7 (1970): 163–74.

Sethom, Hafedh. "L'émigration des travailleurs du Cap Bon vers l'étranger." *Revue Tunisienne de Géographie* 1 (1978): 43–64.

Signoles, Pierre. "Evolution et fonctionnement de l'espace migratoire de Tunis: les grands courants migratoires vers la capitale tunisienne." In *Hommage à Gérard Maurer,* 503–42. Poitiers: Centre Interuniversitaire d'Etudes Méditerranéennes, 1987.

———. "Migrations intérieures et villes en Tunisie." *Cahiers de Tunisie* 20 (1972): 207–40.

Stephenson, D. E. "Specialized Labor Migration in Tunisia: Preliminary Conclusions." *Annales Algériennes de Géographie* special issue (1972): 59–72.

Sulejczak, E., and J. Gudowski. "Les migrations rurales vers les villes en Tunisie du nord." *Africana Bulletin* 27 (1978): 65–104.

Taamallah, Khémaies. "L'Evolution de l'émigration tunisienne en Europe occidentale et ses impacts socio-économiques." *Annuaire de l'Afrique du Nord* 20 (1981): 187–201.

———. "Evolution régionale de la population tunisienne résident en France au cours des deux périodes 1962–1968 et 1968–1975." *Cahiers de Tunisie* 27, nos. 107–8 (1979): 277–85.

———. "La situation actuelle démographique de l'émigration des travailleurs tunisiens en France." In *Actes du Colloque "La migration internationale des travailleurs tunisiens,"* 7–30. Tunis: Centre d'Etudes et de Recherches Economiques et Sociales, 1987.

Taamallah, Malika. "Quelques réflexions sur la population active féminine tunisienne de France." In *Actes du Colloque "La migration internationale des travailleurs tunisiens,",* 255–66. Tunis: Centre d'Etudes et de Recherches Economiques et Sociales, 1987.

Taiachi, Hassen. "Mouvements de la population." In *La démographie historique en Tunisie et dans le monde arabe,* edited by Dalenda and Abdelhamid Larguèche, 133–57. Tunis: Centre d'Etudes et de Recherches Economiques et Sociales, 1993.

Toigo, M. "Emigration, développement et dépendance: le cas de Tunisie." *Migrations Société* 6 (1994): 60–89.

Trifa, Chedly. "L'émigration tunisienne historique et quelques aspects socio-démographiques des émigrés." In *Actes du Colloque "La migration internationale des travailleurs tunisiens,"* 31–46. Tunis: Centre d'Etudes et de Recherches Economiques et Sociales, 1987.

Religion

Abu-Zahra, Nadia. "The Rain Rituals as Rites of Spiritual Passage." *International Journal of Middle East Studies* 20 (1988): 507–29.

Ben Achour, Yadh. "Islam perdu, Islam retrouvé." *Annuaire de l'Afrique du Nord* 18 (1979): 65–75.

Ben Hamza, Kacem. "Croyances et pratiques en Islam populaire: le cas de Matmata." *Revue de l'Institut des Belles Lettres Arabes* 45, no. 149 (1982): 87–111.

Binsbergen, Wim M. J. van. "Popular and Formal Islam and Supra-local Relations: The Highlands of North-western Tunisia, 1800–1970." *Middle East Studies* 16 (1980): 71–91.

Cheikha, Jemaa. "La polémique religieuse dans les études universitaires: Faculté des Lettres-Section Arabe." *Revue de l'Institut des Belles Lettres Arabes* 49, no. 158 (1986): 327–32.

Fontaine, Jean. "La religion dans trois revues tunisiennes (septembre 1977–juillet 1978)." *Revue de l'Institut des Belles Lettres Arabes* 43, no. 146 (1980): 345–52.

Grazzini, F. "La Iglesia en Túnez después de la independencia." In *El cristianismo en el Norte de Africa,* edited by Henri Teissier and Ramon Lourido Diaz, 183–91. Madrid: MAPFRE, 1993.

Hopkins, Nicholas. "L'Islam populaire dans l'Egypte et la Tunisie rurales: l'imaginaire et structures sociales." *Bulletin du Centre d'Etudes et de Documentation Economique et Juridique* 26 (1989): 227–40.

Hours, F. "A propos du jeûne du mois de Ramadan en Tunisie." *Orient* 13 (1960): 43–52.

Meziou, Kalthoum. "Pérennité de l'Islam dans le droit tunisien de la famille." In *Le statut personnel des musulmans: droit comparé et droit international privé,* edited by Albert Bastenier, 247–74. Brussels: Bruylant, 1992.

Saadaoui, Ahmed. "Deux sanctuaires israélites de Testour." *Arab Historical Review for Ottoman Studies* 5–6 (1992): 97–106.

Sebag, Paul. *Histoire des juifs de Tunisie, des origines à nos jours.* Paris: L'Harmattan, 1991.

Talbi, Mohamed. "L'expression religieuse dans la presse et les revues tunisiennes aujourd'hui (1984–1985)." *Maghreb Review* 11 (1986): 1–18.

Tessler, Mark. "The Political Culture of Jews in Tunisia and Morocco." *International Journal of Middle Eastern Studies* 11 (1980): 59–86.

Udovitch, Avram, and Lucette Valensi. "Communautés juives en pays d'Islam: identité et communication à Djerba." *Annales Economies, Sociétés, Civilisations* 35 (1980): 764–83.

———. *The Last Arab Jews: The Communities of Jerba, Tunisia.* Chur: Harwood, 1984.

Urbanization and Housing

Abdelkafi, Jellal. *La médina de Tunis: espace historique.* Paris: Centre National de la Recherche Scientifique, 1989.

———. "Le concept d'espace historique et la problématique de réhabilitation: étude de cas sur la médina de Tunis." In *La réhabilitation des cités anciennes,* edited by the Association Bou Regreg, 155–63. Casablanca: Wallada, 1990.

———. "La réponse de l'état au processus d'urbanisation." In *Tunisie au présent: une modernité au-dessus de tout soupçon?,* edited by Michel Camau and Jellal Abdelkafi, 253–85. Paris: Centre National de la Recherche Scientifique, 1987.

———. "Tunis: les conditions de l'urbanisation." *Maghreb-Machrek* 80 (1978): 63–73.

Akkari, Jenina. "L'habitat traditionnel de Jerba. Un problème d'avenir. Essai de réamenagement de certains menzels pour leur intégration dans la vie contemporaine." *Revue de l'Institut des Belles Lettres Arabes* 40, no. 139 (1977): 67–80.

Aziz Tagina, Mohamed. "Réflexions sur le processus d'urbanisation en Tunisie: le cas de Gafsa." *Revue Tunisienne de Sciences Sociales* 21–22 (1970): 87–110.

Barbar, Aghil. *Urbanization in Tunisia.* Monticello, Ill.: Council of Planning Librarians, 1981.

Belhedi, Amor. "Le système urbain tunisien. Croissance urbaine et structure hiérarchique." *Revue Tunisienne de Géographie* 21–22 (1992): 177–91.

Chabbi, Morched. "Etat, politiques urbaines et habitat spontané. Le cas de Tunis, 1960–1980." In *Etat, ville et mouvement sociaux au Maghreb et au Moyen-Orient,* edited by Kenneth Brown et al., 249–65. Paris: L'Harmattan, 1989.

———. "Politiques d'habitat et modèles de développement: le cas de Tunis (1960–1984)." *Annuaire de l'Afrique du Nord* 25 (1986): 37–50.

Curuchet, M. *A Self-Help Housing Project in Rural Tunisia in Retrospect.* Uppsala: Scandinavian Institute of African Studies, 1987.

Dammak, Oum Kalthoum. "Aspects de l'urbanisation dans un gouvernorat à dominante rurale: le gouvernorat de Zaghouan." *Revue Tunisienne de Sciences Sociales* 94–95 (1988): 169–209.

Davies, Howard M. "The Role of Surplus in the Process of Development and its Impact on Urbanism: The Case of Tunisia." *Maghreb Review* 3 (1978): 23–31.

———. "Urbanism: The Use of Surplus in the Spatial Organization of Tunis, Part 2." *Maghreb Review* 3 (1978): 21–26.

Despois, Jean. "Essai sur l'habitat rural du Sahel tunisien." *Cahiers de Tunisie* 28, nos. 113–14 (1980): 231–52.

Dlala, Habib. "Etude de quelques aspects du problème de l'habitat en Tunisie." *Revue Tunisienne de Géographie* 5 (1980): 41–59.

Dubois, René Edouard. "Un problème de développement urbain: le Kef (Tunisie)." *Cahiers d'Outre-Mer* 26 (1973): 129–49.

Fakhfakh, Françoise. *Une banlieu de Tunis depuis l'indépendance: l'Ariana.* Tours: Centre National de Recherche Scientifique, 1977.

Fakhfakh, Moncef. "Les difficultés de la planification urbaine: le cas de Sfax." In *Les politiques urbaines dans le monde arabe,* edited by J. Metral and G. Mutin, 217–24. Lyon: Maison de l'Orient, 1984.

Fakhfakh, Muhammad. "Croissance urbaine et environnement dans le district de Tunis." *Géographie et Développement* 8–9 (1989): 57–77.

Lawless, Richard. "Social and Economic Change in North African Medinas: The Case of Tunis." In *Change and Development in the Middle East. Essays in Honour of W. B. Fischer,* edited by John I. Clarke and Howard Bowen-Jones, 264–79. London: Methuen, 1981.

Lawless, Richard and Allan Findlay. "Tunis." In *Problems and Planning in Third World Cities,* edited by M. Pacione, 94–126. London: Croom Helm, 1981.

Liauzu, Claude. "Crises urbaines, crise d'Etat, mouvements sociaux." In *Etat, ville et mouvements sociaux au Maghreb et au Moyen-Orient,* edited by Kenneth Brown et al., 23–41. Paris: L'Harmattan, 1989.

Micaud, Ellen. "Urbanization, Urbanism and the Medina of Tunis." In *Sociology of "Developing Societies": The Middle East,* edited by Talal Asad and Roger Owen, 215–225; 236–37. London: Macmillan, 1983.

Miossec, Jean-Marie. "Activités tertiaires supérieures et organisation spatiale du centre de Tunis: le sens d'un élargissement." *Bulletin de la Société Languedocienne de Géographie* 20 (1986): 319–37.

———. "L'évolution des quartiers centraux de Tunis." In *Eléments sur les centres-ville dans le Monde Arabe,* edited by Jean-François Troin, 131–50. Tours: URBAMA, 1988.

———. "La politique d'habitat en Tunisie depuis l'indépendance." *Annuaire de l'Afrique du Nord* 25 (1986): 17–35.

———. "Recherche urbaine et politiques urbaines en Tunisie." In *Middle Eastern Cities in Comparative Perspective,* edited by Kenneth Brown, Michèle Jolé, Peter Sluglett, and Sami Zubaida, 115–40. London: Ithaca Press, 1986.

———. "Urbanisation des campagnes et ruralisation des villes en Tunisie." *Annales de Géographie* 94 (1985): 38–62.

Miossec, Jean-Marie, and Pierre Signoles. "L'évolution récente du système urbain tunisien." *Maghreb-Machrek* 96 (1982): 67–88.

———. "Les politiques urbaines en Tunisie." In *Les politiques urbaines dans le monde arabe,* edited by J. Metral and G. Mutin, 183–202. Lyon: Maison de l'Orient, 1984.

Miyaji, Mieko. "Modern Muslim City and Family Change: A Tunisian Case." In *Urbanism in Islam,* edited by T. Yukawa, 295–327. Tokyo: Research Project "Urbanism in Islam" and The Middle Eastern Culture Center in Japan, 1989.

Paddison, Ronan. "Commercial Structure and Change in the European Quarter: A Comparison of Tunis and Rabat." In *Eléments sur les centres-ville dans le Monde Arabe,* edited by Jean-François Troin, 91–102. Tours: URBAMA, 1988.

Pompei, S. "Problèmes de l'urbanisation dans le Sahel." *Cahiers de Tunisie* 12 (1964): 147–63.

Sethom, Hafedh. "Agriculture intensive et urbanisation accélérée sur le littoral oriental du Cap Bon." *Revue Tunisienne de Géographie* 6 (1980): 153–62.

Signoles, Pierre. *L'espace tunisien: capitale et état-région.* 2 vols. Tours: Institut de Géographie, 1983.

———. "L'armature urbaine tunisienne: forces et faiblesses, et son rôle dans le développement national." *Revue Tunisienne de Géographie* 1 (1978): 67–96.

———. "L'évolution des fonctions métropolitaines de Tunis: la part réciproque de capitale nationale et de métropole-relais." *Bulletin de la Société Languedocienne de Géographie* 20 (1986): 177–96.

————. "Tunis et l'espace tunisien." In *Enjeux urbains au Maghreb: crises, pouvoirs et mouvements sociaux,* edited by Claude Liauzu et al., 205–15. Paris: L'Harmattan, 1985.

————. "The Urban Structure of Tunisia: Strengths and Weaknesses and Its Role in National Development." In *Urbanization: Early Development, Current Trends and Prospects,* edited by L. Unikel, 165–93. Mexico City: Colegio de México, 1981.

Signoles, Pierre et al. *Tunis: Evolution et fonctionnement de l'espace urbain.* Tours: Conseil Scientifique de l'Université, 1980.

Stambouli, Fredj. "Urbanisme et développement en Tunisie." *Revue Tunisienne de Sciences Sociales* 4 (1967): 77–107.

Sugier, Clémence. "Urbanisme et sociologie: la Médina de Tunis." *Cahiers de la Méditerranée* 20–21 (1980): 37–42.

Tekari, Béchir Chebab. "Habitat et dépassement du droit en Tunisie: les constructions spontanées." *Annuaire de l'Afrique du Nord* 25 (1986): 165–73.

Toyn, R., and G. Brierley. "An Examination of the Form and Function of Tunisian Urban Centers." In *Field Studies in Tunisia,* edited by R. Harris and Richard Lawless, 57–63. Durham: Department of Geography, University of Durham: 1981.

Vigier, F. *Housing in Tunis.* Cambridge: Harvard University Graduate School of Design, 1987.

Woodford, Jerome S. *The City of Tunis: Evolution of an Urban System.* Wisbech, Cambridgeshire: Middle East and North African Studies Press, 1990.

Zannad, Traki. "Le vécu urbain entre la théorie et la pratique: le cas de la médina de Tunis." *Cahiers de Tunisie* 34, nos. 137–38 (1986): 366–77.

Women and the Family

Bartels, Edien. "'Les jeunes mères sont comme des chattes': tourments et possessions par les esprits chez les accouchées de la campagne tunisienne." *Revue de l'Institut des Belles Lettres Arabes* 49, no. 157 (1986): 3–29.

Bchir, Badra. *L'enjeu du féminisme indépendant en Tunisie: modèles et pratique.* Cahiers du CERES: Série Sociologique 21. Tunis: Centre d'Etudes et de Recherches Economiques et Sociales, 1993.

Beaujot, Roderic. "Libération de la femme et marché matrimonial en Tunisie." *Population* 41 (1986): 853–58.

Belhassen, Souhayr. "Femmes tunisiennes islamistes." *Annuaire de l'Afrique du Nord* 18 (1979): 77–94.

Brown, K. L. "The Campaign to Encourage Family Planning in Tunisia and Some Responses at the Village Level." *Middle East Studies* 17 (1981): 64–84.

Chater, Souad. *Les émancipées du harem. Regards sur la femme tunisienne*. Tunis: La Presse, 1992.

Chelhi, Mouinne. "The Modern Tunisian Woman Between Hysteria and Depression." In *Women of the Arab World: The Coming Challenge*, edited by Nahed el-Gamal, 110–16. London: Zed Press, 1988.

Cherni-Ben Said, Zeineb. "La femme tunisienne et l'indépendance nationale." *Revue de l'Institut des Belles Lettres Arabes* 50, no. 159 (1987): 115–34.

Durrani, Lorna. "Tensions and Conflict in the Tunisian Family." *Maghreb Review* 2 (1977): 13–17.

Ferchiou, Sophie. "Organisation sociale et participation des femmes à la vie publique en Tunisie." *Annuaire de l'Afrique du Nord* 26 (1987): 433–49.

———. "The Possession Cults of Tunisia: A Religious System Functioning as a System of Reference and a Social Field for Performing Actions." In *Women's Medicine: The Zar-Bori Cult in Africa and Beyond*, edited by I. M. Lewis, Ahmed al-Safi, and Sayyid Hurriez, 209–18. Edinburgh: Edinburgh University Press, 1991.

Ghanmi, Azza. *Le mouvment féministe tunisien, 1979–1989*. Tunis: Chama, 1993.

Gmati, Farida. "Femme et famille en Tunisie." In *L'avenir de la famille au Moyen Orient et en Afrique du Nord*, 127–38. Tunis: Centre d'Etudes et de Recherches Economiques et Sociales, 1990.

Haddad, Radhia. "L'action de l'Union Nationale des Femmes de Tunisie." *Confluent* 25 (1962): 682–90.

Hadraoui, Touria, and Myriam Monkachi. *Etudes féminines: répertoire et bibliographie*. Casablanca: Le Fennec, 1991.

Hochschild, Arlie. "Le travail des femmes dans une Tunisie en voie de modernisation." *Revue Tunisienne de Sciences Sociales* 4 (1967): 145–66.

Labidi, Lilia. *Çabra Hachma: sexualité et tradition*. Tunis: Dar al-Nawras, 1989.

Mahfoudh, Dorrah. "La syndicalisation des femmes en Tunisie." *Peuples Méditerranéens* 44–45 (1988): 29–47, 339–40.

Mahfoud-Draoui, Dorra. "L'AFTURD ou comment développer la recherche sur les femmes?" *Revue de l'Institut des Belles Lettres Arabes* 54, no. 168 (1991): 325–28.

———. "Formation et travail des femmes en Tunisie: promotion ou aliénation?" *Annuaire de l'Afrique du Nord* 19 (1980): 255–88.

Marzouki, Ilhem. *Le mouvement des femmes en Tunisie au XXème siècle: féminisme et politique*. Paris: Maisonneuve et Larose, 1993.

Rejeb, Souad et al. "La mère au travail et son enfant: Simple sondage sociologique." *Revue de l'Institut des Belles Lettres Arabes* 54, no. 167 (1991): 85–93.

Tessler, Mark, Janet Rogers, and Daniel Schneider. "Women's Emancipation in Tunisia." In *Women in the Muslim World,* edited by Lois Beck and Nikki Keddie, 141–58. Cambridge: Harvard University Press, 1978.

Waltz, Susan. "Another View of Feminine Networks: Tunisian Women and the Development of Political Efficacy." *International Journal of Middle East Studies* 22 (1990): 21–36.

———. "Women's Housing Needs in the Arab Cultural Context of Tunisia." In *Women, Housing, and Community,* edited by W. van Vliet, 171–83. Aldershot: Avebury Press, 1988.

Zamiti, Khalil. " 'Kifah' sur les monts Khroumir: sexualité, espace et société." *Peuples Méditerranéens* 48–49 (1989): 25–44, 329.

Zamiti-Horchani, Malika. "Tunisian Women, Their Rights, and Their Ideas about These Rights." In *Women of the Mediterranean,* edited by M. Gadant, 110–19. London: Zed Books, 1986.

About the Author

Kenneth J. Perkins is a professor of Middle Eastern and North African history at the University of South Carolina. He holds a Ph.D. in Near Eastern Studies from Princeton University. A specialist in the nineteenth- and twentieth-century history of the Maghrib and the Sudan, he is the author of *Qaids, Captains, and Colons: French Military Administration in the Colonial Maghrib, 1844–1934* (New York: Africana Press, 1981); *Tunisia: Crossroads of the Islamic and European Worlds* (Boulder, Colo.: Westview Press, 1986); the first edition of the *Historical Dictionary of Tunisia* (Metuchen, N.J.: Scarecrow Press, 1989); and *Port Sudan: The Evolution of a Colonial City* (Boulder, Colo.: Westview Press, 1993). He is the translator and annotator of Lucette Valensi, *Le Maghreb avant la prise d'Alger* as *On the Eve of Colonialism: North Africa before the French Conquest* (New York: Africana Press, 1977); and the coeditor of *The Maghrib in Question: Essays in History and Historiography* (Austin: University of Texas Press, 1997). Professor Perkins has also published articles in *Revue d'histoire maghrébine, African Studies Review,* and *Middle East Studies* (London).